Islam in the Era of Globalization

Globalization, modernity, and identity are fundamental issues in contemporary Islam and Islamic studies.

The essays in this volume present in-depth discussions of the most important questions surrounding these issues. The book uses both theoretical approaches and practical experiences to elaborate the core themes. The book also represents a step towards a new synthesis in Islamic Studies, namely the cooperation of scholars representing diverse disciplinary traditions and various geographical origins and specializations, including both Muslims and non-Muslims.

Islam in the Era of Globalization reflects the wide diversity that characterizes contemporary Islamic Studies. The case studies cover regions stretching from China and South-East Asia, passing through Tajikistan, to diaspora communities in the Carribean. There is significant participation of intellectual voices from all areas concerned, providing a real contribution to the academic exchange between the Muslim and the Euro-American worlds.

Johan Meuleman is a lecturer at the Universiteit Leiden, a research fellow of the Leiden-based International Institute for Asian Studies, a professor by special appointment of Islamic History at IAIN Syarif Hidayatullah, Jakarta and the president of the Islamic University of Europe Foundation in the Netherlands.

ISLAM IN THE ERA OF GLOBALIZATION

Muslim attitudes towards modernity
and identity

Edited by Johan Meuleman

RoutledgeCurzon
Taylor & Francis Group

First published 2002
by RoutledgeCurzon
11 New Fetter Lane, London EC4P 4EE

Simultaneously published in the USA and Canada
by RoutledgeCurzon
29 West 35th Street, New York, NY 10001

RoutledgeCurzon is an imprint of the Taylor & Francis Group

Publisher's Note
This book has been prepared from camera-ready copy
provided by the editor.

© 2002 Johan Hendrik Meuleman; individual chapters
© the individual contributors

Printed and bound in Great Britain by MPG Books Ltd, Bodmin

British Library Cataloguing in Publication Data
A catalogue record is available for this book from the British Library

Library of Congress Cataloging in Publication Data
A catalog record for this book has been requested

ISBN 0–700–71691–2

Contents

vi

Acknowledgements

The origin of this book was the First International Conference on Islam and the 21st Century, organized in 1996 by the Indonesian-Netherlands Cooperation in Islamic Studies (INIS) at Leiden University, the Netherlands. The conference had been conceived as an encounter of Muslim and non-Muslim specialists of Islam from all over the world. INIS thereby endeavoured to extend to a wider circle its unique experience of scholarly cooperation between Dutch, mostly non-Muslim, specialists of Islamic studies with their Indonesian counterparts, mainly Muslims, in a post-colonial situation characterized by an attitude of mutual respect and interest, and by the steady development of Muslim communities in the Western world. The participants in the conference originated primarily from Indonesia and the Netherlands, but they also came from other South-East Asian and European countries, from the Middle East, from other parts of Africa and Asia as well as from North America. In total, almost 100 scholars attended the conference and seventy-odd papers were presented. From the papers presented at the conference, a selection has been made for this publication. The main criterion for this selection was the quality of each paper and its interest, both from the viewpoint of the general theme of the conference, Islam on the eve of the twenty-first century, and from the viewpoint of certain sub-themes or questions around which the papers might be grouped. Because it throws some additional light on some of the questions discussed in the other papers, the editor has added a paper entitled "South-East Asian Islam and the Globalization Process", which he presented at the conference "Emerging Trends in Islamic Thought. Islam, Civil Society and Development in Southeast Asia", jointly organized by the Islamic Studies Program and the Indonesian Studies Program at The University of Melbourne and by the Centre for Citizenship and Human Rights at Deakin University and held in Melbourne, Australia on 11 and 12 July 1998.

The 1996 conference would never have taken place without the hard work of an organizing committee consisting of Dr Dick Douwes, Drs. (MA) Yvonne A. van Genugten, Dr Nico J.G. Kaptein, Jennifer A.H. Trel, and Drs. Cathelijne B.W. Veenkamp, all staff members of Leiden University for INIS. They were supported by a steering committee consisting of Prof. A. Malik Fadjar, M.Sc., Director-General for the Development of Islamic

Institutions, Ministry of Religious Affairs, Indonesia; Dr M. Atho Mudzhar, Director for the Development of Islamic Higher Education at the same ministry; Prof. P.Sj. van Koningsveld, chair of Islam in Western Europe, Leiden University; Prof. R. Kruk, chair of Arabic, Leiden University; Prof. R. Peters, Chair of Islamic Law, University of Amsterdam; Prof. C.H.M. Versteegh, chair of Arabic, Catholic University of Nijmegen; Drs. H. Murni Djamal, M.A., programme director of INIS on behalf of the Indonesian Ministry of Religious Affairs; and Prof. W.A.L. Stokhof, programme director of INIS on behalf of Leiden University. Dr Tarmizi Taher, minister of religious affairs, Republic of Indonesia; Drs. W.J. Deetman, chairman of the Second Chamber of Dutch Parliament; and Prof. L. Leertouwer, rector of Leiden University graciously agreed to become member of the advisory committee. Too many other persons to name them all explicitly also contributed to the success of the conference.

Financial support was offered by the Ministry of Education, Culture, and Science of the Netherlands; the Ministry of Religious Affairs of the Republic of Indonesia; the International Institute for Asian Studies, Leiden; the Leiden University Fund; the Research School CNWS, School of Asian, African, and Amerindian Studies; and the City of Leiden.

Last but not least, it would have been impossible to present this volume in its final form without the meticulousness of the English language editor, Mrs. Rosemary Robson, B.A. (Hons) and the expertise of Drs. Dick van der Meij as an editorial adviser.

Note on References

In order to combine the advantages of various reference systems used in academic publishing, in the present volume references are given as short footnotes, mentioning just the main part of the author name, the abridged title — rather than the year of publication —, and the relevant page number(s). Full references may be found in the Bibliography, common to all contributions. In this Bibliography, works are classified according to the alphabetical order of the main part of the author names. For Western, Chinese, and similar names, this main part is the family name (e.g. "Brown, John", under the letter b; "Mao Zedong", under the letter m). Names containing no family name, such as traditional Arab and Javanese ones, are classified according to the personal name of the author, not, for example, according to patronymics (e.g. "Abdurrahman Wahid", not "Wahid, Abdurrahman"). Because only one author refers to archival documents and few to manuscripts, no separate sections for these types of documents have been created in the Bibliography. Other unpublished works have also been included in the unified bibliography, together with published references. Further details about the references and Bibliography will be evident to the reader without special explanation.

The Contributors

Azyumardi Azra was born in West Sumatra, Indonesia. After undergraduate studies at IAIN (State Institute for Islamic Studies) Syarif Hidayatullah, Jakarta, he was awarded a Fulbright scholarship and moved to Columbia University, New York, where he took two MA degrees and a PhD. His dissertation was on networks of Middle Eastern and Malay-Indonesian *'ulamā'* in the seventeenth and eighteenth centuries. He has published many articles and collections of papers relating to the history and other aspects of Islam in South-East Asia. At present he is a professor of Islamic history and the president of IAIN Syarif Hidayatullah.

Kees van Dijk was born in 1946 in Rotterdam and studied social anthropology at Leiden University. He is affiliated with the Royal Institute of Linguistics and Anthropology (KITLV), Leiden as a researcher and is professor of the history of Islam in Indonesia at Leiden University.

Howard M. Federspiel took a PhD in Islamic Studies from McGill University, Montreal. He has led several educational development projects in Indonesia. At present he is a professor of political science at the Ohio State University and is associated with the Institute of Islamic Studies at McGill University. Among his publications on Islam in South-East Asia are *Popular Indonesian Literature of the Qur'an*.

Mohan K. Gautam was born at Kasganj, Etah, Utar Pradesh, India. He took an MA in social anthropology from Lucknow University and wrote a dissertation on the search of identity of the North Indian Santal at Leiden University, where he has been lecturing for almost four decades. His fields of interest are the comparative study of religions, ethnicity, socio-linguistics, and North Indian languages and literature. Among the regions covered by his publications are South Asia, East and South Africa, as well as the Caribbean. He is also a writer of Urdu and Hindi literature.

Dru C. Gladney is professor of Asian studies and anthropology at the University of Hawai'i at Manoa. A PhD in social anthropology from the University of Washington, Seattle, he has been a Fulbright Research Scholar twice, and has conducted long-term field research in China, Central Asia, and Turkey. Among his books are *Muslim Chinese: Ethnic Nationalism in the People's Republic* and *Ethnic Identity in China: The Making of a Muslim Minority Nationality*. He also works as a consultant to the World Bank, the UNHCR, the Ford Foundation, the National Academy of Sciences, and the UNESCO.

Colette Harris was born in Great Britain and spent the first twenty years of her professional life as a gambist, violist, and early-music performance practice specialist. After a few years in a second career as computer programmer, she decided to retrain as a gender in development specialist. In 2000 she received her PhD from the University of Amsterdam with a dissertation entitled *Control and Subversion: Gender, Islam, and Socialism in Tajikistan*. She has published extensively on gender relations in Tajikistan. In the course of her six years working in Tajikistan, she helped establish the local NGO, Ghamkhori, and its Khatlon Women's Health Project. In February 2001 she took over the post of programme director, Women in International Development at Virginia Technical University in the USA.

Riffat Hassan was born in Lahore, Pakistan. She studied English and philosophy at St. Mary's College, Durham University, England. She then moved to the United States, where she has held various academic positions. At present she is a professor of religious studies at the University of Louisville. She has presented her call for a "feminist theology" of Islam in many countries. She has been involved in various fora and action programmes to combat the misuse of religion to justify discrimination against women. She is the founder and president of the International Network for the Rights of Female Victims of Violence in Pakistan (INRFVVP).

Iik Arifin Mansurnoor was born in Ponorogo, East Java, Indonesia. He studied at IAIN Sunan Ampel, Surabaya, then, after a brief period of study in Cairo, took his MA and PhD at McGill University, Montreal. In 1988 he was appointed a senior lecturer in the History Department of the University of Brunei Darussalam, which he has led since 1992. His main research interest is the history of Islam in South-East Asia.

Nico J.G. Kaptein read Islamic Studies at Leiden University. He is a lecturer at Leiden University in the framework of the Indonesian-Netherlands Cooperation in Islamic Studies (INIS) and researcher at the International Institute for Asian Studies (IIAS) in Leiden. His dissertation on the early history of the birthday festival of the Prophet Muhammad in the Middle East and the Maghrib was written and translated into English, Indonesian, Bosnian (forthcoming), and Arabic (forthcoming). For several years his main research theme has been the process of fatwa issuing in Indonesia and its national and international context.

Azza Mostafa Karam is an Egyptian who has worked as an activist, scholar, and trainer in the fields of gender, development, human rights, democratization, conflict, and political Islam. She founded the gender and the Arab world programmes at the International Institute for Democracy and Electoral Assistance (IDEA) in Stockholm; then was appointed a programme manager at the Centre for the Study of Ethnic Conflict, and a lecturer in politics at the Queens University of Belfast. Currently she is the director of the women's programme at the World Conference on Religion and Peace (WCRP) in New York. Her books include *Women, Islamisms and the State*.

Jamal Malik was born in Peshawar, Pakistan. He read Islamic Studies and political science at the Universities of Bonn, Heidelberg, and Bamberg, Germany. He lectured at the Ecole des Hautes Etudes en Sciences Sociales, Paris; Oberlin College, Cleveland, Ohio; and the University of Derby. Since February 1999 he has held the chair of religious studies - Islamic Studies at the University of Erfurt, Germany. He is the author of *The Colonialization of Islam* and many other publications on various aspects of Islamic literature and culture, colonialism, cultural representation, and Muslim minorities.

Muhammad Khalid Masud was born in India. At the time of Partition, he fled with his parents to the newly created Pakistan. He took an MA in Islamic Studies from Punjab University, Lahore, then took another MA and wrote his dissertation on al-Shāṭibī's philosophy of law at the Institute of Islamic Studies, McGill University, Montreal. From 1963 to 1999, he held various positions at the Islamic Research Institute, International Islamic University, Islamabad, Pakistan, including those of head of the Islamic Law and Jurisprudence Unit and editor of the journal *Islamic Studies*. In 1999 he was appointed academic director of the Leiden-based International Institute for the Study of Islam in the Modern World (ISIM).

Johan Hendrik Meuleman was born in Haarlem, the Netherlands. He studied history and philosophy at the Vrije Universiteit (Free University) of Amsterdam. During his professional career he spent eight years as a lecturer and researcher in Algeria and ten years in Indonesia, with a special interest in Islamic history, Islamic thought, and the development of contemporary Muslim societies. At present he is a lecturer at Leiden University in the framework of the Indonesian-Netherlands Cooperation in Islamic Studies, a research fellow of the Leiden-based International Institute for Asian Studies (IIAS), a professor of Islamic History at IAIN Syarif Hidayatullah, and the president of the Islamic University of Europe foundation, the Netherlands.

Mohamad Atho Mudzhar was born in Serang, West Java, Indonesia. He studied at IAIN Syarif Hidayatullah, Jakarta, took master degrees in Australia and the USA, and finally obtained a PhD from the University of California in Los Angeles. He held several positions in the Indonesian ministry of religious affairs, among them the position of director of Islamic higher education. Since 1997 he has been the president of IAIN Sunan Kalijaga, Yogyakarta, Indonesia. He is especially interested in the social history of Islamic law and has published on the fatwas issued by the Indonesian Council of *'Ulamā'* among other subjects.

Muhamad Hisyam was born in Cilacap, Central Jawa, Indonesia. He studied history and culture of Islam at IAIN Sunan Kalijaga, Yogyakarta and sociology of religion at the University of Indonesia, Jakarta. In 2001 he defended a dissertation on the *pangulu*s (religious officials) in Java under the colonial administration at Leiden University. At present he is head of the Division of Religion and Philosophy at the Centre for Social and Cultural Studies of the Indonesian Institute of Sciences (LIPI). His publications mostly concern the history of Islam and Muslim society in Indonesia

Lukas Werth is a German social anthropologist with special interest in religion, cosmology, and kinship in South Asia. His dissertation was about the Vagri of Tamil Nadu, a nomadic community. He lectured in the Institute of Ethnology (Social Anthropology) at the Free University of Berlin and then became associated with the Humboldt University of the same city, working for a research project on Sufism in Pakistan.

Mark R. Woodward was born in Austin, Texas, United States. He received his BA, MA, and PhD in cultural anthropology from the University of Illinois, Urbana-Champaign, and studied the history of religions at the University of Chicago Divinity School. He has conducted ethnografic research focusing on religion, politics, and modernization in Indonesia, Burma, and Singapore. He is currently associate professor of religious studies at Arizona State University in Tempe.

Introduction

The present volume offers a selection from the papers presented at the First International Conference on Islam and the 21st Century, organized in the framework of the Indonesian-Netherlands Cooperation in Islamic Studies (INIS). This conference offered scholars and experts from various disciplines and institutions the opportunity to meet and combine theoretical approaches with practical experiences relating to fundamental tendencies in contemporary Islam. Islam, in the conference title as well as in the present introduction, is used as a general term denoting not only Islam as a religion, but also the community of its adherents, their society, thought, and culture, characterized by a combination of unity and diversity that is one of the main sources of its interest as an object of study.

The studies presented in this book reflect the wide diversity that characterizes contemporary Islamic Studies. Just looking at the origins of the authors, seven are citizens of the two countries cooperating in the INIS project. Apart from these four Indonesian and three Dutch authors, three authors originate from another important Muslim country in Asia, Pakistan, and one from India although at present they are all living in the West. Two are from other European countries, three from the United States of America, and one from Egypt. From a thematic point of view, the majority of the papers concentrate on Asia, mostly Indonesia, one relates to the Muslim communities of South Asian origin in Surinam, Trinidad, and Guyana, and two address more general topics. To a certain extent, this reflects the actual presence of Islam in the contemporary world and signifies a welcome shift from the focus on the Middle East in traditional Islamic Studies. Although most papers are based on a detailed study relating to a particular country or region, one of the main questions addressed during the conference and in this publication is precisely the interaction of various communities and the impact of global developments.

The various contributions in this volume are concentrated on a certain number of central questions. The following survey of these questions will orient the reader, through the study of this collection, towards some of the fundamental issues of contemporary Islam and contemporary Islamic Studies. Most of these questions relate to one or more core themes, which run like a thread throughout the whole book. These core themes are globalization,

1

modernity, and identity. In conformity with these themes, the book has been arranged into three parts. However, these sections are not strictly separated and several contributions are relevant to more than one of the fundamental issues of the volume, whose very interrelationship justifies their presentation within one volume.

Globalization

The first series of questions raised in this collection of texts relates to the globalization process and its counterpart, localization. This is not the place to enter at length into the almost global discussion on globalization and the divergent definitions and analyses abounding about the phenomenon. Although often a fashionable catchword, convenient for attracting readership or academic subsidies, the term really refers to one of the most fundamental of the processes that characterize the contemporary world. Globalization may be defined as the process leading towards an increasingly strong interdependence between increasingly large parts of the world, resulting in the phenomenon that events and developments in one region influence most other regions. Processes that did display similar tendencies have existed earlier in world history, but the unprecedented speed of relations — in transportation, information, and communication — is often quoted as the quality that makes contemporary globalization the special phenomenon many hold it to be.

Several contributions included in this collection emphasize that the relationship between the contemporary globalization process and Islam is complicated. In my contribution on South-East Asian Islam and the globalization process, I explain that globalization is not a totally new process, especially in relation to Islam. With this in mind, this contribution of mine proposes a distinction between two possible understandings of globalization, namely as the intensification of the involvement in universal Islam (i.e. away from Javanese or Bengal particularity, for example) and as a movement towards a more or less uniform, global civilization (i.e. away from particular reference to Islam or the Muslim community). It is also argued that a clear picture should be obtained of the different positions Muslim communities may occupy in various types of contemporary globalization processes, namely what may be called positions as (co-) actor,

2

as re-actor, or as victim. Certain re-active mechanisms in the Muslim world might be called Islamic counter-globalization.

The thesis that globalization is not a totally new process is confirmed by Azyumardi Azra. In his analysis of Indonesian Muslim discourse, he emphasizes the important role played in its development by the interaction between Indonesia and the Middle East, which began several centuries ago.

Kees van Dijk discusses celebrations and dress codes displaying the differences and interaction between international, local, and Islamic culture in the Indonesian Archipelago. He explains that for several centuries this region has been exposed to the influence of several, competing sets of values and norms. The Western model has not been the only force to intrude itself into the Archipelago. This author points out that the most recent globalizing trend has tended to be related to international Islam. Another important conclusion of Van Dijk is that, in reality, the various globalizing tendencies were only one pole of a dialectic of globalization and local appropriations. This conclusion is supported by the contributions of Muhamad Hisyam and Jamal Malik, which will be presented in the following section.

In his case study on Brunei, Iik Arifin Mansurnoor sheds some additional light on the relationship between globalizing trends and local traditions. He shows that this tiny sultanate, as many other Muslim countries, has increasingly become part of global Islam. Various religious, intellectual, and political networks, both formal and informal, have been instrumental in this process. Of particular interest is this author's contention that, in its exposure to diverse external forces, Brunei has been able to develop what might be called a bargaining power precisely because of its straightforward insistence upon its own, traditional version of Islam. However, he doubts whether this country will be able to maintain its particular interpretation and expression of Islam under the continuing pressure of global systems.

After having seen that globalization is neither a uniform nor a unipolar process, we are led to the question of whether contemporary globalization will induce a reduction in diversity within Islam. Van Dijk states that the opposite might be the case: individual countries may become even more diverse as a consequence of the globalization process. Nico Kaptein, however, speaking of the unifying role of fatwas in Indonesian history, arrives at a different conclusion: he expects that the process of Islamization, i.e. the same form of globalization of which Van Dijk is analysing some other aspects, will lead to a reduction of cultural diversity.

Modernity

The second set of questions concerns the relationship between Islam and modernity. These questions are primarily inspired by the widespread conviction that this relationship is problematic. Although those who possess an objective knowledge of world history will admit that the Muslim civilization once occupied a top position in the scientific and intellectual fields, the dominant opinion is that modernity was born in the West and that Islam is either incompatible with modernity or, to quote the milder standpoint, that it may import modernity by emulating foreign models. This opinion is partly based on the more general idea that the whole world is on the way towards a uniform pattern of life and that the West will forever occupy its centre. In my contribution on globalization in South-East Asian Islam, referred to in the previous section, I explain that this idea, once very popular, has increasingly come under fire. Several other authors propose a more balanced position on the relationship between Islam and modernity as well.

In his comparison of the Christian and the Muslim attitudes towards modernity, Mark Woodward argues that it is Islam indeed which is more open to modernity than Christianity. Whereas modernity in the Christian West has led to secularization, disenchantment, or fundamentalism, Indonesian Muslims, he argues, accept modernity and at the same time continue to provide their experiences with meaning and their society with cohesion on the basis of their religion. He explains this difference in attitude by stating that from the Christian point of view the basic problem of modernity is cosmological, but for Muslims it is primarily sociological. In other words, modernity has been a radical threat to the entire Christian world view, but among Muslims it has led only to controversies about the right social order.

In his critical analysis of the concept of modernity in the context of Pakistan, Lukas Werth joins Woodward in arguing that whereas the specific Western form of modernity may lead to problems in a Muslim environment, this does not mean that various institutions and attitudes associated with modern life may not be adopted by Muslims. Woodward and Werth both substantiate their theoretical positions with concrete examples observed during anthropological fieldwork. Woodward underpins his argument with case studies of Javanese Muslims and Werth bases his one on a study of Muslims in the Punjab. In order to avoid the unjustified application of the

Western concept of modernity outside its proper domain, he suggests the term modernization for the development of those modern phenomena he has observed in Muslim Pakistan.

Azza Mostafa Karam draws our attention to the fact that particular understandings of modernity tend to be forced upon Muslims. She concentrates on the case of Muslim women in Western academia. Through an analysis pointing out the connection between educational and discursive practices and power relations, she explains the delicate position of this category of people, firstly as Muslims in a non-Muslim environment, secondly as women in a male-dominated environment.

In her contribution treating the question of whether Islam is a help or a hindrance to women's development, Riffat Hassan also demands a critical analysis of the concept of modernity. Her point of departure is the question of how it was possible that in the country of her youth, Pakistan, which professed its commitment to both Islam and modernity, manifestly unjust laws could be implemented, especially in relation to women. She considers theological misconceptions to be the main reason for this injustice and is thereby led to a feminist reconstruction of Islamic theology. On the other hand, this author underscores the selectivity of the Western interest in Islam and Muslims. She elaborates her argument by explaining that this selective interest sustains an unbalanced, negative image of Islam and its adherents and leads to Islam being considered at the most a negative factor on the way to modern development. This opinion has been combined with the widespread opinion that the processes of globalization and modernization would ultimately lead to a reduction of the role of religion in public life everywhere. Hassan explains that, compelled by the actual facts of recent history, some Western social scientists are beginning to concede that Islam is one of the factors which should be considered in development projects. Although an improvement compared to the dominant tendency not to take religion into consideration at all in the analysis of social transformation processes, this still falls short of Hassan's own standpoint that Islam is the very matrix of all factors — economic, ethnic and other — that influence the life of Muslims.

Colette Harris does not go as far as Hassan. Instead in her analysis of Muslim views on population in Tajikistan, she arrives at the conclusion that Islam as such in not the main factor in the high fertility rates, but this role is occupied by the social traditions that have grown around Islam and which, for their part, evolve continuously in response to socio-economic and political factors. This apparent difference of opinion stems partly from the fact that these authors address a different problem: Hassan basically opposes the opinion that nothing positive can be expected from Islam on the way to a better future; Harris opposes the tendency to ascribe a negative demographic phenomenon to Islam as a religion.

Identity

Yet a third series of contributions addresses the question how Muslim communities construct and reconstruct their identity in this period of fundamental transformations and increased interaction with other civilizations and modes of thought. This complex question is closely connected with a number of other fundamental issues, including those discussed in the two preceding sections. Iik shows how the small sultanate of Brunei has preserved its own identity in spite of, and partly through, its interaction with international Islam. Werth explains that Punjabi Muslims, although they participate in certain global modernizing trends, maintain a specific identity. Van Dijk shows how the Indonesian Muslims have built and adapted their identity under the impact of successive waves of foreign culture.

Several authors relate this question to another important research theme, namely the relationship between state and what is nowadays often called "civil society". Avoiding any discussion of the theoretical and ideological background to this concept, civil society may be defined in a general way as the population of a country, with their organizations and initiatives, as partner or adversary of the state, with its agencies, agents, and policies at various levels. In our context we basically refer to the Muslim community or communities at large and the *'ulamā'* or specialists of Islamic religious sciences with their various institutions, associations, and aspirations.

The interaction between state and civil society is strongest in the field of the institutions Muslim society has developed in order to preserve, implement, and elaborate its values and principles. The most important of these institutions are related to education — proposed as one of the main themes for the 1996 conference — and law. Several authors address the relationship between state and society in regard of these institutions. Through their contributions, they help develop a more balanced view on the relationship between Islam and the state, dismissing as simplistic the popular opinion that within Islam state and religion are inextricably bound up with each other, whereas one of the essential characteristics of modern society is their separation. This questionable opinion is one element of the more general belief that a fundamental contradiction exists between Islam and modernity, discussed in the previous section.

Jamal Malik's contribution on the interaction between the Islamic religious scholars and the state in the development of contemporary Pakistani education connects these interrelated questions with the issue of globalization. This author points out that state intervention has become increasingly important in education. On the one hand, this process seems to be part of a uniformizing trend found almost anywhere on the globe nowadays, in Muslim and non-Muslim countries alike. In other words, it is part of the first of both possible understandings of globalization I distinguish in my text on South-East Asian Islam and globalization. On the other hand, this process is part of a tendency towards a more universal type of Islam. Malik points out the fact that state authorities, Muslim avant-gardists, and Islamists aspire to achieve a type of universalizing Islam that contrasts with the Islam for which the traditional religious scholars stand. He adds that these traditional specialists seem to have learned how to make use of the state-sponsored Islamization process for their own benefit. As a consequence, this author predicts, the traditional religious scholars and their institutions might well play a crucial role in the adaptation of globalizing and modernizing developments to specific local needs and situations.

In his contribution on religious identity and mass education, Muhammad Khalid Masud shows that even in the past the relationship between state and the Islamic religion was complicated and not uniform. He too argues that in the most recent periods this relationship has become stronger rather than weaker. A particular situation exists when a non-Muslim government administers Muslim communities. Masud compares the attitude to Islamic and Muslim education in the state of Pakistan, which is formally based on Islam, to that in the United Kingdom and in the Netherlands. He shows that even between these two Western states the situation differs. Another important conclusion of this author is that the dominant type of Muslim mass education, in various countries, causes Muslim communities to define their identity in an exclusivist way.

In his analysis of the transmission of knowledge about Islam in the Popular Republic of China, Dru Gladney contrasts the role of state-sponsored and mosque-sponsored educational institutions in the construction of the identity of Chinese Muslims. He explains that the fact that both types of

7

institutions have interacted but remained separate has led to continuing misunderstandings and misrepresentations.

Another contribution which connects the questions of identity construction, the relationship between state and civil society, and the role of education is my text on the Indonesian State Institutes for Islamic Studies (IAINs). It highlights the particular position of these institutions at the interface of state and civil society. In addition, it analyses the interaction of Western, Middle Eastern, and national references in their development. Finally, it points out that these institutions are located at a crossroads from yet a third point of view, namely between specifically religious learning and general education and science.

Besides education, the second domain in which questions of identity and the interaction and competition between state and civil society are of particular importance, is law.

Muhamad Hisyam is particularly interested in the interaction between religion and state in the development of the Islamic courts in Indonesia. He argues that this interaction is based on an ambiguous relationship which lies at the core of a series of conflicts: on the one hand, the effectiveness of Islamic law requires state intervention; on the other hand, state intervention is typically inspired by the interests of various groups as well as by the interests of the state itself.

Mohamad Atho Mudzhar concentrates on another important aspect of Islamic law, the issuing of fatwas, i.e. informed opinions on legal matters. He analyses the interaction of the government, *'ulamā'*, and society at large in the case of the Indonesian Council of *'Ulamā'*.

Returning to the international aspects of the process of identity construction, it is interesting to note that the authors of all contributions presented in the section on globalization pay special attention to issues such as the production of knowledge and the role of Islamic texts and Muslim discourse in this connection. Azyumardi precisely defines the object of his analysis as discourse, a concept referring to both the content and the form and structure of writing and speaking in particular circles on a specific category of subjects. In this case, the religio-intellectual discourse of Indonesian *'ulamā'*. He explains that for a long time now, this discourse has been supported by international networks, whose centre has shifted from its traditional location, Mecca and Medina, to Cairo and may recently even have shifted beyond the Middle East. The importance of international intellectual networks and the processes of recentring or even multiplication of centres they undergo is also highlighted in the contributions of Van Dijk and Kaptein and my own text on the IAINs, all relating to different aspects of Indonesian Islam. Similar issues for the whole South-East Asian region are discussed by Iik and by Howard Federspiel.

The last-mentioned author offers an analysis of the heterogeneous and changing references turned to by various groups of South-East Asian Muslim intellectuals. He is especially interested in the respective influence of Middle-Eastern, Western, South Asian, and local sources on their writings.

An original topic is taken up by Mohan Gautam. He discusses the complex way a Muslim community originating from an Asian country where Islam was already in a minority position has developed its identity, in successive periods, after it migrated and became a new minority in the Americas. In his contribution on the Caribbean Muslims of Indian origin, this author explains how, first, Indian Islam was imbued with regional particularities and, later, their different origins have made the Caribbean Muslims of Indian, African, and Javanese descent into separate communities.

Closing Remark

At the end of this introduction, let us return to the apparent difference of opinion between Hassan and Harris on the role of Islam in social transformation. Above, this divergence was partly attributed to the fact that these authors address a different problem. However, there is another aspect to the difference in the conclusion at which both these authors arrive. Whereas most authors in this volume limit themselves to a scholarly analysis, some Muslim authors go beyond and write out of involvement with Islamic and general human ideals. This is clearly the case with Hassan. She combats both misogynous traditions in Muslim society and an unbalanced image of Islam in the West. She therefore calls on Muslim women to adopt not a re-active but a pro-active attitude in society. Then, Karam opposes the combination of Western arrogance towards Islam and male dominance in Western academia. Finally, Masud, through his argument that the present development of religious mass education produces a negative attitude towards religious pluralism and diversity, advocates an attitude which is more in conformity with the contemporary global community. These three authors combine their involvement with a solid scholarly analysis and it is precisely this combination which makes their contributions a most valuable part of this collection of texts, whose richness lies in the diversity of approaches by which a common set of fundamental questions is addressed.

Johan Meuleman

Part One

Globalization

South-East Asian Islam
and the Globalization Process

Johan Meuleman

Introduction: Discourse on Globalization as a Global Fashion

Over the past few years, discourse on "globalization" has become trendy. Many consider globalization one of the fundamental processes of the present and of the near future. The rapid and comprehensive spread of this idea itself appears to be a clear indication of its truth. A person who has been living in South-East Asia for the last decade or so might at first suppose that the fashion of speaking about globalization is particular to a certain group of semi-intellectuals and popular writers, who happen to have read one or two American publications on "megatrends" or similar concepts that attempt to explain the history and future of mankind in a few catchwords. A simple search for titles containing the word *globalisasi* in the on-line catalogue of the National Library in Jakarta yields fifty-two works, *globalisation* one — by a foreign author — and *globalization* twenty-one — of which three are by Indonesian authors. However, a similar search in the Nederlandse Centrale Catalogus (Dutch Central Catalogue) yields fifty-four for *globalisasi*, of which a large part relate to publications by Indonesian authors available at the library of the Royal Institute for Linguistics and Anthropology (KITLV) in Leiden, ninety-one for *globalisation*, 263 for *globalization* and two and thirty-four for the Dutch equivalents *globalisatie* and *globalisering* respectively.[1] Furthermore, during a recent visit to France I discovered that the term *mondialisation* — not *globalisation* — had become widely mentioned in newspapers. Still more recently, at a seminar on Islamic Studies held two weeks before the original version of this text was presented in Pattani,

---

[1] Search on 6 July 1998, one week before the original version of this text was presented. It is interesting to note that the oldest work among those containing the word *globalisasi* in their title dates from 1990 and that most works in this category were published starting in 1993.

Thailand, I learnt a new term: *'awlamah*, being the Arabic equivalent of "globalization".[2] And we could go on for a long time in a similar vein.

Globalization and the History of Islam

If we define globalization as the process towards an increasingly strong interdependence between increasingly large parts of the world, resulting in the phenomenon that events and developments in one region influence most other regions, we may argue that it is not something as new as this recent discourse might have us believe. Islam, for instance, has played a prominent role in globalization processes since its very origin. This role was not accidental to Islam, but was instead one of its fundamental attributes. It affected political, economic, and cultural life.

This is thrown into particularly sharp relief when we look at the expansion of Islam to South-East Asia. Many historians emphasize the role of an international commercial network, stretching from North Africa to East Asia, in this expansion. At a time when commerce within Europe and the role of the Mediterranean as a bridge between Europe, Africa, and Asia declined,[3] the Indian Ocean became the centre of a new trade network, dominated by Muslim traders. The South-East Asian islands acquired a prominent position within this new "global system". This theory, which has already achieved classical status, has recently received further support from André Wink, Denys Lombard, and Anthony Reid. Wink draws our attention to the Indian Ocean as the axis of a world system and goes on to analyse "*al-Hind*" — understood as South and South-East Asia — as a world in itself.[4] Lombard studies the island of Java as a crossroads in an international economic and cultural system.[5] Reid relates the Islamization and Christianization — two processes he regards as fundamentally variants of the same phenomenon — of large parts of South-East Asia during the "Age of

---

[2] In its published form: Jihād Muḥammad Abū Najā, "Manāhij al-taʿlīm al-islāmī fī Tāyland", 243.

[3] Although this decline was not as absolute as the famous Belgian historian Henri Pirenne contended. See for the debate on the so-called Pirenne thesis Hübinger, (ed.), *Bedeutung und Rolle des Islam*.

[4] Wink, *Al-Hind*.

[5] Lombard, *Le carrefour javanais*.

Commerce" (1450-1680, most intensely 1570-1630) to integration of their areas into larger commercial and cultural systems.[6]

Convincing though these arguments may be, we should not conclude that the development of an international trade network was the only factor in the Islamization of South-East Asia. This has been underscored by Jacobus Cornelis van Leur in his dissertation on pre-colonial and early colonial Asian trade. He argues that a particular combination of commercial and political factors coincided to bring about the Islamization of South-East Asia.[7] In this framework, he is most insistent that these factors were not purely external, internal transformations also certainly contributed to this process. Lombard confirms the role of internal changes.[8] Given these data, it is plausible to maintain that, at least at this stage of "globalization", South-East Asia did not only play a passive role and that the process was the result of interaction between the centre and the periphery of a developing global system.

After commercial relations had played an important role in the expansion of Islam and the unification of the various parts of the Muslim world at an early stage, the way was paved for the development of a network of scholarly relations and mystical organizations which served to strengthen this unity. Anthony H. Johns has emphasized the role of this network in the further development of Islam in South-East Asia.[9] After the Muslim world disintegrated politically and its commercial power had been broken by Portugal, Holland, France, and England, this spiritual network continued to function unimpaired. The fear of Dutch and other colonial authorities about contacts between their Muslim subjects and their co-religionists in the Holy

---

[6]He regards the development of a unified order of monks, under royal control, in Theravada Buddhism in other parts of South-East Asia as being a similar process to a certain extent. Reid, *Southeast Asia in the Age of Commerce*, esp. vol. 2, chapter 3 ("A Religious Revolution").

[7]Van Leur, "On Early Asian Trade", 110-6.

[8]In a tentative theory which, to my knowledge, he never elaborated or strengthened by further research, Lombard explains the fact that Islam hardly spread beyond the insular part of South-East Asia and, even within this part, only from about the fourteenth century AD, by the transformation of the regions in question at that period. This was when they changed from being agricultural and inward-oriented societies into maritime and outward-oriented ones (Lombard, "L'horizon insulindien"). This theory is quite attractive, but needs further research. S.O. Robson, for example, has argued that, at least in the case of Majapahit, the theory which relates Islamization to the transformation of an agricultural into a maritime society is not convincing (Robson, "Java at the Crossroads").

[9]Johns, "The Role of Sufism"; *idem*, "Islam in Southeast Asia".

Land is well known. Recent research has confirmed the importance of this type of network between the Hijaz and South-East Asia.[10]

These facts abstracted from the history of Islam, especially in South-East Asia, militate against considering globalization to be a totally new phenomenon.

Modern Western Expansion and Its Limits

In spite of the development and continued existence of this spiritual network, from about the fifteenth or sixteenth century AD the centre of the world economy moved towards Europe. The Muslim world had previously attained a high level of scientific development, a refined civilization, wealth, and even the formation of a capitalist sector and a bourgeois class.[11] However, despite these advantages it was Europe that experienced the technological and social leap that indirectly transformed it into the centre of an ever wider and stronger new global system.

Instead of the Muslim system which preceded it, it is this "modern world system", as it is often called after the title of Immanuel Wallerstein's influential study of it,[12] that is frequently cited as evidence that globalization is not a recent phenomenon.[13] Wallerstein writes that since the sixteenth century the world has progressively become one integrated system. He emphasizes that the basis of this unification was economic and that economic integration has been faster than its counterpart in other fields. He is quick to point out that this unification has not been accompanied by equality. On the contrary, the "modern world system" was characterised by the contrast between a centre — Europe, later "the West" —, a secondary zone depending on the centre, and a periphery in which only limited influence was exerted by the centre.

European and later also Western progress and expansion led to the formation of a vision that all societies and states were located somewhere on the way towards the same, Western pattern of life, be this in the political,

---

[10]Cf. in particular Azra, *The Transmission of Islamic Reformism*.

[11]On the formation of a capitalist sector, see, among other references, Rodinson, *Islam et capitalisme*, esp. 45 ff.

[12]Wallerstein, *The Modern World System*.

[13]Cf. Ahmed and Donnan, "Islam in the Age of Postmodernity", 2.

cultural, social, or economic field. This view had its origins during Enlightenment and later appeared in various forms in the works of otherwise such disparate authors as Auguste Comte, Karl Marx, and Max Weber. Its influence was strong on colonial policy and on orientalism, including Western analyses of Islam. Finally, it was reflected in the ideas of many political, social, and economic scientists as well as in the development policies of a large number of countries during the period after the Second World War.[14] In this respect, the similarity between liberal politicians and scholars and their Marxist adversaries was striking.

From about the middle of the 1960s, and even more markedly since the 1970s, this broad tendency to link Western expansion — or the expansion of communism — to a process towards uniformity on the Western or communist model began to be abandoned. The prime target for attack was the idea of Western uniformity. This was criticized because of a number of related factors: the failure of development policy for the Third World based on this vision; the political and military failure of the West, in particular the USA, in Vietnam;[15] new developments in Western philosophy that stressed the differences and ruptures between various paradigms, epistemes, and discourses, or which were critical of Western "logocentrism";[16] and a renewed interest in particular, non-Western values and a stress of specificity in the non-Western world, most clearly in the Muslim world.[17]

Not only has the vision that the whole world is on the way towards a uniform pattern of life become the object of criticism, but also the idea that the West would forever occupy the centre of the expanding global system has recently come under fire. The latter criticism has been supported by a number of specialists on Western expansion. Among them was the prominent

[14]Well-known representatives of this tendency are Walt Whitman Rostow and Karl Wolfgang Deutsch. Strange enough, Rostow's development theory, and more especially his ideas about the "take-off era", continued to serve as reference in New Order (Soeharto-led) Indonesia. His ideas are expressed in Rostow, *The Process of Economic Growth* and other publications. Deutsch formulated development as a process in which "countries are becoming somewhat less like Ethiopia and somewhat more like the United States" (Deutsch, "Social Mobilization", 495).

[15]Cf. Kessler, *Islam and Politics*, 18 ff.

[16]Reference is made in particular to the works of Thomas S. Kuhn, Michel Foucault, and Jacques Derrida.

[17]So-called Muslim fundamentalism is the best known, but not the only variant of this phenomenon.

French historian, Fernand Braudel. He had been influenced by Wallerstein and was greatly interested in long-term transformations in international mechanisms of dependency and interdependency. On the basis of historical research, he concluded that economic and political systems and their centres have always been in a state of flux, changing slowly but inexorably. At the time of (Western) classical civilization, its centre was located around the Mediterranean, then it moved to the Middle East, and from the end of the European Middle Ages it moved back again to — Southern then Western — Europe and finally crossed the Atlantic Ocean to North America. At a seminar held in Leiden, the Netherlands in 1975, he predicted that the centre might switch back to Rotterdam.[18] Another prediction that was very popular until the recent economic crisis hit South-East Asia and Japan was that the centre would switch to the Pacific Rim or the Asia-Pacific region. Today there seems to be less evidence to support such an assumption.

At the same seminar, an Israeli political scientist, Samuel Eisenstadt, emphasized that modernization — a concept often associated with globalization and uniformization — was not necessarily identical to Westernization. He argued that the modernization process, which started several centuries ago with European expansion, has not consisted only of the export of European or Western civilization to other regions, but that this Western expansion has also induced a series of reactions in the non-Western world that combine various Western and local elements in the symbolic, political, economic and still other fields.[19]

In this context, it is interesting to indicate the view of the British social anthropologist, the late Ernest Gellner, who agreed with Eisenstadt that modernity is not equivalent to "Westernity". More precisely, he argues that Islam, more than other religions, is very compatible with modernity.[20] As is often the case with Gellner's theories, this one is as fascinating as it is open to question. On this occasion we cannot go into a critical discussion of his underlying theory that, until the modern era, Islam is in continuous state

---

[18]This lecture has been published in English translation as Braudel, "The Expansion of Europe"; see esp. p. 27. Braudel has studied the successive shifts of the centre of world economy in more detail in his monumental *La Méditerrannée et le monde méditerranéen* and *Civilisation matérielle, économie et capitalisme*.

[19]Eisenstadt, "European Expansion".

[20]Gellner, "Flux and Reflux"; *idem*, "Foreword" to Ahmed and Donnan (eds), op. cit.; *idem, Conditions of Liberty*.

of oscillation between a "scripturalist" and a "pastoralist" pattern.[21] It should be remembered that to define "modernity" or to determine compatibility with the modern era, Gellner exclusively uses criteria that are borrowed from modern Western civilization rather than from the Muslim world: universalism, scripturalism, participation in the holy community by all on equal footing, and rational systematisation of social life.[22] In other words, Gellner has only gone halfway in his criticism of the view that modernity equals "Westernity".

Another widespread assumption related to the concepts of globalization and modernization was that these processes would ultimately everywhere lead to a reduction in the role of ethnicity and religion in public life so that these would no longer be dividing factors in societies and states. This prediction too has seemed highly debatable in the light of recent developments in various regions. The clearest and best-known case is that of the Balkan region. Here, ethnicity and religion have quite suddenly emerged as the ultimate forces determining the relations between people and this in a negative rather than a positive way. However, deeper analysis shows that reaction against excessive centralization and unequal positions between various groups and regions lie at the bottom of what are superficially ethnic and religious phenomena.

Turning more specifically to South-East Asian Islam, similar developments have manifested themselves in Southern Thailand and the Southern Philippines. The Malaysian scholar, Wan Kadir Che Man, has shown that theories on economic and political development or state formation, especially these from the 1960s and 1970s, which predicted the end of ethnicity as a factor in public life, have been proved wrong in these regions. He considers analytical models based on the notions of internal colonialism, cultural division of labour and ecological competition — all within a single state — to be more useful and closer to reality.[23] He also

---

[21]In the modern, colonial and post-colonial, states, the urban, scripturalist centre, as the result of modern communication, military, and transportation technology, forever succeeds in firmly establishing its domination, and therefore its type of Islam, on the whole state territory (*locus citati*). For a short criticism of this type of analysis contrasting a "scripturalist" and a "folk" form of Islam, see Meuleman, "Indonesian Islam between Particularity and Universality", 106 f.

[22]Gellner, "Flux and Reflux", 7.

[23]Man, *Muslim Separatism*. For the internal colonialism (i.e. colonialism, within one state, of peripheral regions by the centre region) and cultural division of labour model the

thinks that religion is a source of inspiration and political ideology and a basis for social mobilization, and not a basic cause of the conflicts between the central authorities and the Muslim minorities in these regions.[24] Another interesting conclusion drawn by this author is that, at least in these cases, modernization, in the form of increases in social mobilization, indeed intensifies — not reduces — ethnic tension.[25]

The Contemporary Globalization Process

So far we have seen that several viewpoints relating to earlier processes of globalization and associated concepts such as modernization have recently been challenged. These considerations will be helpful in our discussion of the contemporary process of globalization, which is distinguished from earlier forms of large-scale expansion and unification by many authors.

In their own contribution to a collection of papers they have edited under the title of *Islam, Globalization and Postmodernity*, Akbar S. Ahmed and Hastings Donnan explain the term globalization as referring principally to "the rapid developments in communication technology, transport and information which bring the remotest parts of the world within easy reach".[26] It is this rapidity of relations that, according to these and several other authors, distinguishes contemporary globalization from earlier forms of expansion. As a clear point in case relating to Islam, they refer to the Rushdie affair of early 1989.[27] Ahmed and Donnan add that the domination of the cultural aspect in global mutual influence seems to be a characteristic of contemporary globalization, in contrast to the economic and political aspects which predominated in previous expansion processes.[28] In reality, however, the domination of cultural aspects is at the most relative. Salient

author refers in particular to Michael Hechter, for the ecological competition model to Michael T. Hannan. See especially the "Introduction. Theoretical Considerations" (1 ff.) of op. cit.

[24] See esp. op. cit., 174.

[25] See esp. l.c.

[26] Ahmed and Donnan, "Islam in the Age of Postmodernity", 1, referring to Anthony Giddens.

[27] L.c.

[28] Op. cit., 2 f.

examples of the impact of globalization, such as the penetration of McDonalds and other USA-based fast food restaurants or North and South American television series all over the world, at first sight seem to be cultural phenomena. Such a snap judgement would be incorrect as behind them are economic processes such as foreign capital investment and growing purchasing power of part of the Third World consumers. Moreover, the repercussions of the recent Asian economic crisis on the future course of the globalization process appear to be far stronger than the impact of films, hamburgers and other cultural goods.

Returning to the Balkan conflict, referred to above, the impact of globalization is unequivocal. A large part of the world population followed the events and many governments and international organizations became involved. Many people outside the region felt concerned. Pertinently, this last phenomenon shows precisely that, in addition to globalization as a form of unification, the polarization between various groups, in this case Muslims and non-Muslims, has been intensified at a global level.[29] Nevertheless, however strong this polarization, it is not absolute: many non-Muslim inhabitants of Western Europe tended to sympathize with the Bosnian-Muslim side of the conflict, which appeared to be the primary victim. This fact tends to be ignored in non-European Muslim circles, partly because of their disappointment with the attitude of Western governments. Cogently, one of the basic aspects of the dissolution of Yugoslavia precisely is a sharp refusal and reversal of unification and globalization, in this case at the level of one state. The Gulf War of early 1991 also showed a tendency towards global polarization between Muslims and non-Muslims, but here factors relating to regional strategies and government interests blurred this polarization.[30]

The preceding discussion warns us to beware of oversimplifying the analysis of globalization. Firstly, we have seen that globalization is not an entirely novel phenomenon. On the other hand, the contemporary globalization process has its own particularities, relating mainly to the rapidity of contemporary communication and transport. Secondly, we have understood that globalization is not just a process of one fixed centre, progressively expanding its influence and pattern of life over the rest of the

[29]Cf. op. cit., 8.
[30]Cf. l.c.

world. Therefore, a solid analysis of the globalization process requires a distinction to be made between action and reaction, as well as between "actors", "re-actors", and "victims". It is not impossible that one region, society, or group may act as actor, re-actor and/or victim at the same time, depending on the perspective.

In attempting to locate Islam in the process, it may be added that, as a religion and a civilization, it is fundamentally in support of globalization and indeed has played a prominent role in globalization processes during earlier periods of history. Therefore, basically it should be capable of accommodating to the contemporary globalization process. Various mechanisms, in particular the haj, the circulation of religious and scholarly texts, education in general, and the mystical orders, contribute to the global character of Islam, at least within the community of its adherents. In recent times, these mechanisms that unify the Muslim world have strengthened considerably, but the question of Islam and its relationship with the contemporary globalization process is complicated. To find an answer, a distinction has to be made between two possible understandings of globalization, namely as the intensification of the involvement into universal Islam (i.e. away from Javanese or Malay particularity, for example) and as a movement towards a more or less uniform, global civilization (i.e. away from particular reference to Islam or the Muslim community). In addition, referring to the distinction made before, it is important to determine to what extent the position of the Muslim community in these contemporary globalization processes is that of (co-) actor, re-actor (moving in opposition to the globalization process in one or both of its understandings) or victim.

The Case of South-East Asian Islam

In the following section, the preceding general observations will be illustrated and elaborated with reference to Islam in South-East Asia. The discussion will be concentrated on, but not limited to, Indonesia.

The General Discourse

As we have seen at the beginning of this text, in Indonesia discourse on globalization was quite noticable during the 1990s. Some of the many publications on this theme that have appeared were inspired by concern about foreign influences and the desire to protect what are considered the national values and traditions. Despite such warning voices, the general tendency in Indonesian discourse was to accept globalization as an inescapable process and to reject exaggerated efforts to close Indonesian society or the economy off from the external world. A point in case is a discussion about the possible impact of the introduction of Internet in the mid 1990s. For a short while, various politicians, security officials, and moralists urged measures to control and limit foreign influence and the flood of information pouring into the country via the Internet. However, voices of that tenor have been heard seldom since and Internet has been widely accepted as a useful and indeed unavoidable tool of information and communication, and protection against any potential discordant influence has remained limited to the creation of governmental and military servers with anti-propaganda against certain unwelcome messages from abroad. The numerous shopping malls that sprang up in almost all Indonesian towns during the last few years do not testify either to any great efforts on the part of Indonesia to close itself off from globalization. These cultural phenomena have their economic counterpart in the open character of the Indonesian economy. During the last years of the Soeharto-led New Order regime, government policy was — at least officially — slowly and surely to reduce existing bureaucratic obstacles to an open economy and the free export and import of capital. The IMF-sponsored economic policy that is meant to help the country overcome the present crisis has only reinforced this tendency. This is not to say that among all circles of Indonesian people there is agreement with this open attitude, but this has been the dominant trend, however, also in Muslim circles.

Looking at the many Indonesian publications which discuss various aspects of the globalization process, most are very general and superficial. Among them figure a number of studies by research offices of the Ministry of Education and Culture and the Ministry of Religious Affairs. These research reports too do not delve deeply and tend to limit themselves to the

23

analysis of industrialization and its effects, which is not necessarily part of globalization.[31]

In order to understand the attitude of the Muslim community of South-East Asia towards globalization and related processes, it is essential to be aware of the existence of two different tendencies. The first is composed of those who, partly in reaction to colonial and later contentions to the contrary, tend to stress the "purity" of their religion. Most of them link this judgment to the fact, as they stress, that South-East Asian Islam is part of and conforms to universal Islam. It could be said that this tendency supports globalization in the first sense defined above, namely intensification of the involvement in universal Islam. For certain, but not all, groups, this tendency leads to a movement of reaction to globalization in the second sense, i.e. to a refusal to become part of a uniform civilization that makes no special reference to the Islamic religion. On the other hand, some in the Muslim community tends to emphasize the particular character of South-East Asian Islam. This attitude is often associated with national pride. The existence of these two, conflicting tendencies is most obvious in Indonesia, but it is not confined to this country by any means.[32]

Education

The nature and development of Muslim education in the region offers specific evidence concerning the impact of globalization and the attitude of the Muslim population towards it. As explained earlier, for centuries South-East Asia has been linked to the rest of the Muslim world by a strong network of educational and scholarly relations as well as by international mystical orders. More recently, the Indonesian State Institutes for Islamic Sciences (*Institut Agama Islam Negeri*, IAIN), of which an increasing number have been created since 1960, have demonstrably shown a broad

---

[31]See for example the series of reports entitled [*Laporan Penelitian*] *Antisipasi Agama Terhadap Trend Globalisasi Pembangunan Regional dan Lokal* [(Research Report) on the Religious Anticipation of the Globalization Trend in Regional and Local Development] written in 1992-1994 by a team of the Badan Penelitian dan Pengembangan Agama, Departemen Agama Republik Indonesia.

[32]For a detailed discussion of this phenomenon in Indonesia, see Meuleman, op. cit., esp. 114 f. For a similar phenomenon in Malaysia, see Abaza, "Islam in South-east Asia", 148 f.

orientation in their curriculum and educational approach: they have been inspired by the Middle Eastern tradition of Islamic higher education, the Western academic tradition, and by the peculiarly Indonesian tradition and needs. Moreover, for at least two decades it has been the policy of the Indonesian Ministry of Religious Affairs to send specialists of Islamic Sciences for postgraduate studies to both Middle Eastern and Western countries.[33] The global orientation of Indonesian Islamic education is therefore strong. Nevertheless, in this context Indonesian Islam acts as a receiver rather than as an actor.

The same tendencies can be observed in the other countries of the region. The difference is that in neighbouring countries relatively more students of Islamic religion are sent to the Middle East, fewer to Western universities. Of particular importance is the creation of the International Islamic University Malaysia or Universitas Islam Antarbangsa Malaysia in 1983 and the International Institute of Islamic Thought and Civilization, established in 1987 as an autonomous institution within this university. Both institutions intend to attract an international public and play a role as co-actor in the contemporary global civilization.[34] One of the youngest and smallest institutes of Islamic higher education in the region, the College of Islamic Studies of the Prince of Songkla University, Pattani, Thailand, has not arrived at this stage yet, but at least it has started to establish relations with similar institutions in South-East Asia or elsewhere.[35]

Literature

In the field of Islamic literature, for several centuries South-East Asia has also been participating in the circulation of numerous religious works. The

---

[33]See Meuleman, "The Institut Agama Islam Negeri at the Crossroads." in this volume and *idem* and Chambert-Loir, "Les instituts islamiques publics indonésiens"; and Meuleman, "IAIN di Persimpangan Jalan".

[34]For a concise survey of the history and nature of these institutes, see Ibrahim Abu Bakar, "A History of Islamic Studies in Malaysian Universities and Colleges".

[35]Evidence for this is the international seminar mentioned in the preceding footnote, organized by this college. In 1996 it sent a first graduate for advanced studies to Leiden University, but his studies failed because of his insufficient mastery of the English language. In 1998 the Prince of Songkla University signed a co-operation agreement with the University of Malaya, Kuala Lumpur, relating to Islamic sciences.

number of foreign works on Islamic sciences in the region has greatly increased since the end of the nineteenth century, in the wake of the improvement of transport between the Middle East and South-East Asia and the establishment of various printing firms. In this field once again, however, South-East Asia is mainly an importer of books — and therefore ideas —, not an exporter. After an analysis of books relating to Muslim women circulating in contemporary Indonesia, of which many were translations from Middle Eastern books, I concluded that the main function of most of these books was to reinforce a tradition — or even create a pseudo-tradition — rather than to develop Islam. I also established that very few of these books were relevant to the actual situation of contemporary Indonesian Muslim women.[36] Surprisingly, the circulation of South-East Asian publications among the different countries of the region is extremely limited. Even Indonesian books are hardly available in Malaysia and the reverse is just as true, although both countries speak variants of the same language. A first step on the way to transform South-East Asia from a mere receiver of foreign books — which sometimes amounts to the position of "victim" of globalization — to an intellectual actor on the global scale has been taken by the foundation in 1994 of *Studia Islamika. Indonesian Journal for Islamic Studies*. The objective of this journal of IAIN Syarif Hidayatullah, Jakarta, is to offer articles satisfying international scholarly standards to a global public. Its articles are in English, Arabic, and Indonesian.

Solidarity Movements

As was stated earlier, the large movements showing solidarity with groups of Muslims who are victims of oppression elsewhere in the world form another aspect of globalization, and, from a certain point of view, of polarization at a global level. The Palestinian and the Bosnian people are the main objects of support by these movements. Many South-East Asian Muslims do not consider their sufferings as merely a remote problem that does not concern them.[37]

---

[36]Meuleman, "Analisis Buku-Buku".

[37]For details on Indonesian Muslim solidarity movements with their co-religionists elsewhere, see Darul Aqsha et al., *Islam in Indonesia*, chapter 1 (5 ff.), *passim*.

Struggle for Autonomy

Among movements for autonomy or independence with an Islamic background, the most important have arisen in Southern Thailand and the Southern Philippines. Above, we have already seen that religion was not the fundamental cause of these conflicts, but rather a source of inspiration and ideology as well as providing a basis of organization. It might be added that the harshness of these conflicts, which may be characterised as reactions to globalization processes, depends on several factors, one of the most important being the policy of the central authorities. The difference in attitude and policy shown by the Thai and Philippine governments towards their respective southern Muslim minorities is one of the factors that explain the difference of the way the conflicts in both countries have developed.[38] This supposition is bolstered by the fact that for the last few years the more tolerant, developmental, and participatory character of government policy regarding the Muslims of Southern Thailand has assuaged the friction in this country. Analysis of the Darul Islam/Tentara Islam Indonesia movement of opposition to the Indonesian central government, which lasted until the early 1960s, also shows, firstly, that religion was more a source of inspiration and basis of organization than the fundamental factor of the movement; and secondly, that a change in the attitude of the central government lessened the conflict and finally resolved it.[39]

Inter-Religious Relations

Until a few years ago, South-East Asia in general and Indonesia in particular was known for the relatively good relations which were maintained between the various religious communities. This was more than just official propaganda. Most Muslims in the region accept a plural society, i.e. with a plurality of ethnic and religious groups and, especially in Indonesia, plurality of religious understanding and practice within the Muslim community

---

[38]Man, op. cit., 177.
[39]See, among other works, Van Dijk, *Rebellion under the Banner of Islam*, 391 ff.

itself.[40] However, various voices have accused at least some of the Indonesian authorities or security forces of the New Order regime of having manipulated the inter-religious relations.[41] Since about 1996, various cases of violence perpetrated by Muslims against places of worship of other communities have shocked public opinion both within the country and abroad. There are some who think that these cases were orchestrated by certain elements of the New Order regime. The recent reform movement that led to the fall of President Soeharto had a large, multi-religious base. Students from the non-denominational Universitas Indonesia, the exclusively Muslim IAIN, the Protestant Universitas Kristen Indonesia, the Roman Catholic Universitas Katolik Indonesia Atma Jaya, and many other institutions demonstrated together, shoulder to shoulder. A sudden conflict which erupted on 23 May 1998 between a group of exclusively Muslim students who in the name of Islam defended the new president, B.J. Habibie, against other students, who were not satisfied with the mere replacement of Soeharto, at that time appeared to be ephemeral — and once more, according to several voices, a result of devious manipulation.[42] More recently, Indonesia has witnessed unprecedentedly large-scale violence between Christian and Muslim communities, in particular in the Moluccas. Although the causes of this wave of violence are still far from being plumbed, there are strong indications that here once again manipulation by groups close to the *ancient régime* have played a determining role.

In the course of this text we have seen that the South-East Asian Muslim community is involved in the globalization process in a number of disparate ways. In this process, so far its position has mainly been that of a receiving, undergoing party. Nevertheless, a few efforts have been made to become a co-actor. These efforts are based on the conviction that South-East Asian Islam may contribute something to global Islam and global civilization in general. Opposition to globalization has remained limited and if, in a few cases, religion has become a factor in processes of resistance against the

---

[40]For a comparison of the attitude towards religious diversity within Islam among the Muslim communities and the governments of Indonesia, Malaysia, Singapore and Thailand, see a case-study on the Darul Arqam: Meuleman, "Reactions and Attitudes".
[41]See for example Ade Armando, "Sialnya, Ada Muchtar Pakpahan".
[42]The group of exclusively Muslim students called themselves Komite Aksi Umat Islam Untuk Reformasi (KAUIR; see *Media Indonesia*, 24 May 1998).

external world or other communities, its role has tended to be secondary to other factors and dependent on particular conditions.

Epilogue: Globalization and the Economic Crisis

The economic crisis that has affected South-East Asia since about 1997, and as yet does not appear to be approaching a solution, can only be explained as resulting from a combination of certain elements of the globalization process and a number of domestic problems. Therefore, it seems logical that any search for its solution should also consider both aspects of the crisis. From the viewpoint of the theme of this text, the economic crisis has had both positive and negative effects. The positive effects are that the tendency towards a greater open-mindedness regarding various groups and ideas domestically and at a global level, the tendency towards a dynamic and harmonious social and political pluralism, and the development of civil society have been stimulated. The negative effect is that the position of this region in the globalization process has become less that of an actor, more that of a re-actor, if not a victim. These effects concern South-East Asia in general, but are strongest in the case of Indonesia, which is also facing the most serious crisis of all the countries in the region. It is here especially that the positive effects of the economic crisis referred to above have been increasingly threatened by an internal struggle for power, which has led to a serious reduction in social harmony and exacerbated the position of Indonesia as a victim of global processes.

2 Globalization of Indonesian Muslim Discourse

Contemporary Religio-Intellectual Connections Between Indonesia and the Middle East

Azyumardi Azra

Introduction

Globalization is, for sure, a new "pet theme" among scholars today. With respect to the history of Islam in Indonesia, however, "globalization" is not really a new phenomenon. In fact, there has been a continuous "globalization" of Indonesian Muslim discourse since relatively early in the history of Islam in the region. The centre of the global system Indonesian Islam was a part of, both religiously and intellectually, was the Haramayn, i.e. The Two Protected Cities, Mecca and Medina.

As I have shown elsewhere, intense religio-intellectual contacts and connections between Malay-Indonesian students or scholars (*'ulamā'*, in Malay *ulama*), and their co-religionists and *'ulamā'* in the Haramayn had a vivid reforming impact on the course of Islam in the archipelago, especially from the seventeenth century onwards.[1] Returning students or scholars, although they were also Sufi thinkers and shaykhs, implanted a more *sharī'ah*-oriented Islam in the Malay-Indonesian Archipelago, which forced the so-called "pantheistic" (or "*wujudiyyah mulhid*") Sufism to cede ground. This is the beginning of the rise of a more scriptural Islam, or, in Reid's terms, "scriptural orthodoxy" in Indonesia.[2] The most important proponents of this new tendency throughout the seventeenth and eighteenth centuries were Nūr al-Dīn al-Rānīrī, 'Abd al-Ra'ūf al-Sinkilī, Muḥammad Yūsuf al-Maqassarī, 'Abd al-Samad al-Palimbānī, Muhammad Arshad al-Banjarī, and Dāwūd b. 'Abd Allāh al-Patānī.

By the end of the nineteenth century new globalizing waves of Muslim discourse reached the shores of the Malay-Indonesian Archipelago. These waves were initially brought into the archipelago mostly by haj pilgrims who

---

[1] Azra, *Transmission of Islamic Reformism.*
[2] Reid, *Southeast Asia in the Age of Commerce.*

31

from the 1870s travelled in ever increasing numbers to the Holy Land. Returning to their villages, these new hajis spread not only the spirit of pan-Islamism, but most importantly distributed Islamic literature of various kinds. No less important was the significant role played by the many established *pesantren*s (traditional Islamic boarding schools) in what Roff once called "intensification of Islam".

Other waves came in the early decades of the twentieth century.[3] This was a new kind of waves which has been categorized by many observers as "Islamic modernism". As might have been expected, these waves originated not from the Haramayn, but Cairo instead.

Heavily indebted to modernist Muslim thinkers like Jamāl al-Dīn al-Afghānī and Muhammad 'Abduh, a new Muslim discourse developed in Indonesia, which was later on crystallized in the establishment of such "modernist" Muslim organizations as the Muhammadiyah (1912), al-Irsyad (1913), and Persis (in the early 1920s).

Nowadays, the globalizing waves that influence Muslim discourse in Indonesia no longer stem only from the Haramayn or even from Cairo. In fact, the respectable position of the Haramayn, so far as Indonesian Muslim discourse is concerned, has been in decline for the last few decades.[4] Other places in the Middle East, or elsewhere in the Muslim world, have recently come to the forefront and, in turn, have left their impact on Muslim discourse in Indonesia. Therefore it might certainly be argued that the historic religio-intellectual contacts and relations between Indonesia and the Middle East have been characterized by a combination of continuities and changes.

This text is a preliminary attempt to delineate briefly the contemporary globalization of Muslim discourse in Indonesia by way of tracing religio-intellectual connections between Indonesia and the Middle East in particular. Special attention will be paid to the impact of such religio-intellectual connections upon contemporary Muslim movements in Indonesia.

[3]Roff, "Islam di Asia Tenggara".
[4]Azra, "'Ulama' Indonesia di Haramayn"; *idem*, "Melacak Pengaruh"; *idem*, "Two Worlds of Islam"; *idem*, "Dari Haramayn ke Kairo"; Abaza, *Islamic Education*.

Internal Resurgence of Islam

The contemporary globalization of Muslim discourse in Indonesia is not an isolated phenomenon. Rather, it is a consequence of some interrelated developments at both the domestic and the international level.

At the domestic level, Islam in Indonesia has undergone several tremendous developments and changes during the last three decades. There is no doubt that the failure of the Partai Komunis Indonesia (PKI — Indonesian Communist Party) has stimulated some kind of "Islamic resurgence" in Indonesia. During the period of Soekarno's honeymoon with the communists, with the exception of the Nahdlatul Ulama (NU — Awakening of the *'Ulamā'*, i.e. Islamic religious scholars), Muslim groups were marginalized, if not suppressed. Some prominent Muslim leaders, including Mohammad Natsir, former leader of the Masjumi (Majelis Sjura Muslimin Indonesia — Indonesian Muslim Deliberation Council), and Professor Hamka, a prominent *'ālim* and writer who later became the first chairman of the Majelis Ulama Indonesia (MUI — Indonesian Council of Religious Scholars), were put into jail by the regime. Not many Muslims dared to identify themselves openly as Muslim; being a Muslim was therefore a handicap, particularly in Indonesian politics.

The fiasco of the alleged PKI *coup d'état* (1965) gave new breath to Muslim life in Indonesia. The pre-eminent role of Muslim organizations in counter-actions against communist elements brought Islam back into the socio-political arena.

Despite some political disappointment among Muslims in the early years of the post-1965 New Order era, Islamic religious life was blossoming. Muslim activists who had been pushed behind closed doors during the communist heyday, now steadily began not only to establish mosques, particularly on university campuses and government offices, but also to form *kelompok pengajian* (Islamic discussion groups), or *majelis taklim* (Islamic learning groups). With these the process of "santrinization"[5] of Indonesian Muslim society began to take place.

The resurgence of Islam in Indonesia during the first half of the 1980s did not proceed smoothly. It was somewhat restrained by the continuing tensions between Muslim groups and the government. Muslims felt that

---

[5]From the term *santri*, used to refer to *pesantren* pupils, but also, more generally, to "orthodox" Muslims.

certain government policies, including the forced fusion of Islamic parties into the PPP (Partai Persatuan Pembangunan — United Development Party; 1973), the controversial Marriage Bill of 1974, and lastly the implementation of the *Pancasila* as the sole ideological basis for all social and political organizations (imposed from 1985), were intended to uproot Islamic influences in Indonesian public life.[6] Some Muslims even considered such policies to be part of a systematic "de-politization" of Indonesian Islam. In spite of the objection of many Muslims, the government succeeded in putting all those policies into effect.

As far as the development of Islam in Indonesia is concerned, the acceptance of the *Pancasila* as the sole ideological basis has led to somewhat surprising consequences, even for Muslims themselves. With its acceptance, the path for Islamic resurgence proved to have been cleared. The relatively long mutual suspicion and tension fostered between the government and Muslim groups now became something of the past. Henceforth Muslims were able to carry out various activities without any restrictions or hindrance. Since then, the *rapprochement* between the Muslim population and the Soeharto government gathered momentum and eventually led to what some observers call the "honeymoon" between the two sides.

The "honeymoon" period, it seems, began openly with the establishment of the ICMI (Ikatan Cendekiawan Muslim se-Indonesia — All-Indonesian Association of Muslim Intellectuals) in late 1990. Chaired by the Minister of Research and Technology, B.J. Habibie, the formation of the ICMI was supported by President Soeharto personally. Since its foundation, the ICMI has been playing a predominant role, not only in the establishment of various new Islamic institutions such as the Bank Muamalat Indonesia (Islamic Bank), the *Republika* daily, and the CIDES (Centre for Information and Development Studies, an ICMI "think tank"), but supposedly also in the appointments of ICMI leaders to high offices such as cabinet ministries or provincial governorships. There have been other favourable developments for Muslims, such as the enactment of laws on national education and on Islamic courts, which put Islamic institutions like the *madrasah* (Islamic school) and *peradilan agama* (Islamic court) on the same footing as their "secular" counterparts, that is, the *sekolah umum* (public school) and *peradilan negeri* (state court) respectively.

---

[6]*Pancasila* (the "Five Pillars") is the name of the official ideology of the Indonesian Republic.

The resurgence of Islam arrived with some significant improvements in Muslim socio-economic life. The liberalization and globalization of the Indonesian economy which began in earnest in the late 1970s have steadily improved the economic conditions of the Muslim population as a whole. As a result, by the end of the 1980s an increasing number of Muslims were able to afford the relatively high expenses of the haj pilgrimage; and in the last few years Indonesia has sent the largest haj contingent from outside of Saudi Arabia. During this period, mosques and other places of Islamic worship have been built in ever-increasing numbers; the *majelis taklim* began to gather in prestigious hotels; and more and more Islamic schools and *pesantren*s have been established in urban areas, no longer just in rural areas as in the past. Keeping pace with these developments, the number of "middle class" Muslims was also increasing; many of them received their advanced education abroad, and are holding important social, political, and economic positions that allow them to enjoy some economic symbols of the middle class.

All these phenomena point to the fact that Islam in Indonesia has become more santrinized and more urbanized, indeed more cosmopolitan. Islam is no longer associated with rural culture and backwardness.

The Global Dimension of "Mainstream" Movements

In many respects, all these developments indicate the rise of a new orientation of Muslim dynamics in the country. Indonesian Muslims, by and large, now employ a socio-cultural rather than a political approach to the development of Islamic life — the latter orientation being so dominant during the Soekarno and early New Order periods. This socio-cultural approach has been strongly advocated since the early 1970s by such leading proponents of the *Kelompok Pembaruan* (renewal group) as Nurcholish Madjid, Harun Nasution, and later Abdurrahman Wahid and Munawir Sjadzali.

The rise of this new orientation of Islam, which to a great extent accords with the so called "de-politization" of Indonesian Islam mentioned above, has puzzled a number of scholars. The Malaysian scholar, Muhammad Kamal Hassan, argues that the *Kelompok Pembaruan* has been stage-managed by the New Order. I would argue, however, that the ideas put forward by leading *pembaruan* thinkers, like Nurcholish Madjid or Harun Nasution, were genuinely conceived by themselves. Nurcholish' ideas of "Islam yes, Partai

Islam no" and "secularization and de-secularization", or Harun Nasution's "neo-Mu'tazilite theology" are clearly in line with the ideas of progress and economic development proposed by the New Order government; but this does not mean that they were simply "engineered" by the regime.[7]

The global dimension of the discourse of the renewal groups is obvious. Nurcholish Madjid was well-versed in various streams of both classical and modern, Muslim as well as Western thought, even before he embarked on advanced studies under the late Fazlur Rahman at the University of Chicago from 1978 to 1984. Since that time, he is said to have been strongly influenced by both Fazlur Rahman and Ibn Taymiyyah. Before long, like his mentor, Nurcholish was being categorized as belonging to the "neo-modernist" group, together with other members of the renewal group[8]. In contrast, Harun Nasution, was heavily influenced by the rational and liberal thought of the Mu'tazilah, particularly as this was reformulated in the modern context by the leading Egyptian modernist, Muḥammad 'Abduh. The most eclectic among these scholars is, of course, Abdurrahman Wahid, whose thought has been influenced by various sources ranging from "traditional Islam" (his NU roots) and liberal Islam (his education and intellectual environment in the Middle East) to contemporary Western intellectual tendencies.

The strongest opposition to, or perhaps more appropriately disapproval of, the "neo-modernist" group has come from the Dewan Dakwah Islamiyah Indonesia (DDII — Indonesian Council for Islamic Propagation), which has more recently become also known as the "Kramat Raya Group".[9] This group was once led by the late Mohammad Natsir, the prominent leader of the banned Masjumi and prime minister during the early years of the Soekarno period. After the death of Mohammad Natsir, the leadership of the DDII passed into the hands of Muhammad Rasjidi, whose activities were greatly limited by his advanced years, however. His inactivity meant that the effective leader of the DDII was Anwar Harjono, a member of the Petisi 50 opposition group.[10] It is important to note, however, that in the second half of the 1990s Anwar Harjono and the Soeharto regime began a reconciliation process. The transformation of the DDII from being a strong critic to a

---

[7]See Muzani, "Mu'tazilah Theology".
[8]Cf. Barton, "Neo-Modernism", 13-24.
[9]After the street in which their headquarters are located.
[10]The "Petisi 50" group is called after a critical petition addressed by fifty prominent Indonesians to President Soeharto in 1980.

supporter of the regime was accelerated by younger DDII leaders, particularly Ahmad Sumargono, who had close relations with several generals, such as Prabowo Soebianto, R. Hartono, and Faisal Tanjung. Ahmad Sumargono, the chief leader of the KISDI (Komite Indonesia untuk Solidaritas Dunia Islam — the Indonesian Committee for Solidarity with the Muslim World), and Husein Umar and K.H. M. Khalil Ridwan became the actual leaders of the DDII because of Anwar Harjono's frail health.[11]

Since the time of Mohammad Natsir the DDII has shown its disapproval of the renewal group. Though Mohammad Natsir never condemned the renewal group publicly, he was obviously disappointed, particularly on the controversial ideas of Nurcholish Madjid. Nurcholish himself was once dubbed the "young Natsir", but later he took a different path. The fiercest public opposition to both Nurcholish Madjid and Harun Nasution came from Muhammad Rasjidi, who wrote special books to express his criticism of each of them.[12]

The DDII aversion to the renewal group was once again expressed in 1993. This time it was triggered off by Nurcholish Madjid's public lecture entitled *Penyegaran Paham Keagamaan di Kalangan Generasi Muda Mendatang* (Refreshing the Religious Belief of the Future Young Generation). In this lecture Nurcholish proposed, among other idesa, a new meaning of "islam" (with undercase i), not only as the religion preached by the Prophet Muhammad ("Islam" with uppercase I), but also as "the attitude of submitting oneself to the Truth". According to this definition, Nurcholish argued, the followers of "islam" are not confined to those who believe in Muhammad's teachings, but also include other people who believe in the perennial Truth of God.[13] This point and other opinions to which he gave voice soon became very controversial issues. The DDII group took the leading role in heated public controversies, and Nurcholish together with his renewal group were pejoratively labelled the "Gerakan Pengacau Keagamaan" (GPK — Movement Creating Religious Confusion) by the DDII group.[14]

[11]Cf. Hefner, "Islam and Nation", 48-9.
[12]Barton, op. cit., 13-6; Azra, "Guarding the Faith", 110-4.
[13]Madjid, "Beberapa Renungan".
[14]Punning on the standard term Acehnese autonomy activists and other destabilizing groups were called with: *Gerakan Pengacau Keamanan* (GPK — Security Disturbing Group).

Why was (and latently is) the DDII so critical of the *Kelompok Pembaruan*? What are the religio-intellectual sources of the DDII? Does it have any global connection? I would argue that the roots of the DDII criticism and opposition lie in its strong religio-intellectual tendencies towards Salafism. It is well-known that before founding the DDII in 1967, Mohammad Natsir was a leader of the Persis (Persatuan Islam — Islamic Union), a strict Salafite reformist movement established by Ahmad Hassan, of mixed Indian and Indonesian parentage, who was brought up in Singapore. This Salafite orientation was consolidated even more by Muhammad Rasjidi, a long time prominent member of the Muhammadiyah, the largest Salafite organization in Indonesia. As might have been expected, with its pronounced Salafism — called "fundamentalism" by some[15] —, the DDII has strong connections with the Rābiṭah al-'Ālam al-Islāmī, the Saudi-sponsored Muslim international organization. Besides this doctrinal link, there is some evidence that the DDII also subscribes to certain ideas of Sayyid Quṭb and Mawdūdī, two of the most influential leaders of Salafite inspiration.

Global Muslim "Splinter" Movements

Over and above this "mainstream" discourse of Indonesian Muslims, since the 1980s Indonesia has seen the rise of some unprecedented movements. Most of these movements have their origins abroad.

One important factor behind this phenomenon is the spread of new Islamic literature in Indonesia. In the wake of the fascination engendered by the historic success of the Iranian revolution of 1979, many books written by Iranian "secular" intellectuals as well as *'ulamā'* began to be translated into Bahasa Indonesia. Since this epoch it has been easy to find Indonesian versions of books by such authors as 'Alī Sharī'ātī, Seyyed Hossein Nasr, Ayatullah Khumaynī, Muhammad Ḥusayn Ṭabāṭabā'ī, Murtaḍā Muṭahharī, and Muḥammad Bāqir al-Sadr. Indonesian translations of various works written by revivalist authors like Mawdūdī, Ḥasan al-Bannā, Sayyid Quṭb, Muḥammad Quṭb, Abū al-Ḥasan al-Nadwī, Muḥammad al-Ghazālī, and Maryam Jameelah are also available. These have been followed by translations of books by M.M. Azami (Muḥammad Muṣtafā al-A'zamī),

---

[15]Muzani, "Di Balik Polemik".

Yūsuf al-Qaradāwī, Mutawallī Sha'rāwī, and 'Abd Allāh Nasīḥ 'Ulwān. Another group of translations is represented by works of Fazlur Rahman, Naguib al-Attas, Isma'īl al-Farūqī, Akbar S. Ahmed, Muḥammad Asad, Mohammed Arkoun, Bassam Tibi, Ziauddin Sardar, Fatima Mernissi, and Alija Izetbegovic. Not least important, some books produced by "orientalists" have also been translated. The list includes works by Montgomery Watt, Bernard Lewis, N.J. Coulson, G.E. von Grunebaum, Edward Said, W.C. Smith, I. Goldziher, Annemarie Schimmel, Maxime Rodinson, John Esposito, Edward Mortimer, and C.E. Bosworth.[16]

There is no doubt that the publication of these books contributed significantly to the increasing plurality of Indonesian Muslim discourse. It indicates that the religio-intellectual discourse of Islam in Indonesia is becoming more widely exposed to global perspectives irrespective of their own nature, not only those propounded among Muslim scholars themselves, but also those put forward by outsiders (non-Muslim intellectuals) who have sometimes been the object of darkest suspicion in Muslim circles. In the final analysis, the publication of translated works has stimulated the rise of a new breed of Muslim movements in Indonesia.

The publication of translated works, however, is not the only factor in the rise of the new Muslim movements in Indonesia that will be discussed in detail below. Cultural exchanges between Indonesian Muslims both at home and abroad also play a significant role. As Mona Abaza has convincingly shown us, many Indonesian students in Cairo in the last two decades have been increasingly pulled into the "fundamentalist" lap.[17] At the same time, many Indonesian Muslim students, pursuing advanced studies in Western countries, for various reasons, have also undergone a kind of intensification of Islam. Many of them are now also attracted to Islamic ideas unpopular or even unknown in Indonesia in the past.

Therefore, when these students have returned home ever since the early 1980s, they introduced what they had gained abroad. They have adopted not only these unfamiliar Islamic ideas, they have also embraced the framework and methodology of Muslim movements they saw and became involved in abroad. Many returned with a new Islamic way of dress, particularly the *jilbāb* (veil) and *jalabiyyah* (long robe for men). They have also introduced organizations of a new style known as "*usrah*", under the leadership of an

---

[16]Azra, *Perbukuan*; cf. Von der Mehden, *Two Worlds of Islam*, 72-91.
[17]Abaza, op. cit., 91-101.

"*imam*" or "*amir*". There is a strong tendency among them not simply to question the belief and practice of mainstream Muslims, but also to reject government authority. This attitude is manifested by phenomena such as their refusal to return the *salam* (that is, the Islamic greeting "*Assalamu'alaykum warahmatullahi wa barakatah*) of other Muslims; their conducting of marriages only through their "*imam*" or "*amir*" without formal registration with the office of Muslim marital affairs; and their burning of resident identification cards.

Another important factor in the development of new movements is the cultural exchange that occurred in Indonesia itself through the visits of foreign Muslims, either for missionary reasons or otherwise. These foreigners have established their organizations or networks among Indonesian Muslims. It appears that one of the most active foreign Muslim groups in Indonesia is the Tablīghī Jamā'at, which originates from India.

At this point it is apposite to introduce a discussion of some of the most important contemporary movements in Indonesia which have clear global connections.

Shi'ism

For a long time a number of scholars supposed that Shi'ism used to have a strong influence in Indonesia, particularly in the early years of the spread of Islam in the country. I have argued that there is not sufficient evidence to support this assertion.[18] Were there some "Shi'ite" influences, they would have been very superficial. Undoubtedly, Shi'ism has become popular in Indonesia only recently, particularly after the Iranian revolution, which, as mentioned above, was followed by Indonesian translations of works by Shi'ite intellectuals and scholars.

Many observers and government authorities assume that Shi'ism has gained followers, particularly among young Indonesian Muslims. Ahmad Barakbah, a Qum graduate, claims that there are some 20.000 Shi'ites in Indonesia nowadays.[19] However, it is difficult to assess the exact number. It is said that one of the leading "Shi'ite" intellectuals in Indonesia is Jalaluddin Rahmat, a celebrated lecturer at the Pajajaran University of

---

[18]Azra, "Syi'ah di Indonesia".
[19]Nurjuliyanti and Subhan, "Lembaga Syi'ah", 21; Alkaff "Perkembangan Syiah", 62.

Bandung. Despite the fact that Jalaluddin Rahmat himself has never openly admitted that he is a Shi'ite, he plays a pivotal role in explicating Shi'ite doctrines to various circles. Furthermore, he has been involved in heated debates with certain Sunnite individuals and groups who considered the increasing popularity of Shi'ism a menace to Sunnite orthodoxy.

A further indication of the increasing popularity of Shi'ism in Indonesia is the growth of some forty "Shi'ite" institutions in Jakarta, Bogor, Bandung, Malang, Jember, Bangil, Samarinda, Pontianak, and Banjarmasin. It appears that the centre of these institutions is Jakarta, which reportedly has at least twenty-five Shi'ite institutions. All these institutions are devoted to missionary and educational activities. The most prominent among them is perhaps the Mutahhari Foundation in Bandung. This foundation, led by Jalaluddin Rahmat, has an Islamic senior high school called "SMA [senior high school] Mutahhari", which has become one of the most favourite schools in Bandung in the last few years.[20] Besides its educational activities, the Mutahhari Foundation issues the journal *Hikmah*, which publishes many translated articles written by Shi'ite *'ulamā'* and intellectuals.

Another noted Shi'ite institution in Bandung is the Jawad Foundation. In addition to conducting regular courses on Ja'farite *fiqh*, the Jawad foundation first published a "magazine" called *Bulletin al-Jawad*; later this name was changed into *al-Ghadir*.[21] Yet another important institution often associated with Shi'ism in Bandung is the Mizan publishing house, which takes care of the publication of many translations of books written by Shi'ite intellectuals and scholars. In the middle of 1996, at a book launch sponsored by another publisher in Jakarta, there were voices urging that Mizan's allegedly Shi'ite-oriented publications be boycotted. Sofar, Mizan itself appears to keep aloof from such allegations and actions, and it also publishes many works by non-Shi'ite authors.

One of the leading Shi'ite institutions in Jakarta is the Muntadzar Foundation which was established in 1991. Like the Jawad Foundation in Bandung, the Muntadzar Foundation was established by some Shi'ites. Therefore, the initial programme of the foundation was the study of the "*madhhab* [*fiqh* school] of the *ahl al-bayt* [lit. the family (of the Prophet Muhammad)]", i.e. Islamic jurisprudence in the Shi'ite tradition. Now the

---

[20]Cf. Sarnapi, "SMU Plus Mutahhari".
[21]See Nurjulianti and Subhan, op. cit., 25.

41

Muntadzar Foundation claims to have at least 400 members from all over Jakarta. Its activities are not confined to studying Shi'ite *fiqh*, but also include education at the kindergarten, primary school, and junior and senior high school level.

In Bogor, a Shi'ite institution called the Mulla Sadra Foundation was founded in 1993. Like other such institutions, the Mulla Sadra Foundation originally devoted itself to studying the *ahl al-bayt fiqh* school. But later the foundation expanded its activities to include education and the provision of various social and health services. Pesantren al-Hadi in Pekalongan, a town in Central Java, has a similar background. This *pesantren* was established by Ahmad Barakbah in 1989. The *pesantren* adopted the educational system of Qum. All its nine teachers were graduates from Qum in Iran and Pesantren al-Hadi now has 112 students, most of whom come from outside Java.

Jama'ah Tabligh

The Tablīghī Jamā'at or Jamā'ah al-Tablīgh wa-al-Da'wah was founded in India by Shaykh Mawlana Muhammad Ilyas in 1930. It is believed to have been introduced into Indonesia in 1952, but it only began to gain momentum in this country only in the early 1970s, especially after the construction of its mosque in Kebon Jeruk, Jakarta, in 1974. Now, according to Ahmad Zulfakar, the chief leader of the Jama'ah Tabligh — as it is called in this country — in Indonesia, the movement has its branches in all twenty-seven provinces of the pre-1999 administrative division. My own observation tends to confirm this. At a recent observation in Sawangan, a suburb in South Jakarta, I found a small community of Jama'ah Tabligh, living in peaceful co-existence with other Muslims. According to a local resident, the movement was brought to their village by some Pakistani and Bangladeshi Muslims who later on married local women.

The Jama'ah Tabligh is known for the distinctive appearance of its adherents. Most — if not all — Jama'ah Tabligh members wear Middle Eastern style clothes; men wear *jalabiyyah*, and women wear a fully closed veil. Men also let their beard grow. The adherents also take a *siwāk* — a kind of vegetable toothbrush believed to have been used by the Prophet Muhammad — everywhere they go. They also have adopted what they believe to have been the Prophet's way of eating; a communal meal served in a *nampan* (common dish), using hands only to eat.

Distinguishing itself from most other contemporary Muslim "splinter" movements which tend to be more political, the Jama'ah Tabligh is a completely non-political movement. It is said that its only concern is to spread what its members believe is the correct Islamic way of life through missionary activities. In their eyes talking about politics is *harām* (impermissible); the same goes for talking about *khilāfiyyāt* ("minor differences") between Muslims, asking for charity, or condemning the government. Every member of the Jama'ah Tabligh has the obligation to conduct *khurūj* (lit. "go outside") at least once a year in order to spread their message, e.g. by door-to-door propaganda. The expenses for the *khurūj* are the responsibility of the participants themselves. Also once a year they have an *ijtimā'* or meeting. It is during this great gathering that prominent leaders from other countries, mainly from India and Pakistan, give what they call *ceramah pencerahan* ("enlightening speeches").

Darul Arqam

This is undoubtedly the most politically controversial Muslim movement not only in Malaysia — where it was firstly established — but also in Indonesia. Founded in Kuala Lumpur, Malaysia, in 1968, by Imam Ashari Muhammad al-Tamimi, since the late 1970s the Darul Arqam movement increasingly gained its followers from among middle and higher strata of Malaysian Muslim society, including many students and a number of high-ranking officials or members of their families. The main objective of the Darul Arqam is the application of a total Islamic way of life. Towards this end, the Darul Arqam established exclusive communities, where it could implement its teachings, not only religiously, but also socially and economically. It was relatively successful, particularly in its economic enterprises, which, according to some observers, were well on the way to becoming a challenge to UMNO political and economic ventures.[22]

It is difficult to know exactly when the Darul Arqam began to spread in Indonesia. Nevertheless, there is no doubt that the movement became increasingly popular in this country throughout the 1980s and early 1990s. It appears that the Darul Arqam spread all over Indonesia, with prominent centres in Jakarta (Depok), Bogor, and Bandung. The followers of the Darul

---

[22]Cf. Meuleman, "Reactions and Attitudes".

Arqam are mainly young people and university graduates. Until 1990, the Darul Arqam was by and large not regarded as a national threat, mainly because mainstream Muslim organizations in Indonesia had not yet questioned its interpretation of Islam or its activities. The controversy began publicly only on 17 April 1990 when the Indonesian Council of 'Ulamā' (MUI) for the province of West Sumatra issued a fatwa declaring that the teachings of the Darul Arqam were deviating from Islam and therefore asked the authorities to ban the movement. The Fatwa Commission of the national MUI soon followed suit; in 1991 it issued a similar fatwa, and on August 13, 1994, the national MUI declared the Darul Arqam doctrine to be deviant and, therefore, proposed that the Indonesian Attorney General should ban the movement. The office of the Attorney General was reluctant to do so and left it to each provincial prosecutor's office to decide whether or not to issue a ban. Most provinces chose to do so.[23]

As far as the Darul Arqam controversy is concerned, it is important to note a marked difference between various Muslim mainstream organizations in Indonesia on the issue of whether or not the Darul Arqam was a deviant movement and, therefore, whether or not measures should be taken against it. Some organizations believed that the Darul Arqam had strayed from the path of Islamic teaching and, therefore, should be banned. This group consisted of the Muhammadiyah, the DDII, and the Ikatan Masjid Indonesia (Association of Indonesian Mosques). A second group, consisting mainly of organizations affiliated to the Nahdlatul Ulama, were of the opinion that there was nothing wrong with the teachings of the Darul Arqam. If the Darul Arqam were to be banned, they argued, this should not be for religious reasons, but for reasons of national security or in order to preserve the harmonious relationship between different elements of the Muslim population.[24]

It is highly questionable whether the provincial bans were effective. Subsequent observations have confirmed that the Darul Arqam has remained very much alive and relatively unhampered in its activities The New Order authorities seemed to ignore it to the extent that it caused no further "disruption" to inter-religious harmony, which indeed is one of the principles of religious policy in Indonesia.

---

[23]Meuleman, op. cit.; Azra, *Darul Arqam: Tradisionalisme vs Reformisme*; *idem*, "Darul Arqam: A Historical Reflection".
[24]Meuleman, op. cit.

After the fall of Soeharto the Darul Arqam seems to have regained momentum. Although it took a low profile after the controversy mentioned above, its adherents are now coming out more into the open. At present their distinctive dress can be observed in many mosques in various Indonesian cities, including the Istiqlal Mosque and the Grand al-Azhar Mosque in Jakarta. They now publish their own tabloid entitled *Kebenaran*, which is sold in many mosques, particularly on the occasion of the Friday congregational prayers.

Hizb al-Tahrir

According to a report this group was introduced into Indonesia in 1978. Before long, it had gained some popularity among students on university campuses in Jakarta, Bandung, Surabaya, Yogyakarta, and Bogor. The Hizb al-Tahrīr was established in 1952 in Lebanon by Shaykh Taqī al-Dīn al-Nabhānī. Al-Nabhānī himself was known as a thinker and politician, who formerly worked as a judge at the Supreme Court in Jerusalem.

The main objectives of the Hizb al-Tahrīr are to perpetuate the true Islamic way of life globally and, most importantly, to re-establish the *khilafah* (caliphate), which is believed to have been the most suitable and effective political system by which to achieve Muslim unity.[25] To achieve these goals, the Hizb al-Tahrīr seems to have little difficulty in resorting to radicalism. This is why it soon became one of the most popular movements among disenchanted students and young people, not only in the Middle East, but also among Muslim students pursuing their degrees in Western countries.

In Indonesia, however, the Hizb al-Tahrir — as it is called here — appears to have moderated its attitude. In other words, it has had to accommodate to and compromise with the conditions of Indonesian *Realpolitik*. Therefore, as one of its members points out, the Hizb al-Tahrir has not yet been regarded as an enemy by the government authorities. This probably has also something to do with the fact that the Hizb al-Tahrir does not insist on its members adopting a particular distinguishing form of outward appearance such as wearing a beard or a *jalabiyyah*. Hizb al-Tahrir members are apparently critical of established Muslim organizations, such as the Nahdlatul Ulama and the Muhammadiyah, which they consider not to be

---

[25]Dekmejian, *Islam in Revolution*, 88-91, 195.

real *da'wah* (propagation of the Islamic faith) movements. As one member of the Hizb al-Tahrir asserts: "Their [NU and Muhammadiyah] concern is not to transform Indonesia into a fully Islamic society; what they have been doing is simply to improve Muslim education."

Besides all those groups mentioned above, there is still a large number of smaller groups which are loosely organized in *kelompok pengajian* or as *usrah*. In terms of their origins, most of them have been inspired by similar groups operating outside Indonesia, but a small number of them are some kind of "splinter groups" of established mainstream organizations, including the Muhammadiyah, the NU, and the Himpunan Mahasiswa Islam (HMI — Association of Muslim University Students). Most of them are politically motivated and oriented in one way or another, though sometimes in a very subtle way, but a minority is more religiously oriented, like student Sufi groups.

From Quietism to Activism: Radicalism in the Post-Soeharto Era

Most of the Muslim splinter movements discussed above restrained themselves and shunned the limelight during much of the Soeharto era. In fact, they made some adjustments to their ideological position — at least temporarily — for two reasons. Firstly, splinter movements — especially those with a political orientation — domesticated themselves in order to survive the repression of the New Order political machine which would not tolerate any movement it believed could create religious, social, or political conflicts. Within the framework of the notorious *SARA* policy[26] and the introduction of the *Pancasila* as the sole ideological basis of all Indonesian religious, social, and political organizations, the Soeharto regime did not allow Indonesians to confront sensitive issues regarding ethnicity, religion, race, and social class. The Soeharto regime also took harsh measures against organizations that adopted any other "ideology" — including Islam — instead of the *Pancasila*. Secondly, non-political movements such as the Shi'ite

---

[26]*SARA* stands for *Suku, Agama, Ras, dan Antargolongan* — tribe, religion, race, and [relations] between [social] categories.

46

group and the Jama'ah Tabligh tended to adopt a kind of *taqiyyah*[27], keeping their religious beliefs and practices not too obvious. This was done mainly to avoid controversies and conflicts with mainstream Muslim organizations.

The fall of President Soeharto in May 1998, following the monetary, economic, and political crises, undoubtedly was a great stimulus for the splinter movements that had survived his regime and induced them not only to appear in public, but also to consolidate and spread their organizations. Moreover, new "hardline" groups proclaimed their existence publicly, creating a new tendency among Muslim movements in Indonesia and widespread concern among mainstream Muslims.[28] Some of the most prominent of these numerous new groups are the Laskar Jihad (Jihad Troops), the Front Pembela Islam (FPI — Islamic Defence Front), and the Angkatan Mujahidin Indonesia (Indonesian Troop of Mujahidin — i.e. *jihād*, or "holy war" fighters). Of the older Muslim splinter movements, the Hizb al-Tahrir organized an international conference on its favourite theme, the caliphate, in Jakarta in 2000.

It appears that all these movements, now emerging from the closet, are independent of any connection with any of the Muslim political parties that have proliferated in post-Soeharto Indonesia.[29] In contrast, there are rumours that certain hardline groups have been sponsored by, or at least are in close connection with certain circles of the Indonesian military and have received financial support from a number of ambitious entrepreneurs who had amassed large fortunes during the *ancien régime*. Obviously, it is very difficult to verify these rumours. However, the extremist attitude of these groups cannot be denied. The Laskar Jihad, for instance, has become known for dispatching its fighters to the Moluccas in defence of the Muslims against alleged Christian violence and expansion. The FPI has aroused public concern by its frequent attacks on discotheques, nightclubs, and other dens of alleged social iniquity.[30]

---

[27]Dissimulation (of one's faith), an attitude recommended in case of danger, especially in the Shi'te legal tradition.
[28]Azyumardi, "Islamic Perspective on the Nation-State"; *idem*, "Sustaining the Transition", 8 ff.
[29]Azyumardi, "The Islamic Factor in Post-Soeharto Indonesia".
[30]Azyumardi, "Sustaining the Transition", 18; Bamualim et al., *Laporan Penelitian Radikalisme Agama*, 22 ff.

The information available and analyses of this tend to show that domestic transformation processes and conflicts, both at the national and at the regional levels, are the primary factors in the emergence of these radical groups, but international dimensions do exist. A point in case is the Indonesian Hizb al-Tahrir, which is part of an international organization. The leader of the Laskar Jihad, Ja'far Umar Thalib, studied in the Middle East and he as well as various of his followers have reportedly received a guerrilla training in Afghanistan.[31] This Afghan training, believed to have been set up originally by United States secret services in order to combat the Soviet influence in this Central Asian country, is known to have played a role in various countries in the formation of groups that use violence in the name of Islam. More pertinent to our theme, Noorhaidi Hasan, referring to analyses by Olivier Roy of what this French author calls "radical neo-fundamentalism", indicates the international discourse of the movement designated by this term as one of the constituent elements of radical Muslim groups in contemporary Indonesia. This international discourse throws into question the nation-state, which has great difficulties preserving national solidarity while facing globalization. Noorhaidi too, however, considers domestic factors the primary ones in the emergence of these radical groups in Indonesia.[32]

It is important to point out that not all splinter movements consist of hardliners or radicals. The Shi'ites and the Jama'ah Tabligh, for instance, seem to remain non-political, despite the fact that the Shi'ites have publicly declared the foundation of a nation-wide organization that aims to spread Shi'ism in the country. The Dar al-Arqam has also become increasingly visible, but it appears that it puts more emphasis on the religious and spiritual well-being of the Muslim population than on political activities. The Jama'ah Tabligh has remained as peaceable as before.

In passing, it is worth mentioning that some of the Muslim parties and organizations create or revive martial arts youth wings which have the potential to transform themselves into radical organizations. The Partai Kebangkitan Bangsa (PKB — Party for the Rise of the People) and the Nahdlatul Ulama (NU), for instance, have consolidated their Banser Ansor

---

[31]Bamualim et al., op. cit., 40-6.
[32]Noorhaidi, "Islamic Radicalism", 12.

(Bantuan Serba Guna Ansor — *Ansār*[33] Assistance Units for All Purposes); the Partai Persatuan Pembangunan (PPP) has reinvigorated its Gerakan Pemuda Ka'bah (Ka'bah Youth Movement). This phenomenon is not characteristic of Muslim organizations only. The Partai Demokrasi Indonesia-Perjuangan (PDI-P — Struggle-Indonesian Democratic Party) has also formed groups known as the Satgas (Satuan Tugas — Task Force) PDI-P or by other names, whereas the Pemuda Pancasila (*Pancasila* Youth) and other organizations closely related to the central social-cum-political organization of the Soeharto era, the Golkar (Golongan Karya — Functional Groups), have functioned as pressure groups on various occasions since the New Order.

Concluding Notes

The sudden proliferation of splinter and hardline groups in contemporary Indonesia should lead one to question the reasons behind this new tendency. For students of Indonesian Islam, this new tendency is not only unexpected, it could even lead them to question the image of the moderate and "smiling" face of Indonesian Islam. In their eyes, the new tendency seems to bring Indonesian Islam closer to Middle Eastern Islam, in which the existence and proliferation of such groups was considered characteristic. Furthermore, the rise of such groups is thought to threaten the future of democracy in Indonesia.[34]

I would suggest that the proliferation of these splinter groups is closely related to two important phenomena. Firstly, the euphoria of political Islam after a long period of repression during the Soeharto regime stimulated the development of these groups. The liberalization of Indonesian politics since the interregnum of President Habibie provides yet a further impetus to such groups to establish themselves. Secondly, the continued political struggle between fragmented political groups and the disappointment about the delay in economic recovery during the presidency of Abdurrahman Wahid is another factor. The weakness of the Abdurrahman government seriously limits law enforcement. This, in the final analysis, makes it easier for hardline groups to hold sway in society.

---

[33]Helpers, the term used for the inhabitants of Medinah who assisted the Prophet Muhammad and his Meccan followers after they took refuge in this town.
[34]Azyumardi, "Sustaining the Transition".

Looking at the *raison d'être* of hardline groups in particular, I am not pessimistic about the future of both moderate Islam and democracy in Indonesia. These groups are not supported by the mainstream of Indonesian Muslims. Even though these groups are henceforth free to preach their ideas and practices, they are failing to attract a significant following. Lastly, their sudden proliferation, visibility, and radicalization are taking place only in the time of uncertain transition towards democracy. Therefore, once Indonesia attains a new equilibrium in this painful transition, most — if not all — of these hardline groups will lose momentum.

3 The Indonesian Archipelago from 1913 to 2013

Celebrations and Dress Codes Between International, Local, and Islamic Culture

Kees van Dijk

Introduction

In 1995 Indonesia celebrated the fiftieth anniversary of its Independence. It was an enormous feast. At home almost every night for days at a stretch Indonesians could watch films on television depicting the heroic struggle of the Generation of 1945 and the extremely gruesome atrocities committed by Dutch soldiers. But when we compare the atmosphere in 1995 with that of 1970 or 1945 this is not the most striking point about the celebrations. More noteworthy is it that they were a clear testimony to the growing prominence given to Islam in Indonesian society in the last two decades. In the capital Jakarta, for instance, women from all over Indonesia had come to the Senayan Stadium to participate in a mass meeting of religious instruction groups, while a few weeks after August 17th, the Istiqlal Mosque was transformed into the venue for a grand Islamic festival and exhibition. When Indonesia celebrated the twenty-fifth anniversary of its Independence, the Islamic stamp was much less visible. The country had just embarked on a series of five-year plans and was recovering gradually from the shock of the alleged *coup d'état* of September 1965, which marked the rise to power of the New Order. Religion was being endorsed by the new authorities as a sign of good citizenship, and consequently an upsurge of religious activities was indeed observable, but these were far less pronounced than they are nowadays. Public celebrations were still mostly secular.

Pausing for a moment to ponder upon what has been happening the last few years in Indonesia calls to mind other periods in Indonesian history when a similar phenomenon of outpourings of greater Islamic zeal have produced a higher attendance at religious gatherings and influenced the way people behaved in public. For centuries the Indonesian Archipelago, and in this respect it is no exception, has not been immune to rivalry between different sets of values and norms vying with each other for the loyalty of the inhabitants. Contacts with the Indian world, with the Middle East, and with Europe, and at present, of course, with the United States of America, have brought with them the introduction and selective adaptation of foreign cultural traits and beliefs, including political concepts. At times the contacts with the outside world have had far-reaching consequences. The introduction of Hinduism and Buddhism, the dissemination of Islam, and the penetration of European ideas since the sixteenth and seventeenth centuries can all be cited as evidence. These influences from abroad have been strong, and have changed the outlook of Indonesian societies, without them losing their own distinctive identity.

A Turning Point in Dutch Colonial Power

The Centenary of Dutch Independence in Face of the Eastern Awakening

At times domestic competition or rivalry about what should constitute the dominant cultural stream has been quite intense. The following discussion will not go into the older conflicts and disputes which have resulted in new cultural equilibriums in Indonesian history, only to be contested again almost immediately after they were reached. It will concentrate on what happened during the twentieth century, and may pause to speculate a little about what is in store. The original plan was to take August 17th, 1945, as a point of departure, but it was later decided to go back a few more decades to the years around 1913; a moment incidentally when not the Indonesians but the Dutch were celebrating their Independence, commemorating the fact that one hundred years earlier, in November 1813, they had been liberated from French occupation. It was an era which, when contemporary sources are consulted, calls to mind disturbing parallels with our present day and age. At the end of 1913, when the Dutch parliament in The Hague discussed the colonial budget, one of its members, M. Tijdeman, called attention to the rise of nationalism all over the world, linking this phenomenon to the increase in volume of world traffic in the previous decades.[1] Being a Dutchman of his day and age, naturally one of the examples to which he alluded was the "awakening" of the East and of the peoples of the Indonesian Archipelago, and when turning his attention to Europe he mentioned the nationalist

[1]*Handelingen* 1913-1914, II, 149.

aspirations of the Poles and the Finns. He did not mention the Balkans, but there was no need to do so. Slav nationalism was the talk of the day and only recently had led to two Balkan Wars, with Serbs, Greeks, Bulgarians, and Montenegrins fighting the Turks, and each other. Only weeks earlier Dutch army officers had been assigned the task of commanding and organizing a gendarmerie in Albania to keep at bay the various population groups opposing the establishment of this new state, headed by a puppet of the Great Powers, Prince Wilhelm Friedrich Heinrich von Wied (1876-1945). Within a couple of months this involvement in a peace-keeping force in a country plagued by internal strife and religious antagonism was to end in disaster.

As can be construed from Tijdeman's reference to the awakening of the East, Indonesian societies by that time were changing structurally as well as in appearance. The transformation had come suddenly. These were the years in which it must have looked to many a Dutchman in the Netherlands Indies as if the writing was on the wall and the structure of the old familiar society was giving way to a new one. Though people at all times and in all places may experience their own epoch as unique because of the political, economic, and technological changes inherent in it, developments were taking shape, first in Java and a little later in the other islands of the Archipelago, which really did signify a radical departure from the past. Some of these — the acceleration of communication, reformist movements in Islam, the growth of the printing industry, social democratic propaganda — had been set in motion earlier and gradually gained momentum to reach full force after 1900; other ones were unprecedented. Up to the turn of the century there had been almost no political activity in the colony at all, but then, within a couple of years, it seemed that throughout the length and breadth of the Netherlands Indies people were demanding a fundamental overhaul of colonial society. It was useless to turn one's back on what was happening and try to ignore it. The thoughts that were expressed, the demands that were made, the many public meetings that were held, not to mention the turmoil and enthusiasm that were created by newly founded organizations, made it plain that the Indies were poised on the brink of something new. All population groups, including the Europeans, were affected by the changes. On every side, the Dutch Resident of Surabaya noted in 1913, "among the Natives, even among the Europeans and the

Foreign Orientals, there hangs a pall of anxiety".[2] That same year the Advisor for Native Affairs, G.A.J. Hazeu, stressed that, in the wake of the galloping pace of modernization, the colonial administration had to come to terms with the fact that those who not so long before had been merely dubbed the "lesser civil servants" or the "small people" had begun to realize they were human beings too, demanding decent treatment.[3] The pace was such that the Dutch members of the corps — and many of their compatriots — found it difficult to adjust to changing circumstances. Or, as Hazeu, commenting once more on internal developments, remarked in August 1916: "They may be hard put to do so but the civil servants must come to terms with the undeniable fact that within an unbelievably short span of time the whole intellectual and political atmosphere here in this country has undergone huge alterations; no harsh decisions to ban people will provide a magic formula to conjure up the fine(?), quiet days of the past again, nor can such measures stem the rising stream of modern political life, and all that appertains to it".[4]

These were the years in which a modern nationalist movement took shape. Indonesians embraced Western forms of organization: trade unions and nationalist associations, complete with statutes, written regulations, a subscription fee, and often also newspapers and periodicals. This modernization and turning to the West was accompanied by a fairly abrupt change in dress codes, which made the fact that a new era had arrived all the more conspicuous.

Dress Codes as an Indicator of Cultural Interaction and Transformation

Up to the end of the nineteenth century the Dutch had succeeded in keeping society in the Indies well-compartmentalized. All ethnic and racial groups were subjected to their own specific rules. Dutch men and Dutch women were free to move about in the Archipelago as they pleased and dressed in public in the European fashion. There was a growing tendency to conform to a European middle-class ideal of refined behaviour and social intercourse. Depending on the circumstances, some or all of their prerogatives were also

[2]*Sarekat Islam Lokal*, 296.
[3]Hazeu to Idenburg 14 Feb. 1913 (*Bescheiden* 1913).
[4]Hazeu 21 Aug. 1916, (ARA, Ministerie van Koloniën, Verbaal 22 Nov. 1916-6).

accorded to those indigenous Indonesians who shared their religion, to those who were the legally recognized offspring of a Dutch male and an indigenous female (the so-called Indo-Europeans), and to the indigenous ruling class.

The lives of the rest of the colonial population were very different. There were regulations dating back to the seventeenth century which obliged indigenous Indonesians to adhere to their ethnic costume: Chinese had to dress as Chinese, while Arabs had to wear Arab attire. Life for the two last-mentioned groups was even more restrictive as they had to live in special wards, and were not free to travel as they wanted. The only notable exception made to the dressing codes was that pertaining to the Indonesians who had made the pilgrimage to Mecca. The colonial administration allowed them to dress in such a way that it was plain to everybody that they were a haji, which in those days meant that they adopted Arab garments. The Dutch were reluctant to concede even this, and till the end of the nineteenth century, each time Islamic-inspired unrest plagued Java, voices were raised arguing for this right to be curtailed or abolished. Were the hajis not conspicuous in society by their appearance, critics claimed, it might become more difficult for them to incite the population against Dutch rule.

Dress at that time was clearly a religious statement, and to a certain extent also a political one. Right from the very first contacts Indonesian Muslims resisting the expansion of Dutch authority had stressed the Islamic background of their struggle by adopting codes of dress and behaviour. Soon this was to become a political declaration in a wider sense as well. Though it is difficult to generalize on this point, there are indications that for a long time indigenous Indonesians were quite happy to dress as they did, not showing much inclination, indeed even an aversion, to the adoption of either European attire or other aspects of European cultural expression, including ways of greeting and furniture. Exceptions were the elite who, but only on specific and well-defined occasions and under certain circumstances, imitated European manners and dress, and sat on chairs. Probably we should not read to much into this. During those moments when they entered the European world, communicating and mixing with Dutchmen and other Europeans, they, as did Dutchmen, liked to follow the international trend, looking to France for the latest fashion, and so on. In other functions, acting in an Islamic capacity or as indigenous administrators and rulers, by their dress and behaviour they stressed Islam or local culture.

This system broke down early in the twentieth century. The change was partly instigated by Japan, which had become a power to be reckoned with economically and politically by 1900. In 1895 it had beaten China, and only the concerted action by Germany, France, and Russia had kept her from making territorial gains on the continent. Having built up an impressive navy and army and a developing industry, Japan had become an equal partner with the European powers and the United States. The Netherlands, not exactly a mighty European state, was forced to accord Japanese residents and visitors full European status in the Netherlands East Indies. I would not have mentioned this point, had the elevation of the legal status of Japan in the Netherlands East Indies in 1899 not made the Arab and Chinese communities, still discriminated as Foreign Orientals in their legal description, restless. They demanded to be treated in the same way as the Japanese were, to be free to move where they wanted to go, and to settle where they desired, and probably, though that was not yet a major issue, also to determine for themselves the fashion in which they chose to dress.

In China, and a little later in the Archipelago as well, European attire had become a symbol of modernization and also of protest. In view of the prevailing dress codes in the Netherlands East Indies, as early as 1898 people had begun to wonder how the colonial administration should react when, as part of the political reforms then being contemplated in China, the pigtail were to be banned by imperial edict and European dress to become the norm. Were the Netherlands East Indies to remain a time warp, the only spot in the world where Chinese were still forced to wear the pigtail? The subject, which was first raised in a European newspaper, also reached the Chinese-Malay press, though much of the irony was lost in the process.[5] Fifteen years later the revolution in dress was a fact. Chinese in the Netherlands East Indies reacted *en masse* to the news of the Chinese revolution in 1912 by cutting off their pigtails, which the colonial administration had forced them to wear until then, and by donning European attire. *Pakean Europa*, European clothes, and shoes *model Europa* were in great demand. The Chinese, as the Dutch consul-general in Singapore observed, "endeavoured to imitate, with some degree of success, such

[5] *De Locomotief,* 7 Dec. 1898; *Bintang Soerabaia,* 5 Jan. 1899.

European habits as dress, coiffure, the calendar, and Sunday rest to mention a few of these."[6]

These words were an attempt by the Dutch consul-general to deflate stories current in the Straits' press about large-scale unrest in the Netherlands Indies. The self-assurance with which Chinese in Java had welcomed the revolution in their homeland and the arrogance some of them showed towards indigenous Indonesians, sometimes even towards Europeans had provoked a negative reaction from the Javanese and made some Dutchmen rub their hands with glee at the anti-Chinese aspect of early nationalism. The attitude adopted by some Chinese contributed to the growth of the Sarekat Islam, Indonesia's first nationalist organization which enjoyed massive support and stories about impending violence and anarchy, of which Chinese (and Europeans) were to be the victims, began to circulate, leading among other responses to a rise in the sale of fire arms.

As Hazeu had observed, the good old days would indeed never return. What was happening in the Indonesian community was a test for the Ethical Policy, the endeavour to "elevate" the indigenous population which had just been embarked upon by the Dutch authorities. Statesmen in Europe, European civil servants in the colonies, and missionaries had loudly proclaimed that they were bringing Western civilization to the non-Western world. Neither in Holland nor in the Netherlands Indies were people behind hand stressing that a mission had to be fulfilled. The salvation of people in Africa and Asia was to be provided by association with the West, to mention the terms used by the Dutch orientalist C. Snouck Hurgronje. Non-Western people, including Muslims, had to cast off their backward habits. Muslims, he wrote, should be "freed from some of the medieval rubbish, with which Islam has already far too long been burdened".[7] European education was an instrument to assist them in liberating themselves from such benighted aspects of Islam, outside the purely religious sphere, which "hamper, if not render impossible, their participation in the contemporary civilized life of nations."[8] These words were a new garb for the old antithesis between the Islamic East and the Christian West, which could be heard all over Europe. For people like Snouck Hurgronje every indication that — in their daily life,

[6]Report Dutch Consul-General in Singapore, September 1913 (ARA, Ministerie van Buitenlandse Zaken, A-dos. 190, box 452).
[7]Snouck Hurgronje, *Nederland en de Islam*, 79.
[8]O.c., 89.

but not in their religion — Muslims preferred Islamic or Eastern ways to Western ones, was considered a setback on the road to civilization and a clue to anti-Dutch feelings. Such misgivings were exacerbated because a link was suspected between the Ottoman Empire and the fanning up of discontent among Arabs and other Muslims in the Netherlands Indies. For one or another reason Dutch colonial civil servants, Snouck Hurgronje in the van, had come to the conclusion that the Ottoman Empire was a centre of Islamic subversion scheming to undermine Dutch authority in the Archipelago. In part, he believed, this had been made possible because of "the thousand-fold increase in means of communication".[9] Sending children to Constantinople for their education — which was not a frequent occurrence, but nevertheless caused real forebodings in the Netherlands — loomed in Dutch eyes as a hall-mark of anti-Dutch sentiments; a Turkish fez was a clear sign that the loyalty of its wearer was with the Turks and not with the Dutch; while visiting Constantinople in 1906 a brother of the sultan of Kutei, Prince Sosronegoro, incurred obloquy because while in that city he continued to wear his traditional Indonesian headgear which had a fez-like shape.

It might easily be imagined that in such a strained climate the adoption of Dutch dress and Dutch behaviour would be applauded as a clear sign that association was on its way. Matters were not that simple. One of the stumbling-blocks was the dress regulations which had not yet been rescinded at the beginning of twentieth century. Not much later they were to die a silent death as the trend among Chinese and native Indonesians to dress "Western" became so widespread that it was impossible to enforce the rules. Fighting a rearguard action there were some Dutchmen for whom rules remained rules, which had to be obeyed till they were revoked. Quite apart from these diehards not everybody was overjoyed by these outward manifestations of association, as some saw them as a threat to their own social status and as flying in the face of traditional custom. Not a little of this reaction came from the higher strata of the indigenous bureaucracy. Greatly opposite in this respect is the story about the reaction to a decision in 1898 by the Dutch Resident of Surabaya to allow indigenous Indonesians to wear shoes when cycling. The Javanese regent protested. The wearing of shoes by common people, he stressed, was in violation of custom, and detrimental to the prestige of Europeans and of Javanese civil servants.[10]

[9]O.c., 111.
[10]*De Locomotief* 9 June 1898, 19 Nov. 1898.

About a decade later Western dress and speaking Dutch (or for that matter demanding to sit on a chair and not to squat on the floor) by ordinary people became associated with the more radical expressions of modern nationalism, and in an extension of this with discourteous behaviour and lack of respect for superiors. For younger indigenous Indonesians Western customs had become a way to defy and escape traditional manners, characterized by rigid codes of conduct. In the early 1910s in particular, there are many press reports about indigenous civil servants and employees getting into trouble because they had gone to work in Western clothes, spoken to their superiors in Dutch and not, for instance, in Malay or Javanese. Stories also appeared about Dutchmen, who stammeringly replied in Malay when indigenous Indonesians addressed them in excellent Dutch.

These examples concern the reactions of the establishment, but in Indonesian society at large the copying of Western dress also posed problems, testifying in fact to an opposite effect. Dressing in Western style did not always have to result in a reprimand or worse from the superior, it also had its advantages. The stories just mentioned are counterbalanced by others. Many Indonesians had the experience of discovering that, if under similar circumstances, they on one occasion they wore indigenous dress and on another one they opted for Western clothes, on the latter occasion they were treated more politely and in a more friendly way by Europeans and servants. By donning trousers, shoes, and a jacket, indigenous Indonesians so to speak transmogrified into Indo-Europeans, while Eurasians became more European.

Yet, in entering the Western realm in Western attire indigenous Indonesians also had to forfeit something. Muslims abandoned their outward and visible identification with Islam, while they and other nationalists seemed to forsake their own indigenous culture. Western dress became a symbol of nationalism, of defiance of the colonial overlord, and of the much sought-after modernity. The down side — and Western education posed the same dilemma — was that it seemed to distract from nationalism and Islam. Why copy the manners of the colonial, infidel ruler instead of stressing one's own identity? For some the answer was unequivocal. They refused to abandon the attire of their ethnic group, or that associated with Islam. Others tried to solve the problem by stressing that Western or European dress had nothing to do with submission to the foreign overlord; it was, as some preferred to call it, international dress, part of international culture and of modern times.[11]

In those years the way people dressed was a real cause for controversy; in particular when Islam is added as a third element in the cultural spectrum, in addition to Western and local styles. Though specific Islamic ways of clothing had an identity of their own, traditional dress was seen as more than merely representing their own Indonesian culture, it also had associations with Islam. To reverse the formulation, Western attire was considered by some to deviate from correct Islamic codes, which local dress, though opinions might differ on this, did not. The matter attracted such interest as the elite no longer had the monopoly in the choosing between Islamic, Western, and indigenous cultural elements, as it had been before 1900. It had turned into a question for society at large. The debate of the 1910s was in fact the start of a discussion which has endured to the present day, debating whether long trousers and a neck-tie are fitting garments for an Indonesian Muslim, in particular when this enters into the religious sphere, for instance for visiting a mosque. Before World War II in particular, at times the topic led to heated discussions and aroused intense social conflicts. To this day *kaum sarungan*, "wearers of sarongs", is used as a term to denote a particular group. Sarongs and sandals as opposed to trousers, neck-tie, and shoes still, generally speaking, set apart a specific group of Muslims, even within the devout Islamic community. For some these items of dress have remained conventional clothing, for others they were transformed into a symbol of social and religious backwardness, of which they wanted no part. Within the larger cultural debate the proper norms, values, and beliefs, the choice of dress, because of its visibility, was one of the topics upon which attention focused.

Around 1910 Western dress and Western habits had been embraced enthusiastically by students and lower-ranking civil servants, but within a few years a new alternative for expression of membership of a wider group presented itself. The founding of the Sarekat Islam created an atmosphere in which greater stress was laid on correct Islamic behaviour. Social pan-Islamism, as the Governor-General's advisor for native affairs, D.A. Rinkes, called this, received a wider welcome. In dress, forms of greeting, not to

---

[11]See for instance Soeriokoesoemo, "Taal en kleding", 10. Soetatmo Soeriokoesoemo, by the way, was at the same time inclined to favour traditional dress. With respect to men he still wavered; with respect to women he was absolutely against adopting Western dress.

mention menu, he observed, Muslim customs were being more widely followed, while the fashion of copying Western manners was no longer as pronounced as it had been a few years before. There was, Rinkes reassured, no cause for concern, only room for a "certain sadness", as people had to stand by and watch how association with European culture was being delayed, if not obstructed.[12] This did not assuage the worries of all. Dutchmen began to dread that a day of reckoning was near, fearing that they were to be murdered in Sarekat Islam uprisings. The resurgence of Islam went deeper than the traits mentioned by Rinkes. Moral abuses such as gambling and prostitution were combatted, while in some places — but such instances seem to have remained an exception — Sarekat Islam members tried to prevent festivities being enlivened by *wayang* performances and *gamelan* music, cultural manifestations associated with Javanese and not with Islamic culture. Elsewhere, for the first time Dutch employers were confronted by demands to allow their Muslim employees to go to mosque on Friday. In part they had to blame the colonial administration for such insistence. It had allowed Christian missionary activity to expand, and this too can be seen as a global phenomenon, giving missionaries more freedom to enter Muslim regions once completely out of bounds to them. Some Dutchmen who did not see eye to eye with this trend claimed that missionaries had become too militant.[13] It was rubbing salt into the wound that Governor-General Idenburg, to the consternation of some, decided to promote Sunday rest. In August 1910 he had issued two official circulars, one condemning the holding of festivities on Sunday, especially during the hours of divine service, the other urging civil servants to prevent markets in their areas being held on a Sunday. The Chinese might have wanted to follow the Dutch in making Sunday a holiday; but it seemed inevitable that Idenburg's circulars could not but motivate Muslims to stress the special position Friday holds in their religion.

Distinction and Combination of Cultural References

Some people had no problem electing one of what seemed three options: full assimilation with Western culture, Islam, or their own ethnic background.

---

[12]Rinkes to Idenburg 13 May 1913 (*Adviezen*, 35).
[13]*Handelingen* 1913-1914, I, 36.

Those in support of the last option laid stress on the non-Islamic background of the indigenous culture, of which certain forms of *wayang* and *gamelan* were popular examples. In Java some people began to extol the glory of the pre-Islamic past and lament the harm Islam had done to the culture of their forefathers.

For others, however, and they were and probably are in the majority, the question was more complicated, if simply for the fact that it is difficult to set the three cultural spheres clearly apart. A pioneer of the nationalist movement, Tjipto Mangoenkoesoemo, for instance, praised Islam for the stress it laid on equality but attacked it for the threat it posed to Javanese art. He preferred certain, more relaxed Western manners to the way Javanese etiquette rigidly dictated intercourse between people of different rank, but was no longer completely convinced of the benevolent influence of Dutch culture after, during his exile in The Hague in 1913, he had watched crowds of drunken people in the streets celebrating the fact that one hundred years earlier Holland had been liberated from the French. Such coarseness made him long for the refinement and intimacy of Javanese family life, and the customs that surrounded the end of the fasting month.[14]

When he was allowed back in Java Tjipto Mangoenkoesoemo's choice baffled Dutchmen, including Rinkes. Tjipto Mangoenkoesoemo had begun to glorify Majapahit, the last Hindu-Buddhist kingdom of Java. Not, Rinkes thought, a very wise course of action in view of the fact that Tjipto Mangoenkoesoemo wanted to win over the Javanese population to his political ideals.[15] He should have referred to the Islamic sultanates which had been the successors of Majapahit; and not to a state that, in those days of Islamic fervour, was so detested by Muslims, Rinkes argued.

In spite of Rinkes' reservations, Tjipto Mangoenkoesoemo and his political friends succeeded in attracting popular support among Javanese Muslims, including members of the Sarekat Islam. Rinkes, it seems, had made too clear-cut a distinction between what was considered "Javanese" and what "Islamic". It was the age-old dilemma of where to lay the emphasis on: the Javanese background or Islam; two aspects of Indonesian, or in this case Javanese, culture, between which no clear demarcation line can be drawn. The same remark can be made about the attitude towards Western culture both in the 1910s and at present. This fluctuates between, or at times

[14]*De Expres* 10 Jan. 1914, 24 Feb. 1914.
[15]Rinkes to Idenburg 15 Oct. 1915 (ARA CO V 26-1-1916-32).

combines, admiration for some of its achievements and denunciations of its moral wrongs, execrating its stress on individuality and economic gain, which are claimed to be alien to Asian society.

Since the 1910s, Western culture (though it might be better, as was the case in those days, to speak of international culture), Islam, and regional culture, have continued to be presented as separate alternatives for shaping the outward appearance of Indonesian society. As some Dutch colonial civil servants, watching the new religious fervour sweep their area in the aftermath of the founding of the Sarekat Islam, had expected, the upsurge of Islam soon abated. In secular nationalist circles Western attire, in spite of the doubts initially expressed, became fully accepted. The choice for a symbol of nationalism did not fall on Indonesian dress, but on the *peci*, the fez-shaped black cap. Soekarno especially did a great deal to propagate its use. It was, Soekarno claimed, chosen as such by him in an effort to identify with his poorer fellow countrymen, reinforced by an aversion to the many Western-dressed dandies who populated the cities. As he told Cindy Adams, he launched the idea in June 1921, upset as he was by the "much heated discussion on part of the so-called intelligentsia, who resented the kerchief Javanese men wore with their sarongs, and the *pitji* that *betjak* drivers and other humble people wore."[16] The *peci* was a symbol of his solidarity with the common people, and became one of Islam as well. In Muslim circles throughout the remaining years of the colonial period, the debate continued about which customs used to define and defend the correct Muslim way to dress and behave were Islamic customs and which Arab. Although the question of men's wear figured prominently, female attire, especially the problem of whether head-covering was mandatory, was not neglected.

Indonesian Independence and Its Celebrations

1945: The Plurality of Cultural Spheres

A lot of ink has been spilled about the ideological debate surrounding the proclamation of Indonesian Independence on August 17th, 1945, the second date I have selected as a basis of comparison. As a turning point in Indonesian history, the discussions about the form of the new state and the

---

[16]Adams, *Sukarno*, 51.

place that Islam was to be accorded in it have received ample attention. Likewise the inclusion in the Constitution of 1945 of the *Pancasila* — which gives Indonesia a religious base, but does not specifically mention Islam — instead of the Jakarta Charter — which specifies that Muslims are obliged to follow Islamic law — is well documented. The same can be said about the civil wars that were fought over the orientation the Indonesian state should take and the misery these brought about in their train. Much less has been written about the way such discussions and strife were reflected in everyday behaviour. In a way posing this point is irrelevant. More important issues were at stake in those early years of Independence. The extreme poverty, born of the disruption of the Japanese occupation makes questions about alternatives in material culture superfluous. There was no choice. People had to dress in any garment, if necessary made from gunny sacks, they could lay their hands on. As far as I know, when clothing is deliberately mentioned in contemporaneous reports and scholarly literature it is to illustrate how poor people were in 1945 and 1946 and how severe the shortage of textiles was at that time.

The new political elite of 1945, the former leaders of the nationalist movement, who had opted for Western dress and a *peci* in the pre-war years, continued to dress that way after August 1945. This was already evident during the ceremony in which Soekarno and Hatta proclaimed Indonesia's Independence. Four years later in Yogyakarta, on December 19th, 1949, when Soekarno took the oath to become the first (and last) president of the United States of Indonesia, all males captured in one of the pictures taken on this occasion wore a suit and tie. The only exception is the person holding the Koran. Only the front rows of the people watching the ceremony are shown, and this may not be without significance. As Palmier observes, in the early 1950s dress was a clear indicator of status differences. During public functions — he describes the formal ceremonies to mark the anniversary of Indonesia's Independence in a Javanese town — men of importance wore trousers. Further back in the audience "the more people were clad in sarongs which were the dress of the major part of the population".[17] The same pattern, Palmier notes, could be observed at other public meetings at which "the Western-dressed group were in control of proceedings."[18] In this context Palmier also mentions Islamic organizations

---

[17]Palmier, *Social Status and Power*, 149.
[18]O.c., 154.

such as the Muhammadiyah and the Masjumi, both of which he qualifies as having a modernist orientation. Members and supporters of such groups did not usually object to Western attire and this was precisely one of the points that had brought them in conflict with persons who are often described as being more traditionally oriented Muslims, among whom the Nahdlatul Ulama (in the years when Palmier did his research politically still part of the Masjumi) was the main organizational vehicle. The picture was completely reversed when religious festivities such as the Maulud celebration, a high-day for "traditional" Muslims, were concerned. On such occasions, Palmier observes, the "Western tinge was completely lacking", with the participants all in sarong.[19] So, in the early 1950s Western dress seems to have become generally accepted in the context of the public political life and among the political and economic urban elite. To quote Palmier once more "Javanese young men of the better-off classes (i.e. non-villagers) also wore European dress, though their womenfolk remained faithful to the *kain* and *kebaya* (*kebaya* being the bodice, cut straight across the bottom, of coloured material)."[20]

Palmier's very useful observations indicate the various spheres that should be distinguished, categories which have kept their relevance to the topic discussed throughout the whole of the twentieth century: public and private life; religious and secular gatherings, and those associated with traditional culture; urban and rural setting; differences in wealth; and last but not least the difference between male and female. Each sphere has its dominant cultural expressions. A person who is public, secular, rich, urban and male, for instance is the most likely to adopt Western dress and habits; a person who is private, religious, poor, and female the least. It is the changes within these spheres which indicate developments which are usually captured by terms like Westernization or revival of Islam. In the public sphere, on the streets and during formal political meetings and ceremonies in which the emphasis is laid on Islam, this is to be a clear indication of what people usually call religious revival. The private sphere, within the privacy of a person's own home or during ceremonies accompanying *rites de passage*, shows the greatest resilience when confronted with new cultural alternatives.

---

[19]O.c., 154.
[20]O.c., 26.

1970: The Celebration of National Achievements

This maybe is most aptly illustrated by my two final comparisons, the Independence celebrations in 1970 and 1995. By 1970 the "revival of Islam" had already started, but only modestly; and in the decade which followed part of the devout Islamic community and the government were embroiled in a bitter struggle with one another. Among the most hotly contested issues which aggravated this relationship were a Marriage Act introduced by the government in 1974, which contained stipulations which were not in accordance with Islamic law, and the efforts by the same government to win general acclaim for the primacy of the *Pancasila* as defined in its terms, which also ran into opposition from Islamic circles. In 1970 the headscarf was not as popular as it was to become a few years later, and even it became a bone of contention when the government banned this item of clothing in public schools. Just prior to 1970 the term sarong wearer could still be used, as did the chairman of one of the political parties, the Partai Nasional Indonesia (PNI), in a derogatory way to denote backwardness. Nowadays, in the press the fact that Muslims have stuck to the sarong is merely noted as an indication of a specific cultural, religious sphere to make it clear to the reader which group of Muslims is being written about. Those who wear it have cast off the image of backwardness. Likewise the headscarf has become accepted as normal dress, no longer prohibited from being worn in public schools.

The motto of the Independence celebrations in 1970 was "We want to see what we have already achieved". Jakarta, the national capital, and thus the best place to look to find out what message was meant to be conveyed by the festivities, was the venue for a big parade on August 17th. Almost all the provinces took part in it, joining government departments, private and state companies, and mass organizations and political parties. The groups from the provinces tried to demonstrate the particularities of their own region. Various kinds of oared and sailing boots were borne along on floats; farmers from West Java participated, carrying rice and performing a dance; traditional wedding costumes were shown from Jambi and South Sulawesi, and so on. Jakarta itself was depicted as the city of trade and commerce, of tourism, and of culture. In the afternoon an aubade of secondary school pupils was held. The next day, on August 18th, there was a mass parade of scouts, and a performance of the Jakarta symphony orchestra was staged in the Taman Ismail Marzuki. At the same cultural centre people could watch the popular play *Si Badung, Kapten Frankie* (The Scoundrel, Captain Frankie). Economic development and local culture were portrayed. Islam did not have any special place in these celebrations. *Bedug*s, the large drums used to mark the times for prayer, were beaten to announce the beginning of the festivities, but church bells and sirens played an equal part. If any activity attracted public attention and debate at that time it was the demonstrations against corruption and the preparations for the first national general elections since 1955, scheduled to be held the next year.

1995: The Anniversary in a Global Context

By 1995 time had marched on and the celebrations in August of that year mirrored this new atmosphere. Islamic attire, especially for women, had not only become conventional dress taking its place alongside Western and indigenous clothes, it had gained wide popularity. At least one collection of poems — *Lautan Jilbab* (An Ocean of *Jilbab*s) by Emha Ainun Nadjib, one of the most widely read authors today — takes it as its theme. The number of mosques and prayer houses has increased, special shops selling Islamic garments have sprung up, and Islamic fashion parades have become a frequent event. Islam, very conspicuously, has also made advances into music, including the pop scene. Religious instruction meetings are enjoying great popularity, hence the mass gathering in Jakarta to celebrate Independence. In the wake of the Independence celebrations came the second Istiqlal Festival in Jakarta, a large event held from the end of September till the middle of November 1995. The change bookshops underwent is likewise pertinent. In the 1970s the largest section of many of these was still devoted to books about law and government regulations. In 1995 it was Islamic literature which occupied pride of place in bookshops and took up much of the space. Many of the books sold — some of which have an enormous impression — are translations of books from the Middle East, cheaply priced, dealing with all aspects of Islam, including dress.

This brings us to the international aspect of the topic: the relationship between globalization and Islam which is one of the central themes of this conference. Globalization is a very ambiguous word. Often, even in Indonesia itself, it appears to be used with some apprehension. Local societies have to be protected against its disruptive effects, in which case globalization is associated with Westernization or Americanization, perhaps largely with its more vulgar manifestations. The fact that Westernization or internationalization can result in the loss of domestic values and culture was also realized in the 1910s; a period in which the term globalization had not even been heard of, but when international culture presented a stirring alternative to local and Islamic culture. In Indonesian history and in world history this was a very important period; and many parallels can be drawn with the present day. Fashion — international dress as it was called in those days, part of global culture as it is referred to nowadays — became a world-wide phenomenon, spreading to affect the non-Western world, in particular the youth. In the field of religion there was a revival of Islam; partly reversing the trend of "Westernization" among a section of the Indonesian Muslims. International tensions as well as nationalist feelings in the period ran high, threatening to tear apart whole regions, the Balkans, the Austro-Hungarian Empire, and the Ottoman Empire. The greater interest in Islam in Indonesia and the propagation of an orthodox creed in the early years of the twentieth century must only have been facilitated by an international network of contacts, and more rapid means of communication. The role, for instance, of the progress made in the printing industry, comparable to the present day circulation of cassettes of Islamic music and religious sermons, should not be underrated. Fearful of pan-Islamism, Dutch colonial authorities were worried about the infiltration of subversive periodicals and pamphlets, while on the domestic scene the rise of a nationalist, in part Islamic press was viewed with some anxiety. This shows, as does the present-day stream of booklets from Saudi Arabia and other Islamic countries, that globalization should not be almost exclusively identified with Westernization or vulgarization.

The worldwide confrontation with Western culture in the 1910s did not lead to a uniform world. Islam and the resilience of local culture saw to that. This leads to the question of what the long-term effects of the present intensified possibilities of international contacts will be — for example in the year 2013, at the end of the one hundred years term mentioned in the title of this text. It is impossible to speculate about this. At the time of the birth of the Sarekat Islam, several Dutch colonial civil servants predicted that the greater stress on Islam that accompanied it was only temporary, and later developments indeed saw proof of this. The initial reception of Western culture also slowed down. The world did not become a homogeneous one. The opposite was true. Society became more colourful, offering new alternatives from which to choose or with which to mix. The same can happen again. The outcome of what people call globalization may be that cultures in individual countries will become more diverse. The present revival of Islam may also slow down again, but this closer exposure to its manifestations, which is equally part of globalization, may have lasting effects.

4 Islam in Brunei Darussalam and Global Islam
An Analysis of Their Interaction[1]

Iik Arifin Mansurnoor

The commitment [of the Bruneians] to the Ahl al-Sunna wal-Jama'a in theology and to the Shafi'i school in law as well as their moderate predilection in religious practices have strengthened Islam and enhanced the Islamic presence in the country. This way Brunei Muslims are not easily trapped into divisive religious thought, practice and action... since religious practices in Brunei have been derived through generations from the Ahl al-Sunna wal-Jama'a and the Shafi'i school.
(Md. Zain Hj. Serudin, *Brunei Darussalam*, 196)

Introduction

Brunei Darussalam is a unique political entity in South-East Asia. It obviously maintains the structure and form of a traditional political system. It claims affinity to and origin in Islam, Malayness, and royalty. The sultan has been leader and ruler for the country and for the Muslims. In Brunei the ruler is also the head of Islam. The official version of religious practices is derived from the Shafi'ite school, even though adoption of other opinions is permitted especially if public welfare requires such an undertaking.

In view of the tranquillity and stability of religious life in Brunei, it is interesting to examine the relationship between the emphasis on adopting such a definite religious version and the prevailing calm atmosphere. How has it been possible for Brunei to maintain its religious traditions and at the same time move forward as many other Muslim countries? This text will explore the intellectual networks which encompass the religious elite in the

[1]My thanks are due to several individuals, especially my colleagues and students at the Department of History, University of Brunei Darussalam, Dr. F.R. Kaloko and Dr. Jahan Manan of University of Brunei Darussalam for their invaluable assistance, comments and/or criticism on the drafts of this article. Since not all their views were incorporated into the text, they are not in any way responsible for its shortcomings.

71

country on the one side and religious leaders and institutions abroad on the other side. This study will also examine how far such networks buttress the religious status quo and look into the challenges which Islam in Brunei has faced by joining them.

It should be stated here that Brunei has been enjoying economic prosperity not only because of its oil revenues, but also because of its ability to move with the times and function as a modern state. Despite, or rather because of, its manifest claim to Islamic traditionalism, Brunei optimistically has joined many international groupings and undertaken many steps towards modernization. For example, hundreds of school leavers have continued to join universities and colleges in many parts of the world, including the United Kingdom, Egypt, Australia, Malaysia, and Singapore. Many of its government officials have also been sent abroad for advanced training. At the same time, experts in diverse fields have been invited to come and upgrade the knowledge and skills of Brunei civil servants and officers. Consequently, Brunei has become part of the global system through formal channels and other, more informal, networks. It is therefore argued here that its strength for bargaining with external forces has been derived from its straightforward insistence upon traditional Islam. On the other hand, the continuing influx of new ideas and interlocking ties with global systems raise doubt about the permanence and continuity in the interpretation and expression of Islam in the country.

An underlying thought of this text has been the fact that Brunei, including its expression of Islamic interpretation, has changed greatly without experiencing religious crisis. Indeed, it has adopted various inventions in the administration of Islam and its institutions. In Brunei, no comparable issue of "new faction" (*Kaum Muda*) ever emerged. I have been asking for quite some time: How were Bruneians able to avoid religious conflict, while experiencing and participating in change? Is it mainly because no outside reformer ever came to Brunei to incite debates and conflict? What was the role of the rulers in protecting religious harmony?

Looking at the history of the intellectual tradition in Brunei, one wonders why such an important Islamic centre as Brunei failed to leave massive works comparable to, for example, seventeenth century Aceh. In fact, it was only following the reign of Sultan Muhammad Hassan (1582-1598) that the production of texts became more apparent. Not only the codification of customs and law based mainly on Islam took place, but also the writing of an official genealogy, texts elaborating the complex structure of royal institutions as well as religious texts was undertaken. Yet, the surviving evidences of these intellectual activities remain inconclusive to the stature of Brunei as an important Islamic centre. Whatever the reasons might have been, it is a fact that Brunei had faced serious challenges from external forces since the sixteenth century. Its vast territories at times only added to the burden of the government. By the nineteenth century, Brunei had reached its nadir. Despite the decline, several interesting treatises such as *Syair Rakis*, the translation of Ibn 'Atā' Allāh's *Hikam*, and the completion of *Silsilah Raja-Raja Berunai* [The Genealogical Tree of the Kings of Brunei] were written. The point to be made here is that for a long time Brunei had been part of the larger Islamic world. It enjoyed ties with diverse intellectual-cum-religious centres. How did Brunei play its role in this intellectual network? I have dealt with this question elsewhere,[2] so all that needs to be reiterated here can be said in a few words.

Brunei participated in the intellectual network of Islamic South-East Asia and beyond through different channels. *Tarīqah*s, educational centres, political ties, trading network, religious figures, and personal ties formed important nodes of networks.

Brunei actively pursued participation in the wider Islamic community. For example, in 1807 the sultan of Brunei bought a house in Mecca to accommodate Bruneians, and perhaps also other *Jawi*s, i.e. South-East Asian Muslims, who studied in the holy city. During the mounting pressure posed by the Brookes on Brunei towards the end of the nineteenth and in the early twentieth century, in 1903 Sultan Hashim appealed to the Ottoman ruler for help.[3] Again, during the early part of the British Residency in Brunei, intensive contacts were made with various religious authorities in the Malay Peninsula. The contact centred on cooperation to develop a version of "Mohammedan Law" in Brunei. It should be emphasized that many Bruneians continued to go to different parts of the Islamic world for study and to perform the pilgrimage to Mecca annually. Interestingly, even when the economy was quite modest in the first quarter of the twentieth century, scores of Muslims from Brunei went to Mecca in 1911.[4]

---

[2]See Iik, "Brunei Sebagai Sebuah Pusat Jaringan". For more information on the relations between South-East Asia and the Middle East, see Azyumardi, *Transmission*; Von der Mehden, *Two Worlds of Islam*.

[3]Iik, "Historiography and Religious Reform".

[4]See *Brunei Annual Report (BAR)*, 1911, 12.

In order to facilitate the discussion, this text examines three major entities which link Brunei to the Islamic world and *vice versa*. These are religious, intellectual, and religio-political entities.

Religious Aspects

Pilgrimage

The importance of pilgrimage to Muslims is well-known; but in Brunei it has particular social significance. The Bruneians also paid special attention to the infrastructure of the pilgrimage and its organization. For example, as mentioned before, in 1807 a house in Mecca was bought by the sultan primarily to accommodate the pilgrims. Even today an outsider will easily note that it continues to enjoy high esteem in Brunei society. During the Residency period, Brunei pilgrims joined their counterparts from North Borneo, Singapore and the Malay Peninsula. Usually a pilgrim would leave Brunei Town for Labuan in order to board a ship that transported him to Jeddah via Singapore and Pulau Penang. During the long voyage to Jeddah, Brunei pilgrims would have met many other Malay pilgrims. Even though we have no detailed knowledge about the intensity of such encounters, it is not far-fetched to suggest that they were effective in disseminating current ideas and information about Muslims the world over. The daily activities of the pilgrims on the ship, especially prayers, lectures and other get-togethers made them more aware about their wider ties and concern.

During their stay in the holy places of Mecca and Medina, Brunei pilgrims, like their counterparts from other countries, learned a great deal. On their return, the pilgrims maintained some newly found ideas, lifestyles, and activities.[5] Yet the strict application of the religious norms (*fiqh*) and the belief system (*'aqīdah*) according to recognized schools limited the glaring adoption of religious novelties. For example, a text written in the first decade of the twentieth century warned the Bruneians to be watchful of

---

[5]It is important to mention in this context that the travel by sea caused the pilgrims to stay outside the country much longer than today's pilgrims do. Not only did they spend more than a month aboard the ship alone, but they also had ample time to stay in Mecca, Medina and Jeddah, mainly because of the ship schedule. For more information on a comparable phenomenon, see McDonnell, *Conduct of Hajj from Malaysia*.

"unauthorized opinions" on religious issues.[6] Moreover, in recent time Brunei has officially adopted the Shafi'ite school and the *ahl al-sunnah wal-jamā'ah* as the official brand of Islamic practice and belief system.[7] Other schools are respected and in some cases followed, but no propagation of their controversial teachings can be undertaken. Therefore, most innovations which a pilgrim brought home belonged to the non-central core of religious practices. For example, a pilgrim would have adopted new styles of garment, of cap and of wall decorations/calligraphy. Indeed, no controversial religious leader ever emerged in Brunei from among its pilgrims. Perhaps the only exception was the affair of Haji Muhammad during the early part of the 1840s. So far the religious controversies in the country have originated from the religious movements within the region which lent sympathy to local practices and belief as well as messianism.

Nevertheless, with the growing numbers of pilgrims,[8] there is no guarantee that they remain untouched by foreign influences.[9] The higher numbers of the pilgrims were associated with an increasing diversity in their backgrounds. A growing number of pilgrims were young and well-educated. Their participation in the pilgrimage often led them to become more involved in understanding Islam from new perspectives. For instance, they became interested in reading religious literature written by well-known Muslim authors such as Yūsuf al-Qaradāwī, Abū al-A'lā Mawdūdī, Maryam Jameelah (Jamilah), Buya Hamka, and 'Alī Sharī'atī. More specifically, their

---

[6]Anonymous, Manuscript without title; on Islamic teachings, Brunei, 1325/1907, 106.

[7]See *The Constitution of the State of Brunei* (1959).

[8]Until 1965 the Bruneians officially performed the pilgrimage by sea. For the period before 1955, no detailed report on their numbers has been discovered. For example, a report of 1911 cited that larger number than usual went on haj, including the first pilgrims who have ever gone from Temburong (*BAR*, 1911, 12). From 1955 to 1965 the numbers of the pilgrims ranged from thirty-three (the lowest) to 144 (the highest). The pilgrimage by sea was terminated in 1975. For quite some time, those few who went by plane had to make private arrangements. Only in 1966 did the government of Brunei officially launch a pilgrimage package by air in cooperation with pilgrimage organizers in Singapore and Malaysia. From 1966 to 1974 the numbers of pilgrims who went by sea continued to decline; from 189 in 1966 to thirty-six in 1974. On the other hand, those who went by air were on the increase; from eight in 1966 to 406 in 1974. During the 1970s and 1980s their numbers went even higher; for instance, in 1975 521; 1980 1149; 1985 2684.

[9]It is interesting to note that under the British Residency, *hajiphobia* never influenced the policy makers in the country. For an analysis of parallel phenomena in other parts of South-East Asia, see Von der Mehden, *Two Worlds of Islam*, 3-5.

encounters in the Holy Places with diverse Muslims cannot fail to have affected the personal views on Islam of Brunei pilgrims. It should also be emphasized that the expression of new ideas has to be worked out in a Brunei way, that is without creating a controversy; or else upheld individually. It seems that for many Bruneians the pilgrimage remains strictly a religious observance and personal commitment. This is especially so since the time required for the performance of the pilgrimage has become very short.

Pilgrimage continued to perform its traditional role in Brunei society. It has provided many Bruneians with spiritual satisfaction, an attachment to the wider Islamic world, many concrete ideas about fellow Muslims from various origins, and, generally, a more positive attitude towards their religion. The cutailment of the period of the stay and mingling with other Muslims in the Holy Places, however, allows little opportunity for more serious interaction.

Seminars on Islam

In the past, Bruneians were mostly participants in seminars and conferences held in various other Muslim countries. After independence in 1984, more and more such occasions were held in Brunei. In this section the discussion focuses on academic and religious, and not political, meetings.

For quite some time Bruneians have participated in international conferences hosted by Muslim countries and organizations. Although seminars were organized by diverse countries and organizations, Bruneians made their own choices of the particular seminars they attended. Not only did unfamiliarity with particular countries influence their preference, but the topics discussed were also a crucial factor in their participation. The small number of population of the country had an effect on the relatively limited number of Brunei scholars attending such seminars. For example, Brunei sent a delegation consisting of the mufti and an Islamic judge (*qadi*) to the International Islamic Conference held in Baghdad in 1962.[10] Again, the mufti and the chief judge left for Kuala Lumpur in 1964 to attend an Islamic conference.[11] In December 1964 the mufti and a senior religious official

[10]*Pelita Brunei*, 6 June 1962.
[11]Op. cit., 5 Feb. 1964.

were sent to attend the International Islamic Conference held in Mogadishu.[12] The sending of the Bruneians to international conferences emerged more markedly especially after the Residency system was abolished in 1959. Before that, there was still busy interaction with the world outside. During the 1950s, many Muslim figures and visitors came to Brunei mainly to strengthen ties and to refresh their knowledge about the country. For example, leading Korean Muslims visited Brunei in 1961. They were warmly welcomed in a special meeting organized by the Perkasa.[13] Moreover, in 1962 a delegation from the International Islamic Congress under Dr. I. Khan spent a few days in Brunei.[14] Again, in late 1963 an eminent scholar from Madras visited Brunei, and delivered several lectures.[15] Although it is not possible to divine the exact impact of these encounters and exchanges, it is clear that novel ideas among Muslims were made available at first hand to many Bruneians.

The continued economic growth in Brunei during the second half of the twentieth century allowed Brunei scholars and students to participate more actively in international exchanges in the field of religious studies. The oil boom of the 1970s had a strong and positive impact upon religious life among Bruneians. Despite the appearance of certain religious groups which were suspected by the authorities, in general the period of the 1970s was characterized by more involvement by Bruneians in worldwide Muslim activities. Not only did Bruneians take part in more high-level conferences, but they also organized such activities in their own country. For example, concomitant with the opening of the Islamic Da‘wah Centre in the capital city, an international seminar on the understanding of the concept of *ahl al-sunnah wal-jamā‘ah* was held from 16 to 19 September 1985. And in 1988, a regional seminar on the Shafi'ite school was organized by the Ministry of Religious Affairs. Again, in 1989 an international seminar on Islamic civilization in the Malay world was organized in Bandar Seri Begawan. These occasions provided an opportunity for the Bruneians to show their concern with wider Islamic issues and they also afforded a forum for others to

[12]Op. cit., 6 Jan. 1965. Op. cit., 17 Oct. 1962, 1 presents a brief statement and picture of a visit to Brunei by two officials of the Islamic World Congress (*Kongres Islam Sa-Dunia*), Khaidir al-Husain and In‘am Allah Khan.
[13]Op. cit., 20 Sept. 1961, 3. Perkasa is an abbreviation of Persatuan Kesatuan Islam — Association of Muslim Unity.
[14]Op. cit., 17 Oct. 1962.
[15]Op. cit., 4 April 1963.

discuss common Islamic interests. In most cases international seminars discussing Islamic issues were held by the Ministry of Religious Affairs. Indeed, after the establishment of the University of Brunei Darussalam, several international seminars dealing with different aspects of Islam were hosted by the university. This provides irrefutable evidence that the improvement of the economy and the independence of the country after 1984 contributed to the exertion of Brunei as an important Muslim centre.

Since most international conferences and seminars attracted only intellectuals, their impact could not be of major significance. Ideas disseminated in a conference would take some time to reach a lay Muslim. At the same time, it cannot be denied that conferences have the potential to prepare plans and provide the groundwork for future change among Muslims, including the Bruneians.

Religious Movements: Tarīqas *and Revivalism*

As a part of the wider Islamic world Brunei has always felt the impact of changes occurring among Muslims worldwide. I have argued that Brunei, as an Islamic centre, formed a nodal point in Islamic networks.[16] Religiously inspired activities and institutions formed the strongest link in the networks. They generally persisted and survived against the vicissitudes of political conflict and decline. The intensity of ties and links with the outside world depended very much on the attractiveness and the ability of Brunei to communicate with it. This explains why Brunei was barely excluded from the reformist activities during the early part of the twentieth century. It is primarily because of local initiatives that some degrees of ties were kept alive. This was in contrast to the intensive contacts in the earlier period when Brunei enjoyed power and wealth, especially during the sixteenth and seventeenth centuries. The rapid changes that took place in Brunei following the Pacific War also provided a better opportunity for strengthening ties and relations with the outside world, including the Islamic world. More importantly, by 1959 Brunei ended the Residency system. The sultan thus recovered his full control over the internal affairs of the country, in addition to his authority over religious affairs.

The intensity of contact between Brunei and other Islamic centres can be seen clearly in the influence of religious orders (*tarīqahs*) in the country.

---

[16]Iik, "Brunei Sebagai Sebuah Pusat Jaringan".

For example, the Khalwatiyah order already attracted followers among Bruneians in the seventeenth century. Indeed, a prominent religious official at the time, Pehin Datu Imām Ya'qūb, claimed membership of the *tarīqah*[17] Later, in 1807, Sultan Muhammad Tajuddin ordered the foundation of a Brunei house (*rumah wakaf*) in Mecca. It was originally built for the members of the Sammaniyah[18] and the Brunei pilgrims as well as, I surmise, for students (*muqīmūn*).[19] The building of such a centre indicates the significance of the *tarīqah* in Brunei. Moreover, the translation of Ibn 'Atā' Allāh's *al-Ḥikam* into Brunei Malay by a Bruneian in 1220/1805 clearly shows the influence of the order among the Bruneians. Again, the introduction of the Qādiriyyah wal-Naqshbandiyyah during the later part of the nineteenth century seems to have followed the decline and subsequent unpopularity of the earlier orders in the country. More importantly, the emphasis of the new order on the application of both the *sharī'ah* and Sufism might have served as an extension of the religious reform during the period, or at least the intensification of scripturalism in the country. Indeed, the *tarīqah*s emerged as effective channels of reformist and revivalist ideas all over the Muslim World. Brunei was no exception.

During the Residency period, the emphasis on administrative reform in the religious field did not favour the development of the *tarīqah*s. The *tarīqah*s with their various branches survived, but retained a low profile, as they were adhered to at a personal level.[20] Nevertheless, the impact of the

---

[17]Sweeney, "Silsilah raja-raja Berunai", A74. The propagation of the Khalwati teachings among Malays was undertaken earlier by a well-known peripatetic scholar, Shaykh Yusuf of Makassar (d. 1699), who won the title of *al-Tāj al-Khalwatī* (Van Bruinessen, *Tarekat Naqsyabandiyah*, 34-5; Azyumardi, op. cit., 426-7, 433, 458; Abu Hamid, *Syekh Yusuf Makassar*, 205-18). The link between Brunei and Makassar was more probable since Imam Ya'qub is claimed to have originated from Pinrang (Penderang) in South Sulawesi, see Sweeney, op. cit., A50.

[18]The popularity of the Sammāniyyah in the Malay world towards the end of the eighteenth century was signified by the influence of such books as *Hidāyah al-Sālikīn* and *Sayr al-Sālikīn* written by a Sammani adept, 'Abd al-Samad al-Palimbānī (d. 1788) and *Sabīl al-Muhtadīn* by Muhammad Arshad al-Banjarī (d. 1812). And in Brunei the chains of authority in the Sammāniyyah (*Silsilah al-Ṭarīqah al-Sammāniyyah*) was recorded and circulated, see Iik, "Historiography and Religious Reform".

[19]See op. cit.

[20]In my opinion, several factors caused the *tarīqah* to be practised at a personal level. First, the informality of the *tarīqah* orders did not fit into the legal reform launched by the authorities. Second, the requirement to have a licence to spread Islamic teachings deterred the mushrooming of orders in their full-fledged form. This is despite the fact that

tarīqah-styled expression continued to be prevalent among the religious features of Brunei. The popularity of various forms of *dhikr* is a clear example of this. Indeed, participation in such intense religious experience created a conducive atmosphere for further Islamization, that is a practitioner would be more open to the pursuit of more serious religious knowledge. Such closer attachment to religion undoubtedly had the potential to link the more-involved Muslims in the country with reformist movements in other Muslim societies.

Since the late 1960s, the Bruneians have seen the emergence of various religious activities, if not movements. Most of them were offshoots of parent-organizations abroad.[21] Interestingly, some features of the activities were related to forms of martial arts (*silat*). The most influential grouping at the time was the Nasrul Haq. It grew very fast in the Malay Peninsula following the May 1969 crisis. In Brunei a comparable movement took the form of a martial art association called *Silat Lintau*. It was propagated in the late 1970s by a certain Ishak bin Hassan of the Malay Peninsula. Its impact on Brunei was seen quite strongly among the youth, students, and individual members of the armed forces and the police.[22] Undoubtedly its strict discipline, prominent symbols, and promise of supernatural power were very attractive to many of them. In the early 1970s, a sergeant in the army propagated the teachings of the Mufarridiyyah order. The order won a following among diverse segments of the population, primarily because of its liberal ideas on salvation. When these orders received more support among the misinformed masses, the mufti issued a fatwa condemning them as un-Islamic.[23]

More serious movements emerged in Brunei with the increasing activities of well-known orders. Since the early 1980s representatives of the

---

the *tarīqah* practices survived in local forms or practices for personal religious satisfaction. Third, the structure of Islamic leadership in the country in which the ruler topped the religio-political ladder put pressure on the *tarīqah*s to be run leaderless or to accept the status quo.

[21] Since our focus here is on the Islamic organizations, we put aside the discussion on such groupings as the Baha'is which won converts in Brunei during the 1960s.

[22] Suhaili, *Penyelewengan dari Dasar Aqidah*, 238.

[23] See the Mufti's fatwa no. 39-46/MKB.2/1971; cf. Aishah, *Pusat Da'wah Islamiah*, 147-8.

Ahmadiyyah order,[24] the Jama'at al-Arqam,[25] and the Tabligh movement have extended their preaching to Brunei.

The Tabligh movement — or Tablīghī Jamā'at — has won some following among Bruneians. Their numbers were not very large. It attracted a few but dedicated followers among educated Bruneians. Perhaps because its presence is mainly low profile, the Tabligh did not raise eyebrows among religious authorities.[26]

The leaders of the Ahmadiyyah order formed a branch in Brunei in 1982. Since then it has developed into an active group, providing religious guidance for its followers. It has regular weekly meetings. As a group it has become an effective source of spiritual and socio-religious identification for the increasing numbers of followers.[27]

The influence of the Jama'at al-Arqam — elsewhere also known as Darul Arqam — has been observed in Brunei since the early 1980s. Many Bruneians who joined al-Arqam never formed a formal network linking to its headquarters in Kuala Lumpur. They joined the movements as individuals. The followers of the Arqam in Brunei, however, appeared in public in a way quite similar to that of their brethren in the headquarters. Since they did not formally found a branch in the country, their activities centred on already existing traditional religious patterns. For example, they organized meetings concomitant with religious gatherings (*majlis*) such as *tahlīl*, *tadārus*, and *rites de passage*. As their numbers increased, regular meetings were also held, especially to strengthen the bond between members and to spread the teachings of the movement. Nevertheless, the stronger nucleus revolved around the individual family. It was here that the Arqamis of the country first implemented the religious model established by the leaders in Sungai Pencala in Kuala Lumpur.

When the leadership of the Arqam initiated a few controversial teachings around 1988, their impact upon the Arqamis in Brunei was not insignificant.

---

[24]For more information on the Ahmadiyyah order (*ṭarīqah aḥmadiyyah*) in the broader context, see Hamdan Hassan, *Tarekat Ahmadiyah di Malaysia*. This order should not be confused with either the Qadiani or the Lahore Aḥmadiyyah. The Ahmadiyyah order has its headquarters in Egypt.

[25]For more information on the Jama'at al-Arqam, see Nagata, *Reflowering of Malaysian Islam*.

[26]For more details on the Tabligh activities in Brunei see Aishah, op. cit.

[27]For more information of the Ahmadiyyah in Brunei see Razali, "Tarekat Ahmadiyah-Idrissiyah"; Aishah, op. cit.

The notorious view upheld during the period was that Muhammad al-Suhaimi will emerge as the Saviour (*al-Mahdī al-Muntazar*) of the Muslims. The Arqamis became more exclusive and acknowledged the supreme authority of the Arqam leader, Ustadh Asy'ari Muhammad.[28] This can be seen, for example, in the prestigious position given to his picture in the houses of the Arqamis.[29] Many Arqamis even went to Sungai Pencala to attend special gatherings (*majlis al-yaqadzah* [Arabic *majlis al-yaqazah* — lit. awakening, alertness council]) led by the *ustadh* to reveal those who sinned. They were effective in making the Arqamis more humble to him. When the Arqamis appeared to be more aggressive in their winning of followers and in upholding their newly acquired ideology, on 12 February 1991 the Brunei government banned the propagation of the Arqam teaching in the country.

The Arqam phenomenon in Brunei shows clearly the enthusiasm of the population for Islamic activities. More specifically, it confirmed the link between Brunei and many other Islamic centres.

Brunei also actively participated in enhancing Islamic resurgence during the second half of the twentieth century. The concerted efforts at improving Islamic education and restoring institutions during the 1950s were but a Brunei response to the ongoing awakening in the Islamic World. In Brunei, it was the ruler who took the initiative and sponsored many changes in religious administration and activities. The restoration of Islam as the official religion of the state, as enshrined in the 1959 Constitution, was a statement that Brunei had a firm commitment to Islamization. Indeed, during the 1960s more concrete steps towards the spirit of the 1959 Constitution on Islam were the foundation of more religious schools, the opening of religious classes for adults, the revamping of the mosque committees,[30] the publication of religious literature and the return of newly educated Bruneians from many higher education centres in the region and the Middle East. They were soon appointed to key positions in the religious bureaucracy. Some even published fresh and stimulating articles on Islam.[31] Moreover, in 1967 the

---

[28]*Ustadh*, from Arabic *ustādh*, means teacher.

[29]Aishah, *Pusat Da'wah Islamiah*, 193.

[30]In 1964 the Islamic Council of Brunei formed a central committee of mosques. It became a model for local mosque committees throughout the country. In 1970 the number of mosques reached forty with seventy-seven officials, including fifty-four imams (see Aishah, op. cit., 318).

[31]See *Pelita Brunei*, 1966.

sultan called upon the Bruneians to strive after the implementation of Islam as a way of life.[32]

Although Brunei never witnessed the emergence of an Islamic party, the echo of Islamic revivalism can be seen in many features. First of all the opening of religious schools since 1956 has created the opportunity for girls to be fully enrolled in religious instruction. Accordingly, Brunei women who became mothers since the mid 1960s had a much better knowledge of scriptural Islam. In the long run they were more prone to adapt and practise features of orthodox Islam, including those relating to the education of their children and to their public appearance and mode of dressing. Indeed, by the late 1970s, for example, more and more Brunei women covered their heads in public.[33] Islam has become the language of public discourse in Brunei. Even those who had advocated a secular lifestyle showed respect for the return to the pristine teachings of Islam.[34] Religious gatherings and lectures became usual features in government departments and, after independence, ministries.[35] The initiatives of the ruler in bringing Brunei closer to the Muslim World had a great deal to do with the formal adoption of Islamic leaning in the government circles.[36]

The advent of the fifteenth century of the Islamic calendar contributed to the awakening of Muslims worldwide. The dawn of the new century created an opportunity to evaluate the past achievements and hold discussions and meetings on the subject. In Brunei special sessions and parties were held in conjunction with the coming of the new century. As part of the belief in a renewal every new century, the fifteenth century after the *hijrah* was welcomed and it was hoped it would signify a new prospect for

---

[32]O.c, Dec. 1967.

[33]I got this impression when comparing pictures of the 1950s, 1960s, 1970s, and 1980s, as well as my own personal observation of Brunei students in Cairo during the mid 1970s and those in recent times.

[34]Aishah, op. cit., 338-40.

[35]A senior officer in the Department of Religious Affairs complained in December 1979 that many prominent Bruneians wanted to negate the role of Islam in public life, among other things by encouraging the opening of more places for entertainment. Yet it was these same persons who felt uneasy about the juvenile delinquency and thus advocated "quite seriously" the provision of Islamic teaching to the public (quoted in op. cit., 338, note 14).

[36]Since independence Brunei has become member of various international and regional Islamic bodies and organizations, including the Organization of the Islamic Conference. Moreover, the Islamic influence on government officers grew stronger, see articles by Badaruddin 1982 and 1983.

Islamization. Events in the Muslim World for the past decade and optimism about the development in many Muslim countries had a positive impact upon commitment to Islamic teaching in the country.

Intellectual and Educational Dimensions

Study Abroad by Bruneians

The intellectual training undergone by the Bruneians in various Islamic educational centres formed the strongest link between the Muslim World and Brunei. If in the past Bruneians, like their South-East Asian co-religionists, had gone to Mecca for higher study, after the Pacific War they attended al-Azhar University for their university education. Indeed, it is interesting to note that the leadership of the Department of Religious Affairs, and later the Ministry, has been dominated by al-Azhar-trained scholars. We are not interested in examining the impact of this particular orientation on society or the possibility that the development was a result of the religious orientation in the country. Rather what is worth examining is the relationship between such a religious study orientation and the magnet of the Muslim World.

Following the revival of the Wahhabite movement during the 1920s, Bruneians opted for positive withdrawal. The extent of their intellectual contacts in the Holy Cities was curtailed, outside the formal pilgrimage seasons. Under such circumstances, al-Azhar with its open approach to *madhhab*ism provided a more conducive environment for study for Bruneians.[37] Indeed, the Brunei graduates of al-Azhar continued to influence the prevailing religious system and uphold the status quo, while introducing changes from within.

Having achieved greater scholarship, these al-Azhar-trained scholars had no difficulty in building ties with other Muslim scholars internationally. Before joining al-Azhar University they had studied at the Al-Junid

---

[37]It is necessary to note here that during this period Mecca continued to attract many students from South-East Asia. Some of them, in fact, emerged as prominent scholars at home, see Noer, *Modernist Muslim Movement*; Dhofier, *Tradisi Pesantren*.

Religious School (Sekolah Arab Al-Juned) in Singapore,[38] and the Islamic College of Malaya in Kelang, Malaysia.[39] Brunei scholars completing their first degree at al-Azhar enjoyed access to a variegated academic circle. The years of interaction with different colleagues opened their minds to new and wider horizons. Indeed, a Brunei student in Cairo reported in 1961 that his stay in Cairo not only introduced him to purely religious subjects but also to diverse other disciplines, and even to nationalism and military drills.[40] Moreover, various collections of writings and poems written by Brunei students abroad, including Cairo, indicate that they read widely and participated in current scholarly debates and developments.[41] Similarly, in her study on Indonesian students in Cairo, Mona Abaza noted that these students brought home with them outlooks nurtured by diverse social, intellectual, political, and cultural exchanges during their long stay in Egypt.[42] Nevertheless, the strongest link maintained by these graduates was with their *alma mater*. For most of the experts in the different religious disciplines this was al-Azhar University, whereas middle rank officials generally completed their higher studies at religious institutions in Singapore and Malaysia.

Despite their erudition in religious scholarship, Bruneians who graduated from al-Azhar opted for the evolutionary approach towards reform in the religious field. It is interesting to note here that in 1953, a religious organization, Ikhwan al-Muslimin, was founded in Brunei. It had nothing to do with al-Ikhwān al-Muslimūn of Egypt. Is it possible, however, that the adoption of the name was inspired by the popularity of the Egyptian Ikhwan during the period?[43] Indeed, the Ikhwan of Brunei set up various activities which had an innovative orientation. For example, they actively organized public celebrations on salient occasions in the Islamic calendar, including the

---

[38]The first batch of Brunei students joined this institution in 1950. It consisted of three students, including the present minister of Religious Affairs. The sending of Bruneians to Al-Junid continued until 1983, when Brunei Arabic Secondary School graduates were directly admitted to al-Azhar University, without attending preparatory years at Al-Junid.

[39]The three students who finished their Islamic secondary education joined the Islamic College in 1956. They were followed by others until the early 1970s.

[40]*Pelita Brunei*, 19 March 1961, 2.

[41]On these collections see, for example, Yahya M.S., *Perjalanan Malam*, especially 76-9, 118-55; *Puisi Hidayat*; *Pakatan: Antologi Sajak*.

[42]Abaza, *Changing Images*.

[43]The popularity of the name Ikhwān al-Muslimūn in the Malay World and its association with innovative Islamic activities and modern organization around this period can be seen in the Malay Peninsula, Singapore, and North Borneo.

public celebrations on salient occasions in the Islamic calendar, including the birthday of the Prophet Muhammad, the *hijrah*, and the sending down of the Koran. Curiously, during this period no Bruneian had graduated from al-Azhar.

Writings and Publications

The higher rates of literacy achieved through modern education increased the circulation of written materials. Knowledge has become more and more a public domain thanks to the availability of and interest in written materials and various publications. Although in the past many Bruneians were literate in Arabic scripts, they enjoyed only limited access to reading materials. Knowledge, especially religious, was transmitted generally and most of the time in an oral fashion. The intellectual erudition of many Bruneians through the introduction of religious classes and modern education paved the way for the provision of reading materials on various subjects, including religion. The graduation of many Bruneians from higher institutions of religious learning facilitated the writing of religious texts and studies attuned to local conditions. Indeed, during the 1960s more works on Islam were written by Bruneians, in different forms, than ever before.

The return of Brunei graduates to the country was usually followed by employment in public offices. For example, the Azhar graduates during the 1960s joined the Department of Religious Affairs (DRA). Although these graduates were soon occupied with office duties and administrative responsibilities, many continued to devote part of their time to writing. As can be seen in the religious column of the *Pelita Brunei* of this period, these graduates contributed highly informative and novel views on Islam and society. More specifically, under the sponsorship of the DRA, the religious publications became more frequent and regular. For example, since 1962 the DRA has been publishing a quarterly journal, *Majalah Jabatan Hal Ehwal Ugama*. Its contents include various religious topics, the mufti's views and features of DRA activities. In 1964 another series, *Sinaran Suci*, was published. It was designed to respond to the popular need for religious teachings. During the 1970s, more publications were introduced by the DRA, including a religious journal, *al-Huda* (a new name for the *Majalah*) and a series on Koranic exegesis, *Tafsir Darussalam*. The role of the newly graduated Bruneians in these undertakings was obviously significant.

Interestingly, a score of books on Islamic literary works by Bruneians were published during this period.[44] Several books and monographs were published after 1979 in conjunction with the celebration of the advent of the fifteenth century after the *hijrah*. Moreover, as explained before, during the 1980s a number of religious seminars were organized in the country. They brought together experts in specific fields from around the country to discuss various religious topics. On several occasions the participants were international experts. The bulk of the proceedings of such seminars were published by the DRA. Yet, the fast growing publications of religious materials cannot be separated from the general trend of Islamic revivalism in the country and beyond. The impact of Islamic revivalism could be seen clearly in the speeches and actions of the leaders, political elite and religious scholars of the country.

Several examples can be cited to illustrate the increasing influence of the Brunei graduates of al-Azhar University. As I argue elsewhere, the predominance of the Azharis in the DRA was structural and consequential.[45] The official adoption of a "moderate" version of Islamic practice restricted contacts to certain educational centres. The Azhar continues to enjoy the highest position in the list. Since the majority of the religious leaders had been educated at al-Azhar, it only follows that the future cadres be sent to the same institution. It goes without saying that publications on religious subjects came from the works of the Azhar graduates. This can be seen in the writings of the former mufti, Pehin Mohd. Zain, Pehin Abd Hamid, Pehin Yahya, Pehin Abd Aziz Juned, Dato Abdul Saman and Pehin Badaruddin. All belonged to the top religious officialdom.[46] It should also be mentioned here that in addition to religious training at al-Azhar, all these leaders-cum-scholars had joined religious schools in Singapore and Malaysia. Some spent time in higher learning institutions in the West. For example, Dato Abdul Saman completed his post-graduate programme at the University of Birmingham following his graduation from al-Azhar.

The division of scholarly labour in the field of Islamic Studies in Brunei is worth noting. Despite the strong expression of Islam in public life, writing on Islamic subjects in Brunei has become the sole domain of fully trained

---

[44]Among them were *Puisi Hidayat*.

[45]Iik, "Socio-Religious Change"; *idem*, "Recent Trends".

[46]So far no detailed study of the intellectual tradition among modern Brunei writers exists.

religious scholars. It is true that some Brunei students who had completed secondary religious school opted to pursue non-religious careers. Nevertheless, it is exceptionally rare for Bruneians who have not undertaken a religious training to write on religious issues. The emergence of numerous writers on Islam who have engaged no higher religious education in other countries seems not to have encouraged their counterparts in Brunei. I do not see that the predilection has anything to do with the type of religious practice and understanding held in Brunei. It has more to do with the formal regulation about the spreading of Islamic teaching. A teacher on Islam is required to have a teaching licence. It is argued that the present arrangement has contributed positively to the religious harmony and stability in the country. Religious innovations are discussed internally and if necessary introduced slowly and quietly. Open religious polemics and debates have never taken place.[47]

Visits and Exchanges

As part of the Muslim World, Brunei has played an increasingly important role in reinvigorating Islamic brotherhood. Historically, the spread of Islam to the region was due mainly to commercial exchanges. The acceptance of Islam intensified the link between Brunei and other Islamic centres. The link was further strengthened by religious, economic, and social networks.

The presence of Muslims from other countries created opportunities for stronger social ties. In the past, many foreign Muslims from the Middle East and India took up residence in Brunei, and some even married local women. Indeed, such social ties also took place between the Bruneians and the inhabitants of neighbouring countries. Islam added a new factor to the continuing process of interplay. The intensity of ties eased the transfer of ideas and innovation from and to the country. After the Pacific War, the better provision of communication and improving economic condition facilitated the exchanges between Bruneians and other Muslims. Perhaps the diversity of exchanges has decreased concomitantly with the decreasing

[47]It should be mentioned that in the 1830s and 1840s religious controversies were allowed to be pursued and recognized. For more information on this, see Iik, "Contemporary European Views of the *Jawah*", 181-82.

numbers of non-Malay Muslims residing in the country.[48] The marriages of Brunei men with foreigners have not faced discouraging factors. I should quickly note that the impact of such social ties has been rather limited during the modern period, particularly with the increasing growth of economic and religious exchanges, not to mention the crucial role of the state.

In the economic field Brunei has enjoyed an enhanced position since the Pacific War. Brunei derives its financial strength from oil. The spending of economic surplus and the development of the country eventually brought many Bruneians into contact with outsiders, including Muslims. First of all, the financial capacity introduced many Bruneians to and made them aware of diverse achievements of other Muslims. Some of them have been adapted for the benefit of Bruneians and the country. A good example can be seen in the foundation of new mosques. Many of the mosques were built on a combined concept of Brunei-Islamic architecture and a more modern style, inspired partly by new developments in other Muslim countries. Moreover, the wealth of the country has attracted many traders and businessmen to Brunei, or at least they have developed business interest in it. Of course, we should not exaggerate the role of such men in spreading religious teachings, but those Muslims who are involved in such economic ties contribute indirectly to the development of new religious ideas and forms of expression in the country.[49]

The religious ties between Bruneians and their fellow Muslims have been primarily strengthened through different channels, however. The strongest, as we have seen, existed in the field of education. Again, the per-formance of the pilgrimage in Mecca and the participation in seminars has contributed significantly to the intensification of such ties. Moreover, Bruneians have visited various Islamic centres in order to strengthen ties. When on official duties to other countries, many Bruneians have taken advantage of visiting educational institutions, research centres, and religious establishments. This is corroborated by evidence from journals and

---

[48]It should be mentioned, however, that the number of foreign workers in Brunei in 1991 reached almost 70,000 out of the total population of 260,000. By 1996 it was projected that their number would reach 86,400 i.e. 28.7 per cent of the estimated total population (foreign and national residents) of 300,600 (see *Demographic Situation & Population Projections*, 1994, 43-4). However, in the middle of 1999 the number of foreign workers was estimated at 38,300, i.e. 11.6 per cent of the estimated total population of 330,700.
[49]The development of new financial institutions in Brunei will be discussed below.

newspapers published since the mid 1950s.[50] Conversely, the visits of Muslim religious, not to mention political, leaders to Brunei have been common during the same period. During the late 1950s and early 1960s, Annuar Musadad and Hamka from Indonesia frequently visited Brunei to deliver religious sermons and speeches.[51] Other visitors have come from among Muslim minority communities such as Indian, Korean, Chinese, and Philippine Muslims.[52] The Bruneians have shown their concern about the state of Islamic affairs among these minorities. For example, when the Muslims of Taipeh completed the foundation of a mosque in the city in 1960, Brunei sent a delegation to the opening ceremony.[53]

The Bruneians have paid special attention to the major Islamic events and figures. For example, in 1967 during the 1400th celebration of the sending down of the Koran (*nuzūl al-qur'ān*), the Bruneians held a seven-day religious gathering which included public speeches by Egyptian, Indonesian, and Malaysian scholars.[54] Earlier, in 1965, a special religious gathering was held to commemorate the well-known Muslim philosopher and poet, Muhammad Iqbāl.[55] All these occasions and events not only impressed the participants but also improved the understanding of the public on the importance of Islamic brotherhood and ties.

Administrative and Religio-Political Features

Unification of the Islamic Calendar

It is a fact that Muslim writers in the past consistently referred to the Hijri calendar when mentioning dates. The Hijri calendar thus became an important symbol for their intellectual identity. However, the presence of the West in Muslim lands also brought changes in calendar use. More and more

---

[50]See *Borneo Bulletin, Pelita Brunei* and *Salam* published during the period. For example, in 1962 and 1967 prominent Bruneians visited such centres in Singapore, Perlis, Kelantan and Johor (*Pelita Brunei*, 21 Nov. 1962, 6; 19 Aug. 1967, 6; 6 Sept. 1967, 2).

[51]*Pelita Brunei*, 2 Dec. 1959, 2; 19 Oct. 1960; 2 Nov. 1960, 1.

[52]See op. cit., 4 Dec. 1963, 4; 6 Nov. 1963, 3; 7 Nov. 1962, 6; 6 Dec. 1961, 5.

[53]Op. cit., 6 April 1960. Even in 1966, the Bruneians contributed $20,000 to the foundation of the Kuching mosque, (op. cit., 23 Feb. 1966, 1).

[54]Op. cit., 30 Aug. 1967, 2.

[55]Op. cit., 3 March 1965, 8.

Muslims became accustomed to the Gregorian calendar. Yet they continued to refer to the Hijri calendar when counting the beginning and the end of the *Ramadān* (fasting month), the Islamic new year, and the month of the pilgrimage (*Dhū al-Hijjah*). The Hijri calendar is lunar. Muslims hold that the beginning of the month is based on the sighting of the "baby crescent" (*ru'yah al-hilāl*). Opinion differs on how to have authentic sighting. The majority assert that the sighting can be made only through naked eyes. Some maintain that the scientific calculation (astronomy) is the best way to decide the beginning of Hijri months. Even within one school, opinions about the beginning of particular months can vary. On the basis of these differences, Muslim leaders attempted to develop a unified Islamic calendar.

Various meetings and seminars were held in order to establish a standard Islamic calendar. Previously the Muslims had started their fasting month in accordance with the announcement made by the local rulers or religious leaders. The increasing communications with Mecca, especially in conjunction with the pilgrimage season, encouraged Muslims to adjust their calendar of the month of *Dhū al-Hijjah* in accordance with the beginning of the pilgrimage season. Since the mid 1970s, various seminars at regional and international level have been organized to patch up major differences. In South-East Asia the religious officials from Indonesia, Malaysia, and Singapore met for the first time in 1974 to discuss matters related to the Islamic calendar.[56] They even succeeded in producing a *Ru'yah* Estimation Agreement. Furthermore, the first international conference on the Hijri calendar was held in Istanbul in 1978.[57] The conference came up with several recommendations, including the formation of a commission which would be responsible for the mobilization of efforts towards the unification of the Hijri calendar. Brunei participated in the sixth and seventh conferences held in Mecca in 1985 and Jakarta in 1987 respectively.

Brunei has been active in all these undertakings. Although it preserves its full right to determine the beginning of Islamic months, especially *Ramadān, Shawwāl,* and *Dhū al-Hijjah,* Brunei has joined regional and international bodies which have worked towards the unification of the

---

[56]Since 1984 Brunei has been officially represented in such meetings.

[57]The full member participants during the conference included representatives of Algeria, Bangladesh, Indonesia, Iraq, Kuwait, Qatar, Saudi Arabia, Tunisia and Turkey. In the 1987 conference representatives from states such as Bahrain, Brunei Darussalam, Malaysia, Pakistan, Sudan, United Arab Emirates, Jordan and the Organization of the Islamic Conference attended as observers.

Islamic calendar.[58] At present Brunei has agreed to consider any sighting of the first moon from neighbouring areas with a similar geographic location. Its religious officials regularly attend meetings on these matters with their counterparts from the neighbouring countries, in particular Indonesia, Malaysia, and Singapore. Because of its geographical position and high humidity, the sighting of the new moon cannot often been made satisfactorily. Only on rare occasions has it been achieved. In the past, the beginning of the Hijri months, especially the *Ramaḍān* and *Shawwāl* was determined by the completion of the previous months to thirty days.

Moreover, the use of the Hijri calendar in public has come into vogue in the country. Its dates are usually cited together with the Christian (Gregorian) calendar. It appears that this trend is emerging in conjunction with the increasing public expression of Islamic identity in Brunei. It can be argued, of course, that the latest development only put the sidelined practice back into practice.

Islamic Conferences and Committees

Although Brunei has enjoyed full control over its foreign affairs only since 1984, it unofficially participated in many international Islamic forums. For example, during the 1960s and 1970s various religious leaders of Brunei participated in international Islamic conferences such as those held in Baghdad, Mogadishu, Cairo, and Kuala Lumpur. During this period Brunei participation was rather low profile. The situation has greatly changed since Brunei fully regained independence in 1984.

Brunei quickly joined various international Islamic bodies. Concomitant with its official admission into diverse regional and international organizations such ASEAN, the United Nations, and the Commonwealth, Brunei became a full member in the Organization of the Islamic Conference (OIC). Indeed, shortly after its admission, the sultan attended the summit conference of the OIC held in Casablanca on January 16, 1984.[59] By formally joining the OIC, Brunei also has access to OIC affiliates such as the

---

[58]Interestingly, during the early 1970s a fatwa was issued in the country commenting negatively on the attempts to unify Islamic holidays, see *Mimbar Fatwa*, vol. 1, Siri Rangkaian Islamiah, no. 8, 43-63.

[59]Again, during the December 1991 summit conference of the OIC in Dakar, the sultan participated actively.

Islamic Development Bank (IDB) and the Islamic Economic and Social Council (ISESCO). For example, in 1989 Brunei held an international seminar on Islamic civilization in the Malay world in cooperation with the ISESCO.[60] The seminar was attended by prominent Muslim and non-Muslim scholars from all five continents. And, as we shall see shortly, Brunei has taken advantage of the experience of the IDB in running Islamic banks to set up its own Islamic financial and banking system.

At the regional level, Brunei has actively taken part in various Islamic committees and bodies. For example, it lost no time in joining the forum of senior religious officials of Indonesia, Malaysia, and Singapore. With the admission of Brunei the forum, which was set up in 1974, has four member states. The forum was originally designed to develop better cooperation in the field of Islamic calendar, especially regarding the beginning of the months of *Ramaḍān*, *Shawwāl*, and *Dhū al-Hijjah*. Lately the forum has included in its agenda various religious and social issues concerning the general affairs of Muslims in the region. Moreover, the closer cooperation between the members has led to the holding of more activities in Brunei with the support of other members. A good example of such activities is the organization of two regional seminars on the concept of *ahl al-sunnah wal-jamā'ah* and Islamic values held in September 1985 and October 1988 respectively. During the seminars papers were presented by Muslim scholars from Brunei and other South-East Asian countries.

The active participation of Brunei in various Islamic organizations at the international and regional levels has many positive effects upon Muslims in the country. Better knowledge and information about Brunei's link with Muslim countries and about their affairs through its participation in various Islamic organizations and committees has made Bruneians more aware about their link to the Muslim world. Accordingly, Bruneians have grown more eager to learn about them and to develop closer contact with them. Again, the structural links developed at a state level made it easy for Bruneians to extend their links from the "old friends" to new Muslim countries. As a small country Brunei has the advantage of being accepted as a member of various Islamic organizations. Indubitably, Brunei's wealth adds weight to various projects of these organizations.

---

[60]In this case the ISESCO was represented by its affiliate, the Research Centre for Islamic History, Art and Culture, which has headquarters in Istanbul.

Despite its openness and diplomatic warmth, Brunei is fully aware about its own limitations. It is true that Brunei has established diplomatic ties with many Muslim countries, including Saudi Arabia, Egypt, Malaysia, Indonesia, Oman, and Iran. It has also joined other Muslim countries in giving support to Muslims in Palestine, Afghanistan, Bosnia-Herzegovina, and Kosovo. Again, it has set up various symbols of Islamic revivalism, including the opening of Islamic financial centres. Yet, Brunei has continued to declare its commitment to a long established version of Islamic practice and belief system in the country. At the same time, interestingly, diverse changes have taken place in the organization and administration of Islam in the country. They have taken place smoothly without using new labels. Thus, despite changes in the expression of Islam in the country, Brunei maintains its commitment to the beaten path.

New Economic and Financial Institutions: the Islamic System

The increasing pressure on many Muslim countries to have an Islamic system of finance led to the establishment of several new financial institutions. The tremendous price hike of oil and the following financial boom enjoyed by Muslim oil-producing countries after 1973 forced many Muslim governments to reform and modernize their financial and monetary system. For example, since the mid-1970s attempts have been made among various Muslim circles to run an Islamic banking system. Indeed, the Muslim World League held several seminars on Islamic economics during the period. A positive response to the idea of having an Islamic banking system came from Dubai when the Islamic Bank of Dubai was founded in 1975. Before the end of the 1970s no less than seven new financial institutions using an Islamic system were established, mostly in the Middle East. Outside the Middle East, Pakistan and Malaysia took similar steps when an Islamic system of banking was introduced into the existing banking system in 1981 and 1983 respectively.

In Brunei concrete steps towards the foundation of Islamic financial institutions took place from the end of the 1980s, after a period of Islamic revival, several aspects of which have been described before. In response to increasing numbers of Islamic banks founded in many Islamic countries, in

1987 a committee for the foundation of Islamic Bank in Brunei was formed.[61] More specifically, a definite plan for establishing an Islamic system in banking took place after the ruler announced his support for the enterprise in late 1990.[62] Indeed, a year later, in September 1991, an Islamic savings bank, known as *Tabung Amanah Islam Brunei* (TAIB), was established. It was modelled mainly on the existing example founded earlier in Malaysia. The primary aim of the institution was to provide financial services and business transactions in an Islamic way.[63] The success of the TAIB in attracting customers led to another major step in the Islamization of the financial system when on January 13, 1993 the International Bank of Brunei was restructured to become the Islamic Bank of Brunei.

Although Brunei Darussalam was not among the early protagonists of the Islamic financial system, it did not want to be left behind its brethren. Its participation in the increasingly popular and successful system shows that Brunei is well aware of its ties with the wider Muslim World.

Religio-Political Issues

Political solidarity among Muslim countries has been regarded by many scholars as shallow and non-substantial.[64] Expressions of solidarity were often considered as lip-service, thus rarely materialized. This tendency is traced back to the internal structure of modern Muslim governments and to their relations with the established states, particularly those of the West, as well as their relations with their Muslim neighbours. Yet, in the past few years, when the economy of many Muslim countries has improved, at the same time enjoying political stability, concrete common actions were, indeed, undertaken. For example, the Muslims did take virtually a common stand on the Afghan issue in the early 1980s when the Soviet Union had interfered in

[61]Abdul Aziz, *Islam in Brunei*, 186.
[62]"As a nation with a strong Islamic basis, we have the obligation to take steps forward presenting ourselves among other countries which have set up [Islamic financial] enterprises" (*Sebagai sebuah negara yang mempunyai teras keislaman yang kuat, maka kita adalah wajib melangkah ke hadapan turut menampilkan diri bersama-sama mereka yang telah memulakan usaha*), quoted in op. cit., 190-1.
[63]Op. cit., 188.
[64]Landau, *Politics of Pan-Islam*; Israeli, *Fundamentalist Islam and Israel*; cf. Esposito, *The Iranian Revolution*.

Afghan affairs. Again, concrete actions were taken by diverse Muslim countries to help their brethren in Bosnia-Herzegovina and most recently Kosovo. Their solidarity towards their co-religionists in these two countries, as we all know too well, did not stop at the moral solidarity alone.

In the case of small countries like Brunei, options to build "independent" foreign relations may be rather limited. Indeed, as an author has put it, foreign policies of such countries are heavily influenced by external factors.[65] However, it is interesting that Brunei has succeeded in steering a more realistic approach to solidarity among Muslim countries. It has never failed to join common stands adopted by other Muslim countries on contemporary issues among Muslims.

Brunei has strongly supported the rights of the Palestinian people. The support was shown clearly in the speech by the Brunei ruler, when Brunei was admitted to the United Nations as the 159th member state in 1984.[66] For Brunei the overall solution of the Palestinian question was the only answer to the political crisis in the Middle East. As a member state in the OIC, not surprisingly Brunei has been applying the general policy of the organization towards Muslim countries. Similar straightforward approaches were adopted in dealing with the Soviet's interference in Afghanistan and the independence of Bosnia-Herzegovina.[67] Nevertheless, Brunei faces a dilemma comparable to other Muslim countries when dealing with political crises among Muslim countries. For example, while Brunei had adopted cautious approaches to the Gulf crises, it joined other Muslim countries in calling for the end of the war between Iran and Iraq. Again, Brunei called for an immediate peaceful solution to the Kuwait crisis in order to establish peace in the region as a whole. Although Brunei officially condemned the Iraqi annexation of Kuwait, it strongly urged for negotiation and a political

---

[65]See Shafruddin, "Ide Kenegaraan dan Negara Kecil", 339-40.

[66]The speech was delivered in the U.N. General Assembly on 31 September 1984. For details see Mohd. Jamil al-Sufri, *Liku-Liku Perjuangan*, 293. A similar echo was also expressed by the Minister of Foreign Affairs during the 1990 Gulf crisis, see *Pelita Brunei*, 28 Nov. 1990. For Brunei, one crucial problem at the root of the crisis, which required an immediate solution, was the right of the Palestinians to exercise their freedom.

[67]Before the campaign for substantive support for the struggle of the Bosnian people in 1993, Bruneians had mobilized funds for victims of the May 1991 cyclone in Bangladesh. It should be added that during the recent Kosovo crisis a massive campaign and concerted efforts were undertaken by all levels of society in Brunei Darussalam to mobilize funds for the Kosovo refugees.

solution to the crisis. Indeed, the idea of Muslim unity was reiterated time and again by Brunei in various OIC meetings.

With the increasing awareness of the Bruneians about their brethren in other Muslim countries, they began to realize their importance. Therefore, diplomatic ties were formally established with many of these countries. At least six Muslim countries have permanent representatives in Brunei. It will be interesting to analyse, on the occasion of another study, how the official positions towards Islamic issues have been accommodated by and moulded in public opinion.

Summary

Brunei pays special attention to its position as a Muslim state. It has played a significant role among Muslim countries. It is also participating in the diverse networks operating among Muslim states and communities. Although Brunei has definitely opted for a particular version and expression of Islam, it has never closed its doors to more intensive communication with other Muslim countries. I do not see that its predilection for a particular version of Islam, as claimed by G. Braighlinn,[68] was merely to serve a political contingency. The widespread adoption of the traditional approach to Islam, in fact, has led the political leaders to accommodate it within Brunei polity. It is pertinent to point out that the religious revivalism among Muslims worldwide has had a positive impact on Bruneian religious attitudes in that it has made Islam more meaningful and relevant. Following the more recent religio-political development and socio-economic change in the region, Brunei has pro-actively responded to new challenges. However, this is another topic which requires further study and can be dealt with more appropriately on another occasion.

By adhering to a well-defined belief system and religious practices, Brunei has maintained a relatively stable religious life. The strength of its religious bureaucracy has been effective in limiting the influence of controversial ideas and figures. Some might argue that, despite its success in achieving religious uniformity and stability, Bruneians may still be prone to new religious movements. The religious establishment seems to be aware of such challenges as suggested by their positive response to various

---

[68]Braighlinn, *Ideological Innovation under Monarchy*, 64-5.

developments in the Muslim World. Attempts in the country have been made to show that Bruneians are joining their Muslim brethren to live Islamically within the modern world.

Fatwas as a Unifying Factor in Indonesian History

Nico Kaptein

Introduction

A fatwa (Arabic *fatwā*) is a piece of religious advice, given by a mufti (*muftī*: fatwa giver) at the request of one or more Muslims who regard this mufti as authoritative. The giving of fatwas is called *iftā'*, while the asking for fatwas is called *istiftā'*. Many fatwas from throughout the Muslim word have been preserved, and every day new fatwas are issued. These texts have the following form: first, the question to the mufti is mentioned, followed by the mufti's answer, giving his opinion from the point of view of the — in his view — authentic sources of Islam. The size of a fatwa may vary from a few lines to an entire treatise. Because fatwas are given on request, they present a picture of all kinds of issues which are of topical interest to Muslims, and might give an insight into the tension between the Islamic ideal, as formulated by the authoritative muftis in their fatwas on the one hand, and all kinds of practices which were carried out in daily life on the other.

As a matter of course, many fatwas from Indonesia are also still extant. The present text, as an example, will start with a discussion of a number of fatwas which deal with a case of conditional repudiation in Batavia in 1298/1880 and mention some of the formal characteristics of these and other fatwas from the end of the nineteenth century, in order to shed some light on the institution of *iftā'* in Indonesia. It will then go on to mention some formal characteristics of fatwas which were recently issued in Indonesia, and discuss the similarities and dissimilarities between the fatwas from these two different periods.

Some Fatwas from the End of the Nineteenth Century

It is useful to start our discussion by presenting a case of conditional repudiation which occurred in Batavia at the end of the nineteenth century,[1] because this case brings to light a number of important characteristics of the institution of *iftā'* in the Netherlands East Indies in this period. This case has been well documented in a small, lithographic booklet which contains copies of the relevant documents and thus forms a dossier of the pertinent issue. The original documents are in Arabic, while the connecting passages and some summaries of relevant texts are in Malay. The booklet once formed part of the personal library of the famous Dutch orientalist C. Snouck Hurgronje (1857-1936), who spent the years 1889-1906 in the Netherlands East Indies in the service of the Dutch colonial administration as Advisor for Native and Arab Affairs. During this period Snouck Hurgronje collected an enormous number of printed and handwritten works, and after his death in 1936 this collection was bequeathed to the Leiden University Library.

The booklet mentions neither where it was published nor when. On page 1 there is a statement that the case began in AH 1298, which corresponds to AD 1880/1881. Therefore, the publication date will have to be set not too long after this year. The booklet has no title, and I will refer to it as *Segala Soal Jawab* (abbreviated as SSJ), because these are the first words mentioned on the cover, followed by a few lines in Malay to indicate the contents of the booklet. In translation these lines read as follows:

> These are all questions and answers pertinent to the issue that it is not permitted to confirm a repudiation on the sole basis of a document drawn up by witnesses who have since died. [This issue] has been sent to Mecca the Venerated and has been approved of by the mufti of Mecca and by other *'ulamā'*[2].

The booklet specifically deals with a case of conditional repudiation (*ta'līq al-ṭalāq*). In large parts of the Netherlands East Indies at the time it was customary that, immediately after the conclusion of a marriage contract, the

---

[1]This section leans partly on Kaptein, "Sayyid 'Uthmân", where the entire case is discussed in more detail.

[2]Ini segala soal jawab atas masalah tiada harus mehukumkan talak dengan semata-mata tulisan saksi-saksi yang telah mati. Maka telah dikirim ke Mekah al-musharrafah dan telah ditashihkannya oleh mufti Mekah beserta lain ulama lagi.

husband stated that his wife would be repudiated, should he not fulfil certain conditions which had been specified in the contract.

The case started in 1298/1881 when a woman asked a district *imam* (*imam distrik*) to affirm that she was divorced from her husband, who had left her to go on a sea voyage and had subsequently been absent for approximately ten years. Although the *imam* who had concluded the marriage (*menikahkan*) between the woman and her husband, as well as the witnesses who had been present when the marriage had been concluded, had since died, in the marriage registration book (*buku nikah*) was a written *ta'līq* formula "as is usual according to the customary law of the province [*adat negeri*]", with the signature of the husband (*tekannya suami*) under it, thus supplying the evidence needed to dissolve the marriage. Despite this written evidence, the *imam* to whom the woman had turned, did not confirm the repudiation because he was aware of texts issued by *'ulamā'* which forbade the giving of a verdict solely on the basis of written evidence without the verbal testimony of the witnesses.[3]

The issue moved a stage further when the *imam* presented the case to Sayyid 'Uthmān (1822-1914), the well-known Batavian scholar of Arab descent, who was one of the most productive Islamic scholars in the Netherlands East Indies in his day, and in 1889 was appointed the "Honorary Advisor for Arab Affairs" to the Dutch colonial administration. The booklet contains the question (in Arabic) to the Sayyid asking whether or not the wife had been repudiated in this instance,[4] as well as his extensive answer which forms the major part of the booklet and which denies the validity of the *talāq* under the circumstances given.[5]

Thereafter, this answer was discussed in a fatwa council (*majlis fatwa*) which undoubtedly took place in Batavia.[6] The majority of the participants supported Sayyid 'Uthmān's view. However, on the basis of the principle of emergency (*ḍarūrah*), a part of a Koranic verse (*sūrah* 2:185b), and a quotation from a *fiqh* manual (the *Fath al-mu'īn* by the sixteenth-century scholar Zayn al-Dīn al-Malaybārī), three of the persons composing the *majlis*

---

[3]*SSJ*, 8-9.
[4]Op. cit., 1-2.
[5]Op. cit., 2-7.
[6]Cf. op. cit., 10.

were of the opinion that the marriage could be dissolved on the basis of the written document without requiring the presence of the witnesses.[7]

After this gathering the district *imam* gave his decision to the woman, to wit that he could not confirm her repudiation.

Moving on to a higher level, the case was sent to Mecca, where it was presented to two authoritative Muslim scholars for arbitration, to wit Nawawi Banten and Ahmad b. Zaynī Dahlān. The former scholar was born in Banten, West Java in 1813 and left Java when he was about fifteen years old in order to settle in Mecca to study, eventually winning fame as a scholar and teacher. Although he spent the rest of his life until his death in 1897 almost entirely in Mecca, he was very influential in Indonesia through his students and his books.[8] The latter was mufti of the Shafi'ites from 1871 until shortly before his death in Medina in 1886. He received questions from Shafi'ite Muslims all over the world and was held in high esteem in the Netherlands East Indies. He was the teacher of many prominent *'ulamā'* from the Netherlands East Indies, among them Sayyid 'Uthmān.[9] Both Nawawi Banten and Ahmad Dahlān stated with regard to the Batavian case under discussion that the repudiation could not be confirmed.[10]

Such a request for confirmation by a higher religious authority is not unusual in the history of Islam in South-East Asia at this period of time. This confirmation is an interesting phenomenon within the institution of *iftā'*, and is called *tashīh*, perhaps best to be rendered with "official approval". In this particular case, the *tashīh* of Zaynī Dahlān has been preserved and reads as follows:

> The contents of this answer [by Sayyid 'Uthmān], namely that a repudiation without legal proof, but based on the custom (*'amal*) of a piece of writing lodged with the authorities is not valid, are a true account which accords with what is right and the texts mentioned in the answer are sufficient. May God reward the person who gave this answer .... Ahmad b. Zaynī Dahlān, mufti of the Shafi'ites in the Protected City of Mecca ....[11]

[7]Op. cit., 9.
[8]Snouck Hurgronje, *Mekka*, 268-72, 278.
[9]Snouck Hurgronje, "Een rector der Mekkaansche universiteit", 67-68.
[10]*SSJ*, 10-1.
[11]Op. cit., 7.

I have dealt with this case extensively, because it gives an unique insight into how it reached Mecca, and how the intellectual relations between Mecca and the Netherlands East Indies were maintained. It is important to note that this case, in which a legal dispute eventually led to the request for a fatwa from Mecca, is certainly not a unique example. In fact, we come across requests from Indonesian Muslims to the leading Meccan muftis quite often, and even an entire collection of Meccan fatwas given at the request of Indonesian Muslims is known. This collection is entitled *Muhimmāt al-nafā'is fī bayān as'ilah al-ḥadīth*, "The precious gems dealing with the explanation of questions about current topics", and contains some 130 fatwas in Arabic and Malay, referring to all kinds of subjects.[12] Although the precise identity of the persons who asked for these fatwas cannot be traced, it is clear that the issues dealt with were of topical interest to Indonesian Muslims, and for this reason it seems likely that, at least for an important number of the fatwas, similar to the case of conditional repudiation just discussed, the requests for a fatwa reached Mecca only after the issue had been debated at home in Indonesia first. The interesting thing about the repudiation case is that the entire process can be traced, while this can not yet be done with the fatwas from the *Muhimmāt al-nafā'is*, because the "local" fatwas have not been preserved. However, in many cases the discussion on the pertinent issue will have followed the same pattern. In other words: in many cases, the Meccan fatwas for Indonesian Muslims were only the tip of the iceberg.

The very fact that Indonesian Muslims turned to Mecca for religious guidance and education confirms the characterization of Mecca and, more in particular, of the colony of Indonesian teachers and students who lived there, as "the heart of the religious life of the East-Indian Archipelago".[13] Thus, from Mecca there was a constant stream of Islamic views pouring into the Netherlands East Indies in the form of fatwas and these form an interesting chain in the intellectual relationship between the Middle East and South-East Asia. The next section will deal with the impact of this stream of fatwas on the Netherlands East Indies, not in individual cases, but as an institution.

[12]Kaptein, "Meccan *Fatwâs*".
[13]Snouck Hurgronje, *Mekka*, 291.

The institution of *iftā'* in the Netherlands East Indies

In order to asses the significance of the legal institution of *iftā'* for the Netherlands East Indies properly, it is necessary to give some details about its legal system. This system was pluralistic in character, in the sense that different systems for various sections of the population existed side by side. This traditional plural organization was affirmed in the Government Regulation ("*Regeringsreglement*") of 1854. In seeking to establish the place of indigenous Indonesian law within this Regulation, Article 75 is highly significant. This article stated that the administrators of native law would apply the "religious laws, institutions and customs of the natives, in so far as they are not in conflict with generally recognized principles of fairness and justice". In real terms this meant the functioning of different legal systems alongside each other: regionally differing laws for natives and "foreign orientals" (the Arabs and the Chinese) on the one hand, and Dutch statute law for the Europeans and others equated legally with them on the other hand.[14]

The predominant view of the Dutch administrators on what this indigenous legal system was, changed in the course of the nineteenth century. In the first half of this century the Dutch administrators of the Netherlands East Indies thought that the laws which regulated indigenous society were basically Islamic. This explains why in this period a number of classical *fiqh* handbooks formed part of the curriculum in the Dutch educational institutions where the future civil servants were trained. Quite a few of these books, like the *Kitāb Tuḥfah* by Ibn Ḥajar al-Hàytamī, the *Mir'āh al-ṭullāb* by ʿAbd al-Ra'ūf al-Singkilī and others, were partly or entirely published by the colonial government. These books were published in order to understand, and consequently to exercise better control over the native population. Although there was already an awareness afoot that there were local "deviations" from this law system, the general conviction at that time was that the indigenous society was basically ruled by Islamic law, supplemented by local customs, called *adat* (from Arabic *ʿādah*), in as far as these had legal consequences. This paradigm changed towards the end of the nineteenth century, when the perspective was turned upside down: it was no longer thought that the *shariʿah* formed the foundation of society, but

[14]Sonius, "Introduction", LVIII.

instead the *adat* which was supplemented by a number of rules coming from Islamic law.[15] It is generally assumed that this conceptual change was first recognized by the above-mentioned C. Snouck Hurgronje (1856-1936), who is credited with having coined the term adatrecht ("*adat* law") in his 1893-1894 book on the Acehnese.[16]

Once this inversion in the relationship between *adat* law and Islamic law had gained recognition, the study of *adat* law was made into a separate academic discipline, first and foremost as a result of the efforts of C. van Vollenhoven (1874-1933).[17] Within the conceptual framework of *adat* law the Netherlands East Indies were divided into nineteen separate geographical regions, which were regarded (or perhaps better: declared) as consisting of ethnographically and culturally homogeneous peoples. Within this framework Islamic law did not exist as a category *sui generis*, but was only taken seriously in as far as elements of it had been "received" into a particular *adat*. This conceptual predominance of *adat* law had, of course, political consequences: by stressing *adat* law the differences between the various ethnic unities in the Netherlands East Indies were confirmed, while supra-ethnic unification was obstructed. In short: on a national level the promotion of the *adat* law meant in real terms a *divide et impera* policy.[18]

To conclude this section, it is possible to place the constant stream of Islamic views from the Middle East into the Netherlands East Indies in the form of fatwas against the background of the legal philosophy and system just sketched. If we do so, it will be clear that these fatwas with their appeal to all Muslims from the entire Archipelago had a supralocal impact and transcended the regional law circles. In this way, the institution of *iftā'*, in conjunction with other Islamic institutions, like the Islamic courts, and Islamic educational institutions, enhanced the predisposition amongst the

---

[15]Boland, "Historical Outline", 8-9, 20-2.

[16]Op. cit., 20. As far as I know, the legal publications and professional correspondence of Mr. L.W.C. van den Berg have never been studied with regard to this issue. There is a strong possibility that this scholar attributed more legal force to the *adat* than is generally assumed, and that he is in fact one of the pioneers of this new perception of the relationship between *adat* law and Islamic law.

[17]This binary opposition of *adat* and Islam was later questioned and refined by a number of scholars, like Taufik Abdullah. In an important article in 1966 this Indonesian scholar stressed that the *adat* in Minangkabau was not in opposition to Islamic law, but had developed as a synthesis of *adat* (in the antithetical sense) and Islam, and that *adat* in this sense was much wider and included Islam (Roff, "Islam Obscured?", 10-1).

[18]Op. cit., 13-4.

native peoples of the Archipelago to accept Islam as a organizing principle for nationalistic politics. For this reason, the institution of *iftā'* will have promoted the unification of the native population of the Netherlands East Indies.

Final Remarks

At the end of this study it might prove interesting to go briefly into contemporary *iftā'*. In present-day Indonesia various institutions issue fatwas, like the national Majelis Ulama Indonesia, which was founded in 1975 at the initiative of President Soeharto; regional Councils of *'Ulamā'*; and Muslim organizations, like the Nahdlatul Ulama (at various levels) and the Muhammadiyah.[19] For this reason, we might say that the institution of *iftā'* is alive and kicking nowadays. However, when present-day *iftā'* is compared with that from the end of the nineteenth century, one difference is particularly striking[20]: As we have seen above, at the end of the nineteenth century, the native population from the Netherlands East Indies regarded Mecca as "the heart of the religious life of the East-Indian Archipelago". Nowadays, Mecca still plays an important role, namely as the place in and around which the yearly pilgrimage takes place. However, Mecca is no longer regarded as the most important place to study, and consequently has lost its position as the intellectual centre of Indonesian Islam, which was still well and truly entrenched at the end of the nineteenth century. This is also reflected in contemporary fatwas for Indonesian Muslims: in general, these fatwas are no longer addressed to muftis in Mecca, but to qualified countrymen or national institutions.

As far as the unifying function of the nineteenth century *iftā'* is concerned, this function seems to have continued to be active up to the present day. Even when fatwas contradict each other, the possible contradictions should be perceived as a sign of the flexibility of the system, and not as a menace to its unity. Generally speaking, any fatwa asked for implies the recognition of the validity of Islamic discourse, and in this sense *iftā'* has contributed and still contributes to the deeper Islamization of Indonesian society. It is to be expected that with the ongoing process of

---

[19]Atho, *Fatwas*, 3-4.
[20]Other differences, like a different legal methodology, are left aside here.

Islamization, local cultures will loose many of their particular features and cultural diversity in Indonesia will shrink.

Part Two

Modernization

6 Modernity and the Disenchantment of Life
A Muslim-Christian Contrast

Mark R. Woodward

The difference between your country and mine is that in the United States the power elite is very modern, but has no use for religion. In my country we want to combine modernity and Islam. We understand that life is more than a natural process, it is a gift from God.
(Dato Abdul Majid Mohamed, Ambassador of Malaysia to the United States, at an October 1994 conference sponsored by the Phoenix Chamber of Commerce)

Introduction

Modernization theorists, following Max Weber, have generally assumed that the "disenchantment of life" was an essential component of the process of rationalization which gave rise to the modern era. Traditional cosmologies in which God(s) and hosts of lesser spiritual beings play active roles in the natural environment and human affairs gradually give way to an impersonal and mechanistic cosmology and its sociological counterpart, the functionally rationalized bureaucratic social order. The persistence of traditional religions and their periodic resurgence are understood as examples of incomplete modernization or alternatively as revivalistic responses to rapid cultural change. Or, so goes the theory.

In *Defenders of God*, Bruce Lawrence characterizes modernity as: "the emergence of a new index of human life shaped, above all, by increasing bureaucratization and rationalization as well as technical capacities and global exchange unthinkable in the pre-modern era."[1] He describes modernism as "the search for individual autonomy driven by a set of socially encoded values emphasizing change over continuity; quantity over quality;

[1]Lawrence, *Defenders of God.* 1.

111

efficient production, power and profit over sympathy for traditional values or vocations, in both the public and private spheres. At its utopian extreme, it enthrones one economic strategy, consumer oriented capitalism, as the surest means to technological progress that will also eliminate social unrest and physical discomfort."[2] To the extent that "technical capacities" and "global exchange" are the material consequences of the ideology of modernism, religion is marginalized. If, as many assume, the relationship is causal, the marginalization of religion in both public and private life is a necessary pre-condition for modernity.

The global religious resurgence of the 1980s and 1990s and particularly the rapid growth of fundamentalist movements in Christian, Muslim, and Hindu cultures raises serious questions concerning the validity and predictive power of modernization theory. In this text it is argued that the disenchantment of life, which *is* characteristic of modern Christian theology, is not a necessary component of modernization. Rather, it is the result of the conflict between Christian and scientific ways of knowing which dates from the sixteenth century. the emphasis of Christianity on cosmology and cosmogony combined with a tendency towards literal readings of scripture produced a conflict between those Lawrence terms "defenders of God" and proponents of science and secular philosophies which continues to haunt the Western world. Lawrence and other scholars engaged in the study of religious responses to modernity have focused primarily on fundamentalist and secularist responses to modernity. In this text I will be concerned with the ways in which contemporary Indonesian Muslims have attempted to find a middle ground between the spiritual emptiness of secularism and the rigid authoritarianism of fundamentalism.

The Islamic world-view differs fundamentally from that of the Christian West. The world-views of Muslims and Christians are shaped by the interaction of sacred texts and local cultures. The nature of textuality in the two traditions has had a subtle, but profound, influence on the ways in which they have, and to a certain extent can, approach modernity. One of the most basic differences between the two great traditions is the fact that the Koran is not a cosmological text or a universal history in the same sense that the Bible is. This distinction is apparent even in the ways in which the two texts are ordered. The Christian Bible begins with the creation of the world, and

[2]L.c.

moves in chronological order to its ultimate destruction. While the Koran often touches on cosmological, cosmogonic, and historical themes, the order of the text is determined by the length of the individual chapters. Consequently, the Christian Bible can be, and often is, read as a chronologically ordered history of the universe in which "modernity" is a missing chapter. It is far more difficult to read the text of the Koran in this way.

This difference has significant implications for the ways in which modernity is, and can be, understood by Muslims and Christians. For Christians, the basic problem of modernity is cosmological. In the Muslim world the problems of modernity are primarily sociological. Most recent studies of modern Islam have focused on competing visions of how to define an Islamic society in the context of the modern secular world. In this text I will be concerned with the ways in which the *spiritual* dimensions of Islam continue to provide meaningful experience and social cohesion for Muslims in an increasingly modern Indonesia. It will be argued that a modern Islam, unlike a modern Christianity, need not be a disenchanted Islam. While in the West modernism and religion appear to be locked in an eternal struggle, in Indonesia a person can be both profoundly modern and profoundly Muslim.

This text consists of two parts. The first describes the religious crisis which has been produced by cosmological conflict in the Christian West and three major responses to it: 1. secularization; 2. disenchanted religion; and 3. fundamentalism. The second argues that in Indonesia, and the Muslim world more generally, modernization does not necessarily entail the disenchantment of life. The Koranic distinction between naturalistic and religious causality and the subsequent Sufi division of reality into external, material states (*lahir*) and internal, spiritual states (*batin*) enables many Indonesian Muslims to avoid the conflict between religion and science common in European thought.[3] God and lesser spiritual beings remain active in a world which is increasing understood in scientific terms. In the conclusion it is argued that, owing to the fact that, as Mircea Eliade has suggested, concern for the sacred is a fundamental quality of humanity, an enchanted modernity, such as that which appears to be emerging in Indonesia, may in the long run prove to be more stable than the secular

---

[3]On the distinction between naturalistic and religious causality, see Rahman, *Major Themes of the Qur'an*, 4, 66 ff., 91.

modernities of the Christian West. While the social, economic and political problems of modernization are real, it is at least possible that in the Muslim world social change will not entrap the human spirit in what Max Weber termed the "iron cage" of Western capitalism.[4]

Religion and Modernity: Western Social Scientific and Theological Perspectives

Secularization

The concept of modernity has been among the central concerns of the social sciences almost from their inception. In different ways Karl Marx, Emile Durkheim, Max Weber, Sigmund Freud, and the evolutionist tradition in anthropology and sociology represented by Herbert Spencer and Edward Tylor were concerned with the social and historical transformations which led to the secularized industrialized nation-states of Western Europe and North America. While individual theorists differ greatly, their works rest on the assumption that the characteristics and development of human societies are to be explained naturalistically. There is, in short, no room for God in Western social thought. Religion is among the social facts which must be explained. In a very different sense modernity has also been among the central concerns of theology. If the social sciences have sought to explain religion in non-religious terms, modern theology has sought to redefine its place in societies and systems of authority which have ceased to be overtly religious.

Social scientific theories of religion as well as Western notions of "religious freedom" are products of the European "Enlightenment". As Daniel argues, pre-Enlightenment attempts to understand Islam and other non-Western religions were phrased in Christian theological terms.[5] Attempts to understand non-European religions on their own terms, or in

---

[4]Weber, *The Protestant Ethic*, 181.
[5]Daniel, *Islam and the West*. Attempts to explain "other" religions are in no sense unique to the European intellectual tradition. Heresiography is an element of many traditions, including that of Muslim Java. However, it has been from European discourse about others that both the history of religions and anthropology developed.

terms of non-theological theoretical constructs, arose largely as the result of the gradual decline of Christian theology as the paradigmatic structure of Western thought. The rise of science and the consequent falsification of traditional geo-centric cosmologies, Darwin's assault on the Biblical theory of creation, the critical and historical examination of Christian sacred texts, as well as increased awareness of the religions of Asia, the Americas, and Africa all contributed to a theological crisis. As Claude Welch put it "At the beginning of the nineteenth century the theological problem was, simply, 'How is theology possible?'"[6]

Jeffery Hopper attributes the decline of Western Christianity to the ways in which scripture was understood in the pre-modern era.[7] The Bible was considered to be the source of all knowledge and a standard against which truth could be judged. Any challenge to Biblical authority was an affront to all aspects of the faith including the central teachings of faith and redemption. Hopper cites the crisis surrounding Galileo's astronomy as a critical turning point in Western history. Galileo's astronomy was, and was understood by the Church, as a direct attack on both geo-centric cosmology and the veracity of Biblical texts according to which the sun moves and the earth does not. Cardinal Bellarmine, writing in 1615, understood the issue clearly. He observed: "to affirm that the sun is really fixed in the center of the heavens .... is a very dangerous thing ..... injuring our faith and making the sacred Scripture false."[8]

The Church took a strong stand against Galileo. It lost. Hopper puts it this way: "But the scientific findings of Galileo and others were inevitably so much more powerful in their impact upon the minds of the educated that the power of the Church was doomed. The authority claimed by both philosophers and theologians and claimed for scriptures in many areas of human existence was destined to be greatly reduced and restricted. ...... The truth of Christianity that had long been assumed would also come into question. It would be some time after Galileo before all of this would become manifest, but some church leaders were quick to see a very real threat."[9]

---

[6] Welch, *Protestant Thought*, 59.
[7] Hopper, *Understanding Modern Theology*.
[8] Quoted from op. cit., 20.
[9] L.c.

The religious crisis which began with Galileo and Copernicus and continued through the time of Darwin and beyond had implications beyond the narrow confines of academic theology. It called into question the veracity of Biblical cosmology and narrative which were the linchpins of the traditional Christian world view and faith. Eliade has argued that cosmology is the core of pre-modern religion and that celestial archetypes are models for human action.[10] Michael Polanyi and Harry Prosch observe that for religion to be accepted, the myths on which it is founded must be at least plausible.[11] By demonstrating that the traditional cosmology was not merely implausible, but simply false, questions were also raised about the soteriological teachings of the Church such as grace, redemption and salvation.[12]

Eighteenth-century Enlightenment thinkers often attacked religion as irrational and cruel. Welch observes that with the growth of science and rational philosophies, the fundamental teachings of Christianity (and other religions) such as miracles and original sin came under increasingly sharp attack. He refers to the criticism of thinkers like David Hume, Denis Diderot, Voltaire, and Max Müller.

Of the numerous responses to this intellectual and spiritual crisis, four are particularly significant for understanding the development of contemporary scholarly discourse about religion: 1. the staunch defence of Biblical myth; 2. natural theology which understands the world as a form of divine revelation; 3. the theological tradition of Schleiermacher which has attempted to formulate a non-cosmological understanding of Christianity; and 4. the rejection of tradition characteristic of the Enlightenment.

The Enlightenment and the rise of science did not lead to the death of theology as some had hoped or feared. Theologies continued to be developed, but were confronted not only with alternative theologies, but with the idea that religion itself could be dispensed with. Since the Enlightenment, the central problem for theology has been to arrive at formulations of Christianity which avoid the problem of falsification. Natural theology and Schleiermacher's non-cosmological faith are among the most important

---

[10]Eliade, *Mythe de l'éternel retour.*
[11]Polanyi and Prosch, *Meaning,* 158-60.
[12]This crisis was as acute for Protestant Christianity as it was for the Roman Catholic tradition, and perhaps more so because Protestant scholastic theologians, unlike their Roman Catholic counterparts insisted on a literal understanding of Biblical narrative.

examples. Alternatives include an ultimately intellectually futile rearguard defence of Biblical narrative, and the abandonment of religion as a way of knowing. Biblical literalism continues to be a significant voice in confessional Christian discourse, but has almost no impact on the social sciences or modern theology. For the social sciences, which chose to abandon theology as a way of knowing, religion has become one of many objects of study.

Antagonism between science and religion was a central feature of nineteenth-century thought, the context in which the modern social sciences developed. Generally speaking, social scientists have placed themselves on the secular side of the debate. In their anti-theological stance, the social sciences are the heirs of earlier Enlightenment critiques of religion. With few exceptions they would answer the question "How is theology possible?" with the assertion that while it may be possible, theology is a subject without an object. Most regard religion as human phenomena which must be explained in human or other natural terms. While the range of theoretical explanations of religion which have been proposed is enormous, most share the assumption that the claims religion makes about the cosmos and the human condition are ultimately false, and that we live in a world in which claims that God(s) and other "supernatural" beings and forces influence the course of human and natural events are curious relics of a previous, pre-modern age. As Edward Evan Evans-Pritchard observes, early theories of religion were attempts to discern its origins. They were, however, simultaneously critiques of religion, because if it can be shown that religious ideas are derived from the interpretation of the natural or social phenomena, it follows that the claims of any possible theology are false.

Anthropological and other social science theories of religion did not grow directly from anti-religious polemics, but rather from Enlightenment speculation about why it should be that generation after generation of humans would accept the absurd propositions of religion as truth. In other words, theories of religion assume the prior validity of some version of the Enlightenment critique of religion. The question which arises is then why do people accept the untrue as truth and what, if any, human purposes does this serve. Writing in 1748, Montesquieu, who understood the development of human society as governed by "laws" similar to those of nature, observed that religion serves useful social purposes, particularly when its forms correspond with prevailing social and political institutions. The Enlightenment polemic against and attempts to explain religion mark a fundamental development in Western thought. For those scholars rooted in this tradition, the study of religion is a quest for human rather than cosmic truth. As Evans-Pritchard puts it: "He is not concerned, *qua* anthropologist, with the truth or falsity of religious thought. As I understand the matter, there is no possibility of his *knowing* whether the spiritual beings of primitive religions or of any others have existence or not, and since that is the case he can not take the question into consideration."[13]

The French and American Revolutions helped to establish Enlightenment thought as the ideological foundation of the modern world order. As William Miller has shown, the question of what role religion should play in the American political system was hotly debated. While some of the framers of the United States constitution advocated a system which affirmed the truth and prerogatives of Protestant Christianity, the majority, among them Thomas Jefferson, favoured a secular state in which citizens could freely exercise any religion — or none at all. Jefferson advocated a clear distinction between civil rights and religious duties. Interestingly his rhetoric establishes a link between scientific ways of knowing and secular, democratic ways of living. He wrote: " ... that our civil rights have no more dependence on our religious opinions than our opinions in physics or geometry; that therefore the proscribing any citizen as unworthy of the public confidence by laying upon him any incapacity of being called to offices of trust and emolument, unless he renounce this or that religious opinion, is depriving him injuriously of those privileges and advantages to which, in common with his fellow citizens, he has a natural right;" and in a less formal style: " ...it does me no injury for my neighbor to say that there are twenty gods , or no god. It neither picks my pocket not breaks my leg."[14]

Disenchanted Religion

Secular politics was as radical a way of living in the world as secular science was as a way of knowing it. Together they established rational inquiry as the paradigmatic structure of Western modernism. As Lawrence notes, the shift from religious to secular paradigms had profound implications for all

---

[13] Evans-Pritchard, *Theories of Primitive Religion*, 17.
[14] Thomas Jefferson, quoted in Miller, *The First Liberty*, 85 f.

subsequent ways of religious knowing and living. Religious people may reject the secular paradigm, but they ignore it at the risk of sinking into obscurity and irrelevancy.

What can be termed "modern Christian theology" presumes the validity of much of the Enlightenment critique of traditional cosmological religion. The history of modern Christian theology and its struggles with both science and traditional religion has a long and complex history which is beyond the scope of this text. Here it will suffice to note that, by the beginning of the nineteenth century, the burning theological issue was not the denunciation and repression of scientific thought but, as the German theologian, Friedrich Schleiermacher put it: "to create an eternal covenant between the living Christian faith and an independent and freely working science, a covenant by the terms of which science is not hindered and faith not excluded."[15]

Schleiermacher was the founder of the hermeneutical tradition which continues to be among the primary methodologies of modern Christian theology. He devised hermeneutics to salvage Christianity from the intellectual insolvency and spiritual void of Protestant Biblical literalism. Schleiermacher's mode of textual exegesis focused on a subjective understanding rather than literal reading of scripture. Schleiermacher articulated two ways of knowing or encountering textual materials: a grammatical mode which examines the precise literal meaning of a text and a feeling (Gefühl) of its ultimate significance. Hodges characterizes Schleiermacher's hermeneutics as follows: "he finds that the understanding of a literary whole has two aspects, both necessary and co-ordinate in status, but different in aim and method, viz. grammatical and psychological understanding. The aim of grammatical understanding is to remove ambiguities in, and to wring the last drop of meaning from, the words and phrases which constitute the outward appearance of the work. The aim of psychological understanding is to go behind this outward appearance to the 'inner form', the living principle or idea in the author's mind, of which the written text is the expression."[16]

The same forces which were behind Schleiermacher's efforts to salvage Christianity gave rise to an increased appreciation of the truth claims of non-Christian religions and laid the groundwork for contemporary religious

---

[15]Cited in Welch, op. cit., vol. 1, 63.
[16]Hodges, The Philosophy of Wilhelm Dilthey, 12.

relativism. In 1799 Schleiermacher wrote: "If you want to compare religion with religion as the eternally progressing work of the world spirit, you must give up the vain and futile wish that there ought to be only one; your antipathy against the variety of religion must be laid aside, and with as much impartiality as possible you must join all those which have developed from the eternally abundant bosom of the Universe through the changing forms and progressing traditions of man."[17]

Schleiermacher's theology is deeply religious in an almost mystical sense. It is, however, spirit- rather than text-centred. The success of Schleiermacher's theological programme among academic theologians led to an increasing distancing of liberal Christianity from its textual roots, while continued scientific advances distanced theology from the natural world. The result has been an academic discourse in which there is little room for the person of Jesus Christ and the miraculous narrative surrounding his birth, preaching, death, and resurrection.

Some modern theologians go so far as to argue that God, to say nothing of the myriad of lesser spiritual beings such as saints and angels or Satan and his minions, does not act in the world. Others, including Hopper, reject traditional Christian understandings of salvation and eternal life, arguing that, because it is a natural human desire, hope for eternal life betrays a lack of faith and trust in God and consequently must be denounced as idolatry. He is equally harsh in his treatment of doctrinal and liturgical formulations. Still other modern theologians, including those associated with the California-based Jesus Seminar *vote* on such basic questions as "Did Jesus actually rise from the dead?", generally answering in the negative. Others rewrite scripture in gender-neutral terms. The decentring of Christian texts in modern theologies is possible, and indeed necessary because, as Gordon Kaufman puts it, the texts are regarded as mythological, while God, Christ and salvation are treated as symbolic concepts, the meanings of which change in course of human history.[18]

[17]Schleiermacher, *Über die Religion*, 242.
[18]Kaufman, *Theology for a Nuclear Age*.

Fundamentalism

These theologies build on Schleiermacher's in that they are rooted in a personalistic faith encounter, rather than in the textual tradition and in their self-conscious attempts to appeal to "modern" secular intellectuals. In a recent edition of the popular American news magazine, *Time*, the Anglican bishop and liberal Protestant theologian, John Spong, put it this way: "There are a whole lot of literal concepts out of the Bible that have long ago been abandoned. I'd like to think Christianity is something that would appeal to people who are well educated and who are modern people."[19] I suspect that most Muslims will find this approach to religion completely unacceptable. So do many Christians.

The very features of modern Christian theology which make it compatible with science and with Jeffersonian political philosophy make it difficult, if not impossible, for the majority of Christians to comprehend, much less accept. They have also led to the marginalization of academic theology in American public life. Secular intellectuals are not inclined to accept the truth claims of any theological formulation. Traditional Christians find the detextualization and relativization of the faith disturbing, if not heretical.

Contrary to the predictions, and in some cases hopes, of social theorists and modern theologians, traditional text-centred religion has not disappeared. It adapts to, confronts, ignores, and/or seeks to transform modernity in a complex variety of ways which are not entirely predictable. While there may be modern individuals, there are no fully modern societies. As Eliade observes, even in the most radically secularized societies people continue to live in "imaginary Universes" which have little practical value. The reason for this is that religions provide what appear to be plausible solutions to basic human questions which, owing to its own epistemological foundations, modernity, and particularly science, cannot address. These are what Paul Tillich calls questions of ultimate concern. Among them are those of origins and meaning of life and of death. While modernity seeks for naturalistic explanations, many individuals look for a sense of meaning and certainty which secular modernism and modern Christian theology cannot provide.

[19]*Time*, 145, 15 (10 April 1995).

Even in the most modern of societies many cling to and yearn for the certainty of traditional religion and look to God, lesser spiritual beings and supernatural forces and powers to solve problems that science can not. Many find the moral relativism implicit in modern theology to be both dangerous and wrong. Conservative and Evangelical theologians reject modernism, clinging to a text-centred understanding of the core doctrines of the Christian faith and a Biblical understanding of sin and morality. At least until recently the power and intellectual elites of Euro-American societies have treated these competing voices with disdain. "Mainstream" churches, "mainstream" media, and "mainstream" politicians alternatively mock and fear adherents of traditional world views.

Bishop Spong's call for a modern Christianity is included in a side-bar in an article entitled: "The Message of Miracles" the headline of which reads: "As the faithful hunger for them, scholars rush to debunk and to doubt." A less "respectable," but widely read publication (*The Weekly World News*), ran a related headline the same week: "New Wave of Biblical Miracles in America!" While *Time* sought to debunk or explain away popular fascination with supernatural causality, *The Weekly World News* described the following as "fact": "Man walks on water," "Angel leads child out of Tennessee inferno," "Nurse brings the dead back to life," "Housewife feeds hundreds of poor people with three loaves of bread," "Holy water rains down on Missouri town".

The contrast between *Time* and *The Weekly World News* is but one example of what James Hunter calls the American "Culture War".[20] Hunter argues that in the contemporary United States there is a basic, and seemingly unbridgeable, chasm separating those who hold world views rooted in Enlightenment social and scientific thought and others whose understanding of the world is rooted in interpretations of Biblical narrative. These radically different paradigms give rise to opposed views on questions ranging from abortion to prayer in school to politics and the arts. He finds little room for discussion or compromise — only a struggle to turn alternative visions of America into social and political realities. Hunter's "culture war" is the most recent example of a struggle between secular and religious ways of knowing and living that dates to the days of Cardinal Bellarmine and Galileo. The fact that there is, or at least would appear to be, no middle ground between

---

[20]Hunter, *Culture Wars*.

extreme secularism and fundamentalism is largely the product of the role of creation narratives in Biblical texts and the systematic retreat of "modern" theology from the problem of supernatural causality.

Pre-modern Christians understood the Bible as the source of all knowledge. It is at once cosmogony, cosmology, history, and science. Almost from the beginning secular science and religion have regarded each other with hostility. With the advance of secular sciences, theology slowly, but steadily retreated from its position of authority to become either a compliant voice dominated by secular philosophies or a defiant cry speaking from the political and intellectual margins of Euro-American society. A middle ground, in which the causal claims of both science and religion can be granted serious consideration, does not appear to have been acceptable to either side. Hunter concludes that it may be unrealistic to expect that even begrudging mutual tolerance and respect can be achieved. He regards the current culture war as a potent threat to American public life and as one that has the potential to produce increasing levels of civil unrest and violence. This is a grim prospect for a society in which the technological and other material benefits of modernity are so broadly distributed and which has, perhaps mistakenly, considered itself to be what Clifford Geertz would term a model for a modern democracy.

Towards an Enchanted Modernity: Islam and Secular Knowledge in Contemporary Indonesia

As an intellectual system or way of knowing, modernity involves viewing the universe and the human condition as an interrelated sets of naturally and socially occurring phenomena. It is the realization that, in principle, natural phenomena can be explained by empirically testable theories and that human societies are the creation of human beings. This does not, however, mean that there need be a single modernity. There is no reason to expect that modernization necessarily produces secular, liberal, democratic capitalist societies. The assumption that it does, or at least should, is an element of what Robert Bellah calls the "civil religion" of contemporary Euro-American states.[21] The normative quality of modernization theory so apparent in the

---

[21]Bellah, *The Broken Covenant.*

arguments of scholars ranging from Marx to Durkheim to Talcott Parsons can be understood as the theological legacy of pre-modern European theology combined with evolutionary social thought of the late nineteenth century. It presumes that there is an ideal social order which modernization can and should produce.

The disenchantment or secularization of the world, or portions of it, does not necessarily mean that religion is to be abandoned, although this is of course one possible modernity. The central issue is that of restricting the domains of knowledge and action to which religion applies or in Geertz's terminology reducing the scope of religion. In particular, modernity leads to a greatly diminished role for religious cosmologies both as systems to explain the natural order and as models for social and political institutions. The diminution of religious cosmologies allows scientists, philosophers and political thinkers a level of freedom of inquiry and action unknown in societies in which there are "religious tests" by which intellectual efforts must be evaluated. What is important is not whether a given scientific theory is correct, or a political philosophy functionally rational, but that they are to be evaluated, accepted, acted upon, rejected, or ignored on the basis of evidence instead of dogma. The degree to which modernization leads to secularization is determined as much by the characteristics of religion as by modernity itself. In those cases where religious assumptions give rise to a confrontational stance, the explanatory power and technological advantages of modernity lead to a devastating critique of religion. If the truth claims of religion and modernity concern different classes of phenomena and address different questions, Schleiermacher's quest for a "covenant" between religion and science can be concluded without resort to the degree of secularization current in the "Christian" West.

The comparison of Euro-American and Indonesian cases indicates that modernization is a process through which scientific and humanistic theories supersede religion as the principles upon which social and political institutions are founded. But in even the most modern societies religion does not disappear. In considering the relationship between religion and modernity as intellectual and social paradigms, the relevant question is not only that of the degree to which religions survive and flourish in modern or modernizing contexts, but also that of the ways in which religious and secular ways of knowing and living are integrated and/or juxtaposed. It is here that Indonesia and the United States, Christianity and Islam differ greatly. While in the United States and the larger Christian civilization of which it is a part, religion and modernity are juxtaposed and seemingly irreconcilably opposed, in Indonesia Islam and modernity show signs of reaching a stable compromise in which science and religion are integrated into a single system in which either, or a combination of both, can be used to provide meaningful explanations for social and natural phenomena.

Lawrence argues that fundamentalism can be understood as a response to modernity and as a rejection of the ideology of modernism. Fundamentalists make sophisticated use of the technological products of modernity to combat its ideological and intellectual foundations. It is in a sense ironic that fundamentalists seek to overturn modernity with its own technological products. The goal of fundamentalism is not a return to a pre-modern golden era, but rather the use of modern technology and bureaucratic social systems to give legal force to scripturally based codes of conduct. As Geertz and Bassam Tibi observe, there is a basic tension between fundamentalism and rationalism in modern Islamic thought.[22] In a similar vein, Tibi observes that fundamentalism provides the basis of a critique of the contemporary order but offers no clear alternative. He argues that the seeming tension between Islam and modernity can be resolved and fundamentalism overcome only if Islamic theologians succeed in creating an "Oriental Islamic variant" of a world technological/scientific social order.[23] Christian understandings of the Bible as a universal history, cosmology and cosmogony give rise to an "all or nothing" or "zero sum game" struggle between religion and science. Islamic understandings of relationships between religious and worldly affairs leave room for a more principled compromise.

The Koran and Hadith - the foundational texts of Islam - do not constitute a universal history or cosmogony in the same sense that the Bible does. Fazlur Rahman puts it this way: "The Quranic cosmogony is minimal. Of the metaphysics of creation the Koran simply says that the world and whatever God decided to create in it came into existence by his sheer command."[24] While the foundational texts of Islam make it clear that all that exist is the product of Allah's creative powers, there is no Islamic Book of Genesis. The Prophet Muhammad did not claim to be a scientific

---

[22]Geertz, *Islam Observed*; Tibi, *Die Krise des modernen Islams*.
[23]Tibi, op. cit., 186.
[24]Rahman, op. cit., 65.

authority and encouraged the quest for empirical knowledge of the natural world. While it stresses natural causality, the Koran also makes it clear that when it suits his purposes Allah can suspend the laws of nature he has established in order to bring humanity towards Him. Rahman observes:

> "Besides natural causation, however, there is another, more ultimate causation, bestowing upon natural processes in their entirety a significance and intelligibility that natural processes viewed in themselves do not yield. This higher causation is not a duplicate of, nor is it an addition to, natural causation. It works within it, or rather is identical with it — when viewed at a different level and invested with the proper meaning."[25]

This perspective motivates an Islamic natural theology in which understanding nature is a way of coming to know Allah.

The Sufi tradition of Islamic mysticism, which has long exerted a powerful influence on Indonesian thought, builds on this dualistic concept of causality, to establish the distinction between interior (*batin*) and external (*zahir*) realities and ways of knowing and experiencing religion and the world. [26]"Modernity" can be accepted, and indeed embraced, as an element of the phenomenal world (*zahir*) without challenging the external, mystic truths of the realm of *batin*. In Indonesia, it is widely believed that the realm of *batin* is, in principle, not subject to empirical observation. It can be felt only through a subtle sense called *rasa*. Because it is non-empirical, that which is *batin* cannot be falsified by scientific observation of the external world. This theory of knowledge has direct implications for the ways in which Javanese and other Indonesians understand modernity. Beliefs in spirits, supernatural causality, sacred geography, and cosmology are all *batin*. They are often described as being "irrational". However, the Javanese concept of irrationality is very different from that current in the West. Simply put, in Java, to say that something is irrational does not mean that it is not true. It is rather an appeal to a higher, spiritual truth which is beyond ordinary human comprehension. This dualistic theory of knowledge allows Indonesian Muslims to integrate science and religion in ways which are far more difficult for Christians. It allows for a fully rational, scientific

---

[25]Op. cit., 66.
[26]See Woodward, *Islam in Java*.

approach to the material world, which is still, however, subject to the intervention of interior spiritual forces. The problem is not one of which theory of causality is correct, but rather which one is operative at a particular time and place.

In the remainder of this text I will be concerned with the inter-relation of religious and naturalistic concepts of causality in contemporary Indonesian texts and in the lived experience of Javanese Indonesians of varying religious orientations. It is argued that the Koranic understanding of causality described by Fazlur Rahman plays a significant role in contemporary Indonesian world views and that it allows Indonesians to resolve Schleiermacher's problem of the inter-relation of science and religion without falling into the spiritual dilemmas posed by the juxtapositioning of textual literalism and disenchanted religion. Much of the data that will be discussed is anecdotal. No claim is made that it is systematic or representative of Indonesia as a totality, but only that it is representative of the views of Javanese Indonesians encountered in nearly two decades of ethnographic and textual research.

There are few, if any, secular Indonesians in the sense that there are secular Americans or Europeans. Devotion to God is as central to the Indonesian political system, and to Indonesian identities, as the separation of religion and politics is to the United States. The storm of criticism evoked by Nurcholish Madjid's use of the term *sekularisasi*, by which he meant only the clarification of which domains of human action are properly understood as being religious and *not* secularization in the Western sense of the term, is indicative of the fundamentally religious character of Indonesian life. Not only is Indonesian life fundamentally religious, it is religious in a traditional, enchanted sense, in which Allah and other spiritual beings are active participants in human and natural affairs.

Divine Intervention in Human Affairs: Spiritual Powers and Indonesian History

Pre-modern Javanese and other Indonesian historical texts often refer to the pervasive influence of divine will and the activities of spiritual beings in the course of history. The introduction of Western historiography in the nineteenth and early twentieth century added a new dimension to Indonesian historical awareness, but did not lead to the demise of the traditional view that Allah and lesser spiritual beings and powers play major roles in the day-to-day life of the nation. Nowhere is the Indonesian understanding of Allah's role in the course of human events more obvious than in written and especially oral accounts of the Independence struggle. The Islamic modernist Syafruddin Prawiranegara put it this way:

> ".... I see this clearly as God's will. So all this talk about man's self determination is not true, in fact its nonsense. It was God's determination. God has decided: 'It's time you were independent!' Otherwise, it would have been impossible. And if we had to fight for our independence physically, just with weapons, we would have found it impossible to win against the Dutch ... it was divine will that we become independent, and God willing, we can settle everything with his help, so long as we remember him."[27]

Syafruddin Prawiranegara's analysis is more elegant than most, but typical in the sense that it combines elements of materialistic and religious reasoning. He attributes to divine intervention what a highly developed and trained sense of material rationality tells him would have been impossible. Other accounts of the independence struggle I heard in Yogyakarta and Surakarta mention the spiritual powers of various Islamic leaders and the late sultan of Yogyakarta, Hamengkubuwana IX, those of amulets, charms and magical heirlooms (*pusaka*), and the intervention of Gusti Kangeng Ratu Kidul and other powerful spiritual beings as contributing factors. Very few attribute the success of the Indonesian forces to military and political factors alone.

A study of the constitutional history of the sultanate of Yogyakarta by K.P.H. Soedarisman Poerwokoesoemo is an telling example of the role of religion in Indonesian historiography.[28] The author was a Dutch-trained lawyer, mayor of the city for twenty years, and a close associate of Sultan Hamengkubuwana IX. Like many upper class Javanese of his generation, Poerwokoesoemo received a thorough Western education and was fluent in Dutch. He clearly understood the central role of modern education in national development and sent his children and grandchildren to study in the

---

[27]Cited in Wild and Carey, *Born in Fire.*
[28]Poerwokoesoemo, *Daerah Istimewa Yogyakarta.*

United States and Australia. Several hold advanced degrees from prestigious universities. He strongly supported the efforts of organizations such as the Muhammadiyah and Taman Siswa to bring modern education to the Indonesian people. After his retirement from public service he served as rector of Universitas Janabadra, a private institution specializing in legal education.

Pak ["Mister"] Poerwo, as he was known in Yogyakarta, was also an authority on Javanese mysticism, serving his family and close associates as a spiritual guide and mystical healer. He was a Javanist Muslim whose spiritual teachings focused on the necessity of leading a moral life, and the purification of the soul through fasting and meditation. Pak Poerwo emphasized the mercy and compassion of God and his role in actively guiding the course of human events. He was also convinced of the power of saints, ancestors, and spiritual being to intervene in human affairs. He regularly sought aid and guidance from the spirits of the sultans of Yogyakarta, making frequent pilgrimages to the royal graves at Imo Giri, and from Semar, the spiritual guide of Arjuna in the Javanese *wayang purwa* (shadow play).

The purpose of his history of Yogyakarta is to explain the position of the sultanate in the Indonesian Republic. The greater part of his work consists of a painstaking account of the legal foundations of the status of the sultanate as a "special region" within the Indonesian republic. The reader would not necessarily know that the author was Javanese or that the work could be read as a religious text. The authorial voice of the final chapter shifts from that of Soedarisman Poerwokoesoemo the legal scholar to that of Gusti Pangeran Hario Poerwokoesoemo the Yogyakarta prince and Javanese mystic. Here he speaks of Yogyakarta as the sacred centre and *axis mundi* of Indonesia, of the Indonesian revolution as the continuation and culmination of the struggle between Sultan Agung and the Dutch East India Company, and of the modernist organizations the Muhammadiyah and Taman Siswa as evidence of the continued central role of the city in Indonesian historical glory. I had the privilege to discuss this theory of history with Pak Poerwo at considerable length in the late 1970s. On this occasion he also expressed his conviction that the future of Indonesia depends on a combination of increasing the level of technical and scientific education and maintaining close contact with God, saints, and the forces of the spirit world.

The success of economic and technological development programmes, which are the foundation of the New Order's modernization strategy, are widely believed to depend on the will of Allah as well as human efforts in education, finance, and technology transfer. This is true in both the highest levels of the Indonesian government and in the villages and *kampung* (urban neighbourhoods) in which the vast majority of Indonesians live. Despite his consistent emphasis on long-term development planning President Soeharto is a deeply religious man. He is widely believed to attribute his rise to power as a manifestation of the will of Allah, and in his autobiography asks God for the external and internal power necessary to complete the struggle for development.[29] The relationship between religion and development is also a frequent theme in the speeches and biographies of B.J. Habibie, former minister of research and technology and state president of Indonesia from 1998 to 1999. Habibie was Indonesia's leading advocate of high technology development strategies. He was, however, also the leader of the All-Indonesian Association of Muslim Intellectuals (Ikatan Cendekiawan Muslim Se-Indonesia — ICMI), which seeks to combine Muslim piety with technical knowledge and education.

This combination of piety and programmatic development is not restricted to official and semi-official discourse. It is a pervasive element of Indonesian life. Two examples will suffice to illustrate this point. The first is a sign I noticed at a Yogyakarta mosque during the Islamic fasting month of Ramadan in 1979. It read "Bring Success to the Five-Year Development Plan Through Fasting." From the perspective of Western technical theories of knowledge this is incongruous. But when I inquired with the leaders of the local community concerning its meaning, they explained that development must be understood not only as the product of human action, but also a blessing from Allah. They added that fasting alone would not ensure the success of development planning, but that there was little hope of obtaining the goal of a just and prosperous society, without Allah's blessing and that this could be obtained only by living in accordance with His commands, which included fasting during the month of Ramadan. The second concerns what is perhaps the most important symbol of technological progress in the late twentieth century — the American mission to the moon.

---

[29]Soeharto, *Soeharto*, 560 "Saya mohon kekuatan lahir batin kepada Tuhan Yang Maha Esa dalam perjuangan kita melanjutkan pembangunan ini."

Lawrence mentions a rumour, which circulated throughout the Muslim world, that while walking on the moon Neil Armstrong heard a noise, which he later learned was the Islamic call to prayer, and subsequently converted to Islam. Lawrence regards this rumour as an element of the tension between Islam and modernity, with Muslims arguing that while the technological age was "ordained by Allah for the benefit of all humankind," the United States had rejected Allah's call, forcing Armstrong to hide his conversion to Islam for fear of losing his government job. Some Indonesians accepted this account of Armstrong's encounter with Allah at face value, others were more sceptical. The Laboratorium Islam Sunan Ampel, a modernist Muslim think tank in Surabaya, launched a full scale, rationalist investigation into the report.[30] Significantly, the possibility that Armstrong has heard the call to prayer on the moon and subsequently become a closet Muslim was not denied. This is indicative of a traditional, religious understanding of God's ability to intervene in human and natural affairs. The question the Surabaya organization posed was rather: Was it in fact the case that the call to prayer had been heard on the moon? To determine the veracity of the account, the Surabaya think tank wrote numerous letters to the American Embassy in Jakarta, NASA, and to Armstrong himself. Given the negative responses they concluded that Armstrong has not heard the call to prayer on the moon and that, unfortunately, he has not become a Muslim.

Modernity and Religion in Everyday Life

The integration of modern, materialist, and religious, spiritual understandings of causality is a pervasive feature of everyday life in contemporary Indonesia. Spiritual powers and beings are believed to influence the lives of individuals as well as the course of social and political history. At critical points in their lives, Indonesians regularly turn to religion for comfort and assistance. Appeals to religious concepts of causality and for the intervention of spiritual beings and forces are not stigmatized in the way they are in the modern West, but rather, respected as an appropriate response to problems for which there is no apparent "naturalistic" solution. Indonesians routinely combine spiritual and bio-medical remedies for health problems and seek the

---

[30]See Aljufri, *Panji-Panji Muhammad SAW.*

aid of Allah, saints, spirits, and powerful religious figures in a quest for solutions to life's problems. Students pray and seek the blessing of saints and ancestors to prepare for university examinations. Spirit mediums as well as the police are consulted in attempts to recover lost or stolen property. Religious teachers are asked to bless houses and businesses and to ensure dry weather for weddings, theatrical performances and other public events. These are but a few examples of the combination of religious and naturalistic modes of understanding and acting apparent even in the lives of the most seemingly modern individuals.

Three examples will suffice to illustrate this point. All concern conversations with individuals who consider themselves to be pious Muslims and who, in different ways, are proponents of modernist solutions to the challenges facing contemporary Indonesian society. In keeping with anthropological practice pseudonyms will be used to safeguard their confidentiality. The first is a university professor, the second an engineer who operates a successful heavy construction firm, and the third one of the leaders of a Muhammadiyah mosque in Yogyakarta.

Pak Fendi is a biological scientist and a lecturer at a major Indonesian university. In many respects his understanding of modernity is similar to that of B.J. Habibie and other Muslim scientists whose views shape the agenda of ICMI. His doctoral research focused on the application of American methods of livestock production in the Indonesian agricultural system. He has always held that the adaptation and diffusion of modern technology and scientific methods hold the key to the establishment of the "just and prosperous society" which is the goal of Indonesian development policy.

I met Pak Fendi in the United States, when we were both graduate students and discovered that we shared mutual interests in Indonesia, religion and agriculture and the curious fact that we are both "*anak desa*" from deeply religious families who, by somewhat similar paths, had found our ways from the settled traditional world of rural villages to a modern university setting. While both of us studied for our MA and doctoral exams, Pak Fendi and his wife also fasted. When he completed his studies and was preparing to return to Indonesia Pak Fendi planned a trip across the United States to visit historical places. When he asked where they should go I suggested Washington D.C., New Orleans, Yellowstone Park, the Grand Canyon and other "typical" American tourist attraction. I was somewhat surprised to learn that *his* plans included Arlington National Cemetery,

Springfield Illinois, Independence Missouri, Hot Springs Georgia, and Mount Rushmore and that he was concerned that Grant's Tomb in New York is empty (*kosong*). I did not understand until much later that what he had planned was not so much a vacation trip as a pilgrimage tour to seek the guidance and blessing of Lincoln, Truman, Roosevelt, and Kennedy, whom he considered to be America's most sacred leaders. I was equally surprised by his insistence that I visit my father's grave prior to my first trip to Indonesia.

In Indonesia Pak Fendi often escorted me on trips to the graves of Javanese kings and Indonesian heroes. Immediately prior to the fasting month of *Ramadan* we journeyed to his father's grave to show respect and seek blessing and guidance. He explained to me that, in order to implement the scientific methods he had learned in the United States, it was often necessary to appease the spirits and to seek the aid of *kiai*s (traditional Islamic scholars) who, like rural Javanese, remained strongly attached to the old ways of doing things. When Pak Fendi's young son fell from a tree and broke his arm he took him to a clinic, but subsequently brought a *kiai* from a local *pesantren* (Islamic boarding school) to his house to recite portions of the Koran "just in case" the fall had been caused by a angry spirit or ghost. He also warned me against travelling to Bali or the jungles of Kalimantan which he, and many other Javanese, believe to be inhabited by powerful, but dangerous, (*gawat*) spirits. Pak Fendi's understanding of relationships between material and religious causality resembles the Koranic system described by Fazlur Rahman and those of Poerwokoesoemo and other Javanese intellectuals. He explained that in his development work he had once been called on to supervise the construction of an irrigation system. Much to the surprise of the engineers, the construction of one of the dams failed several times. After several attempts to find a technical solution Pak Fendi consulted a village *dukun* who told him that the dam had been built too close to the shrine of the village guardian spirit and that it would be necessary to perform a "*bersih desa*" rite to appease him. After the rituals were performed the dam was successfully completed. Pak Fendi explained that because there was no possible naturalistic explanation for the dam failures, the *dukun* must have been correct even though he had no modern education and was completely unscientific.

Pak Karim is a civil engineer who heads a large Indonesian construction firm. I met him at a conference sponsored by the Phoenix Chamber of

Commerce and the ASEAN Ambassador's Tour of major United States business centres. The purpose of this tour was to promote investment in the ASEAN countries and closer economic and commercial ties between the United States and the countries of South-East Asia. The Phoenix conference consisted of a series of presentations concerning financial regulations, trade and investment policies, tariff and non-tariff barriers, regional security issues, technology transfer — and many other concerns shared by "modern" and "modernizing" nation-states. Religion was not mentioned in any of the formal presentations. One would not have known from the "official" programme that Indonesia and Malaysia are overwhelmingly Muslim countries. Pak Karim confirmed, and expanded upon Ambassador Abdul Madjid Mohamed's characterization of the role of religion in American life, quoted at the opening of this text. Over coffee and *kretek* (cigarettes of tobacco mixed with cloves), he explained that it was best that his American business partners remain ignorant of the importance of Islam in Indonesia because they "tend to associate religion with superstition and Islam with fanaticism."[31]

Pak Karim explained that in Indonesia things are very different. He explained that business people and others with substantial resources had an obligation to promote the modernization of Islam. He is particularly proud of his attempts to bring computers and other modern technological aids to a small *pesantren* in West Java. His view is that the selective use of "high tech" can facilitate the study and promulgation of Islamic values and help Indonesia to avoid the spiritual disease of secularization which has infected the West. He firmly believes that a combination of modern education and technology and Islamic piety and values holds the key to the future of Indonesia as a leader in the Pacific Basin area. When I asked why he had chosen to support a particular *pesantren* he responded that it was because of the great sanctity of the leading *kiai*. The *kiai*, he explained has been blessed by Allah with the ability to memorize the entire Koran and to pass these skills on to his students. He has also been blessed in other ways, including the ability to use divine power to interrupt the normal process of natural causality. Pak Karim recounted an incident concerning a theatrical performance he had arranged to celebrate his daughter's wedding to which

---

[31]When the topic of our conversation shifted from "modernity" to "religion" the language of conversation shifted from English to Indonesian.

important political and business leaders had been invited. The performance was to be held out of doors. When the sky darkened threatening rain which would have forced cancellation of the affair, or worse still a poor attendance, Pak Karim summoned the *kiai* to recite portions of the Koran and pray for its success. Despite the fact that much of the Jakarta area was drenched by a monsoon storm, the area surrounding Pak Karim's house remained dry. Pak Karim concluded that this was one of a number of events he had witnessed that were inexplicable, and did not make sense, in scientific terms and could only be interpreted as the consequence of divine intervention in the natural world.

Pak Fendi and Pak Karim can be numbered among the modern elite of Indonesia. Both have high levels of "modern" education and play significant roles in the diffusion of "modern" technology and scientific rationalism. The third case, Pak Asan, is somewhat different. He is representative of an older strain of Indonesian modernism which links Islamic renewal (*tajdid*) with material progress and rationalization. Before he retired he was the headmaster of a Muhammadiyah secondary school in the Yogyakarta area. While he has some modern education, he still defines himself primarily in terms of the Muhammadiyah reformist ideology, which emphasizes a combination of Islamic scripturalism and scientific rationalism. He was also one of the principle benefactors of the mosque in the neighbourhood in which I lived and my neighbour for more than a year.

While Pak Asan donated the land on which the mosque was built, it is a community mosque. He explained that when he first moved to the *kampung* there was no mosque and that consequently many people neglected the Friday prayer and other religious duties and that during the 1960s communism had flourished. He and a small group of friends first constructed a *langgar* (prayer room) and, when they had sufficient funds, a small mosque. While all of these individuals are reformists, there are a large number of traditional *santris* and *kejawen* Muslims in the community.[32] While Pak Asan promotes the reformist agenda he is careful not to criticize the practices of his neighbours overtly and always attempts to stress the religious and social benefits of reformism instead of criticizing the impiety

---

[32]The term *santri* is used for particularly pious or strict Muslims, especially those educated in the *pesantren* tradition. *Kejawen* is the Javanese mystical tradition.

and — from a reformist perspective — "non-Muslim" beliefs and rituals of his neighbours.

I first met Pak Asan in the summer of 1978. At that time I was conducting a general survey of religious belief and ritual in the vicinity and asked him what must have appeared to be striking naive questions about the fundamentals of Islam and the history and organization of the mosque. His replies to my questions were brief, though always polite and informative. At the time I was struck by the fact that what he said sounded almost exactly like a reformist polemic — which it was. When I asked him about traditionalist Islam, which in Java includes the veneration of saints, visitation of graves, ritual meals, the use of sections of the Koran as amulets and the like, he replied that this was not the true Islam and that I should not pay any attention to it. Our initial conversations left me with the impression that the Muhammadiyah promoted, as Geertz and Peacock have described it, a highly rationalized, disenchanted form of Islamic fundamentalism.

The following January I settled myself down in Pak Asan's *kampung* for a full year and he became one of my main interlocutors during my fieldwork. Almost from the beginning it became clear that Pak Asan's understanding of Islam was neither as fundamentalist, nor as disenchanted as I had initially suspected. I arrived in Yogyakarta a few days prior to the *Garebeg Malud* (Arabic *mawlid al-nabī* — birthday of the Prophet) which is one of the most important traditionalist holy days and the occasion of a major state ceremony. Many reformists are opposed to any celebration on this day, regarding it as an unacceptable innovation which was not part of the practice of the Prophet Muhammad or his companions. They are strongly opposed to the *slametan* (ritual meals) Javanese hold on this day. The *Malud* was not observed at the mosque. The following Friday the sermon concerned reasons why it should not be observed and how "The Real Islam" does not put the Prophet Muhammad on one level with God. I was struck by the fact that many of my other informants, and most of the residents of the *kampung*, did celebrate the Malud and especially by one statement that holding a *slametan* on this day is the mark of a true Muslim. I asked Pak Asan about this about a week later. His reply sparked the first of what was to be a long series of conversations about the nature of Islam and his personal view of Islamic reformism. He stated that the reformist view is correct — the *Malud* is not a part of the "True Islam" — but that none the less it must be considered Islamic in some sense and that people who celebrate it think that they are acting in a Muslim manner. He continued that they were not unbelievers but that they were "still ignorant".

Pak Asan often delivered the sermon (*khutbah*) at the Friday prayer and religious lectures at "*pengajian*" — evening meetings that expound upon the basic principles of Islam which are an important part of Indonesian reformism. Pak Asan's style of religious discourse was remarkably consistent. His sermons and other public statements never deviated from the "reformist position". In addition to these positive statements, he condemned the veneration of tombs as "worshipping rocks and trees", stressed the fact that Allah's mercy and obedience to his commands rather than any type of mystical experience held the key to the attainment of a "good life" in this world and salvation in the next, and discouraged any form of religious practice which was not firmly rooted in the Koran. He also stressed the value of work, and at one time said in English (which he does not understand) "God helps those who help themselves." He considered the acquisition of "modern" knowledge, which he termed "knowledge of the external world" as a religious duty because it enables humans to help themselves.

Taking these statements at face value would lead one to believe that Pak Asan had a very clear, systematic, fundamentalist view of religion and of the proper relationship between humans and Allah. His public statements focused on ethical and behavioural aspects of religion. In the ways in which he described relationships between religion and rationality Pak Asan appeared to approach Weber's "ideal type" of this worldly asceticism. I found what I thought to be Pak Asan's understanding of Islam interesting in part because it appeared to confirm the observations of previous scholars and appeared to be so different from those of my other neighbours in the *kampung*.

The *kampung* in which I lived is one of the oldest in Yogyakarta. It is located within the *kraton* (palace) wall (*benteng*) and is believed to be home to numerous spiritual beings as well as human residents. Almost everyone had encounters with spirits at some time or the other. Some of the spirits were helpful, others could be troubling, particularly if offended, while a few were thought to be dangerous and evil. I considered Pak Asan to be more "modern" than most *kampung* residents in part because he did not appear to be troubled by, or concerned with his non-human neighbours. As an anthropologist I was very concerned with spiritual beings and attempted to conduct something of a census. I was surprised to the point of disbelief when one of my other neighbours told me that if I wanted to know about those who lived in the vicinity of the mosque I should ask Pak Asan. When I asked how this could be true given Pak Asan's "modernity" and "rationality" my informant told me that Pak Asan had befriended a very powerful spirit who lived in his house, and who helped him in various ways.

My first inclination was to treat this statement as malicious gossip and as an example of the ways in which *kejawen* Muslims attribute worldly success to the aid of spiritual forces. I was very reluctant to raise the issue with Pak Asan, for fear of offending him, and of looking stupid. Several weeks later I asked him indirectly about the "Islamic view" of Javanese belief in the power of spiritual beings. Pak Asan responded by quoting *surah* al-Jinn according to which Muhammad was sent to bring the word of Allah to *jinn* (spiritual creatures) as well as to humans. Pak Asan explained that there is nothing "un-Islamic" about *jinn* and other spiritual beings. They are described at length in the Koran and Hadith. Some of them are Muslim, and come to pray at the mosque, while others are ignorant or unbelievers. His view is that there is nothing wrong with communicating with spirits, but that worshipping them, as he believes many Javanese do, is a major sin. He continued that human/spirit contacts could not be considered Islam in the technical sense of the word (submission to Allah), but that because they are, like people and animals, among the creatures created by Allah, it was only natural to interact with them in some way. When I asked about the *jinn* that our neighbour claimed lived in his house, Pak Asan answered matter-of-factly that he had known the *jinn* for many years. It is among the few Muslim *jinn* living in the area and was happy to learn that Pak Asan planned to build a mosque. It helped him to drive away non-believing (*kafir*) *jinn* who tried to interfere with the construction project and over the years had helped in numerous ways. Pak Asan pointed to the fact that he, unlike many of the other *kampung* residents had not built a wall around his house to deter thieves, explaining that he did not need one because the property was protected by the *jinn's* power. The *jinn* also helped him to perform exorcisms for other members of the community who are occasionally bothered by non-Muslim *jinn* and other evil spirits.

When I asked Pak Asan if his relationships with the spirit world were in conflict with the modernist teachings of the Muhammadiyah, he stated emphatically that this was not the case. As a matter of public policy, the Muhammadiyah emphasizes a combination of Koran-centred piety, modern education and social welfare. Pak Asan's view is, however, that because the world is inhabited by spirits as well as humans, it would be foolish, if not impossible to ignore them. Just as Muslims are obligated to turn to the Koran and Hadith for knowledge about how to conduct social relationships, they should turn to Islam rather than Javanese magic for guidance in dealing with the spirit world. He concluded by explaining that Muslims have much to learn from the West, that they are obligated to take what it good and reject that which is harmful, but that science and Western technology are of little use in dealing with this and other spiritual aspects of reality.

Conclusions

During my initial stay in Indonesia I was, like many anthropologists, primarily concerned with traditional forms of what Geertz calls "local knowledge". I had come to study the ideological foundations and ritual expressions of the Javanese theory of kingship and had suspicions concerning the "authenticity" of "modernized" forms of Javanese culture and religion. Despite, or perhaps because of, their own modernity many anthropologists secretly long for the days when a journey to the East was a sojourn among peoples untouched by what the Islamicist and historian of religions Marshal Hodgson called the "Great Western Transmutation". We continue to search for remote villages, islands, and mountain enclaves in which local cultures have evaded the forces of modernity. This tendency is only in part the product of a rational, scientific agenda to document the variety of human cultures. It is also a form of cultural escapism and the product of the European Romantic flight from modernity. The time for such studies is rapidly passing, if it has not already passed. The power and technological advantages of modernity are such that few, with the possible exception of anthropologists and other Western Romantics, would wish to escape it. In many respects the spread to modern ways of knowing can be compared to that of great religions, Islam, Christianity, and Buddhism in the pre-modern era. Just as the interaction of transcultural religious ideas and local cultures has produced rich and variant local Islams, Christianities, and Buddhisms, modern education has, and is, producing multiple modernities. What they share is a common way of understanding and acting upon the natural world.

In the West modernity has meant the displacement of religion, both as a way of knowing and as the dominant social and political paradigm.

139

Religious people have been pushed to the margins of Western societies. At most religion is a "private" faith.

Pak Fendi, Pak Karim, and Pak Asan taught me much about Indonesia and Islam. They also caused me to reflect on Western society and the problems and promises of modernity. Modern ways of knowing are not necessarily in conflict with religious understandings of the world. They are, however, incompatible with the literal reading of Biblical texts required by many conservative Christians. A thoroughly anti-modern understanding of causality lies at the heart of Biblical teachings of salvation. As in so many cases, the writings of the Apostle Paul provide a key to understanding the dilemma of modernity in the Christian West. Paul's logic establishes a powerful connection between the soteriological message of the Christian Gospels and the cosmogonic mythology of the Hebrew Bible.[33] It has the unintended consequence of subjecting both teachings to radical falsification at the hands of modern science. The problem for modern theology has been to preserve the soteriological half of the equation in face of overwhelming evidence that the literal truth of cosmogonic mythology can no longer be maintained. Centuries of conflict bear witness to the fact that there is little middle ground between scientific and religious apostasy. Hunter's "Culture Wars" and the increasing polarization of American society along religious lines are sociological consequences of this theological controversy.

Islam does not have this problem. The point is not that Islam, unlike Christianity, proclaims a purely naturalistic theory of causality. It is rather that in Islam, divine intervention in the natural order of things is understood as a break in the normal course of causality. The fact that cosmogonic mythology is not tied directly to the soteriological teachings of Islam avoids the problem of radical falsification. For Muslims the problem of modernity is sociological not cosmological. While Christianity explicitly abrogates the legal system of the Hebrew Bible, Islam remains very much a religion of law. However, as the history of Islamic jurisprudence clearly demonstrates, sociological components of religion have proved to be far more flexible than cosmogonic truth claims. Generations of Muslim scholars have recognized *shari'ah* (Islamic law) as an ideal system of human conduct ensuring

---

[33]In *Corinthians* 15:20 Paul links the doctrine of salvation directly to the account of cosmogony included in *Genesis* 1-3 by equating death will the "fall" of Adam and life with the person of Christ.

happiness in this world and in the life to come. On the other side, Muslim scholars have accepted the legitimacy of governments which establish conditions in which the Muslim community is free to fulfil its religious obligations as legitimate. Indonesian scholars including Nurcholish Madjid and Abdurrahman Wahid who recognize the Constitution of 1945 and the *Pancasila* as an acceptable basis for a Muslim government are contemporary examples of this long tradition.[34] The question of secularism, a way of life independent of religious conviction, does not arise in discussions about these matters. The question is how, and not if, people should live in accordance with the will of Allah.[35]

Given the enormous technological advances brought on by the Great Western Transmutation, many in the West are inclined to view their own societies as "models for modernity". Weber realized more clearly than most that Euro-American formulations of modernity have engendered a spiritual crisis of major proportion. He describes modernity as an "iron cage" in which material forces determine the lives of individuals. He elaborates:

No one knows who will live in this cage in the future, or whether at the end of this tremendous development entirely new prophets will arise, or there will be a great rebirth of old ideas and ideals, or if neither, mechanized petrification, embellished with a sort of convulsive self-importance. For the last stage of this cultural development, it might be truly said: "Specialists without spirit, sensualists without heart; this nullity imagines that it has attained a level of civilization never before achieved."[36]

Weber's assessment of the spiritless character of modern life builds on a combination of Paul's insistence on the centrality of cosmogonic mythology in Christian soteriology and ethics and the scientific advances of the nineteenth and twentieth centuries which subjected this mythological complex to radical falsification. Weber knew little of Islam, and nothing of Indonesia. While the religious and technological problems confronting modernizing societies cannot be ignored or underestimated, there is at least

---

[34]*Pancasila* (the "Five Pillars") is the name of the official ideology of the Indonesian Republic.
[35]See Nurcholish "Islamic Roots of Modern Pluralism", and Woodward, "Conversations with Abdurrahman Wahid".
[36]Weber, op. cit., 109.

hope that Islamic understandings of cosmogony and causality will enable Indonesians to construct an enchanted modernity in which "old ideas and ideals" remain powerful forces and in which "purely mundane passions" will be held in check by the spirit of Islam.

7 Pakistan

A Critique of the Concept of Modernity

Lukas Werth

Introduction

The consequences of what we are used to call "modernity" are nowadays being more and more felt all over our world: nation-states, industrialized modes of production, modern technologies, global systems of communication, international finances and markets, to name some of the features commonly associated with the concept, increasingly influence even the remotest corners of our globe, and serve to describe contemporary conditions in general. This essay questions the adequacy of this approach by looking at some features of a limited area in Pakistan, mostly the Potwar, concentrating on the micro-level of social interaction, looking at questions like marriage, status, or personal attachments, secular and religious. The perspective of an anthropologist, confined to a local dimension of daily interactions, may have the advantage of taking account of the identities of persons and their immediate social contexts. Is it hoped that this perspective will serve to indicate a particular social context in which Islamic features are expressed, and will hint at some problems of broader relevance concerning Muslim societies, although a thorough comparison with the Muslim world in general is beyond the scope of this essay. Nevertheless, the Muslim population addressed here does not submit to the parameters of modernity, and is not likely to do so in the foreseeable future. The institutions and technical features of modernity which have long found their way into Pakistan may more profitably be linked with a process of "modernization", to be distinguished from "modernity" as a cultural dominant. This distinction may enable us to question the sweeping adoption of Western cultural concepts for the description of contemporary situations in any given niche. The dominant lines along which the perception of reality in Pakistan is organized, and which formulate directions for the dreams, the ideals, and the lines of development of the society, follow patterns which have to be inspected in their own right. Simply to apply categories taken from a particular context to people elsewhere, without scrutinizing at least the context in which they are used, may cause these people to feel alienated from a discourse which leaves them no chance to formulate their identities in proper categories.

Before proceeding, let me give a small example which has a direct relevance to the topic of this essay: the idea of modernity, often used with a strongly positive connotation, is frequently tried to be recovered within the realm formulated by the intellectual framework of Islam. The idea of modernity is then required within the religious sphere of Islam itself: the opposition between modernity and tradition is equated with the advance of the Islamic world view over heathen Arabia, of which the mental condition is captured by the term *jaheliyyat*, a word which has tended to acquire the general meaning of the condition of being ignorant of the written world. It should be noted how thoroughly the notion of modernity has become transformed by this adaptation: the full circle described when a notion crucially informed by the secular movement of the Enlightenment is restated in religious terms is only the beginning. Tradition, in the common usage of the term as the opposite of modernity, here is made to encompass again within its own realm a concept characterized by the dynamic it gains from the very opposition to forces restricting change, and unified world views in general.

The social reality in the West is manifold, and, of course, the same is true for a country like Pakistan. Many other dimensions beside modernity (or postmodernity) as such are found in Western life styles, and in the same way the social topics in a country like Pakistan certainly incorporate much more than may be addressed in this paper. Therefore, if we are planning to speak about the roles of families in Pakistan, it should at once be obvious that family life and its values have by no means disappeared from the scope of Western ideals. In any case, making such a statement one would at least wish to compare more specific settings, and not to talk simply of the "West". A bit more about the perils of comparison will be said in a moment. We may, however, evoke Walter Benjamin's notion of the dreaming of epochs for a moment to state the idea that there are general guidelines in societies which formulate general dimensions and directions in which societies move, or which organize social reality in a somewhat similar way as magnets organize pieces of iron which come into their field. There are bound to be plenty of residuals (or conflicting influences) in any social setting, but the organizing themes, referred to also as "ideology" or "cultural dominant", which are mostly taken for granted by those within their domains and therefore not recognized as such or discussed, formulate the distinct quality of the social reality of a society. In this text when we look for such a dimension within what is effectively a very confined area within Pakistan, the question will arise of whether its formulation does not simply amount to yet another construction of otherness, to forming a mirror image of Western categories, a way of representation which has been dubbed "orientalism". This problem is connected with the term modernity itself: nobody wants to be excluded from a form of living or an overarching concept which is propagated by many users of the term as the only possible one in the contemporary world, which has achieved global dimensions and moved beyond local confinements, as the term "globalization" indicates. However, something is ignored by these concepts and the very terminology, a symptom of which is the deep unrest filling those who feel their own concepts and their identity are being twisted in the process of being attuned to a formulation of a reality which is not theirs. What is proposed here, therefore, apart from a scrutiny of the terminology of modernity, is to point out the possibility of alternative forms of living in the contemporary world which may be captured by a vocabulary which only enters a dialogue with the dominants of modernity secondarily, a dialogue which ineluctably cannot be avoided at a time when isolated units indeed have ceased to make sense. Nevertheless, this essay will at least allude to a construction of social reality which is informed by other parameters.

This text will concentrate on the situation in the Pakistani Punjab. Most of what will be related was gathered in the Potwar, the area around Islamabad, the modern capital of the country. The discussion of this Muslim society will not centre so much on any postulated entity of Islam as such, but on how it is implemented to construct social reality. Some readers may also miss conventional categories like those of Great Tradition and Little Tradition, or "high Islam" and "folk Islam": this is because the notion of Islam (or, for that matter, Christianity) which underlies this discussion sees Islam not as a set of principles basically complete in themselves, but as a set of general guidelines the particular interpretation of which is of crucial importance. This text will also not dwell mainly on the problems commonly associated with Islam and modernity, like fundamentalism, the factual possibilities of an Islamic state, the juridical system, or Islam and democracy, but rather describe some important contexts in which persons construct their identities in daily life, and which basically inform their world view and very orientation.

Pakistan

Notions commonly integrated within the framework of modernity are by no means absent in Pakistan, as is shown by its very existence. The decision to fight through and found the state of Pakistan was based on the idea of an Islamic nation, and emerged within the Indian struggle for independence. Men like Muḥammad 'Alī Jinnāḥ and "Mawlānā" Abū al-A'lā Mawdūdī strove to find a new Muslim identity in a changing world, and to assert Muslim rights against the colonial administration as well as against a Hindu majority. Both formulated a new political dimension to Islam, and the latter's ideas particularly influenced Islamic revivalism all over the Muslim world.[1] In its short but turbulent history Pakistan has seen a variety of different governments, and over long periods its government has been in the hands of army generals - as it is now again, as these lines are revised. Muḥammad Ḍiyā' al-Ḥaqq (Zia ul-Haq) in particular also strove to implement Islamic ideals politically, for which he is held in quite high esteem by many people.[2] However, the concentration on the political dimension does not adequately portray the general situation.

In order to capture conditions in contemporary Pakistan, to concentrate on such questions as fundamentalism means to isolate questions about religion and separate them from other features of life. Therefore, Ernest Gellner, for instance, sees fundamentalism as one of three basic opportunities offered to deal with existential questions.[3] Inspiring as his discussion is, he treats the issue essentially from the perspective of Western philosophy, and tends to equate the stronger shades of Muslim faith with what is commonly called fundamentalism: his argument presumes two essentially antagonistic strands in Islam, one of saints and ecstatic practices, associated with the rural areas; the other of scholars and a reformist purity, associated with urban areas and higher strata of population, and this latter strand is, according to

---

[1] See Nasr, *Mawdudi*.

[2] Prosaically, he probably just wanted to take the wind out of the sails of the Muslim reformist zeal of the Jamā'at-i islāmī party.

[3] Gellner, *Postmodernism, Reason and Religion*, 2.

Gellner, now becoming universal. It is the modern fundamentalism which is rendering the world of saints obsolete. Yet, in Pakistani elections, the party of which the ideals come nearest to this understanding of the term (Jamāʿat-i islāmī) regularly earns surprisingly few votes, although the Islamic faith remains unquestioned among the Muslim population of the country, and its influence is ubiquitous. The term "fundamentalism", which is not liked by many of the people so described, is a Western concept, originally created to deal with Western categories (a certain brand of American Christians), and serves to classify only within a Western, in fact modern framework.[4] Applied to the conditions in Pakistan, the quality of the Muslim faith seems to evade us if conceptualized in this way. Saints are not disqualified or obsolete in contemporary Pakistan, nor are they pre-eminently associated with the rural sphere (indeed this was not the case in the past either). There are reformist movements in Pakistan, and the saints are by no means uncontested, but some of them engage themselves in discussions about the quality of Islam which may aptly be termed reformist.[5] The quality of this faith is not correctly depicted in Gellner's bold historical strokes.

Yet another example serves to illustrate the inadequacy of "orientalist" concepts like fundamentalism: in the initial pages of his work, Gellner mentions the contrast between taking the words of holy scriptures literally or, in the face of the contradictions which arise regarding scientific (modern!) knowledge, merely allegorically. The religious discourse in the area of my fieldwork, however, is simply not or not foremostly structured along this distinction, but pays heed to such matters as science or modernity in a different way: rather than treating them as antagonistic, it incorporates them into its own realm. It is therefore a frequently stated belief that the astronaut who took the first steps on the moon had become a Muslim afterwards. Einstein's notion of the relativity of time is evoked to explain how the Prophet could remain in paradise three days, taking no more than an instant of terrestrial time. Other features of contemporary life, too, are encompassed by a religious cosmology: dancing performances on television are taken as signs of the imminence of the Day of the Last Judgement (qiyāmat), of which it is said that then there will be dancing in every house. Therefore, science and technology are made to serve a religious world view: their achievements are generally taken by educated people as signs of the

---

[4]See Giddens, *Beyond Left and Right*, 85.
[5]See Gilmartin, *Empire and Islam*, 58 f.

greatness of God. The meaning of religion as such is generally not disputed, but provides fixed points of reference which make it possible for people to find a moral orientation. Secularization is virtually invisible in contemporary Pakistan.

Therefore, aspects of what we commonly identify with "modernity" in contrast to "tradition" in Pakistan form part of an integral development within a world construction which does not postulate the existence of something outside itself. It should immediately be noted that a consequence of this situation is likely to be a lack of critical evaluation or ideological analysis. The leaders of the Muslim movements which eventually led to the foundation of Pakistan developed their thoughts to a considerable degree by means of a debate with Western systems of thought, and this does account for the emergence not only of Muslim modernist thinkers like Sayyid Ahmad Khan, but also of a revivalist like Mawlānā Mawdūdī. In his excellent book on the latter's thoughts, Reza Nasr shows that they are not simply based on antagonism (which is what springs most readily to mind at first glance), but on a critical examination of the actual situation of Indian Muslims which necessitated, in his opinion, a reformulation of the political dimension of Islam.[6] Mawdūdī developed thoughts similar to those expressed in the examples above, using which he tried to accommodate Western science in a Muslim world view.[7] His work clearly incorporates a scrutiny of Muslim tradition, but it is also evident that his conclusions are guided not so much by his intention of constructing a new edifice based on the rejection of tradition, but rather by his intention of reconstructing an ideal Muslim identity, or a re-invention of tradition.

These were the pioneers, but the situation in which these generations of thinkers found themselves were different from that at present. As has been mentioned, the actual influence in contemporary Pakistan of the party founded by Mawdūdī, Jamā'at-i islāmī, has become marginal.[8] Contemporary Islamic faith has assumed a quality which relies on a more implicit indigenous formulation of tradition, in itself usually not the object of critique. This by no means precludes the fact that in many respects the situation in Potwar as well as in contemporary Pakistan in general also

---

[6]Nasr, op. cit.

[7]Op. cit., 53.

[8]If other parties seek coalitions with this party, as it happens in contemporary politics, it is not so much because of its influence, but rather because of its supposed ability to carry out mass demonstrations and bring politics to the streets.

achieves a global dimension, and even in its villages people increasingly take part in an international discourse brought to them by modern means of the dissemination of information. Its dependence on an international market and politics has been acutely felt by the Pakistani population for the last few decades, and people routinely leave the country to earn money, or even settle permanently abroad. However, the items of modernity are incorporated into a discourse which derives its structure from other sources. The people of Pakistan treat the objects and icons of modernity within their own framework of reference, and construct their world in a different way: the common self-understanding in Pakistan, ideology and world view, are extrinsic to the notions of modernity. Change or the idea of the new as such is not considered a value in Pakistan, and the features of modernity are not conceived to be in opposition to traditional ones. The coming of Islam, both to the world and to South Asia, is the one great transformation which looms large in the minds of the people. As in medieval Christianity, the fact of once having been converted continues to be part of the construction of social and personal identity. As Clifford Geertz describes with respect to Indonesia, Islam also continues to serve as a new explanation for existing categories.[9] The implications of being Muslim are broad enough to include South Asian categories as well as those commonly associated with modernity. There is no necessity to construct a rift between the present and the past, or between tradition and modernity. The creation of the state of Pakistan itself also is not seen so much as a break with the past, but rather, insofar as it is idealized, as a fulfilment of an earlier promise, or as the concretization of much older structures. A case in point is Aitzaz Ahsan, who tries to argue for a separate identity for the area of contemporary Pakistan, which has existed since time immemorial.[10]

The image of the West prevalent in Pakistani urban middle-class circles is informed by this emphasis on continuity rather than change: it is in many respects one of moral chaos and absurdity. Western women in particular are thought to be devoid of any morals. Behind this muddled and obscure surface, however, Pakistanis often feel that "this chaos must have a reason", as a retired brigadier in Rawalpindi once explained to me. The picture then again becomes theocentric: a hidden conspiracy is frequently thought to exist which secretly rules the world and has made a pact with Satan. These views

[9]Geertz, *Islam Observed*.
[10]Ahsan, *The Indus Saga*.

correspond to some subaltern Western views which find themselves at odds with developments introduced by modernity, like some brands of American fundamentalist Christians, or, it seems, circles like those which produced the Oklahoma bombing of 1995. American books produced by these circles rife with theories about Jewish conspiracies (the *Illuminati*) are handed around in Pakistan, and lead here to the production of other works with the same tendency. Significantly, although in the West such views are entertained by groups who find themselves at the fringe of society, in Pakistan they are a common idea of a form of living conceived of as foreign, entertained by the educated urban middle class (note that here the phenomenon commonly labelled "globalization" is touched upon).

Pakistani society might therefore also be described as being in a state of rapid development or transformation, but the dynamics of this process are different from those in the West. And here again, describing the state of affairs in modern Pakistan, we may find ourselves entangled in a familiar difficulty, namely trying to formulate a different reality in terms deriving from our own culture. This problem becomes even more obvious when we move closer to daily reality to see how Islamic categories are actually applied to other, indigenous ones, which they also inform and modify. Pakistan today orients itself officially towards the Middle East, and relations with India are to a large extent antagonistic and hostile. However, in the Punjab (as in the Sind), South Asian categories form an important, albeit little recognized, dimension of daily life. They provide a framework for the identity of persons in which the boundedness in collectives is generally more emphasized than it is in the West. If we refer here to the thoughts of Louis Dumont concerning Western individualism, let me immediately hasten to say that this by no means implies that individuals as such, individuality, or personal qualities are not recognized in South Asia — as some authors seem to imply.[11] In the case of Pakistan, we have to qualify Dumont's ideas carefully to see how Islamic notions interact with South Asian ones. To develop this theme further, the best point of departure is in the context of kinship and family to show how contemporary life in the rural and urban Punjab is informed, and identities are shaped by spheres which tend to be marginalized in modernity.

[11]See e.g. Mines, *Public Faces, Private Voices*.

150

The Context of Kinship

In Pakistan, childhood is looked upon as the happiest period of life, because it is free of the duties and the sorrows which are inevitably part and parcel of adulthood. This is a common topic in songs and poems, and also is commonly stated in daily life. From the outset, however, sons are regarded very differently from daughters. This difference may already be observed in most families when the children are still mere toddlers: sons are often given food first, and are served by their sisters. A son chooses his food, makes demands a daughter would not dream of, strolls around while his sister gets used to the discipline of daily duties, and commands his sisters from an early age. In poorer families frequently only sons, not daughters, are sent to school. A son will soon learn to look after the honour of the women of his household: if, for instance, a small boy scolds his mother for not covering her head in public, she may be proud of him and tell others how much her son already cares for the family's honour. Sons are fervently desired by parents, because they carry on the family and, apart from their rights, they also have duties: in contrast to many Middle Eastern Muslim societies, women given away in marriage are never completely separated from their kin. Their brothers retain a certain responsibility for them, expressed, among other ways, in gift exchange, and the sister always has in her brothers a place to turn to in times of marital distress.[12] In such a situation, from early childhood onwards, sisters also learn to look for their brothers for support, and to love them and to care for them.

A brother's responsibility for his sisters may be considerable. An elder brother, even if he is a man in a good, settled position, may be expected not to marry until some of his sisters are married, because he is supposed to pool the money he earns with that of his parents to cover the expenses of his sisters' marriages, and share his parents' sorrows: once he is married, his attention will be diverted, because he will have his own family to take care of. A son is regarded as the extension and continuation of his father and mother, he shares their responsibilities and takes care of them in their old age, whereas a daughter is, as it is often said, a guest in her parents' house. Frequently a family also invests everything in one son to send him abroad

---

[12] Tapper, *Bartered Brides*, 16 f. introduces this as a distinguishing criterion between two different types of Muslim parallel cousin marriage, the other type consisting in handing women over completely to the family into which they are married.

to work. The economy of Pakistan is heavily influenced by this practice. Working abroad, in the rich countries of the Arabian peninsula or somewhere in the West, is virtually the only chance for a man without a distinguished education, or capital to invest, to earn enough money to escape a lifetime of scraping to make ends meet. Without these possibilities there would be considerably less money to invest in Pakistan, and its internal consumption would probably drop drastically. However, although we are witnessing a process of globalization here, from the perspective of Pakistan it is integrated into a context foreign to individualist notions of modernity: men frequently work abroad for their whole families, building a material basis for all their siblings who in their turn connect their own position to that of their brother abroad.

Space does not allow to describe other gender differences; it is enough to say that the role of Pakistani (and other Muslim) women tends to be widely misunderstood in the West. A particular obstacle to any understanding is constituted by the fact that, although the realms of women are far more separated from those of the men than in the West, the female gender is generally not considered to form an opposition or antagonism to its male counterpart: the relationship is rather one of mutual completion within a larger whole. The concept of the *pardah* ("curtain"), the hiding of women from the public sphere, associated with a cultural understanding of shame, tends to be interpreted by the West as an extreme deprivation of women's liberty. Notwithstanding this view being partly followed by Muslim authors like Fatima Mernissi, this grossly underrates the central role of women in the large and important context of family and kin in societies like that of the Punjab in Pakistan.[13] Women operate within their own sphere in which men should not mix. The Punjabi derogatory term for a man, *janānā*, means precisely somebody meddling or taking an interest in women's affairs. And women's decisions, like those regarding marriage, are vital to their families. Here we encounter a notion of persons who are not meant to be alone, and not so much supposed to find their own ways and form their relations with others in a plurality of free-floating individuals (admittedly a somewhat extreme description of Western conditions), but who locate themselves within a larger context made up of entities with essentially different qualities, in which they form a part of a group at least as much as an individual entity. In the sphere of gender, we already meet an important

[13]Mernissi, *Peur modernité*.

theme in Punjabi Muslim culture, namely a complex negotiation in daily life between participation and sharing on the one hand, and self-assurance on the other. The latter, however, as we shall see, occurs primarily with reference to a social totality (and, of course, to God). To expatiate on this theme, it is neccasary to examine the concept of marriage.

Marriage anywhere in Pakistan is generally not a matter of individual choice, but depends on parents' decisions, and on those of a wider circle of kinship. Traditionally, in the villages, marriage is commonly conducted within kin and status groups cognate with castes, *birādarīs*.[14] A common way in which the term is used refers primarily to a network of cooperation between households which is expressed in several contexts, like mutual invitations to marriages and other ceremonies, and a network of gift exchange for which the women are largely responsible. At least in villages, matches for marriages are sought mainly within this context, and preferably among a family's nearest relatives, primarily therefore, in accordance with Islamic law, among the first cousins. There is no preference, as it is reported for other Muslim societies, for a father's sister's daughter; indeed, if anybody, a maternal cross cousin is preferred.[15] Generally, people try to marry their children off to relatives who are as close as possible and to give them to those families with whom other marriages have been conducted before. A common way in which this strategy is expressed is to exchange two pairs of brothers and sisters (Punj. *vaṭa-saṭa*), or otherwise marrying more than one of a couple's (often many) children into the same house. The way the strategy is debated also shows how marriage is conceived of as integrated in a social context: both men will try to make their marriage work, because if one fails, the other husband is also likely to divorce his wife, as he sympathizes with his sister and wants to take revenge on his sister's husband's sister who is his wife. Men usually have more sympathy for their sisters than for their wives, and the latter possibility is often also stated as an argument against *vaṭa-saṭa*. Despite such stumbling blocks, the practice is widely followed, and it tends to create very closely knit kin groups in which people are related to each other in several ways. In one

[14]The term is derived from the Punjabi term for brother, and members of a *birādarī* are thought to be of common descent.
[15]The data of Eglar, *A Punjabi Village* implicitly show a preference for the mother's brother's daughter, and the hitherto unpublished thesis of my wife, Anjum Alvi, *Bearers of Grief*, confirms this observation and incorporates it into a systematic theoretical framework.

153

village at least ninety per cent of the marriages were found to take place with cousins, and wherever possible, people tried to exchange their children according to the *vaṭa-saṭa* system. Sometimes considerable disadvantages, like the bridegroom having to wait until his early forties to marry, were accepted in the course of pursuing this strategy.

The spirit of this traditional pattern prevails not only in the villages, but also in urban environments. The situation there is, as might be expected, more fractured, and other interests have to be taken into consideration. There is a great deal of family mobility both within and between the urban centres of Pakistan, and in Rawalpindi with its army headquarters, for instance, live people from different states as well as those people and their descendants who moved during the partition from India to Pakistan. The latter also intermarry with the Punjabi population. Many people, however, moved from villages into the urban areas relatively recently in serach of work, and this process continues. They often entertain strong links with the places from which they hail, keep houses there, even invest money to build new ones, and go back to the villages for occasions like marriages, including those of their children. Sometimes they settle back in their villages in old age, particularly when they were in army or government service elsewhere; activities which did not allow them or in which it was not necessary to develop strong links in the places in which they worked. Even when living in the cities, these people mostly continue their pattern of marriage and only reluctantly give their children in marriage outside their *birādarī*. Relatives tend, if circumstances allow it, to live together in one neighbourhood or area.

Circumstances may compel families to look outside the circle of their relatives for their children's marriage partners. This situation is not too uncommon nowadays, but the way people deal with it is telling: first, it is very often only the second choice of parents if they have to look outside their kin for marriage partners for their children. Good, long-time neighbours and friends may also present a real choice of a group to marry into, or at least they may suggest acquaintances of their own. It is regarded as a real friend's service to find a marriage partner for a child. Marriage offices have become common in Pakistan, but they are generally considered a last resort; divorcees and widowers sometimes search for spouses through them, or people who for some reasons find themselves in social isolation or difficulties, come from abroad, or look for spouses for certain purposes, like getting residence permits for other countries through the marriage.

In all these cases, even if young people marry on their own initiative, a marriage once conducted opens the way to other unions between the same families. The family into which to marry is at least as carefully chosen as the bride or groom, because through the marriage a lasting link between the families is established. People in Pakistan generally have many children to care for, and frequently siblings of the first couple will successively also marry each other. They in turn will probably, once they have children of their own, again try to marry them to their cousins. People frequently try to marry their children off to their relatives even where they themselves did not follow this pattern: two sisters, for instance, married to unrelated husbands, will almost certainly try to marry some of their children to each other.

The idea of forming bonds by exchange is therefore a leading notion in marriage in Pakistan, one which is actively pursued not only in traditional, rural contexts, but generally. The concept of the *birādarī* as an endogamous unit is preserved in cities as well, and even when people look for marriage partners outside, its principle is still adhered to: marriage is a means to form and maintain units of interaction; to share a social identity with the in-laws permanently.[16]

To understand how this notion of marriage is connected with other values of the society, we have to look inside family and kinship networks to single out leading concepts of responsibility, participation of status, and the nature of status and power.

Status generally is among the first things to be expressed in communication, and is an important aspect of a person's self-representation, but people in Pakistan participate to considerable extent in the status of their social context. To understand this more fully, we have to return to the concept of the *birādarī* which implies a common status of the collectivity of its members, and we have to keep in mind that it is primarily marriage through which the continuation of a *birādarī* as a concrete entity is secured. The term no longer implies, as it did one or two generations ago, a position within a fixed pattern of hierarchical interaction of endogamous groups in certain localities. It does, however, imply a certain status according to its position: highest are these groups who are considered to be the descendants

---

[16]The idea of a marriage market is another notion which is frequently referred to nowadays; however, it is conceived of as a substitute if marriage through exchange within the traditional circle does not work, and it is derived from the idea of exchange, a metaphor informed by the notion of collective interaction.

of the Prophet, the *sayyid*s; other *birādarī*s emphasize their position by making a claim to royal descent, for example by calling themselves *rājput*.[17] Generally, the *birādarī*s which traditionally constituted (and still constitute) the land-holding groups (*zamīndār*) in their places of origin enjoy a high reputation, whereas the reputation of the traditional service castes (*kami*) reputation is lower. The word *kamīna* ("mean", "low"), derived from *kami*, is a common term of abuse.

In urban contexts and frequently also in the countryside, fixed status positions no longer constitute the core function of the *birādarī* concept. In marriage, even with non-relatives, the reputation of the *birādarī* is still an important point, but primarily the concept provides a pattern of identification and solidarity. The practical extension of a *birādarī*, or the relevant circle of kin varies, but a person's social status as well as practical possibilities open to him or her in life are closely associated with it. Therefore, a person's circle of kinship has a common status defined through the *birādarī* or caste (*zāt*) to which it belongs, but normally the positions of its members vary greatly. There are some men who have achieved a higher position in their profession, and their relatives turn to them for many matters of practical help in daily life: whether they want a job, or have trouble at their work, or need a place in college for their son. Regularly, if one man acquires an influential position, for example in a bank, some of his relatives will also be employed there, and he will be able to place his relatives in other positions to which he has access through a network of favours. the extent to which this system is officially entrenched may be seen by the fact that there are reserved places for students in sought-after educational courses like medicine allotted to politicians, who may name persons for these places — including their own children. Influential men are often able to procure a visa for young men to send them abroad to work, or settle cases in court. This construction is also noticeable in other spheres of Pakistani life, like rural development: whether villages get facilities like metalled roads, a water supply, electricity, telephones, medical dispensaries, school facilities and colleges, may depend on the initiatives of single men who are connected with them, and through their efforts and connections introduce these facilities to them.

Client relations of this sort form an important part of the structure of *birādarī*s today, and influential men in a person's kin group are frequently

---

[17]This term, of Hindu origin, means "son of a king", and originated from what is nowadays the Indian state of Rajasthan, where it is the name of the royal castes.

referred to in conversations, and their position, assets and status are described. The general background of, for instance, a guard in a bank, and any influential men in his kin group, are known in his environment, because his treatment partly depends on these factors. In this way men participate in the position of their relatives; frequently, if poor people from a village visit cities, they stay in the houses of their rich relatives. They may live there often for any indefinite period, doing household or serving work, but their position will be different from those of common servants, and in the cases I witnessed, they addressed their elder relatives by the respective kinship terms, and were likewise addressed by the younger ones. The course of a person's life may be decided to a large extent by kin relations of this sort, even his or her marriage may be fixed by influential relatives.

Conversely, influential men themselves form their positions through the support they may give to others, and through their relations with them. They may be rich, but their power is normally based less on material wealth than on social influence. A man's wealth is often very much used to express his status: commoditization in this way has become a prominent feature in Pakistan. Technological goods are cherished, and the houses built by wealthier people in the cities testify to a great concern with the outward demonstration of material prosperity. Here, individual competition is obvious. But it is not all conspicious consumption. The line between commodities and gifts is narrow in Pakistan, and contexts of gift exchange account for large sectors of material transactions. Secondly, the way commodities are used seems to differ from the West. To express it in a somewhat simplified opposition: whereas in the West material goods are used to construct the identity of a person, and wealth is mostly associated with these material aspects, in Pakistan goods underline social position, and wealth and position are associated much more directly with power over and influence on persons than in the West. Social relations are not geared to deal with commodities; the situation tends to be the other way round.[18]

For this reason, the extent to which persons are bounded within collectives seems to play a central role in their reputation, sometimes to a startlingly greater extent than their individual capacities would seem to justify. The term *safārish*, which means "using one's influence in speaking on behalf of somebody", so prominent in Pakistani discourse, often, but not

---

[18]The market for consumer goods should reflect this situation. This topic might be worth a separate study.

always used with negative connotations, is symptomatic of the general situation. *Safarish* is not only done for relatives, but is instead a general feature of the society. Cogently, *biradaris*, the categories providing a common identity, are, however, in their contemporary form among the most important social preconditions for this type of discourse. *Rishvat*, bribe, should also be seen in this context. This is the common way of exploiting the resources of an official position, to which one has access to a large extent because of one's social background. It is interesting to note that this social disease — it is seen as such by most people in Pakistan — has encroached most inexorably on the social contexts and institutions established by the British colonial government.

Client relations of the sort outlined may be regarded as negative phenomena, and some of their expressions, exemplified by the terms *safarish* and *rishvat*, are indeed also frequently viewed critically in Pakistan, and the deficit of justice and efficiency in the institutions, politics, or economics of the country are deplored. Lack of space means it is impossible to elaborate this point in this essay, but it must at least be mentioned that what is said here is not meant to forestall criticism, but instead to outline a more profitable understanding of the ideological dimensions of Pakistani society. Once this step has been taken, it may then be employed to commence a critical discourse which, however, does not simply take the own premises for granted.

The different views which the people of Pakistan generally hold on such matters are revealed when we turn to other aspects which belong, according to this analysis, to the same complex, but are regarded as main positive values. Therefore, marriages inside the *biradari* are, according to a common saying, conducted in heaven, and relations formed or underlined by them, as are kin relations in general, are considered very important. A lack of regard for these factors in the West is generally remarked upon critically. A person's identity is connected with his or her kin through the participation of his or her relatives' status to a large degree, and the pride of important persons in the kinship is as positive as the pride of those on whom other persons depend.

If there is a conclusion to be drawn from the discussion of the context of kinship, it is that the idea of equality in Islam, expressed in the last speech of the Prophet, in which he emphasized that all men originate from Adam and are brothers, has to be interpreted carefully, although it is often emphasized in relation to foreigners. Also, if a person belonging to a *kami birādarī*, considered as low, is asked to which *birādarī* he belongs, the answer is often: "We are all Muslims." Such statements are less often heard among people with a higher background, and the notion of the common bracket of Islam expresses more a feeling of belonging together in relation to outsiders than a feeling of equality. Being Muslim implies a relationship with God, and the meaning of equality refers primarily to the relationship with Him, and is otherwise reserved for the paradise, the opposite of earthly existence.[19] There is no equality constituted by an independent "natural" dimension of the individual as it exists in the West, as shown, for instance, by David Schneider's analysis of American kinship.[20] In Islam and in the Pakistani world view, there has so far been no necessity to introduce a realm prior to culture or society other than God: therefore, nature is not opposed to culture as it is in the Western sense, but both are defined through their relationship with God. This topic is best explored with regard to the Sufi saints who constitute an essential part of living religion in Pakistan, and most assuredly should be referred to in this context.

The Saints

Notions which resemble Western individualism are found in such contexts which are regarded as being outside society, or rather outside the world. The saints (*pīrs*, *sūfīs*), who have a wide following in Pakistan and play important roles in the country's religious life, provide a case in point. Through their positions they are able to establish patron-client relations with their followers which complement, and sometimes even transcend those outlined above.

A Sufi, like the Indian renouncer, may be seen at least ideally, as an "individual-outside-the-world" — in opposition to an "individual-in-the-world" in modernity.[21] As Dumont has stated, the former is the type of individualism which emerges in a non-modern society, and just this is the ideal role of the *pīr*[22] in Pakistan. In this country shrines and their *pīrs* are linked with features which show their outworldly position: mostly, shrines

---

[19]See Kurin, "Morality, Personhood and the Exemplary Life".

[20]Schneider, "What is Kinship All About?".

[21]For these concepts, see Dumont, *Essays on Individualism*, 26.

[22]Literally: "the elder one". This Persian term is the most common term for Muslim saints in South Asia.

have been and are created away from human settlements, in areas classified as wilderness (*jangal*). The *pīr* shows his independence of worldly things through the austerities he undergoes, like sitting for many days praying at one place, paying no heed to food and drink (*chilla*). A *pīr* often emphasizes the simple food he takes, letting it be known that he subsists on less than what a common men would be able to. He sometimes does not move even outside his house: indeed there are saints who spend their time sitting on their future tombs, and come out only on an annual ritual occasion. A *pīr* is considered to be a friend of God, in a reversal of the general situation in which men are evaluated by their relationship to other men. The *pīr* is therefore removed from normal mortals into the proximity of the divine and his followers (*murīds*), who define themselves in relation to him, acknowledge his superiority. His nearness to God is also shown by his transcendence of social norms and categories: he is able to shelter criminals who ask for his help, and extends his help to high and low. The self-representation of certain categories of *pīr*, the *majzūb*, shows outworldliness in yet other ways: many of them are thought to be enveloped in a holy madness (a condition described by the adjective *mast*), symbols like nakedness show their unconcern for common social norms, and frequently they constantly argue and fight with devil(s) and ghosts in front of their followers. Some *majzūb*s scold their visitors and, according to Athar Abbas Rizvi, they even pelt them with stones and dust.[23] The famous *cūe* associated with the shrine of Shah Daula in Gujrat are people suffering from microcephaly and in most cases severely mentally disabled, who are seen begging in the cities of the Punjab. They are commonly regarded as *majzūb* or *darvesh*, and their blessings are sought after by many people. *Pīr*s often describe themselves as *faqīr*s, a term also used for mendicants.

Cogently, the outworldliness of *pīr*s should not obscure the fact that in contemporary Pakistan *pīr*s are often at the centre of social and political life. The image of a *pīr* is commonly associated with the highest social category, or, keeping with indigenous social classification, caste, those of the *sayyid*s, to the extent that people sometimes speak of "the caste of the *pīr*s". This is far from saying that all *pīr*s are *sayyid*s, but the association demonstrates the merging of religious and social categories. *Sayyid*s are considered to have come from outside South Asia, to be the descendants of the Prophet, and *pīr*s also trace their origin to Muhammad. In this way, sacred descent merges

---

[23]Rizvi, *History of Sufism*, vol. 2, 470.

the two categories and emphasizes a separate position, aloof from society, which in turn is linked to a position outside the world in popular perception.

This position at the social top is expressed in a number of ways. Famous shrines are sometimes palace-like structures, and the *pīrs* command influence over thousands or even hundreds of thousands of followers. They are visited by politicians, preferably on the eve of elections, and in many respects are practically exempted from normal law. They are thought to perform miracles, made possible by their position outside the world and their consequent proximity to God, which in turn gives them status and power in the world. The followers of a *pīr* receive his help and support in spiritual and worldly matters, and he subsists on whatever they give to him. This can certainly be enough to ensure that some *pīrs* of famous shrines are included among the richest people of Pakistan. But again, material wealth is not the main source of their power: *pīrs* have followers who obey them absolutely, who would give their life for them. It is these followers who constitute the real basis of their power, and they are drawn not only from rural or lower, uneducated classes. If the majority of followers of most of the *pīrs* is from these classes, it is probably because the vast majority of people in Pakistan belongs to them. However, urban people with an academic education are also to be found among the followers of saints: if, for instance, a judge is not actually the *murīd* of a saint, he may go to a shrine of a local saint, and pray there for his promotion. Gellner's distinction between an urban Islam of the *'ulamā'* and an ecstatic Islam of the saints, which loses its importance in modernity,[24] does not hold water in South Asia. The saints of Pakistan are, of course, contested, but so are other institutions, and a renewer like Mawdūdī argued, significantly, both against the traditional *'ulamā'* and against the Sufi *pīrs*.[25] His influence today, although readily discernible, seems in many respects to have been reduced again to the traditional realm, and the zeal of many sympathizers of the Jamā'at-i islāmī does not prevent them from visiting Sufi *pīrs*. Quite a few from the latter group take an active part in the contemporary discussion about Islam, thereby demanding leading roles in intellectual life and formulating their own reformist ideas.

The saints act, according to common Pakistani understanding, as mediators between God and mankind, and as such they transcend social categories. However, the relations between them and their followers are not

[24]Gellner, op. cit., 9 ff.
[25]See Nasr, op. cit., 110, 115 f. 122 f.

understandable in a milieu of individualism in which relations are, in the last resort, regarded as secondary to the individuals themselves. The relations between the saints and their followers are also based on mediation and a participation of identities. Apart from sometimes very practical favours, *murīd*s gain from their *pīr*s identity and an orientation in life which is established through the relationship itself. The kinship categories discussed above may be described by similar formal patterns, but the relations with *pīr*s go beyond the limits of the former. They construct a hierarchical relationship between society as such and the world beyond, the realm of God which is prior to society and gives meaning to the latter.

Conclusions

In this essay, an effort has been made to outline some conditions which serve to shape identities in the contemporary Pakistani Punjab, and to show that they continue to be informed by contexts foreign to modernity.[26] The problem seems to be that we tend to presuppose that our conceptual tools are adequate for the description of contemporary dynamic conditions such as those in Muslim countries like Pakistan, where we encounter many of the institutions associated with the modern form of living, like the nation-state, democracy, the military, a market economy, industrialization, and the effects of globalization produced by modern means of transport and information technology. Indeed, we seem to find reflections of global waves in Pakistan, as Dhū al-fiqār ʿAlī Bhuṭṭo (Zulfikar Ali Bhutto) was ultimately swept to power to a significant degree by student unrest so typical for the global situation of the late sixties.[27] However, without intending to look in more detail at these cases here, we may state that in such cases also the conceptual tools of modernity may lead us astray.

It is perhaps useful to outline very briefly how the concept of modernity as a cultural dominant may be grasped. Different beginnings are postulated in the literature: for the history of art and architecture modernity begins often only at the end of the nineteenth century, but usually its origins are located earlier, as with the Enlightenment or the beginnings of

---

[26]The arguments in this essay have been confirmed in discussions with friends in Pakistan, who did not feel themselves misrepresented.
[27]See Waseem, *Politics and the State*, 220 ff.

industrialization in the seventeenth and eighteenth centuries. However, the era termed "early modern times" in history commonly refers to a period beginning at about 1500. And at least one well-known author, Benjamin Nelson, locates the origins of our era in the twelfth century.[28] These differences are not necessarily mutually contradictory, but tend to point to different aspects or dimensions of the concept. This historical perspective also indicates the cultural confinement of this form of living which we call modernity. The dominant values which are found in it today must also be linked to their historical genesis. A cardinal feature of modernity is the break with tradition, or rather the splitting off of traditional from contemporary values. As Jürgen Habermas puts it: modernity "has to draw its normativity out of itself".[29] Anthony Giddens emphasizes "reflexivity", a similar idea describing the necessity of justifying one's action no longer by tradition, but by conscious judgements based on critical evaluations. "Reflexive modernization" (rather than "simple modernization") carries the full impact of the capabilities inherent in the concept of modernization, and, this author argues, is connected with the globalization of life which affects every niche of society with the constant change it brings. Most particularly, individuals actively have to construct and shape themselves. They can no more depend on identities "handed down"[30] to them. Choices constantly occur and cannot be avoided, daily life becomes experimental, and basic questions, like whether to marry or not, whether to have children, or "what one's sexuality is"[31] have to be decided.

The process of secularization is connected with the Enlightenment, and antedates the former notions; it is frequently seen as a precondition for forming one's own life at a critical distance from tradition. Max Horkheimer and Theodor Adorno argue towards that when they construe the opposition between myth and Enlightenment, and it is for them man's inability to find his own self which makes him continuously fall back on myth.[32] Secularization itself and distance from tradition, or reflexivity, may be seen as a symptom of the development of an ideology which ultimately created what we call modernity (or, for that matter, "postmodernity"). This mental disposition is probably best described by the term "individualism" which is

---

[28]Nelson, *On the Roads to Modernity.*
[29]Habermas, *Der philosophische Diskurs*, 16 (my translation, L.W.).
[30]Giddens, op. cit., 82.
[31]Op. cit. 83.
[32]Horkheimer and Adorno, *Dialektik der Aufklärung.*

used here according to Dumont, although this author is paid scant attention to in the discussion about modernity.[33] By this term Dumont refers to the basic ideology which gradually evolved in the Western civilization, its origins lying (partially) in the beginnings of Christianity. "Individualism" is distinguished from "holism",[34] a term referring to non-modern ideologies, and among its basic characteristics is the separation of fact from value. This, Dumont maintains, is specific to Western civilization: its members gradually began no longer to take entities as intrinsically bound up with their evaluations, as value-facts, a view which entails the consequence that moral qualities are irreducibly connected with any entities. Other civilizations emphasize relations, and give primary consideration to the contexts of entities. Identities of persons are not conceived as isolated or independent, and the concept of a collective is not so much that of a plurality of single units, but that of units defined in relation to each other. The concept of birādarī, or zāt (Hindi jāt; commonly translated as caste) illustrates this view, one which modern ideology, Dumont claims, is having trouble in comprehending: "our culture is permeated by nominalism, which grants real existence only to individuals and not to relations, to elements and not to sets of elements".[35] The modern understanding of the person also contains an egalitarian view according to which a person's "real nature" is sociologically prior and implies the assumption of a natural substance which is only secondarily superseded by a cultural code, thus rendering persons essentially equal to each other.

The advantage of Dumont's theory is that it allows to construct a systematic relation between the phenomenon of modernity and other world views. It should also be noted that the concept of "individualism" is not foreign to such notions as a critical distance to tradition or "reflexivity". Rather, it presupposes them: the degree of isolation reached by the modern identity should allow a systematic reappraisal of its position in the world. Similarly, the retreat of religion from daily life seems to constitute a precondition to distance oneself from tradition, and was probably made possible by individualist ideas. Relating the notion of modernity to a larger context also exposes a certain arbitrariness of many of its traits, a reemergence of "traditional" patterns disguised as the very non-tradition. An

---

[33]Reference is to Dumont, *Essays on Individualism*.
[34]Op. cit., 25.
[35]Op. cit., 11.

important point in case is the concept of change, or the idea of the new (which may be seen as an important feature of modernity in its own right). When Giddens maintains that modernity "is not embracing the new for its own sake", but as a condition of a reflexive disposition,[36] he seems to take an inside perspective which analyses modernity according to its own standards. A comparison with other world views, however, shows that change, or the new, has become a value in the West, and in some areas has become deeply engrained in the perception of reality. The concept of the puberty of adolescents, for instance, is connected in Western societies with a challenge of the values of the parents' generation — whereas in other societies this concept as a cultural fact is simply not present.[37] Other examples include the modern conception of art and fashion, which Walter Benjamin defined as the negation of the immediate past. The way how commodities are produced and marketed in industrialism directly depends on the notion of change as a value.

Commodities today have become an indispensable means of dealing with tradition, or acting in a self-reflective way, and their use has long obscured the original, optimistic meaning of a reflective basis of life decisions: in order for individuals to create personal roles for themselves, modern societies are surrounded by the assets which, once they are acquired, are supposed to give shape to their personalities. Clothes, cars, houses, mobile phones, and so on, are bought not only to be used, but as ready-made pieces to build an ideology or *Weltanschauung*: entities traded as commodities have not only gained a neutral value independent of the context in which they are exchanged, but social relations are now geared up to deal with them. Things in particular often seem to be the one point of orientation in the reflexive world of today; they, or better, the need for them is handed down readily from the collective to the individual, and the game of getting them has itself become the handiest way to construct a person's own identity. Typically, assets tend to occupy similar positions in people's world views as do their transcendental or religious values, in the sense that they offer meaning to life. Much of modern creativity goes into advertising, the true art of the modern market society. The whole fashion-oriented and designing part of production also works towards this end, and the oxymoronic postmodern idea of a "free consumer" is an expression of this. In this sense, the idea of

---

[36]Giddens, *The Consequences of Modernity*, 39.
[37]The biological changes are interpreted in very different ways.

the market has attained a centrality similar to religion in other societies. It should be noted that the ideology of individualism is also connected with the idea that the market is based on the assumption of single individuals who are not necessarily in relation to each other, but only compete with each other, and are defined through things.

When discussing such complex and multifaceted phenomena as modernity, it is useful to distinguish between its (ideological) conditions and the material and institutional forms in which they crystallize, like the modern notion of the market and the technological consequences, including industrialism and the production of commodities. This perspective is also made easier by the notion of individualism.[38]

Of course, in modernity man tends, as anywhere else, to form certain images of himself. If modernity is seen as a form of society, we should not forget that the Durkheimian view of society as a relatively harmonious, bounded entity is no longer valid, and least of all in the extremely pluralistic contemporary Western societies. The notion of modernity must be seen as acting on and reacting to other aspects which do not belong to its context: many of our institutions (constitutional monarchies!), and indeed facets of life, represent other values. The reality defined by or included in modernity is a complex and fractured one. We must also pay proper regard to the cultural multiplicity within modernity itself. It is patently obvious that there is a multiplicity of modernities and they all include in themselves and encapsulate many ideas and forms of life which seem to contradict them. However, this does not prevent the posing of the empirical question of whether the different contexts and levels of a society or culture are guided or directed by or derive their meaning in relation to each other from an interpretation of reality we may identify as being connected to the ideological foundations which also were linked to the historical emergence of the phenomenon of modernity, and set it apart from other constructions of reality. For this, the "centres of gravity" of a society have to be identified, its dreams (like Walter Benjamin's notion of dreams of epochs) and developments, like the notion of "postmodernity" or "postmodernism" which

---

[38]Science and the subjection of the world to technology are frequently rated under the positive achievements of modernity, but according to the view supported here, they also belong to its consequences, and do not by themselves constitute aims, but means which may be used for many ends. National Socialism in Germany and the holocaust also provide an example of what modernity may look like (see Baumann, *Modernity and the Holocaust*).

must be visualized, in their eclecticism and fracturing of reality or in their isolating elements from their context, as a consequence, not as an surmounting of modernity.

The society of contemporary Pakistan does not share these directions and dreams, but emphasizes their opposite: it shapes reality by stressing the mutual dependence of its units, and Pakistani people look at Western societies with a feeling of deep estrangement. The term "modernization", in contrast to "modernity", allows a better description of the way Pakistan is taking part in the contemporary world. The first term refers to the symptoms of modernity which are nowadays found all over the world, albeit in varying degrees and mixtures, above all modern technology and its consequences, but also capitalist and industrialist structures and the nation-state. This term does not necessarily imply, however, that these symptoms or features go along with an ideology associated with modernity. It rather infers that different ideologies may be able to handle features of modernities, and that contemporary forms of life are not as uniform as might be assumed judging from the worldwide spread of the features of modernity, nor will necessarily be so. It also does not seem to be a useful exercise to interpret the ideology in Pakistan in terms of what Giddens called "linear modernization" in contrast to "reflexive modernization",[39] if only because this would mean to assume universal steps of some sort of evolutionary development, an assumption which contemporary evolutionary theory tends to discard. "Linear modernity" may well describe the condition of society in the nineteenth century, but it presupposes, for instance, an individualistic ideology, secular tendencies, and a particular line of development regarding the relationship between people and commodities. In Pakistan, social and religious features tend to encompass the assets of modernity: as we have seen, a person defines him- or herself primarily in relation to other persons. Striving for material wealth is certainly rife in Pakistan, but this should not in itself be taken as a sign of the reign of modernity. Commodities do not serve in Pakistan as much to construct identities as to underline demands of status and power, and it is these factors which shape public perception to a large extent.

The notion of Islam must be seen from the same perspective: Pakistan came into existence through an idea inspired by modernity, that of an Islamic nation. The separation from India allowed Islam to gain access to the centre of power, and to define all areas of life without competition from Hinduism.

---

[39]Giddens, *Beyond Left and Right*, 80 ff.

Pakistan has subsequently defined itself in opposition to its larger neighbour. But much of the form of the Islamic creed has to be located within South Asian dimensions: central notions of kinship and caste, the idea of the renouncer, the hierarchical world view these notions imply, make up crucial aspects of Pakistani identity. These form basic ideas which give direction and meaning to the lives of people, while remaining mostly implicit and unstated, because they are taken as self-explanatory. Thus, ideas of status and authority, as they are expressed in kinship, caste, and the relationship between the saint and his followers, are not only reflected in the way various persons are assessed in daily life and in politics, but they also structure the manner of religious perception, because they define a universe of various capacities of persons and shape the understanding of the sacred history of Islam. For instance, all saints are related to the figure of the Prophet Muhammad, as are the *sayyid*s, the highest social category which is itself associated with saints in popular imagery: these links make up a pervading imagery which serves to conjure up not only the ancient heroes of Islam, but also national heroes like Muḥammad Jinnāḥ and politicians like Dhū al-fiqār 'Alī Bhuṭṭo. And, in the context of this essay, it may just be hinted at that, by extension, this view of persons, certainly at odds with the individual of modernity, accounts for much of the perception of the West, where a highly personalized agenda of a hidden conspiracy is imagined to strive for the doom of humanity: a mirror image of the world order defined by Islamic sacred history, of which Satan is in control.

However, the Islamic universe is perceived very much in South Asian terms. Generally speaking, it is inappropriate to describe the Pakistani world view as one in which regional elements have been incorporated into the Islamic faith, or as a situation characterized by syncretism. The reverse is true. The Islamic faith and imagery have been incorporated within the South Asian social universe. We might state that Islam has given new meaning to regional features, but this interpretation would lead us into deep waters, for it is not easy to sift through the multiple layers of meaning identifiable in a particular ideology, which may differ according to contexts as well as according to the perspectives of different persons. The Islamic features we identify in Pakistan form a means of identifying the self and the world, but seem necessarily to depend on other, cultural factors. Space forbids the elaboration of the point by a comparative study, but this seems to be a general condition of the Islamic faith. We must therefore be aware of a possible multitude of lines of development which allow for other cultural dominants dealing with the contemporary world, other than those usefully identified as falling into the fold of modernity: the Muslim world today is not of one kind — nor indeed are distinctions between centre and periphery, global and regional factors, and other similar ones of more than a very limited use — and people like the inhabitants of Pakistan do not necessarily perceive the world in the same way as Western modernity tends to presume.

Different lines of development may probably be identified with certainty only in retrospect, but if we ignore their possibility, the result will not be, as our moral inclination leads us to think, that we communicate on better terms with each other. Differences do have to be taken into account without turning them into antagonisms, if we are to avoid features which we have ignored erupting like a jack-in-the-box.

8 Muslim Feminists in Western Academia
Questions of Power, Matters of Necessity

Azza M. Karam

Introduction

In September 1994 I was in Cairo, attending the International Conference on Population and Development (ICPD) and completing the last phases of my fieldwork. The ICPD was an extremely dynamic forum, wherein Egyptian women — of all political convictions — mobilized and vocalized their interests and demands in an unprecedented manner. It was also a forum which brought together Egyptian and Arab women in what was referred to as "the Arab Women's Caucus". One of the intentions of this caucus was to coordinate the viewpoints and demands of Arab women active within the parallel NGO Forum and to present these in some coherent and effective fashion to their colleagues in the "official" Conference — being held at a distance which was nominally in close proximity to the venue of the NGO Forum, while nevertheless being conveniently distant. Going into the dynamics of the (un)successfulness of this particular Caucus — interesting though they are — would fall outside the objectives of this text. What should be mentioned, however, is that this was an excellent opportunity for me to come into contact with a great many Egyptian and Arab women who shared my self-same position of being activists in the field at the same time as being involved in Western academic research on the women's movements in their respective countries. I met altogether twenty-five women from Egypt, Sudan, Jordan, Palestine, Tunisia, Algeria, Libya, and Iraq. They were a dynamic, interesting, and enlightening mix of different characters, backgrounds, political orientations, and approaches to academic work. But they all had several characteristics in common, especially the Muslim faith — though practised or adhered to very differently. Furthermore, these Muslim women were, either directly or indirectly, involved with Islamic studies in the respective Western universities to which they were attached. Each of them was studying and researching the different kinds of women's activism in her own country and culture, and hence confronting issues of anthropological and social significance in general.

Being involved at the time in the process of writing a dissertation, I myself and ten others of these Muslim women[1] eventually ended up sharing their frustrations, anxieties, and the highlights that surround any process of research. What struck me was an almost uniform and certainly unfailingly consistent observation all of us made. It was an observation that underlined the sense of frustration that we all felt. Because it was difficult to summarize it succintly, we spent hours and literally days afterwards discussing and arguing — sometimes heatedly — about this particular observation. But what was this observation? Basically each of these women confessed a sense of unease about the manner in which their work was regarded by their Western academic colleagues and seniors. It was not only accounts of the hierarchical and sometimes demeaning interpersonal relations within Western academia that I found fascinatingly and frighteningly familiar,[2] but we were all struck by the virtually invariable approach with which our *written texts* were dealt with.

We shared a host of our interactions within academia, many of which were positive. There were many of us for example, who had established a good rapport with our feminist professors and supervisors, and felt that we actually had friends among them. Moreover, we all expressed relief that some of our supervisors were instrumental in providing guidance from a useful distance while we were enmeshed in our active fieldwork. And many shared their positive experiences about the advice and professional guidance given during the laborious refocusing periods that often followed. Nevertheless, we remained disturbed by the results of some of these shared experiences. For in effect, what we had uncovered was a complex system of power relations — admittedly an aspect of any academy. In this case, however, these particular systems of power relations are further complicated

---

[1] The ten women were four Egyptians, three Sudanese, one Libyan, one Algerian, and one Palestinian. Seven of them were busy preparing their MA degrees (meanwhile, five of them have obtained their degrees, out of which three are continuing with their PhD) and three were at various stages of their PhD study (one of them has obtained her degree since). They were attached to universities and/or institutes in the United Kingdom, France, Germany, the Netherlands, and the United States.

[2] A case in point was the struggle we had to go through in order to gain entry and acceptance into certain "men's clubs" within departments, as well as certain "women's clubs". These Arab women in some instances had to face an accumulation of discriminations: gender, ethnicity, and academic hierarchy.

by hegemonic discourses of cultural domination, which inevitably affected the processes of the production of knowledge in which we were involved. Put more simply and rather crudely, these women researchers felt that their research work was being definitively influenced by Western biases within academia, despite the arguments for "objective" science, and freedom of both speech and writing that Western academia, *in comparative perspective*, is famous for.

The Background

In itself there is nothing new in the above considerations. Edward Said's critique, as outlined in *Orientalism* (1978), constituted an academic scrutiny of and denunciation against all forms of misrepresentation and "cultural hostility", latent or otherwise, which Western "studies" of the Orient are based upon. In fact, Said's main theme was referred to again in his later work *The World, the Text and the Critic* (1983), when he states that

> The entire history of nineteenth-century European thought is filled with such discriminations ... made between what is fitting for us and what is fitting for them, the former designated as inside, in place, common, belonging, in a word *above*, the latter, who are designated as outside, excluded, aberrant, inferior, in a word, *below*. From these distinctions which were given their hegemony by the culture, no one could be free. The large cultural-national designation of European culture as the privileged norm carried with it a formidable battery of Other distinctions between ours and theirs, between proper and improper, European and non-European, higher and lower: they are to be found everywhere in such subjects and quasi-subjects as linguistics, history, race theory, philosophy, anthropology and even biology.[3]

In a similar vein, Edmund Leach, in a conclusion to a historical sketch of social anthropology, notes:

> We started by emphasizing how different are "the Others" — and made them not only different but remote and inferior. Sentimentally

[3]Said, *The World, the Text and the Critic*, 13-14.

we then took the opposite track and argued that all human beings are alike; we can understand Trobrianders or the Barotse because their motivations are just the same as our own; but that didn't work either, because "the Others" remained obstinately the Other.[4]

Attempts to avoid cultural obscurities and understand "the Other" varied. One of these endeavours was cultural translation, and specifically translations — and transformations — of language. An attempt that is heavily (and rightly in my opinion) criticized by Talal Asad as necessitating that the anthropologist simultaneously acts as a translator and a critic. Asad argues instead that "[t]he inequality of languages is a feature of the global patterns of power created by modern imperialism and capitalism".[5] Asad proposes that "the anthropological enterprise of translation may be vitiated by the fact that there are asymmetrical tendencies and pressures in the languages of dominated and dominant societies".[6]

Asad further suggests that these processes of asymmetrical power relations are what should be studied in order to determine "how far they go in defining the possibilities and the limits of effective translation".[7] This, to my mind, is not unlike Foucault's articulation of "taking the forms of resistance against different forms of power as a starting point" to analysing relations of power.[8] In other words, what I refer to as the politics of Othering, is *per se* not new, and in fact has been attempted through and within various studies of the Other. It is the relations of power behind these politics which in many respects fashion the direction, the extent, and the contexts in which these politics take place. Hence the importance of highlighting the role and functions of Western academia in the politics of Othering, and in the processes of the production of knowledge.

A Problematic Within the Production of Knowledge

The politics of social research and academia is an important ingredient of the *how* and *why* certain texts are written, and thereby how and why certain

---

[4]Leach, "Ourselves and the Others", 772.
[5]Asad, *Genealogies of Religion*, 199.
[6]L.c.
[7]L.c.
[8]Foucault in Dreyfus and Rabinow, *Michel Foucault*, 211.

forms of knowledge are (re-) produced. Steven Sangren in 1988 had already elaborated that academic politics conditions the production and reproduction of ethnographic texts. He argues,

> Whatever "authority" is created in a text has its most direct social effect not in the world of political and economic domination of the Third World by colonial and neocolonial powers, but rather in the academic institutions in which its authors participate.[9]

Frances Mascia-Lees et al. point out that patriarchal social orders prevail in academia and influence the choice and method of writing. In fact, they argue that some postmodern writings are an attempt by some to "score" higher than others who inhabit the halls of anthropology departments and thereby secure future jobs.[10]

This criticism of male-dominated academia and its eschewed literary and intellectual output resonates with arguments made in both the United States and Britain for the femininization of academia. Adrienne Rich's "Towards A Woman-centred University"[11] attacks the ways in which education is used as a weapon of colonization, while arguing that the solution lies in feminist pedagogy. The latter could, Rich maintains, legitimate personal experience and begin to change the reproduction of knowledge in academic institutions, and the content and priorities of research. Marcia Westkott takes this further by arguing for feminist research that is *for* women rather than *about* women.[12] She also argues that to achieve Rich's call for a "woman-centred university", women have to be at the university and *in positions of power* within the university, in order to bring about change for other women.

In short, a body of feminist pedagogy has emerged and developed, which outlines the problems, strategies, and encounters between feminists/women's studies and patriarchal structures, within academia and the educational field in general.[13] However, I maintain that arguments against the Western androcentric halls of academia, and the body of knowledge and literature concerning feminist pedagogy contain two major flaws — or absences.

---

[9]Sangren, "Rhetoric and the Authority of Ethnography", 412.
[10]Mascia-Lees et al. "The Postmodernist Turn in Anthropology".
[11]In Adrienne Rich, "Toward a Woman-Centred University".
[12]Westkott, "Women's Studies as a Strategy for Change"; cf. Westkott as quoted in Humm, *Modern Feminisms*, 396.
[13]See Luke and Gore (eds), *Feminisms and Critical Pedagogy*.

Firstly, I consider that with all respect and acceptance of validity and importance, there is an overemphasis on the problematic of male/female or androcentric/gynocentric bias in the production of the forms of knowledge. A similar criticism in fact, is levelled by a number of non-Western feminists against Western feminism. Namely, that the latter seems to be preoccupied with focusing on and furthering enmity between men and women. The second absence I see in feminist arguments and the feminist body of knowledge is that they serve to point out above all the problems faced by *Western* researchers in Western academia. What is yet to be done sufficient research on and is of vital importance as pointed out in this text, is the extent to which Western academia, including *Western feminists within academia*, influence research writings by native (non-Western) feminists on their own cultures and inherent feminisms. What unfolds in these situations is a power dynamic, in which the traditional "Other" of Western academia, namely feminists, are dealing with this relatively newer "Other": native non-Western feminists — who study their own societies (in which they are simultaneously self and "Other") from within the halls of Western academia. The complexities involved are compounded if those "native" feminists do not share or profess the same discipline and/or ideology as their Western academic seniors, but are involved in multidisciplinary research agendas.

Keeping this imbalance of power in mind, similar and more radical and vocal criticisms of feminist pedagogy are registered by Black feminists in Western academia. Gloria Hull and Barbara Smith state that

> women's studies has become both more institutionalized and at the same time more precarious within traditional academic structures, the radical life-changing vision of what women's studies can accomplish has constantly been diminished in exchange for acceptance, respectability, and the career advancement of individuals.[14]

What is more, Hull and Smith state clearly that "we cannot change our lives simply by teaching solely about 'exceptions' to the ravages of white-male oppression".[15] In other words, white feminist pedagogy may fall into the same pit as its initial oppressor, and actually end up oppressing "the Other" — using the same techniques. Bell Hooks talks of a similar dilemma when

[14]Hull and Smith as cited in Humm, op. cit., 400.
[15]L.c.

insisting that it is not simply the creation of an alternative or new discipline within academia that will lead to emancipation or freedom from oppressive structures of creating knowledge. In fact, Hooks argues that

> as individual critical thinkers, those of us whose work is marginalized, as well as those whose work successfully walks that elusive tightrope with one foot on the radical edge and one foot firmly rooted on acceptable academic ground, must be ever vigilant, guarding against the social technology of control that is ever ready to co-opt any transformative vision and practice.[16]

Hence the importance of addressing the problems within Western academia, where the production of knowledge by native/non-Western researchers is influenced by the reproduction of certain oppressive means. Based on my discussions with colleagues from different Western universities, we identified certain mechanisms whereby our work is devalued and silenced, and our academic identities Othered and dehumanized. These mechanisms, inherent in the politics of Othering and culled from our experiences, are described in the following lines.

Delegitimation of the native researcher's work by Western academics is not uncommon. In some instances it proceeds by outright denial of the "objective" validity of the work carried out, or simply by ignoring the substantial scholarly input, and sometimes physical *presence,* of the native non-Western researcher. In other instances, aspects of the native researcher's work are simply appropriated as Western ones — thus denying the originality of the ideas presented and ignoring the researcher's labour. The power dynamics render it such that to complain about this is to risk pitting the reputation of established educators against that of the beginning and as yet even untenured researcher. At an obvious disadvantage, the non-Western researcher may and often does choose to remain silent. Yet in other cases, the sources and methods used by the researcher are questioned, "dis-acknowledged" and thus invalidated. One seemingly popular technique is to deny knowledge of and thus importance to, particular indigenous sources that the researcher may wish to rely on. Similarly, misunderstandings and lack of awareness of the situation of the "Other" may prompt dismissal of certain precepts while insisting on other areas of interest which are less valid in different contexts. Such attitudes of denigration and delegitimation from a

---

[16]Hooks, *Yearning*, 132.

position of imposing power and the ultimate right to approve written texts, can lead to the "reification of the silence" of the native researcher as "Other". This academically sanctioned power imbalance highlights serious problems of privilege/underprivilege, that still divide Western feminists from their Southern, non-Western, and native counterparts.

Effectively, what is underlined here is that Western academia is another field where the self/Other issue goes beyond Man/Woman and firmly enters multiple-layered domains of Western academics/Indigenous ("non-Western") academics. The latter is a realm with its specific baggage of power relations, which, in turn, have direct epistemological implications for writing research. One's research is intended not only for the readers — feminist and otherwise — back home and among the general Western audience. In fact, what we — as non-Westerner researchers — must and do keep in mind is that our work has to be read *and approved* by Western academics before it is even legitimized as research material at all. These are very important considerations which one cannot afford to ignore. The implications of this reality for one's own academic and feminist convictions, as well as for the end product of writing are stimulating at best, and frustrating at worst.

I thus continue to be fascinated by the distinction (and discrimination) between "Self" and "Other"[17] — particularly with regard to Western feminist ethnographical theorizing, which in some cases assume certain aspects of that which traditional male ethnography stands accused of. More precisely, the work of white Western feminist ethnographers on "Third World women" — where the distinction between Self and Other is clear-cut — is often regarded as evidently ethnographic. Meanwhile the ethnographic work of "indigenous" feminists is scrutinized on more detailed grounds, in an attempt to question the validity of both the knowledge gathering and writing processes. Western feminist anthropologists and ethnographers are credited with "gendering the fields" and pioneering diversity in ethnographic methodology, as well as resisting traditional male, highly structured knowledge gathering techniques. Yet in my experience, and that of other Non-Western researchers in Western academia, Western feminist criteria for such anthropological/ethnographical work, when carried out by native feminists in their own societies, become more rigid and frustratingly limiting.[18] The expectations are that indigenous

[17]See Bell et al., *Gendered Fields* and Kandiyoti, *Gendering the Middle East.*
[18]See Ong, "Colonialism and Modernity"; Lorde, *Sister Outsider*; Chow, "Violence in the Other Country"; Mohanty et al. (eds), *Third World Women.*

feminist ethnographic writing must be limited in scope (e.g. to life stories only, or to in-depth daily descriptions of particular aspects of life) and must be wary of theoretical material. Put differently, it is as if the indigenous Other is firmly and incessantly being Othered and continuing to be the Other, while to the Western Self is attributed the responsibility of widely researching and ultimately "saving" this Other. Rey Chow succinctly phrases a similar point in the following:

> Vis-à-vis the non-Western woman, the white woman occupies the position, with the white man, as investigator with "the freedom to speak." This relation, rather than the one that says "we are all women," is particularly evident in disciplines such as anthropology and ethnography. What has become untenable is the way Western feminism imposes its own interests and methodologies on those who do not inhabit the same sociohistorical spaces, thus reducing the latter to a state of reified silence and otherness.[19]

Bell Hooks makes a parallel statement when she says,

> When I do write in a manner that is experimental, abstract, etc., I find the most resistance to my choosing that style comes from white people who believe it is less "authentic". Their need to control how I and other people write seems to be linked to the fear that black folks writing in ways that show a preoccupation with self-reflexivity and style is a sign that they no longer "possess" this form of power.[20]

These are but some of the complications involved in writing research in Western academia, which have implications not only for the process of writing itself, but (consequently) also with regard to the manner in which the final presentation of the text to the readers takes place. The Othering of the indigenous author is part and parcel of the entire data gathering and writing process, and has many unresearched consequences vis-à-vis Self/Other relationships.

Most important in my opinion is the necessity of acknowledging the endurance of the politics of Othering in general, and its changing shapes and dimension within Western academia in particular. Moreover, the recognition

---

[19]Chow, op. cit., 93.
[20]Hooks, op. cit., 130.

of the significance and impact of the politics of Othering on the scientific output of knowledge on Islam in general, and on Muslim women in particular, is equally crucial. In the following section I argue for a particular understanding and definition of feminism, aimed at describing an emergent activist-intellectual force, while simultaneously highlighting its role within processes of the production of knowledge.

Muslim Feminisms: Countering the Politics of Othering

Before I describe Muslim feminisms, in order to avoid a great deal of misunderstandings and misinterpretations usually surrounding the term "feminism", I must first clarify what and how I understand feminism to be. I understand and use feminism as *an individual or collective awareness, that women have been and continue to be oppressed in diverse ways and for diverse reasons because of their gender, and attempts towards liberation from this oppression involving a more equitable society with improved relations between women and men.* An investigative category of "women's activism" *per se* is ambiguous, and difficult to use in practice. By identifying and isolating certain forms of women's activism as "feminisms", I am simultaneously highlighting differences, locating specificities, while placing them within a broader frame of reference. The latter facilitates recognition, and by so doing, permits comparison and inquiry. For I do not unceremoniously label all women as feminists — but I take into account disparate nuances, as well as pronounced differences. Indeed, it is in such a gist that I refer to the plurality and heterogeneity of feminisms — as opposed to a single unified and universal philosophy.

The term "feminism" is, to all intents and purposes, one that has originated in the West. Thus, in post-colonial Arab Muslim societies the term is tainted, impure, and heavily impregnated with stereotypes. One of these stereotypes is that feminism basically stands for enmity between men and women, as well as a call for immorality in the form of sexual promiscuity for women. Not only is feminism loaded with negative stereotypes, but some late and present-day religious scholars and intellectuals associate feminism with colonialist strategies to undermine the order of indigenous social and religious culture. In the opinion of such thinkers, colonizers used the "woman question" as a tool with which to attack Islam and portray it as oppressive and backward. Hence, the near total association of "feminism" with abuse of Islam. These stereotypes and associations have proved remarkably persistent. Not so much, I believe, because of the limited element of truth in them,[21] but because such ideas appeal to pre-existing imagery and are effective tools in the attempts to discredit any means that legitimize and justify women's attempts to gain control over their own lives.

One Islamist woman told me that "we must not reject everything Western simply because it is Western. There are some aspects worthy of emulation"[22]. When pressed to give examples, she mentioned Western punctuality and the respect for commitments and meetings. However, I prefer to broaden her point somewhat. What seem today as taken for granted rights (e.g. women's right to vote) were revolutionary when first introduced. Of course, the quest for equal rights with men remains a thorny issue in most contemporary Arab Muslim countries. Hence the call, especially prominent during the lead up to and holding of the United Nations Fourth World Women's Conference (FWWC, Beijing 1995), of "equity" instead of "equality". Though still ambiguous, the main difference between equity and equality seems to centre on affirming women's access to rights which do not necessarily equal those of men, as well as women's rights to differ from those of men without being subjected to any form of hierarchy. The supposedly alternative term of equity was accepted by and actually pushed for by Muslim countries, and it was propagated and discussed during the FWWC by Islamists as well as their "pro-family" religious colleagues.

Whatever the interplay of words and jargon, the mere fact that another term needed to be found to suit the enterprise of women's rights, indicates that the terminology is more problematic than the actual efforts involved. In fact, whereas feminism is refused as a term, some of its meanings and agendas are nevertheless made adaptable by the different actors within different historically and culturally specific contexts. If "feminism" is rejected, this does not mean that a *feminist consciousness* and agenda are absent.

The term feminism itself is in particular questioned by many so-called "Third World" women. Feminist movements have been challenged on the

---

[21]Western feminism, in all its diversity and ranges, cannot be described as having openly advocated sexual promiscuity. Moreover, many who level this accusation have lived in Western countries and must have been able to see, to some extent at least, the range of ideas on sexual behaviour.

[22]Amany Farag, affiliated to the Muslim Brotherhood, personal interview, Cairo, September 1995.

grounds of cultural imperialism, of shortsightedness in defining the meaning of gender in terms of middle-class, white experiences, and in terms of internal racism, classism and homophobia.[23] All these factors combined to make feminism a suspicious identity-definition as well as category of analysis.

Moreover, some criticisms against some Western feminisms are valid. Clearly, Western feminist discourse and political practice are neither singular nor homogeneous in their aims or analysis. But, as Chandra Mohanty argues, there are

> various textual strategies used by writers that codify Others as non-Western and hence themselves as (implicitly) Western. ... The analytic principles ... serve to distort Western feminist political practices, and limit the possibility of coalitions among (usually white) Western feminists and working class and feminists of color around the world. These limitations are evident in the construction of the (implicitly consensual) priority of issues around which apparently all women are expected to organize.[24]

Mohanty elaborates her criticism to identify certain Western feminist assertions on a "monolithic notion of patriarchy or male dominance", which supposedly oppresses all Third World women in the same way. She proceeds to argue that

> It is in this process of homogenization and systematization of the oppression of women in the third world that power is exercised in much of recent Western feminist discourse, and this power needs to be defined and named.[25]

Taking these critical remarks a step further, one could argue that insofar as some Western feminisms have essentialized, homogenized, and universalized the means and outcomes of women's oppression, they have acted as a metadiscourse. As such, they have sought to legitimate themselves by many means. An example of these attempts at legitimation can be seen when some Western feminists rushed to show solidarity with their Iranian sisters who were supposedly "oppressed by the revolution". Received rather coolly by

---

[23]Mohanty, "Introduction", 7.
[24]Mohanty, "Under Western Eyes", 52. f.
[25]Op. cit., 54.

their Iranian counterparts, this zeal for feminist solidarity had later to be tempered somewhat. What is advocated here is a feminism devoid of hegemonic and universalizing characteristics.

Nevertheless, even while sometimes rejecting the label, many women from developing countries from the South have gone on to engage with feminism. Amrita Basu notes that many of these women who believe that feminism is bourgeois or Western go on to identify indigenous alternatives to Western-style feminism within their own cultural and political contexts.[26]

Going likewise beyond the Western paradigm, Kumari Jayawardena, writing about feminist movements in Asia in the late nineteenth and early twentieth century, defines feminism as "embracing movements for equality within the current system and significant struggles that have attempted to change the system".[27] Jayawardena asserts that these feminist movements emerged in two formative contexts. One of these conditions was the formulation and consolidation of national identities during periods of anti-imperialist struggles. The other context was the recreation of pre-capitalist religious and feudal structures in attempts to "modernize" Third World societies.

Hence there are different forms of feminism and different expressions for the activism it advocates, which correspond to the types of oppression women perceive in different parts of the world. I tend to agree with certain postmodern conceptualizations of feminism, which advocate a theoretical outlook that "is attuned to the *cultural specificity of different societies* and *periods* and to that of *different groups within societies* and *periods*" [emphasis added].[28] Other important features of such postmodern-feminist theorizing are its non-essentialism, non-universalism, pragmatism, and even, its fallibility. Most importantly, however, in its foreswearing of a single feminist epistemology, it creates space for contemporary feminist political practices, which would have been previously regarded as unorthodox. It has been maintained that feminist anthropology had already advocated, to some extent, this so-called. "postmodern" understanding of feminisms. Still, I believe postmodernist feminist theoreticians in particular, played an important role in the evolution of feminist critiques of Enlightenment

---

[26]Basu (ed.), *Challenge of Local Feminisms*, 20.
[27]Jayawardena, *Feminism and Nationalism*, 2.
[28]Fraser and Nicholson, "Social Criticism without Philosophy", 34.

discourses, which in turn enabled diverse conceptualizations and articulations of feminisms.[29]

Mohanty also points out that writings on feminism undertaken by women from the developing world have focused on various aspects of the complex interrelationships between feminist, anti-racist, and nationalist struggles. One of these aspects is the differences, conflicts, and contradictions internal to Third World women's organizations and communities.[30] In view of this aspect and in relation to the particular situation of Muslim communities, I propose a distinction between three different "types" of feminist thought and praxis operating in these communities today, namely *secular feminism*, *Muslim feminism*, and *Islamist feminism*. Covering the broad political spectrum, this identification serves to highlight the multiplicity of voices through which women in Muslim societies speak and act. I will not delve here into an explanation of the secular and Islamist feminisms[31]. Instead, I will concentrate on the category of *Muslim feminists*, who are primarily those who wish to maintain their identity as Muslims and who try to develop, from within an Islamic framework, agendas by which to emancipate women. Muslim feminists use Islamic sources, like the Koran and the *sunnah* (the Prophet's actions and sayings), but their aim is to show that the discourse of total equality between men and women *is* valid, from the point of view of Islam. Muslim feminists also try to steer a middle course, between interpretations of socio-political and cultural realities according to Islam, and Human Rights discourse.

Many of them will be proud to be seen as feminists, or at least have no problems with the term, insofar as it describes their main aims. As far as these women are concerned, myself included, a feminism that does not justify itself within Islam, is bound to be rejected by the rest of Muslim society, and is therefore self-defeating. Moreover, Muslim feminists feel that attempts to separate Islamic discourses from human rights discourses (whether they are accused of being "Western" or not) can only lead to serious fragmentation within society, and is thus unrealistic as an option. Such a separation, many argue, succeeds in preventing a process of mutual enlightenment, between the two discourses, and in fact, risks making the

---

[29]See Nicholson, *Feminism/Postmodernism*; Kristeva, "Le temps des femmes"; *idem, Pouvoirs de l'horreur*.

[30]Mohanty, "Introduction" 10.

[31]For further elaboration see Karam "Islamisms/Feminisms" and *idem, Islamisms, Feminisms and State.*

Islamic one more alienating and patriarchal, and the sole domain of political Islam[32]. Moreover, Muslim feminists argue for a form of *ijtihād*,[33] and maintain that women *are* indeed capable of taking on tasks involving the interpretation of Islamic jurisprudence, and providing social and political leadership (previously thought to be the exclusive domains of men). Muslim feminists mediate between competing discourses: secular discourses that call for women's rights from outside any religious frameworks — and which fare much the same way as secular discourses in general are — i.e. losing political ground and cultural legitimacy — and discourses which seek to situate women's rights exclusively and mercilessly within a universalized and essentialized interpretation of religion. Muslim feminist discourses themselves are neither unified nor homogenous, but contain a multiplicity of opinions and varieties of interpretations.

Muslim feminists are not a category whose existence is confined to my imagination. They do in fact exist both within local Muslim communities in their respective Muslim countries and within Muslim migrant communities in Europe. Most importantly, they exist and are working within academic, cultural and political institutions in many parts of the globe. Though very much an emergent cultural discourse and political formulation, Muslim feminists (including those I met and discussed with in Egypt) are actively engaged in the process of producing and disseminating knowledge in Western academia. Their fields of study range from cultural studies to biology and in all of these fields they are trying to counter stereotypes, provide alternative sources of information, and deconstruct existing discourses about Islam and women.

Conclusion

I conclude this text in a rather unorthodox manner. I contend that in the same spirit in which Western feminists have revolutionized Western

---

[32]Prominent and internationally known writers and theorists who advocate this stance, include Fatima Mernissi (from Morocco), Riffat Hassan (Pakistani-American), and Azizah Al-Hibri (Arab-American).

[33]*Ijtihād* is independent inquiry into the sources (i.e. the Koran and the exemplary behaviour of the Prophet Muhammad, the *sunnah*, as transmitted in the Hadith). The main aim of this inquiry is to come up with interpretations of the religious texts that are suitable to the conditions and exigencies of modern day life.

academia by introducing the discipline of women's/feminist studies, Muslim feminists have a similar, yet more complicated task and responsibility ahead of them. Namely, Muslim feminists have to introduce the field of Muslim women's studies to *both* Western and non-Western institutions (i.e. those that as yet lack such a specialization). As far as Western academia is concerned, that is not where the complications end, Muslim feminists have to avoid the pitfalls of imitating androcentric power patterns as mimicked by certain Western feminists.

Moreover, Muslim feminists have to ally themselves with senior professors (men and women) in academia, who in turn, must be willing not only to listen sympathetically, but to cooperate and use their positions of power to alter the Othering process. To reach that stage, Muslim feminists and Western professors — feminists and non-feminists alike — have to go through a process of what Hooks terms "meaningful contestation and constructive confrontation".[34] Actually, it is not only the introduction of a new field of study that is important, but the challenge within both fields of Women's Studies and Islamic Studies, as they exist within Western academia. This challenge will not be easy by any means or gain many adherents. Nevertheless, it remains important to keep in mind that it is only by constructively facing daunting and contestable concerns, that we can move beyond impasses and avoid the pitfalls along the way.

Recognizing the ambiguous consequences of the imbalances in power relations between non-Western researchers and their Western seniors, within Western academia, is a first step towards altering the manner in which knowledge is perceived. Furthermore, the acceptance of a politics of difference — as opposed to a politics of Othering — is, in my opinion, a *sine qua non* of a necessary restructuring of the epistemological validity of the knowledge of "the Other". In other words, an acceptance of a politics of difference is crucial for the radical changes necessary for the production of knowledge. I thus end with a quote from bell Hooks in which she emphasizes

> the need to remain ever mindful of the way certain discursive practices and the production of knowledge are easily appropriated by existing systems of domination .... If we do not interrogate our motives, the directions of our work, continually, we risk furthering

---

[34]Hooks, op. cit., 133.

a discourse on difference and otherness that not only marginalizes people of color but actively eliminates the need for our presence.[35]

---

[35]Op. cit., 132.

Is Islam a Help or Hindrance to Women's Development?

Riffat Hassan

Introduction

Women such as Khadījah and 'Ā'ishah, wives of the Prophet Muhammad, and Rabī'ah al-'Adawiyyah from Basra (the outstanding woman Sufi) figure significantly in early Islam. None the less, Islamic tradition has, by and large, remained strongly patriarchal up to today. This means, amongst other things, that the sources on which the Islamic tradition is based, mainly the Koran (which Muslims believe to be God's Word transmitted through Angel Gabriel to the Prophet Muhammad), *sunnah* (the practice of the Prophet Muhammad), Hadith (the oral traditions attributed to the Prophet Muhammad), and *fiqh* (jurisprudence), have been interpreted only by Muslim men who have arrogated to themselves the task of defining the ontological, theological, sociological, and eschatological status of Muslim women. It is hardly surprising that up till now the majority of Muslim women who for centuries have been kept in physical, mental, and emotional bondage, have accepted this situation passively. A very pertinent fact in this context is that while the rate of literacy is low in many Muslim countries, the rate of literacy among Muslim women, especially those who live in rural areas where most of the population is to be found, is amongst the lowest in the world.

In recent years, largely because of the pressure of laws antagonistic to women which have been promulgated under the cover of "Islamization" in some parts of the Muslim world, women with some degree of education and awareness are beginning to realize that religion is being used as an instrument of oppression rather than as a means of liberation. To understand the powerful impetus to "Islamize" Muslim societies, especially with regard to women-related norms and values, it is essential to realize that of all the challenges confronting the Muslim world perhaps the greatest is that of modernity. Muslims, in general, tend to think of "modernity" in two ways: (a) as a process of modernization which is associated with science,

189

technology, and material progress; and (b) as Westernization which is associated with promiscuity and all kinds of social problems ranging from latch-key kids to drug and alcohol abuse. While "modernization" is considered highly desirable, conversely "Westernization" is considered equally undesirable. What is of importance to note at this juncture is that an emancipated Muslim woman is seen by many Muslims as a symbol not of "modernization" but of "Westernization". This is so because she appears to be in violation of what traditional societies consider to be a necessary barrier between "private space", where women belong, and "public space", which belongs to men. The presence of women in men's space is considered to be highly dangerous for - as a popular hadith states - whenever a man and a woman are alone, *al-shaytān* (Satan) is bound to be there. In the Muslim world today, because of the pressure of political and socio-economic realities, a significant number of women may be seen in "public space". Caretakers of Muslim traditionalism feel gravely threatened by this phenomenon, which they consider to be an onslaught of "Westernization" under the guise of "modernization". They believe that it is necessary to put women back in their "space" (which also designates their "place") if "the integrity of the Islamic way of life" is to be preserved.

Though I had begun my study of theological issues pertaining to women in the Islamic tradition in 1974, it was not until 1983-84, when I spent almost two years in Pakistan, that my career as an activist began. The enactment of the "Hadud Ordinance" (1979) according to which women's testimony was declared to be inadmissible in *hadd* crimes, including the crime of rape, was accompanied by a wave of violence perpetrated on women and a deluge of anti-women literature which swept across the country. Many women in Pakistan were jolted out of their "dogmatic slumber" by the "Islamization" of the legal system which, through the promulgation of laws such as the Hadud Ordinance and the Law of Evidence (1984) as well as the threat of other discriminatory legislation (such as the Law of Qisas and Diyat or "blood-money"), reduced their status systematically — virtually mathematically — to less than that of men. It soon became apparent that the forces of religious conservatism were determined to cut women down to one-half or less of men, and that this attitude stemmed from a deep-rooted desire to keep women in their place, which means secondary, subordinate, and inferior to men.

Reflecting upon the scene I witnessed with increasing alarm and anxiety, I asked myself how it was possible for manifestly unjust laws to be implemented in a country which professed a passionate commitment to both Islam and modernity. The answer to my question was so obvious that I was startled that it had not struck me before. Pakistani society (or other Muslim societies) could enact or accept laws which specified that women were less than men in fundamental ways because Muslims, in general, consider it a self-evident truth that women are not equal to men. Among the "arguments" used to overwhelm any proponent of gender equality, the following are perhaps the most popular: that according to the Koran, men are *qawwāmūn* (generally translated as "rulers" or "managers") in relation to women;[1] that according to the Koran, a man's share in inheritance is twice that of a woman;[2] that according to the Koran the evidence of one man is equal to that of two women;[3] that according to the Prophet, women are both deficient in prayer (due to menstruation) and in intellect (due to their evidence counting for less than a man's)[4].

Since, in all probability, I was the only Muslim woman in the country who had been engaged in a study of women's issues from a non-patriarchal, theological perspective, I was approached numerous times by women leaders (including the members of the Pakistan Commission on the Status of Women, before whom I gave my testimony in May 1984) to state what my findings were and if they could be used to improve the situation of Pakistani women. I was urged by women activists who were mobilizing and leading women's protests in a country under martial law to help them refute the arguments which were being used against them, on a case-by-case or point-by-point basis. Though I felt eager to help, I was not sure if the best strategy was simply to respond to each argument which was being used to deprive women of their human (as well as Islamic) rights. What had to be done, first and foremost, in my opinion, was to examine the theological ground in which all the anti-women arguments were rooted to see if, indeed, a case could be made for asserting that from the point of view of normative Islam, men and women were *essentially* equal, despite biological and other differences.

As a result of further study and reflection, I came to perceive that in the Islamic, as well as in the Jewish and the Christian, tradition, there are three

---

[1]Reference is made here to Surah 4 (*al-Nisā'*): 34.
[2]Reference is made here to Surah 4 (*al-Nisā'*): 11.
[3]Reference is made here to Surah 2 (*al-Baqarah*): 282.
[4]Reference is made here to hadiths cited in Ṣaḥīḥ al-Bukhārī and Ṣaḥīḥ Muslim.

theological assumptions on which the super-structure of men's alleged superiority to women has been erected. These three assumptions are: (1) that God's primary creation is man, not woman, since woman is believed to have been created from man's rib, hence is derivative and secondary ontologically; (2) that woman, not man, was the primary agent of what is generally referred to as "Man's Fall" or man's expulsion from the Garden of Eden, hence "all daughters of Eve" are to be regarded with hatred, suspicion, and contempt; and (3) that woman was created not only *from* man but also *for* man, which makes her existence merely instrumental and not fundamental. The three theological questions to which the above assumptions may appropriately be regarded as answers are: (1) How was woman created? (2) Was woman responsible for the "Fall" of man? and (3) Why was woman created?

It is not possible, within the scope of this short text, to deal exhaustively with any of the above-mentioned questions. However, in the brief discussion of each question which follows, an effort has been made to highlight the way in which sources of normative Islam have been interpreted to show that women are inferior to men.

Women in the Sources of Normative Islam: Three Questions

How Was Woman Created?

The ordinary Muslim believes, as seriously as the ordinary Jew or Christian, that Adam was God's first creation and that Eve was made from Adam's rib. While this myth is obviously rooted in the Yahwist's account of creation in *Genesis* 2: 18-24, it has no basis whatever in the Koran which describes the creation of humanity in completely egalitarian terms. In the thirty or so passages pertaining to the subject of human creation, the Koran uses generic terms for humanity (*al-nās, al-insān, al-bashar*) and there is no mention in it of Hawwa' or Eve. The word "Adam" occurs twenty-five times in the Koran but it is used in twenty-one cases as a symbol for self-conscious humanity. Here, it is pertinent to point out that the word "Adam" is a Hebrew word (from *adamah* meaning "the soil") and it functions generally as a collective noun referring to "the human" rather than to a male person. In the Koran, the word "Adam" (which Arabic borrowed from Hebrew) mostly does not refer to a particular human being. Rather, it refers to human beings in a particular way. As pointed out by Muḥammad Iqbāl:

> Indeed, in the verses which deal with the origin of man as a living being, the Qur'an uses the words "Bashar" or "Insan", not "Adam" which it reserves for man in his capacity of God's vicegerent on earth. The purpose of the Qur'an is further secured by the omission of proper names mentioned in the Biblical narration - Adam and Eve. The term "Adam" is retained and used more as a concept than as a name of a concrete human individual. The word is not without authority in the Qur'an itself.[5]

An analysis of the Koranic descriptions of human creation shows how the Koran evenhandedly uses both feminine and masculine terms and imagery to describe the creation of humanity from a single source. That God's original creation was undifferentiated humanity and not either man or woman (who appeared simultaneously at a subsequent time) is implicit in a number of Koranic passages. If the Koran makes no distinction between the creation of man and woman — as it clearly does not — why do Muslims believe that Hawwā' was created from Adam's rib? It is difficult to imagine that Muslims got this idea directly from *Genesis* 2 since very few Muslims read the Bible. It is much more likely that the rib story entered the Islamic tradition through being incorporated in the Hadith literature during the early centuries of Islam. In this context the following six hadiths are particularly important since they are cited in *Ṣaḥīḥ al-Bukhārī* and *Ṣaḥīḥ Muslim*, which Sunnite Muslims regard as the two most authoritative hadith collections, whose authority is exceeded only by the Koran:

> 1. Treat women nicely, for a woman is created from a rib, and the most curved portion of the rib is its upper portion, so if you would try to straighten it, it will break, but if you leave it as it is, it will remain crooked. So treat women nicely.[6]

---

[5]Iqbal, *Reconstruction*, 83.
[6]*Ṣaḥīḥ al-Bukhārī, Kitāb al-anbiyā'* (Book of the Prophets), Chapter 1, in the English translation by Muhammad Muhsin Khan, Lahore: Kazi Publications, 1971, 346.

2. The woman is like a rib, if you try to straighten her, she will break. So if you want to get benefit from her, do so while she still has some crookedness.[7]

3. Whoever believes in Allah and the Last Day should not hurt (trouble) his neighbour. And I advise you to take care of the women, for they are created from a rib and the most crooked part of the rib is its upper part; if you try to straighten it, it will break, and if you leave it, it will remain crooked, so I urge you to take care of women.[8]

4. Woman is like a rib. When you attempt to straighten it, you would break it. And if you leave her alone you would benefit by her, and crookedness will remain in her.[9]

5. Woman has been created from a rib and will in no way be straightened for you; so if you wish to benefit by her, benefit by her while crookedness remains in her. And if you attempt to straighten her, you will break her, and breaking her is divorcing her.[10]

6. He who believes in Allah and the Hereafter, if he witnesses any matter he should talk in good terms about it or keep quiet. Act kindly towards women, for woman is created from a rib, and the most crooked part of the rib is its top. If you attempt to straighten it, you will break it, and if you leave it, its crookedness will remain there so act kindly towards women.[11]

Elsewhere in my writings I have examined the above hadiths and shown them to be weak with regards to their formal aspect (i.e. with reference to

---

[7]Op. cit., *Kitāb al-nikāh* (Book of Marriage), first hadith of "Bāb al-mudārāh ma'a al-nisā'" (Chapter on Sociability with Women), in Khan's English translation, 80.

[8]Op. cit., same chapter, next hadith, in Khan's English translation, 81.

[9]*Sahīh Muslim, Kitāb al-nikāh*, first hadith of the last chapter ("Bāb al-wasiyyah bi-al-nisā'" [Chapter on Advice in Regard to Women]), in the English translation by Abdul Hamid Siddiqi, Vol. 2. (Lahore: Shaikh Muhammad Ashraf, 1972), 752 (in other editions of Muslim's *Sahīh*, this and the two following hadiths are included in the last chapter of a separate book, *Kitāb al-radā'* [The Book of Breast-feeding]).

[10]Op. cit., same chapter, next hadith, in Siddiqi's translation, loc. cit.

[11]Op. cit., same chapter, next hadith, in Siddiqi's translation, Vol. 2, 752 f. The first "women" in Siddiqi's English translation of this hadith is singular ("woman"), but has here been rendered plural in conformity with the Arabic original.

their *isnad* or chain of transmitters).[12] As far as their content (*matn*) is concerned, it is obviously in opposition to the Koranic accounts about human creation. Since all Muslim scholars agree on the principle that any hadith which is in contradiction to the Koran cannot be accepted as authentic, the above-mentioned hadiths ought to be rejected on material grounds. However, they still continue to be a part of the Islamic tradition. This is due certainly, in significant measure, to the fact that they are included in the hadith collections by Muhammad b. Ismāʿīl al-Bukhārī (AD 810-70) and Muslim bin al-Hallāj (AD 817-75), collectively known as the *sahīhān* ("the two sound/authentic ones") which "form an almost unassailable authority, subject indeed to criticisms in details, yet deriving an indestructible influence from the "ijmaʾ" or general consent of the community in custom and belief, which it is their function to authenticate."[13] However, the continuing popularity of these hadiths amongst Muslims in general also indicates that they articulate something deeply embedded in Muslim culture, namely, the belief that women are derivative and secondary in the context of human creation.

Theologically, the history of women's inferior status in the Islamic (as well as the Jewish and Christian) tradition began with the story of Hawwā's creation from a (crooked) rib. Changing her status requires returning to the point of creation and setting the record straight. Given the way the rib story has been used, it is impossible to overemphasize its importance. The issue of woman's creation is more fundamental theologically than any other. This is so because if man and woman have been created equal by God who is the ultimate giver of value, then they cannot become unequal, essentially, at a subsequent time. On the other hand, if man and woman have been created unequal by God, then they cannot become equal, essentially, at a subsequent time. If one upholds the view that man and woman were created equal by God — which is the teaching of the Koran — then the existing inequality between men and women cannot be seen as having been mandated by God but must be seen as a subversion of God's original plan for humanity.

---

[12]Hassan, Riffat, "Made from Adam's Rib. The Woman's Creation Question", *al-Mushir (The Counselor). Theological Journal of the Christian Study Centre* (Rawalpindi), 27, 3 (Autumn 1985), 147-151.
[13]Guillaume, *Traditions of Islam*, 32.

Was Woman Responsible for the "Fall" of Man?

Muslims, like Jews and Christians, generally answer the above question affirmatively though such an answer is not warranted by the Koran. Here, it needs to be pointed out that the Koranic account of the "Fall" episode differs significantly from the Biblical account. To begin with, whereas in *Genesis* 3 no explanation is given as to why the serpent tempts either Eve alone or both Adam and Eve, in the Koran the reason why *al-shaytān* (or *Iblīs*) sets out to beguile the human pair in the Garden is stated clearly in a number of passages.[14] The refusal of *al-shaytān* to obey God's command to bow in submission to Adam follows from his belief that, being a creature of fire, he is elementally superior to Adam, who is an earth-creature. When condemned for his arrogance by God and ordered to depart in a state of abject disgrace, *al-shaytān* throws a challenge to God: he will prove to God that Adam and Adam's progeny are ungrateful, weak, and easily lured by temptations and, thus, unworthy of the honour conferred on them by God. Not attempting to hide his intentions to come upon human beings from all sides, *al-shaytān* asks for - and is granted a reprieve until "the Day of the Appointed Time." Not only is the reprieve granted, but God also tells *al-shaytān* to use all his wiles and forces to assault human beings and see if they would follow him. A cosmic drama now begins, involving the eternal opposition between the principles of good and evil, which is lived out as human beings, exercising their moral autonomy, choose between "the straight path" and "the crooked path".

In terms of the Koranic narrative, what happens to the human pair in the Garden is a sequel to the interchange between God and *al-shaytān*. In the sequel we learn that the human pair has been commanded not to go near the Tree lest they become *zālim* (perpetrators of *zulm*: unfairness, tyranny, oppression, or wrongdoing). Seduced by *al-shaytān*, they disobey God. However, in Surah 7 (*al-A'rāf*): 23 they acknowledge before God that they have done *zulm* to themselves and earnestly seek God's forgiveness and mercy. They are told to "go forth" and "descend" from the Garden, but in addressing them the Koran uses the dual form of address only once (in Surah 18 (*Tāhā*): 123); for the rest the plural form is used which necessarily refers

---

[14]For instance, see Surah 15 (*al-Ḥijr*): 26-43; Surah 17 (*Bānū Isrā'īl*): 61-64; Surah 18 (*al-Kahf*): 50; and Surah 38 (*Ṣād*): 71-85.

to more than two persons and is generally understood as referring to humanity as a whole.

In the framework of Koranic theology, the order to go forth from the Garden given to Adam or the Children of Adam cannot be considered a punishment because Adam was always meant to be God's viceregent on earth (Surah 2 (al-Baqarah): 30). The earth is not a place of banishment but is declared by the Koran to be humanity's dwelling place and source of profit to it.[15]

There is, strictly speaking, no "Fall" in the Koran. What the Koranic narration focuses upon is the moral choice that humanity is required to make when confronted by the alternatives presented by God and al-shaytān. This becomes clear if one reflects on Surah 2 (al-Baqarah): 35 and Surah 7 (al-A'rāf): 19, in which it is stated: "You (dual) go not near this Tree, lest you (dual) become part of the zālim." In other words, the human pair is being told that if they go near the Tree, then they will be counted amongst those who perpetrate zulm. Commenting on the root zlm, Toshihiko Izutsu says:

> The primary meaning of ZLM [zlm] is, in the opinion of many authoritative lexicologists, that of 'putting in a wrong place.' In the moral sphere it seems to mean primarily 'to act in such a way as to transgress the proper limit and encroach upon the right of some other person.' Briefly and generally speaking zulm is to do injustice in the sense of going beyond one's bounds and doing what one has no right to.[16]

By transgressing the limits set by God, the human pair became guilty of zulm toward themselves. This zulm consists in their taking on the responsibility for choosing between good and evil. As pointed out by Iqbāl,

> the Koranic legend of the Fall has nothing to do with the first appearance of man on this planet. Its purpose is rather to indicate man's rise from a primitive state of instinctive appetite to the conscious possession of a free self, capable of doubt and disobedience. The Fall does not mean any moral depravity; it is man's transition from simple consciousness to the first flash of self-consciousness .... Nor does the Koran regard the earth as a torture-hall where an elementally wicked humanity is imprisoned for an original act of sin. Man's first act of

[15]Iqbal, op. cit., 84.
[16]Izutsu, *Structure of Ethical Terms*, 152-3.

disobedience was also his first act of free choice; and that is why, according to the Koranic narration, Adam's first transgression was forgiven .... A being whose movements are wholly determined like a machine cannot produce goodness. Freedom is thus a condition of goodness. But to permit the emergence of a finite ego who has the power to choose ... is really to take a great risk; for the freedom to choose good involves also the freedom to choose what is the opposite of good. That God has taken this risk shows His immense faith in man; it is now for man to justify this faith.[17]

Even though there is no "Fall" or Original Sin in the Koran, the association of the episode described in *Genesis* 3 with fallen humanity and illicit sexuality which has played such a massive role in perpetuating the myth of feminine evil in the Christian tradition, also exists in the minds of many Muslims and has had an extremely negative impact on the lives of millions of Muslim women. The following comment of 'Abd al-A'lā' Mawdūdī — one of the most influential scholars of contemporary Islam — is representative of the thinking of many, if not most, Muslims:

> The sex instinct is the greatest weakness of the human race. That is why Satan selected this weak spot for his attack on the adversary and devised the scheme to strike at their modesty. Therefore the first step he took in this direction was to expose their nakedness to them so as to open the door to indecency before them and beguile them into sexuality. Even to this day, Satan and his disciples are adopting the same scheme of depriving the woman of the feelings of modesty and shyness, and they cannot think of any scheme of "progress" unless they expose and exhibit the woman to all and sundry.[18]

Though the branding of women as "the devil's gateway"[19] is not at all the intent of the Koranic narration of the "Fall" story, Muslims, no less than Jews and Christians, have used the story to vent their misogynistic feelings. This is clear from the continuing popularity of hadiths such as the following:

---

[17]Op. cit., 85.

[18]Maududi [Mawdūdī], *Meaning of the Qur'an*, vol. 2, 16, note 13.

[19]This expression comes from Tertullian (AD 160-225), a church father from North Africa who wrote: "And do you not know that you are (each) an Eve? The sentence of God on this sex of yours lives in this age: the guilt must of necessity live too. You are the devil's gateway; you are the unsealer of that (forbidden) tree: you are the first deserter of the

[The Prophet] said, "After me I have not left any affliction [sic; "temptation" would better render the Arabic *fitnah*] more harmful to men than women"[20].

Ibn 'Abbās reported that Allah's Messenger may peace be upon him said: "I had a chance to look into Paradise and I found that the majority of the people were poor and I looked into the Fire and there I found the majority constituted by women".[21]

Abū Sa'īd Khudrī reported that Allah's Messenger may peace be upon him said: "The world is sweet and green (alluring) and verily Allah is going to install you as viceregent in it in order to see how you act. So avoid the allurement of women: verily the first trial for the people of Isra'il was caused by women".[22]

Why Was Woman Created?

The Koran, which does not discriminate against women in the context of creation or the "Fall" episode, does not support the view held by many Muslims, Christians, and Jews that women were created not only *from* man but also *for* man. That God's creation as a whole is "for just ends" (Surah 15 (*al-Ḥijr*): 85) and not "for idle sport" (Surah 21 (*al-Anbiyā'*): 16) is one of the major themes of the Koran. Humanity, consisting of both men and women, is fashioned "in the best of moulds" (Surah 95 (*al-Tīn*): 4) and is called to righteousness which requires the honouring of *ḥuqūq Allāh* (rights of God) as well as *ḥuqūq al-'ibād* (rights of creatures). Not only does the Koran make it clear that man and woman stand absolutely equal in the sight of God, but also that they are "members" and "protectors" of each other. In

---

divine law, you are she who persuaded him whom the devil was not valiant enough to attack. You destroyed so easily God's image, man. On account of your desert — that is, death — even the Son of God had to die" (*De culte feminarum* 1.1 cited in Swidler, *Biblical Affirmations*, 346).

[20]*Saḥīḥ al-Bukhārī, Kitāb al-Nikāḥ*, "Bāb mā yuttaqā min shu'm al-mar'ah" (Chapter on What Misfortune of the Woman one Should Be on One's Guard Against), in Khan's translation, 22 (quotation marks added).

[21]*Saḥīḥ Muslim, Kitāb al-riqaq* (Siddiqi: "Book of Heart-Melting Traditions"), first hadith, in Siddiqi's translation, Vol. 4, 1431 (quotation marks added).

[22]Op. cit., same chapter, 11th hadith, in Siddiqi's translation, Vol. 4, 1432 (quotation marks added).

other words, the Koran does not create a hierarchy in which men are placed above women nor does it pit men against women in an adversary relationship. They are created as equal creatures of a universal, just and merciful God whose pleasure it is that they live together in harmony and righteousness.

In spite of the Koranic affirmation of man-woman equality, Muslim societies, in general, have never regarded men and women as equal, particularly in the context of marriage. Fatima Mernissi has aptly observed:

> One of the distinctive characteristics of Muslim sexuality is its territoriality, which reflects a specific division of labor and specific conception of society and of power. The territoriality of Muslim sexuality sets ranks, tasks, and authority patterns. Spatially confined, the woman was taken care of materially by the man who possessed her, in return for her total obedience and her sexual and reproductive services. The whole system was organized so that the Muslim *ummah* (community) was actually a society of citizens who possessed among other things the female half of the population .... Muslim men have always had more rights and privileges than Muslim women, including even the right to kill their women .... The man imposed on the woman an artificially narrow existence, both physically and spiritually.[23]

Underlying the rejection in Muslim societies of the idea of man-woman equality is the deeply-rooted belief that women — who are inferior in creation (having been made from a crooked rib) and in righteousness (having helped *al-shaytān* in defeating God's plan for Adam) — have been created mainly to be of use to men who are superior to them. The alleged superiority of men to women which permeates the Islamic (as well as the Jewish and Christian) tradition is grounded not only in Hadith literature but also in popular interpretations of some Koranic passages. Two Koranic passages — Surah 4 (*al-Nisā'*): 34 and Surah 2 (*al-Baqarah*): 288 in particular — are generally cited to support the contention that men have "a degree of advantage" over women. Of these, the first reads as follows in Mawdūdī's translation of the Arabic text:

> Men are the managers of the affairs of women because Allah has made the one superior to the other and because men spend of their wealth on

---

[23]Mernissi, *Beyond the Veil*, 103.

women. Virtuous women are, therefore, obedient; they guard their rights carefully in their absence under the care and watch of Allah. As for those women whose defiance you have cause to fear, admonish them and keep them apart from your beds and beat them. Then, if they submit to you, do not look for excuses to punish them: note it well that there is Allah above you, who is Supreme and Great.[24]

It is difficult to overstate the negative impact which the popular Muslim understanding of the above verse has had on the lives of Muslim women. Elsewhere in my work I have made a detailed analysis of this verse to show how it has been misinterpreted. For instance, the key word in the first sentence is *qawwāmūn*. This word is most often translated as *hākimūn* or "rulers". By making men "rulers" over women, a hierarchy akin to the one created by the Apostle Paul and his followers in the Christian tradition, is set up in the Islamic *ummah*. Linguistically, the word *qawwāmūn* refers to those who provide a means of support or livelihood. In my exegesis of this verse, I have argued that the function of supporting women economically has been assigned to men in the context of child-bearing — a function which can only be performed by women. The intent of this verse is not to give men power over women but, rather, to ensure that while women are performing the important tasks of child-bearing and child-raising they do not have the additional responsibility of being breadwinners as well. The root-word *daraba*, which has been generally translated as "beating", is one of the commonest root-words in the Arabic language with a large number of possible meanings. That the vast majority of translators — who happen to be all men — have chosen to translate this word as "beating" clearly indicates a bias in favour of a male-controlled, male-oriented society.

The second Koranic passage which is cited to support the idea that men are superior to women is in the specific context of *'iddah* — a three-month waiting period prescribed for women between the pronouncement of divorce and remarriage. The "advantage" men have in this regard is that they do not have to observe this waiting period because, unlike women, they do not become pregnant (the three-month waiting period is for making certain that the woman is not pregnant). That the intent of this verse is to ensure justice

[24]Maududi, op. cit., 321.

201

is made clear by its emphasis that "women shall have rights similar to the rights against them, according to what is equitable."[25]

The reading of the Koran through the lens of the Hadith is, in my opinion, a major reason for the misreading and misinterpretation of many passages which have been used to deny women equality and justice. Hadiths such as the following are often cited to elevate man to the status of "*majāzī khudā*" (pseudo-god):

> And Ibn Ḥabbān said referring to Abū Hurayrah: "A woman came to God's Prophet, may God's blessing and salvation be upon him. She said: 'I am so-and-so the daughter of so-and-so.' He said: 'I know you. What is your problem.' She said: 'My problem concerns my devout paternal cousin, so-and-so.' He said: 'I know him.' She said: 'He has asked for my hand and informed me what the right of a husband in relation to his wife is. If it is something I am capable of, I shall marry with him.' He said: 'His right is such that if blood and pus were streaming from his nostrils and she should lick it up with her tongue, she would not [yet] have given him his due. If it were befitting for a human being that he prostrated oneself before [another] human being, I would have ordered the woman that she prostrated herself before her husband when consummates his marriage because of the privilege He has bestowed upon him in relation to her.' She said: 'By Him who has sent you with the truth, I shall not marry as long as the world remains.'"[26]

A faith as rigidly monotheistic as Islam, which makes *shirk* or association of anyone with God the one unforgivable sin, cannot conceivably permit any human being to worship anyone but God. However, this hadith makes it appear that if not God's, it was at least the Prophet's, wish to make the wife prostrate herself before her husband. Since each word, act, or exhortation of the Prophet is held to be sacred by Muslims in general, this hadith has had enormous impact on Muslim women. How such a hadith could be attributed to the Prophet, who regarded the principle of *tawḥīd* (oneness of God) as the basis of Islam, is, of course, utterly shocking.

[25]Koran, Surah 2 (*al-Baqarah*): 228.

[26]Muhammad Ṣiddīq Ḥasan Khān Bahādur, *Ḥusn al-uswah bi-mā thabata min Allāh wa-rasūlih fī al-niswah* (The Good Example of What Has Been Established from God and His Prophet on Women), Constantinople, AH 1301 (AD 1884), 390. This author mentions that this hadith was collected by al-Bazzār and al-Ḥākim. For details and several similar hadiths see op. cit., 390 f.

Toward a Feminist Theology

Islam as a Religion of Justice

Reference has been made in the foregoing account to the fundamental theological assumptions which have coloured the way in which Muslim culture, in general, has viewed women. That these assumptions have had serious negative consequences and implications — both theoretical and practical — for Muslim women throughout Muslim history up till the present time needs to be emphasized. At the same time, it needs to be borne in mind that the Koran, which to Muslims in general is the most authoritative source of Islam, does not discriminate against women despite the sad and bitter fact of history that the cumulative (Jewish, Christian, Hellenistic, Bedouin, and other) biases which existed in the Arab-Islamic culture of the early centuries of Islam infiltrated the Islamic tradition, largely through the Hadith literature, and undermined the intent of the Koran to liberate women from the status of chattel or inferior creature, making them free and equal to men. Not only does the Koran emphasize that righteousness is identical in the case of man or woman, but it affirms, clearly and consistently, women's equality with men and their fundamental right to actualize the human potential that they share equally with men. In fact, when seen through a non-patriarchal lens, the Koran goes beyond egalitarianism. It exhibits particular solicitude towards women as also towards other classes of disadvantaged persons. And not only this, it provides particular safeguards for protecting women's special sexual/biological functions such as carrying, delivering, suckling, and rearing offspring.

God, who speaks through the Koran, is characterized by justice, and it is stated clearly in the Koran that God can never be guilty of *zulm*. Hence, the Koran, as God's Word, cannot be made the source of human injustice, and the injustice to which Muslim women have been subjected cannot be regarded as God-derived. The goal of Koranic Islam is to establish peace which can only exist within a just environment. Here it is of importance to note that there is more Koranic legislation pertaining to the establishment of justice in the context of family relationships than on any other subject. This points to the assumption implicit in much Koranic legislation, namely, that if human beings can learn to order their homes justly so that the rights of all within it — children, women, men — are safeguarded, then they can also

203

order their society and the world at large, justly. In other words, the Koran regards the home as a microcosm of the *ummah* and the world community, and emphasizes the importance of making it "the abode of peace" through just living.

In my judgement, the importance of developing what the West calls "feminist theology" in the context of the Islamic tradition is paramount today in order to liberate not only Muslim women, but also Muslim men, from unjust social structures and systems of thought which make a peer relationship between men and women impossible. It is extremely important for Muslim women activists to realize that in the contemporary Muslim world, laws instituted in the name of Islam cannot be overturned by means of political action alone, but through the use of better religious arguments. Professor Fazlur Rahman had stated that the tragedy of modern Muslims has lain in the fact that those who understood modernity, did not understand Islam, and those who understood Islam did not understand modernity. In my opinion a greater tragedy lies in the fact that Islam seems to be represented globally - as also so visibly at the conference where this text was presented - by two extreme groups, one presenting Islam in extremely narrow and conservative terms, and the other as being in absolute opposition to human rights as they are defined in Western secular discourse. The majority of the educated Muslims who, in my opinion, tend to be progressive rather than conservative, appear to be marginalized even though it is from amongst such people that the reformers who liberated the Muslim world from colonialism came. Neither the extreme right nor the anti-religious groups which have "hijacked" human rights in many Muslim countries represent the vast majority of Muslims who are religious without being fanatic, narrow-minded, or inclined toward violence and terrorism.

George Santayana has remarked with acute insight that those who do not know their history are destined to repeat it. Stating the same idea in another way, a Muslim scholar once said to me, "If you are going somewhere in a train and you realize after some time that the train has somehow become derailed and is going in the wrong direction, you cannot at that moment get back on the right track. You have first to get back to the point at which you got off-track and then you can get back on-track." Women in general need to know the point at which they became derailed in history in order to reclaim their proper place in the world. I believe strongly that by means of feminist theology it is possible to equip and empower women to combat the gender-inequality and injustice to which they have been subjected for a very long time.

Muslim Women: A Paradigm Shift from Re-active to Pro-active

The United Nations Conference on Population and Development, held in Cairo, Egypt, in September 1994, was an extremely important landmark in raising global consciousness with regard to a number of issues which are central to the lives of women. The conference was particularly momentous for Muslim women who participated in record numbers in this meeting, which was held in one of the most important capitals of the Muslim world. The presence in Cairo of al-Azhar University, the oldest University in the world, of which the fatwas or religious proclamations carry much weight amongst Muslims, added further significance to the venue of this conference.

In an opening session of the conference, three male professors representing al-Azhar University, presented what was labelled "Muslim viewpoints" on the subject of "Religion, Population, and Development". Only a small part of their presentations, however, dealt with the topic of Population and Development which was the subject of the conference. After stating that Islam was not against family planning but that it allowed abortion only to save the mother's life or health, the speakers focused on the status or position of women in the Islamic tradition. The purpose of this panel presentation by high-powered representatives of the most prestigious Muslim university in the world was to pre-empt any discussion on the subject of Muslim women by making the "privileged" position of women in Islam clear to both the Western media (which stereotypes Muslim women as "poor and oppressed") and to Muslim women themselves. In interventions from the floor, however, the "Muslim viewpoints" represented by the three male professors of Al-Azhar University were questioned as voices of Muslim women were conspicuous by their absence in the panel of presenters. Muslim women demanded "equal time" and they got that and more — in subsequent days when a number of sessions were held at the NGO Forum in which Muslim women figured significantly and in which women-related issues were explicated by women themselves.

Women's identification with body rather than with mind and spirit is a common feature of many religious, cultural, and philosophical traditions. However, though women have, traditionally, been identified with body, they have not been seen as "owners" of their bodies. The issue of who controls women's bodies — men, the State, the Church, the Community, or women — has been one of the most important underlying issues of the Cairo Conference. The fact that Muslim women forcefully challenged the traditional viewpoint not only with regard to women's identification with body, but also with regard to the control of the woman's body, indicates that Muslim women are no longer nameless, faceless, and that they are ready to stand up and be counted.

It has now been accepted globally that issues which may appear to pertain primarily to a woman's body, namely that of contraception and abortion, cannot be looked at in isolation from the larger factor of women's over-all development as human beings. However, as pointed out by a number of persons and agencies, the primary focus of the Cairo Conference was on "population" issues focusing on the body, rather than on "development" issues which focus on the whole person.

The challenge before women in general, and Muslim women in particular, is to shift from the re-active mindset in which it is necessary for women to assert their autonomy over their bodies in the face of strong opposition from patriarchal structures and systems of thought and behaviour, to a pro-active mindset in which they can, finally, begin to speak of themselves as full and autonomous human beings who have not only a body, but also a mind and a spirit. What do Muslim women - who along with Muslim men have been designated as God's vicegerent on earth by the Koran - understand to be the meaning of their lives? Reacting against the Western model of human liberation no longer suffices as a pro-active orientation requires a positive formulation of one's goals and objectives. The critical issue on which Muslim women are called upon to reflect, with utmost seriousness, is: what kind of model or models of human self-actualization can be developed within the framework of normative Islam which takes account both of the realities of the contemporary Muslim world and its ideals?

I would like to say a word to those human rights groups in the Muslim world which adopt the position that human rights and Islam are incompatible and that the abandonment of Islam is a precondition for women's liberation from oppression and development. In my judgement, the average Muslim woman in the world has three characteristics: she is poor, she is illiterate, and she lives in a rural environment. If I, as a human rights activist, wanted to "liberate" this average Muslim woman living anywhere from Ankara to

Jakarta, I could not do so by talking to her about the United Nations Declaration on Human Rights, 1948, because this means nothing to her. But it is possible for me to reach this woman's heart and mind and soul by reminding her that God is just and merciful and that, as a creature of this just and merciful God, she is entitled to justice and protection from every kind of oppression and inequity. I make this statement because I have seen the eyes of many Muslim women who have lived in hopelessness and helplessness light up when they realize what immense possibilities for development exist for them within the framework of the belief-system which defines their world.

In the end a word needs to be said about the representation of Muslim women in the West and by the Western media. Since the nineteen-seventies there has been a growing interest in the West in Islam and Muslims. Much of this interest has been focused, however, on a few subjects such as "Islamic Revival", "Islamic Fundamentalism", "The Salman Rushdie Affair", and "Women in Islam", rather than on understanding the complexity and diversity of "the World of Islam". Not only the choice of subjects which tend to evoke or provoke strong emotive responses in both Westerners and Muslims, but also the manner in which these subjects have generally been portrayed by Western media or popular literature arouses questions about the motivation which underlies the selective Western interest in Islam and Muslims.

Given the reservoir of negative images associated with Islam and Muslims in "the Collective Unconscious" of the West, it is hardly surprising that, since the demise of the Soviet Empire, "the World of Islam" is being seen as the new "Enemy" which is perhaps even more incomprehensible and intractable than the previous one. The routine portrayal of Islam as a religion spread by the sword and characterized by "Holy War", and of Muslims as barbarous and backward, frenzied and fanatic, volatile and violent, has led, in recent times' to an alarming increase in "Muslim-bashing" — verbal, physical as well as psychological — in a number of Western countries. In the midst of so much hatred and aversion towards Islam and Muslims in general, the outpouring of so much sympathy, in and by the West, towards Muslim women appears, at a surface level, to be an amazing contradiction. For are Muslim women also not adherents of Islam? And are Muslim women also not victims of "Muslim-bashing"? Few of us can forget the brutal burning of Turkish Muslim girls by German gangsters or the ruthless rape of Bosnian Muslim women by Serbian soldiers.

207

Since the modern notion of human rights originated in a Western, secular context, Muslims in general, but Muslim women in particular, find themselves in a quandary when they initiate, or participate in, a discussion on human rights whether in the West or in Muslim societies. Based on their life experience, most Muslim women who become human rights advocates or activists feel strongly that virtually all Muslim societies discriminate against women from cradle to grave. This leads many of them to become deeply alienated from Muslim culture in a number of ways. This sense of alienation oftentimes leads to anger and bitterness toward the patriarchal structures and systems of thought which dominate Muslim societies. Muslim women often find much support and sympathy in the West so long as they are seen as rebels and deviants with the world of Islam. But many of them begin to realize, sooner or later, that while they have serious difficulties with Muslim culture, they are also not able, for many reasons, to identify with Western, secular culture. This realization leads them to feel — at least for a time — isolated and alone. Much attention has been focused, in the Western media and literature, on the sorry plight of Muslim women who are "poor and oppressed" in visible or tangible ways. Hardly any notice has been taken, however, of the profound tragedy and trauma suffered by the self-aware Muslim women of today who are struggling to maintain their religious identity and personal autonomy in the face of the intransigence of Muslim culture, on the one hand, and the imperialism of Western, secular culture, on the other hand.

While the West constantly bemoans what it refers to as the "rise of Islamic fundamentalism", it does not extend significant recognition or support to progressive Muslims who are far more representative of "mainstream" modern Islam than either the conservative Muslims on the right or the "secular" Muslims on the left. Even after the Iranian Revolution and the "Islamization" of an increasing number of Muslim societies, many Western analysts are still unable or unwilling to see Islam as a religion capable of being interpreted in a progressive way or a source of liberation to Muslim peoples. An even deeper problem is their refusal to understand the pivotal role of Islam in the lives of Muslims the vast majority of whom — in a worldwide community estimated to be over one billion — are "believers" rather than "unbelievers". Compelled by facts of modern history, some social scientists in the West are now beginning to concede that Islam is *one* of the factors which needs to be considered — along with political, economic, ethnic, social and other factors — in planning and evaluating development projects. This approach, though an improvement on the one which does not take account of religion at all, is still not adequate for understanding the issues of the Muslim world or finding ways of resolving them. Islam is not, in my judgment, simply *one* of the factors which impact on the lives of Muslims. It is the *matrix* in which all other factors are grounded. I do not believe that any viable model of self-actualization can be constructed in Muslim societies for women or men which is outside the framework of normative Islam deriving from Koranic teachings and exemplified in the life of the Prophet of Islam. Nor do I believe that any profoundly meaningful or constructive dialogue can take place between "the World of Islam" and "the West" without a proper recognition of what Islam means to millions of Muslims.

10 Muslim Views on Population
The Case of Tajikistan[1]

Colette Harris

Introduction

Along with the Muslim countries of North Africa, the Middle East, and
Eurasia, until recently the Muslim Central Asian Republic of Tajikistan had
one of the world's highest annual population increases. While Islam appears
to play some part as a unifying cultural influence here, we need to beware
of a Eurocentric, neo-colonial tendency to view it as the sole cause of high
birth rates, leaving socio-economic and political factors out of consideration.

The present text starts by looking at how the above factors influence
fertility rates in Muslim countries in general and then proceeds to relate these
to the situation in Tajikistan.

Islam and Population

Nowadays official population policies increasingly tend to abandon the
traditional concept that a large population makes a country powerful, and
adopt the modern one that an overcrowded country is a poor one, and
Muslim countries are starting to take practical steps towards reducing their
birth rates.[2] I start with a history of Islamic attitudes to birth control in

---

[1] I should especially like to thank Dr. Sofia Hafisovna Hakimova and the many other
women of Tajikistan who so kindly helped me with the information on which this text
is based. Where not otherwise noted, the information on Central Asia comes from
interviews carried out in Tajikistan between December 1994 and February 1996. I should
also like to thank Joke Schrijvers for her comments on earlier drafts.
[2] A number of Muslim countries refused to have anything to do with the 1994 UN Cairo
Conference on population, on the not entirely unjustified grounds that Western population
policies in the developing world amount to racism. However, both Lebanon and the
Sudan, which had been among those countries boycotting the 1994 conference, were
present in January 1996 at the Cairo regional conference on family planning, organized
by the International Planned Parenthood Federation (IPPF) Arab World Region. In all,

order to refute the widely-held view that this doctrine is basically inimical to the regulation of fertility.

Islam and Birth Control

The Islamic religion is the only one of the three "religions of the book" to put an emphasis on sexual pleasure. Although male pleasure is considered paramount, Islamic religious texts insist that women also have a right to sexual pleasure.[3] The linking of sex with pleasure presupposes practising it at times other than when a child is desired, so that it is only logical to suppose that, unlike important traditions within Judaism and Christianity,[4] Islam would not forbid the use of contraception.

The Muslim law-givers of the Middle Ages discussed methods of contraception at length, especially al-Ghazālī (AD 1058-1111), one of the most important medieval Islamic authorities on the subject. Even abortion during the first weeks of pregnancy was permissable under certain conditions. The Persian philosopher and scientist, Ibn Sīnā (AD 980-1037), better known in Europe by his Latin name of Avicenna, provides twenty methods of contraception, including ten different types of suppositories and herbs in the third book of his *al-Qānūn fī al-ṭibb* (Code of Medicine), although withdrawal (*coitus interruptus*) was the most popular method.[5]

Up to and including the nineteenth century there was general consensus among Muslim jurists that regulation of natality was permissible and that women had a right to decide how many children they wanted.[6] In this respect Muslim society was far ahead of the West, where contraception was only approved well after the start of the twentieth century and where the Roman Catholic Church has never accepted it.[7] Most Islamic scholars today

representatives from fourteen Arab countries attended and expressed favourable opinions on family planning, pledging to take measures to try to increase support for it within their countries (Hamand, "Working for Change in the Arab World", 5-7).
[3]Musallam, *Sex and society in Islam*, 31-2, 34-6, 107.
[4]The medieval Roman Catholic church was against sex other than for procreation and, therefore, against all contraception. The objection to birth control in Judaism is that it destroys male seed, a terrible sin according to the Bible (see Genesis 38, for instance).
[5]Musallam, op. cit., 17-18, 25, 67.
[6]Omran, *Family planning in the legacy of Islam*; Musallam, op. cit., 28, 37-8.
[7]Women's very physiological capacity for experiencing sexual pleasure was denied in the West in the late nineteenth century and for many years of the twentieth (Scully and Bart,

agree on the acceptability of birth-control methods, although abortion is somewhat more controversial.

Islam and Fertility

High birth rates have generally been associated with poverty and the low status of women. The great majority of Muslim countries, although poor, have considerably higher per capita incomes than most Sub-Saharan African countries with equivalent birth rates.[8] Thus, until recently, the status of women in Islam was held to be the single most important factor affecting them.[9] However, this point of view is now being refuted and replaced with analyses that consider Islam to be only one factor among many (Carla Makhlouf Obermeyer) or that hold that socio-economic and political factors are solely responsible for birth rates (Valentine Moghadam).[10]

My own view is that Islam does play a role here, albeit a less important one than has previously been thought. It does this through the traditions of the *sharī'ah* family code which legitimize male control over women. This has been a major influence on the position of women in all these societies, even in those countries where it is not now incorporated into the legal code. Despite differences of interpretation, its influence tends to have a somewhat unifying effect on Islamic attitudes to gender relations.[11] Where men's status depends on the number of their (male) children, as it may do where they have no other way of gaining it, such as through acquired skills, husbands have good reason to exercise their control over their wives by insisting on large numbers of pregnancies.

Family control over women is also legitimized through the *sharī'ah* and remains generally strong, particularly in those rural areas where extended families predominate. Here socio-economic factors combine with ideology. A family's continued survival and prosperity may be contingent upon its production of large numbers of children, especially of sons. Therefore, both girls and boys are encouraged to put a high value on their future fertility. Older family members, especially mothers-in-law, have considerable input

"A Funny Thing Happened").
[8]United Nations, *The World's Women 1970-1990*, 67-80, 108-11.
[9]Youssef, "Status and Fertility Patterns".
[10]Makhlouf Obermeyer, "Islam, Women, and Politics"; Moghadam, *Modernizing Women*.
[11]Makhlouf Obermeyer, op. cit.

into decision-making relating to the fertility rates of the younger women. This reinforces husbands' desires for sons and results in heavy pressures on women to bear large numbers of children.[12]

This is not to say that Muslim women never play an active part in determining their own family size. Although raised to find their chief identity as wives and mothers, their attitude towards their own fertility also depends on their personal socio-economic circumstances. These may be the chief determinants of whether women will prefer a small or a large family. For instance, despite increasing government pressure towards smaller families, Iranian national policies in relation to the family code threaten women's security and this means that many women find their interests better served by larger families.[13]

The mother-child relationship is usually the strongest personal relationship most people in traditional Muslim societies will have. In a patrilocal society, where girls leave their mothers at an early age to go to live in their husbands' houses and where deep affectionate relations between husband and wife are rarely permitted to develop, it is sons who provide their mothers not only with high status but with the strongest love relationship of their lives. In addition, male children ensure the continuation of the marriage, and guarantee a woman's future and support in old age. For these reasons, women may have as much of a stake in having many sons as other family members.[14]

Political circumstances also play a part both in gender relations and fertility rates. Increasing threats to the cultural identity of Muslim societies, in a world more and more dominated by modernization and poverty as a result of Western policies of development and the global market has put any movement towards gender equality under stress. The Islamic Revolution in Iran, the Iran-Iraq war, and Palestinian resistance to Israel, have all produced a considerable rise in birth rates.[15]

Despite an overall high level, Muslim birth rates are not as uniform either over space or over time as a cursory glance at the statistics would indicate. They display considerable regional variety, with urban/rural

---

[12]See the many case studies of women in Muslim countries, for instance Lajoinie, *Conditions de femmes en Afghanistan*; Mernissi, *Beyond the veil*; Al-Khayyat, *Honour and Shame*; Bouamama and Saoud, *Familles maghrébines*.
[13]Hoodfar, "Reforming from Within", 34-5.
[14]*Cf.* note 14.
[15]Makhlouf Obermeyer, op. cit., 51.

differences being especially marked. It should be understood that the factors that appear to unite Islamic cultures over different geo-political areas are only a part of the story. Each individual Muslim country has its own specificity and the determinants of family size in each one vary with the socio-economic and political circumstances.[16]

Population in Tajikistan

Islamic Traditions and Fertility Rates

Although the Muslim Republics of the Soviet Union have a modern history very different from that of other Muslim countries, these factors continue to play a part in fertility rates in Tajikistan. Children confer status, give material and moral support to their parents, and are considered to contribute to family prosperity.

Long removed from the official legal system, the *shari'ah* family-code still continues to influence daily life. Soviet destruction of the institutions of Islam has not achieved its aim of destroying religious values. However, it has meant that local religious leaders are often ignorant of much of Islamic doctrine, including its positive attitude towards family planning.

Relatively advanced material conditions, including over ninety-five per cent literacy rates among the age group twenty and over, and a higher level of female employment than most non-Soviet Muslim countries, as well as a legal code that encourages sexual equality, have not produced significant advances in gender relations in Tajikistan. Nor has universal education significantly raised skill levels among ordinary Tajik. At the time of independence most skilled jobs were still held by people of European ethnicities.

Young Tajik have their lives organized for them by their families, including in most cases choice of spouse. Fertility is highly esteemed, and brides are encouraged to become pregnant as soon as possible after the wedding. Until the recent civil war, Tajikistan had one of the world's highest birth rates and one of the fastest growing populations — twenty-six per cent

[16]Moghadam, op. cit., 3-5.

per annum in 1990.[17] Rural birth rates of ten to fifteen children per woman have not been uncommon and rates of twenty or more have been registered.

Fertility Rates Before World War II

In the late nineteenth century, Tajik women, much as women in other Muslim countries, were married off at very young ages by their parents and appeared to have little control over most of their lives. However, they were not as downtrodden as they appeared, and may well have been less oppressed than Russian peasant women of the time, with more control over their fertility.[18]

According to figures presented by Bushkov, immediately before the Russian conquest in the 1860s the annual natural increase of population in the region that now comprises northern Tajikistan was around 0.3 per cent. During the first decades thereafter population growth rose to 1.4-2.15 per cent *per annum*, apparently due to higher birth rates and lower mortality rates. By 1926 population growth had fallen and did not start to rise again in most areas until after 1959.[19] The 1926 Soviet census reflects a small number of children per Tajik family.[20]

The evidence for family size before the mid 1920s comes largely from Russian officials, scholars, and physicians, and from Western travellers in the area. According to them infant and child mortality were high, associated with early marriage and pregnancy, poor diet and hygiene, and epidemics of disease[21]. Infertility was estimated at around 7 per cent and due in part to wide-spread syphilis.[22] In northern Tajikistan, at least, it was not uncommon for women of the generation born between 1880 and 1900 to give birth between seventy and twenty times, with as few as nil to two

[17]Republic of Tajikistan, *Human Development Report*, 2.
[18]Harris, "Women of the Sedentary Population", 92.
[19]Although by 1931 the population of Leninabad Oblast was over three times as large as in 1870 (Bushkov, "The population of Northern Tajikistan", 225, 226, 230, 235).
[20]Jones and Grupp, *Modernization*, 98.
[21]Harris, op. cit.; Shishov, *Sarty*; *idem*, *Tadjiki*; Bushkov, op. cit. Some of these epidemics came in the wake of the Russians, for instance, measles. Hitherto unknown in Central Asia, its impact was deadly (reports in *Turkestanskie Vedomosti*, 6, 1824, 37). As late as the 1940s large numbers of young children in Tajikistan were dying from it and even today it is often fatal.
[22]Shishov, *Sarty*, 417, 464, 469; *idem*, *Tadjiki*, 315-6; Jones and Grupp, op. cit. 103-4.

children surviving into adulthood so that actual family size remained small. In the south families were also small at least up to World War II, very probably because of similarly high infant and child mortality rates.

Even without recourse to modern methods of contraception, Tajik were able to take control of their fertility. Women induced miscarriages by means of carrying heavy loads and through the use of herbs. Breast-feeding was used as a contraceptive measure. Before Tajik women began to work outside the home, they would remain with their children all day and would breast-feed for periods of several years, sometimes as many as five. It is uncertain whether parents deliberately limited the size of their families at that time, although it is possible that socio-economic circumstances may have made this desirable. Deliberate regulation of fertility in order to keep family size small in times of economic or other hardship was approved of by the Islamic jurists.[23]

A mid-1970s survey of the ideal family size among married women in rural Uzbekistan, culturally very close to Tajikistan, found that 44.5 per cent of women born at the turn of the century believed that a family should have "the more children the better"; the next most favoured answer was "as many as God gives", while only the youngest women had specific numbers in mind.[24] How many children the older women had given birth to and reared to adulthood was not stated.

Fertility Rates After World War II

Family size in much of Tajikistan remained small up to, and even after, World War II. Prior to the 1950s Soviet resources were never sufficient to provide much medical coverage to the women of Central Asia. After World War II there was a gradual slow advancement in the Soviet economy and by the mid 1960s medical facilities had greatly increased. Soviet statistics show a rise in the number of doctors in Tajikistan from 4.1 per 10,000 in 1940 to 14.9 in 1965, although this was still the lowest rate in the USSR.[25] Epidemics became fewer and less deadly, nutritional levels improved, and infant and child mortality fell. Starting from the 1940s, the huge population

[23]Musallam, op. cit., 118.
[24]Jones and Grupp, op. cit., 36-7.
[25]Ministry of Health, *The system of Public-Health Services*, 118.

losses in World War II, as well as in the famines and purges of the 1930s, together with small or even negative population growth in Russia, led the Soviet state to put pressure on families to have large numbers of children; to this end material inducements were offered to women with many children, including one-time and ongoing monetary payments,[26] medals, prizes, and a generally high status for "heroine mothers", those with ten or more children.

Benefits paid to mothers of large families, cheap housing, free education and health care, free plots of land for members of communal and state farms, and the low costs of essential food stuffs made it possible for most families to afford the economic costs of many children without too much hardship. Although the poorest families nevertheless had a low standard of living, it was still well above the average in most developing countries. In rural areas children provided labour for the private plot and for the house. There was too much work for one or two women to cope with; a constant supply of daughters and later daughters-in-law would greatly lessen the burden. This all meant that the more members a rural family had, the higher would be the living standard.[27]

Women's fertility was also affected by the use of chemicals in agriculture, which became widespread in the last few decades, especially in cotton production, the chief product of Tajikistan. Large amounts of chemicals banned in the West, including DDT and Butifos, were in use on the cotton fields well into the 1980s. These severely affected the health of the women who worked in the fields,[28] even causing lactation failure[29]. With greater use of women in employment outside the home and a lack of breast-feeding facilities for working women both in agricultural and non-agricultural employment, exacerbated by incorrect Soviet breast-feeding practices,[30] this played a part in the inadequacy of lactation as a method of birth-control.

[26]A woman could receive 41.2 per cent of the average annual wage at the birth of her tenth child provided she had at least two other young children (Heer and Bryden, "Family allowances", 156).

[27]Qvortrup, "Modernisation", 107.

[28]Carley, "The Price of the Plan", 10-3.

[29]According to gynaecologist Dr. S. H. Hakimova.

[30]These included separation of mother and child in hospitals, late and incorrect initiation of breast-feeding, and too early introduction of sugar water and juices, all of which affect lactation aversely (according to local UNICEF staff).

I do not have any data as to what sort of access women might have had to traditional medicine, which was largely driven underground by the state, but modern birth-control methods were very hard to come by in the Soviet Union. Abortion was the main method of fertility regulation for the majority of Soviet women.[31] Relatively few Muslims had recourse to this, since it was considered to be a sin. Even though many people believed that Islam also forbade the use of contraception, increasing numbers of women wanted to use the IUD, which had been introduced into Tajikistan around 1980. Women were complaining about constant pregnancy and begging doctors for help. Despite their pleas, the majority did not receive it, either because of insufficient supplies, or because of the refusal of their mothers-in-law and/or husbands to allow them to limit their fertility. Increasing numbers of women were giving birth at intervals of twelve to fifteen months, especially in rural areas.

The urban population had greater access to modern birth-control methods and did regulate their fertility to some extent, especially since the direct costs of large families were greater in the towns.[32] However, much of the urban population still had relatively large families of five to seven or more children. The Soviet system, coupled with institutionalized corruption, meant that personal favours remained as important as in pre-Soviet times and the more members a family had in useful positions and able to help relatives both materially and in more intangible ways, the more that family flourished, although in urban areas larger families did at times bring difficulties in providing sufficient food.

All the factors discussed above contributed to a sharp rise in fertility rates, which shows up in official statistics after 1959 in greatly increased family sizes.[33] By 1979 twenty-five per cent of Tajik families had seven or more children, the highest level in the USSR.[34]

By the time of independence in 1991, the ideology of large families was well established among the local population. There were strong pressures on women to give birth frequently, with those who did not often threatened with

---

[31]Kon, *Sexual Revolution.*

[32]Qvortrup, op. cit., 107.

[33]Craumer, "Agricultural change", 150-3.

[34]Djanko, "Sem'ya i byt narodov Sredney Azii i Kazakhstana", 477. The Northern Oblast of Leninabad had the highest growth rate in the USSR. Between 1959 and 1975 this was 2.9-3.1 per cent and between 1975 and 1986 4.8 per cent (Bushkov, op. cit., 235).

divorce, and women even vied with each other to see who could produce the most children the soonest.

Very different factors influenced the Russian-speaking inhabitants of Tajikistan. Although they tended to have larger families than the inhabitants of Russia, averaging two to three children rather than one to two, this was still much smaller than Tajik families, where only the elite had such small numbers. The reason for this lay partly in a different set of values and partly in their different socio-economic situation. The Russian-speaking population mostly lived in small flats in the cities and worked in industry. Almost all the women were employed in wage labour and this, together with their higher material expectations, meant that any advantages of larger families were outweighed by the disadvantages, government payments for large families notwithstanding. Their different cultural ideology put less value on large numbers of children and more on providing each child with high levels of education and skills and they had frequent recourse to abortion and contraception.

During the last years of the Soviet Union, the government began to be concerned about the rate of population increase in Tajikistan. Despite increasing levels of un- and/or underemployment, living standards remained high enough not to force the great majority of the population out of their native rural areas. Around 81 per cent of all Tajik remained in their place of birth.[35] This meant that the high population rates in Tajikistan could not be made to compensate for the falling rates in Russia; there was little migration from areas of high fertility and low employment opportunities to ones of low fertility and high opportunities, but less attractive living conditions.

Since independence the situation has changed drastically. The breakup of the centralized Soviet economic system had a devastating effect on the already poor Tajik economy and the Civil War of 1992-3 destroyed it almost completely. The emigration of the vast majority of skilled workers from the Republic has hastened the destruction of the little Tajik industry there was.

Under these circumstances, many Tajik men have left their villages, and even the Republic, in search of work. Male rural-urban migration has increased very significantly and even female migration has risen. Both men and women in the poorer families are desperate to limit their fertility.

[35]Djanko, op. cit. 483.

Although their ideal number of children remains between four to six,[36] most young couples know they will not be able to cope with so many without a large improvement in their financial situation and that realistically they should have no more than two[37]. Under these conditions the birth rate is dropping and will continue to do so even further, especially if adequate access to contraceptives can be supplied. Only those families whose economic situation has remained relatively strong or who have benefited from the new situation, can afford to have large families.

Conclusion

Many questions remain unanswered, in particular in regard to the situation prior to 1926. Was there really such a sharp difference in natural population increase after the Russian conquest? If so, what were the causes? Was it related to medical care, dietary changes, or cultural influences? Is the drop in population growth prior to 1926[38] only the result of famine, war, and the generally chaotic situation in the post-revolutionary period? What other influences were at work?

The population explosion in Tajikistan after 1959 appears to have been because of improved medical services, increased prosperity, material incentives for the production of children, and failure of lactation to regulate fertility together with a lack of modern contraceptive methods. However, traditions related to Islam - including high fertility rates as a way to attain high status,[39] coupled with strong male/female control - clearly also made a major contribution and are partly responsible for the great difference between family size in the Tajik and European communities.

It is not clear how the post-Soviet period will affect female status and women's capacity to control their own lives. However, the pressure on women to bear large families has been reduced. The sudden big drop in material circumstances is producing radical change. In the present political

---

[36]Young men want significantly larger numbers of children than young women. This tendency also appears among older married couples (according to research carried out under the auspices of UNICEF in 1995).

[37]Although there is a Tajik saying that two children is no children.

[38]Bushkov, op. cit., 226.

[39]I was told that in order to achieve high political office, for instance as a government minister, it is almost an unwritten requirement to have at least four children.

climate it is impossible to judge how much Islamization in Tajikistan will increase in the near future, what influence this may have on views on family size, and what the likelihood is of the *sharī'ah* family code being re-incorporated into the official legal code. At present Islamization is rather limited except in very small parts of the country and under Rakhmonov's government the republic is set on remaining secular. Nevertheless, the fact that status continues to be bound up with fertility is evident from the fact that those families who think they can afford it, and especially the *nouveaux riches*, still want large numbers of children. However, in a non-socialist future where past levels of reasonable subsistence for the majority are unlikely to return, there is going to be a contest between the traditional value of children as status symbols and support in old age, and modern calculations of the costs of rearing and educating them.

Today families are confused as to how many children they actually want. Some men from very poor families still insist on their wives not using birth control but most have realized they simply cannot continue to produce children without the most basic resources even for feeding them. Year by year it is becoming harder to find these. The better off are beginning to realize that even for them a small family means greater prosperity. The demand for contraceptives is greatly on the increase.

There remains a great deal of research to be done in regard to questions of fertility rates in Tajikistan. It is especially important to carry out research into the attitudes of different social groups towards ideal family size and the use of birth control and to look at who is responsible for decisions affecting the real numbers of children produced and how these decisions are reached.

The demographic trends displayed in Tajikistan over the last decades would appear to confirm Makhlouf Obermeyer's contention that Islam is far from the main factor in high fertility rates. Moreover, the fact that Islamic doctrine is not opposed to fertility regulation, some schools even accepting abortion, means that small-family policies can seamlessly co-exist with the strongly Islamist politics of such a country as, for instance, Iran. It is the social traditions that have grown up round Islam rather than the religion itself that have produced the tendencies to large families in Muslim societies. Such traditions are constantly evolving and respond strongly to socio-economic and political factors, which thus play a very major part in how Muslim populations perceive their fertility needs.

Part Three

Identity

11 The *Mullā* and the State

Dynamics of Islamic Religious Scholars and Their Institutions in Contemporary Pakistan[1]

Jamal Malik

Introduction

Dealing with Islamic society and its educational institutions, the importance of the role of the state is ineluctable, since it is the state that has had a major impact on society in general and on traditional institutions in particular. This is especially true with regard to traditional Muslim education as it has developed, both in content and form, during the last few decades. In this framework, an enduring struggle can be observed between reform-Islam as perceived by state authorities and Muslim avant-gardists and Islamists, on the one hand, and the upholders of Islamic traditions and targets of change, for example the religious scholars, the *'ulamā'* and *mashāyikh*, on the other.

The State and the Reform of Religious Education

The contemporary reform tradition goes back to at least the nineteenth century, when, in the wake of colonial penetration, especially after the upheavals of 1857, the dichotomy between "modernity" and "traditionality" was born[2] and some North-Indian Muslims launched efforts to reorganize Muslim education. Consequently, new and different schools of thought emerged, appealing to specific social groups and tied to particular regions, thereby adding to the religious and societal complexity of South Asia. The

---

[1] The following text is based on Malik, *Colonialization of Islam* and *idem*, "Dynamics among Traditional Religious Scholars".
[2] I do not want to go into this *orientalist* discussion here since a wealth of material has been written on this shift during and after colonial expansion; see Rothermund (ed.), *Aneignung und Selbstbehauptung*.

Deobandis, Barelwis, Ahl-i Ḥadīth, and Nadwah al-'Ulamā' are among the best known of these trends and schools of thought (*maktab-i fikr*), not to mention the folk-religious and mystical traditions.[3]

Although in independent India the institutions of these schools of thought were more or less untouched by the secular state, in Pakistan after 1947 the situation was quite different: political leaders have always been interested in controlling these autonomous communities, since *madāris* (Islamic schools; sg. *madrasah*) traditionally play a crucial role in providing knowledge, and one also imbued with cultural and political significance.

State encroachments in Pakistan started even before Ayub Khan, but were thrust to the fore with his nationalization of religious endowments and schools during the sixties. The proposed institutional affiliation was parallelled by curricular reforms, which engendered a feeling of deficiency and opposition among religious scholars and their students. It was in this context that religious leaders established umbrella organizations of religious schools just prior to the proclamation of the West Pakistan Waqf Property Ordinance 1961. The main tasks of these umbrella organizations were to organize the schools, to reform their curricula, and to expand their range of lessons with modern subjects as well as to standardize the system of examinations and, of course, to counter state power and its nationalization policy collectively.

With the advent of so-called Islamization in the 1970s, state activities touching traditional educational institutions increased in effectiveness. As in other Muslim countries, this has resulted in a new dimension of curricular reform and has ushered in a new phase of institutionalization among traditional establishments. After all, for the first time it was envisaged that the diplomas of religious schools would be recognized. To be sure, their formal recognition was subject to certain conditions: instead of the eight years of the traditional curriculum,[4] religious scholars henceforth were to offer a reformed and modernized curriculum which would last sixteen years. In doing so they would be obliged to follow the suggestions of the "National

---

[3]Compare Metcalf, *Islamic Revival*; Malik: "Muslim Identities".

[4]The traditional eight-year curriculum or *dars-i niẓāmī*, developed in eighteenth century, was not primarily religious but secular and tied to the needs of the functional elite, but had undergone several changes in the nineteenth century rendering it into a purely religious syllabus (compare Haque, "Muslim Religious Education").

Committee on Religious Schools" established in 1979.[5] In this way these institutions were to be modernized, simultaneously legitimizing state policy according to Islamist principles, i.e. on the basis of the concept of knowledge presented by Muslim intellectuals in Mecca at the first "World Conference on Islamic Education" in 1977.[6] The idea of a reformed and universalizing Islam was at loggerheads with the concepts of most of the *'ulamā'*, and this inevitably produced a reaction to these suggestions. Nevertheless, because of the insistent demands by and support of the government — i.a. through zakah (*zakāh* - compulsory alms) money (see below) — and the ultimate promise of equivalence of degrees of religious schools and those of national universities in 1981/82, *'ulamā'* were gradually won over to the potentially positive effects that the Islamization policy would have for them. What they really did, however, was not to subject the curriculum to a radical change. They merely added subjects from the formal primary education system to their traditional curriculum and to gild the gingerbread the English denominations of certificates were given an Arabic nomenclature. Thus, the duration of education was extended from eight to sixteen years, grades one to eight and nine to sixteen representing parts of totally separate systems of education: the first one secular, complemented by "Reading the Koran" and "Basics of Islam", as offered in formal schools at present; the second part continuing the traditional *dars-i nizāmī*. The committee's demands, which were aimed to achieve an integrationist curriculum, were therefore inserted delicately into their new educational courses by the umbrella organizations, and simultaneously the *'ulamā'* seized their chance to show their ability to gain official recognition by merely making minor alterations, thereby finding themselves in a position to exercize increasing influence on the secular sector.

Theoretically, these degrees, once recognized, would open up 3economic mobility and possibilities for promotion to graduates. Laudable though this may seem, as we will see below, no heed was taken of how and where the soon to be officially examined army of *mullā*s would be integrated into the job market and this shortsighted planning rapidly created considerable problems.

---

[5]See Government of Pakistan, *Riport-i qaumī kamūī barā-ye dīnī madāris-i Pākistān.*
[6]See Khan: *Education and Society*, 126 ff.

Parallel to these administrative and curricular reform measures, the economic situation of religious schools was changed for the better by means of money disbursed through the central and provincial zakat funds set up by the government in 1980: ten per cent of the alms thus collected through zakat-deducting agencies was set aside for religious education, if curricular reform and political loyalty were complied with. The additional financial resources enhanced the budgets of religious schools considerably, constituting as much as one third of their annual income, which was placed exclusively at the disposal of the heads of the schools, the *'ulamā'*. Inexorably, these additional receipts produced new expectations and created new patterns of consumption, which, however, could only be satisfied were political loyalty to be demonstrated.

The Anticipated and Unanticipated Effects of Educational Reform

As a result of official interventions with regard to financial support, the formal recognition of degrees and curricular reform, a new dimension can be discerned in the mobility of religious scholars and their centres of learning. At the same time, the respective umbrella organizations have assumed a more formal nature. This prompts the inclination to speak of an expanding indigenous infrastructure which has already produced far-reaching consequences. Firstly, the prospect of zakat basically resulted in a mushroom growth of religious schools, mostly in rural regions. Reacting to this, the government has tried to stem the tide of new *madāris* by implementing different measures, resulting again in new problems. Secondly, the number of the graduates from higher religious schools — not to speak of students in religious schools in general — is at present constantly on the rise, as these institutions now also offer a formal primary level education and their diplomas are officially recognized. Thirdly, the recent process of integration, as an inherent part of the Islamization policy, has fostered a new phase of institutionalization among umbrella organizations so that the number of schools affiliated has increased tremendously (growth rates up to 700 per cent in five years only). Fourthly, the data available on religious schools and their education also shed light on their spatial distribution and the social and regional background of their students: Deobandis in North Western Frontier Province and Baluchistan, Punjab, and some in Sindh; Barelwis in rural areas, where the cult of holy men is most popular (Sindh and Punjab); Shi'ites in the Northern Areas and in some districts of the Punjab dominated by folk religion; Ahl-i Ḥadīth in commercial centres and important internal markets; Jamā'at-i islāmī in urban and politically sensitive areas. Thus, each school of thought has its own reserved area, be it rural, urban, trade-oriented, or even strategic.

This clear — if not exclusive — spatial distribution of schools of thought is analogous to the socio-economic structure of the respective geographical regions. The explanation for the distributive patterns of religious schools therefore lies in the social substratum of the corresponding schools of thought or organizations. The Deobandi, Barelwi, and Shi'ite candidates for graduation may be understood above all as representatives of the traditional sector. Accordingly, they are primarily to be found in traditionally structured areas. As religious schools have some representatives in intermediary social sectors as well — i.e. in sectors economically, socially, and normatively situated between modern (post-colonial) and traditional (pre-colonial and colonial) systems —, they are also settled in zones with a certain degree of official control, such as urban Sindh or other modernized districts, for example the northern Punjab. This is true of members of the Ahl-i Ḥadīth and of the Jamā'at-i islāmī in particular. Hence, a heterogeneity of Islam practised in Pakistan is traceable in regional patterns. This geographical distribution of different schools of thought, which naturally involves political power, has promoted the regionalism of Islam, which challenges and interferes with the enforcement of universalizing normative Islam as is propagated by the avant-gardists and the government.

In the wake of the recent formalization and reform of religious schools — in reaction to the Islamization policy — an increasing trans-provincial north-south migration from rural to urban areas, in particular to Karachi, can be observed. This is a sign of the degree of spatial mobility among the young religious scholars. That students from specific regions look for schools and teachers who comply with their cultural perceptions and ethnic affiliations indubitably fosters the search for corresponding institutions and hence creates identity-giving sub-structures in an urban surrounding which may otherwise be perceived as alien and often hostile. The migrated scholars-to-be now gather in the metropolis and potentially contribute to conflicts that are often religiously and ethnically motivated. The fact that the number of religious schools and their students has grown in a spectacular way in urban, but particularly in rural areas also suggests that cities are not the only locations which have become sites of increasing conflicts. The hinterland has also been inexorably drawn into the sphere of religiously legitimized battles. In other words, the Islamization policy has promoted the institutionalization of different groups, on the one hand, and it has fostered their politicization and even radicalization, on the other hand. Contemporary regimes are neither able nor willing to integrate *'ulamā'* in a productive way, and this marginalizes them even more and causes an even more potent friction within society. The ensuing perspective is not too bright: following the tremendous numerical increase in religious scholars and their centres of learning, a great potential for conflict has taken root because young theologians now pour onto the labour market, particularly in urban areas. For tens of thousands formally recognized religious students, whose degrees are now equivalent to the MA in Arabic/Islamiyat, there is little prospect of employment. So far, in all reform measures, corresponding planning with respect to the labour market has been neglected by government officials and Islamists. Places of employment for these *'ulamā'* are neither available in the courses offered for Koranic studies in formal schools, courses that should underline the promised Islamization of the country, nor in recently established reading circles and mosque-schools that should improve the poor literacy rate. The reason for this lack of planning lies mainly in the prejudice of the bureaucracy itself. The advisor on religious education criticized:

> Reservations were voiced by various officials of the provincial Departments of Education about recruiting `Maulanas´ for the schools on the suspicion that they would divide the students on the basis of their own preferences for a particular `Maktab-i-Fikr´.

He hastened to add that

> these suspicions, however, were proved in the field to be ill-founded. Such suspicions should never be allowed to affect the making of educational policy at any level.[7]

Only in respect to Arabic courses, which have been promoted since 1979, do some young scholars find jobs. These courses are offered first and foremost to Pakistani overseas workers in the Middle East, and they primarily reflect pragmatic financial motives. On the other hand, the military promotes

---

[7]Ali, "Draft Chapter on Islamic Education", 6.

religious scholars. In the medium term, this may lead to new values and structures in this institution, which continues to stand entrenched in the colonial tradition. The new warrior-scholars may fall back on the experience they gained during the guerrilla war in Afghanistan.

With the official support of religious scholars in the 1980s and even 1990s, the political strength of representatives of the traditional sector has increased unmistakably. If these tendencies last — and there is no reason to suggest the opposite — the Islamization policy, or better the politics of de-traditionalization, will ultimately force the politically dominant sector to rethink its own positions. Furthermore, in the near future, the centre may be pushed on the political defensive, a position it could overcome only by violence and in increasing its delimination from the rest of the society. This danger is most rampant when indigenous social and educational structures, such as endowments, alms, and religious schools, still extant and mostly functioning, cannot be adequately replaced and the integration of thousands of unemployed *mullā*s who have access to the masses does not succeed quickly. The Islamization policy could therefore boomerang — "The spirits which they conjured up ...." The conflicts in the rural hinterland, particularly during the last few years, in fact point to a larger encompassing crisis. This crisis is the result of a policy which the Islamists in particular have not taken into account, a policy based on ill-considered and misconceived modernistic perceptions. As a consequence, the bearers and protagonists of different Islamic and Islamist traditions take an isolationist and radical position, a development also taking place in other Muslim regions.[8]

In view of the cultural, religious, economic, and infrastructural potential of traditional institutions in general and religious schools in particular, those who run these establishments may in the long run be able to make a constructive contribution to indigenous developmental processes that may be shaped to fit the needs of the local population. In this way, the very important connection between official ideology, for example Islam, and the social mass base, for example religious scholars, could ultimately be established. This would, however, most probably imply that the *mullā* and his education would not only become the prime representative and locus of the people but would also be present in transnational forums and would therefore determine national and international politics. The coming of the

---

[8]For further readings consult Eickelman and Piscatori, *Muslim Politics.*

mullā will have to be taken seriously in modern democratic states. Indeed, the Talibanization of Afghanistan and the increase of religiously legitimated violence in South Asia are the first outcomes of this tussle.

Religious Identity and Mass Education[1]

Muhammad Khalid Masud

Introduction

Mass communication is turning human societies into a global community. Mass education, in conjunction with print technology, were expected to promote pluralism in this community as there were apprehensions that purely technological societies might lose diversity and the ethical and moral values necessary to human civilization. Dale Eickelman observes that mass higher education has certainly raised some basic questions about self and society, including questions about the place and role of religion in it.[2] It leads to the objectification of religion in people's consciousness. Consequently, it has often given rise to religious activism, generally called fundamentalism. Mass higher education, Eickelman argues, began in the Muslim world in 1950s, but its effects began to be felt in 1980s, particularly in terms of reshaping the concepts of religious identity and authority among groups which generally have come to be known as fundamentalists.

Gilles Kepel also notes a rise of religious activism not only among contemporary Muslim but also among Christian and Jewish societies.[3] He also finds linkages between religious activism and mass higher education. For instance, with reference to Christian societies in the USA, Kepel finds a noticeable increase in the student enrolment among the religious activists, e.g. a ninety-five per cent increase in US evangelical schools between 1971 and 1978.[4] The religious activist groups have also founded religious universities in their respective societies.

Among Muslims, we also find religious activists promoting mass education to reinforce religious identity. The recent growth of educational

[1]The author wishes to dedicate this text to Rev. Jan Slomp and other Dutch scholars who have given a serious thought to the problem of education for Muslim children in the Netherlands.
[2]Eickelman, "Mass Higher Education".
[3]Kepel, *Revanche de Dieu*.
[4]Op. cit., 174.

institutions of higher learning like the International Islamic Universities in Pakistan and Malaysia are illustrations of the Muslim quest for identity through mass education. Disagreeing with the scholars who describe these phenomena as a "revival" of the old forms of religious understanding, as claimed by the religious activists as well, Eickelman regards them as distinctively modern developments.[5] Although these institutions have not been able to replace the old forms of religious understanding completely,[6] yet they have certainly introduced some modern dimensions to mass education. Still, Muslim mass education has not moved towards an open pluralist world view.

This text argues that the continued emphasis on the theological basis of religious identity by modern movements for mass religious education is largely responsible for the faltering progress of a pluralist world view. It has rather given way to religious extremism, and sometimes even to violence. An ideal mass education should aim at an appreciation of religious diversity by means of widening awareness and information about others, at least immediate neighbours. Emphasis on an exclusionist approach to religious identity comes from a sense of insecurity and fear of others. It is symptomatic of a lack of self-confidence. This may be explained with reference to Islamic history.

The Historical Background: *Madrasah*s and Religious Identity

The establishment of large networks of *madrasah*s, especially by Niẓām al-Mulk al-Ṭūsī, a Saljuqid wazir during the Abbasid caliphate in the eleventh century of the Christian era, is the earliest example of mass education in Islamic history. Until recently, most historians explained the foundation of these *madrasah*s from the perspective of religious identity. They argued that these institutions were established on a wider scale to counter the rising Isma'ili *da'wah* (religious propaganda), the establishment of the Fatimid state, and the spread of several other "heresies". George Makdisi, who has studied this phenomenon in depth in his outstanding work *Rise of Colleges*, refutes this explanation. He argues that these *madrasah*s were founded for

[5]Eickelman, op. cit., 643.
[6]Op. cit., 652.

the teaching of law, not theology. Theology was not part of the curriculum; it was instead an extra-curricular activity.

It is significant to note why in this example of mass education, law, rather than theology, was chosen as focus. This may be explained briefly.

Identity in Muslim societies is still defined from several perspectives. Although family, place of origin, language are also markers of identity, yet religion remained the most common denominator. Muslim religious identity has been defined on more than one basis. Besides sectarian denominations shaped by theology, adherence to various Sufi orders and to different schools of law also defined a person's religious identity. Thus religious identity was always pluriform. It is quite common to find the description of a religious scholar in, for instance, the following terms: an Ash'arite in theology, a Malikite in Islamic law, and a Qadirite in Sufism. Sufism and Islamic law differed quite significantly from theology in their conception of religious identity. Islamic law encouraged and honoured difference of opinion. A science of disputation (*'ilm al-khilāf*) was developed and made part of Islamic legal training. The different schools of Islamic law that resulted from this *khilāf* regarded diversity as blessing, not deviation. The jurists respected their opponents and regarded their doctrines as alternate views. A doctrine of *Murā'ah al-khilāf* (concession to the disputed doctrine) actually asked the jurists to accommodate opposite views. *Taqlīd* (adherence to a school of law) defined religious identity from this perspective, but even in its extreme form it did not invoke *takfīr* (declaration of heresy) of the opponents, as the theological definition did. Similarly the Sufi identity was also not exclusive. In fact a person could belong to more than one Sufi order at one and the same time. The theological approach, however, does not allow diversity in religious identity.

Now let us return to the mass education *madrasah*s in the Abbasid period. The question is that when theology was not included in the curriculum, why was it introduced as an extra-curricular activity.

The usual explanation is that some Abbasid caliphs like Ma'mūn patronized the Mu'tazilah and the Greek sciences. The conservative *'ulamā'* were opposed to this. They believed that free thought would weaken the faith as well as the unity of the Muslim community. The Ash'arites, another group of theologians, fought against the Mu'tazilah and eventually won the battle. The Saljuqids were admirers of this group and invited them to teach at the *madrasah*s. There is some truth in this explanation, because the Saljuqids were quite worried about the rise of heresies in the community. Plausible though it may be, historically the explanation is difficult to substantiate. First, the Saljuqids were apprehensive of groups like the Karramiyyah, the Isma'ilis, and the Fatimids and the Ash'arites were not refuting these "heresies". Second, as Makdisi has very convincingly argued, the free thought of groups like the Mu'tazilah was defeated by the conservative Hadith movements headed by Hanbalite scholars, not by the Ash'arites. Third, the triumph of conservative theology took place long before the rise of *madrasah*s.

Theology (*'ilm al-kalām*) came into prominence in Muslim society during the encounter of the traditionalists with the Mu'tazilah, who tried to impose rationalist theology with the support of the Abbasid caliphs al-Ma'mūn, al-Mu'taṣim and al-Wāthiq in the ninth century. The traditionalists resisted this imposition and finally succeeded in earning caliphal support for themselves in the eleventh century. An official orthodox declaration of faith, "Qadiri creed", was issued by the Abbasid caliph, al-Qādir bi'llāh. In this process, theology, or polemics about heresy and orthodoxy, became a prominent subject. Makdisi argues that even jurists like al-Shāfi'ī were compelled to develop a juridical theology to defend their legal position.[7] Prominent theologians were invited to give public lectures at the *madrasah*s. They spoke against heresies and expounded Islamic doctrines about religious identities. Deviations from such defined identities were regarded as heresy and punished. In later periods, prominence was given to theology as the "queen of sciences" when scholarly disputation was developed as a science. The inclusion of theology, particularly as an authoritative science in defining religious identity, had far reaching effects on the subsequent development of Muslim education.

The first target of the theological sciences was philosophy. Ironically, one may compare it with the situation today. Philosophy was a European science introduced by translation from Greek philosophy. Traditional scholars were apprehensive of the introduction of Greek sciences during the Abbasid period. They believed that these sciences were harmful to Muslim religious identity. They feared that the Philosophers and the Mu'tazilah who favoured the teaching of these sciences symbolized a basic change in Muslim outlook. One way to counter these sciences was to exclude their practitioners from teaching by classifying them as non- or ir-religious. That explains why the "science of the classification of sciences" became so important in this

---

[7]Makdisi, "The Juridical Theology of Shāfi'ī".

period. A large number of books was written on this subject. In these books, sciences were divided into traditional (*naqliyyah)* and rational (*'aqliyyah*), sacred (religious, *dīniyyah*) and profane (worldly, *dunyāwiyyah*). Philosophy was a *foreign* science, invariably contrasted with traditional sciences. Seyyed Hossein Nasr observes that these attempts to classify sciences, which became themselves an independent science, were in fact a response to the challenge of accommodating or rejecting these sciences in the Muslim educational system.[8] Al-Ghazālī and others even used the classification to exclude from the curricula certain sciences such as philosophy, mathematics, and physics, which were also sometimes called the rational sciences. In this context it is important to note that even with the division of sciences into religious and non-religious, there were no separate *madrasah*s exclusively for religious education. Later in the sixteenth and seventeenth centuries, under the influence of Iranian metaphysicians philosophy, physics, astronomy, mathematics, and so forth also came to be taught in the religious *madrasah*s in India, Iran, Central Asia, and Turkey. Theology (*'ilm al-ilāhī* or *ilāhiyyāt*) became a regular subject in the *madrasah* curriculum in later periods, and, as will be shown below, it tended to dominate the *dīnī madāris* curricula in Pakistan.

Muslim education came into contact once again with Europe during the colonial period. Again similar apprehensions led Muslims to focus on the issue of religious identity and theology. The Western educational system was introduced by Christian missions or was framed by European utilitarians and liberals, who imposed it with the help of state authority. The situation was comparable in a certain sense with that of the Mu'tazilah in the past. The traditionalists resisted but this time they opted for a different solution: separation of religious education from the main stream. We need not go into the details of the bitter controversy between the supporters and opponents of the introduction of mass education on the European pattern. It is enough to emphasize the fact that the apprehension of the traditional scholars was based on their fear of losing their religious identity in the modern educational system. Their focus and concern for religious identity have led them to resist the introduction of modern sciences and to maintain that *madrasah*s should be exclusively for religious education. Although some *madrasah*s later introduced certain modern sciences, they remained very conscious of the issue of religious identity. In order to safeguard it, they paid more attention

[8]Nasr, *Islamic Sciences*, 14.

to the teaching of theology. The emphasis on theology, initially aiming at opposition to modernity, materialism, and secularism, gradually narrowed it down to sectarian polemics. This will be elaborated with particular reference to Pakistan.

The Case of Pakistan: Division and Exclusivism in Religious Education

At present, several educational systems are co-existent in Pakistan. *Dīnī madāris* (lit. schools of religion), one system of education, are controlled privately by various religious groups and stand out as a separate category. Other educational institutions, classified as English medium schools, are also mostly private. Another category, Urdu medium schools, are mostly run by the government. Besides *dīnī madāris* that are exclusively religious institutions, religious education is also imparted in other schools under the name of *islāmiyyāt*. This subject deals with the creeds, rituals, history, and moral teachings of Islam. It is taught both as an elective and a compulsory subject in schools and colleges. The syllabus of *islāmiyyāt* is divided into three parts: Sunnite, Shi'ite, and common. Students study the common part together and other parts are taught separately by Sunnite and Shi'ite teachers. Efforts to unify the syllabus have not succeeded.

The situation in the *dīnī madāris* can be illustrated by the case of Dar al-Ulum [*dār al-'ulūm*] Deoband, founded in 1867. It distinguished itself by its stress on financial independence from the government as well as on the exclusion of modern sciences from its curricula. Nevertheless it adopted several modern pedagogical methods, such as written examinations, syllabi, classroom teaching, attendance registers for students, and annual convocations. It also benefited from the experience of educationists like Mawlānā Zulfaqār 'Alī, Mawlānā Mamlūk 'Alī and others, who had held positions in the British educational system or had taught in the Arabic College, Delhi, a modern college established on European patterns by the British. In an address in 1874, Mawlānā Qāsim Nanawtawī, the first patron-principal of the Deoband school, explained why Deoband did not favour including modern sciences: "Education in modern sciences is progressing as there are abundant official schools established by the government, to the extent that even the old sciences did not enjoy such success previously in the days of the sultans. However, the traditional sciences (*'ulūm naqliyyah*), i.e., purely religious and Islamic sciences, are declining in a manner that they never did before. Under these circumstances, the (British) subjects found it redundant to institute modern sciences in the curricula of the madaris".[9]

In his history of the Deoband school, Maḥbūb Rizwī explains that, besides the political issues, the major reason for the establishment of the school was that the political decline and syncretist trends in Muslim society in the nineteenth century had corrupted the beliefs and practices of Muslims and it was necessary to establish institutions to educate people in religious matters. The teaching of *'aqā'id* (dogmatics) and *kalām*, and defence of religion and spread of Islam through missionary efforts and education therefore constituted the core of the programme of the school.[10] Naturally, the question of *maslak* (theological position) became extremely significant to the school. Several official statements were made on this point. Rizwī sums up this position as follows: The *maslak* of the Dar al-Ulum Deoband shall be that of *Ahl al-sunnah wa-al-jamā'ah*, Hanafite school [of Islamic law] and the way of its revered founders Mawlānā Muḥammad Qāsim Nanawtawī and Mawlānā Rashīd Aḥmad Gangohī.[11] *Dastūr asāsī*, the basic document of the institution, laid down the following rule: "All members and associates of the Dar al-Ulum are obliged to abide by this *maslak*. No employee of the Dar al-Ulum or its student shall be allowed to take part in any association, institution or public meeting if this participation were harmful to the interest or the *maslak* of the Dar al-Ulum".[12] Deoband established a *Dār al-iftā* ("House for Fatwa Issuance") for the guidance of the people on religious issues. The school also began publishing books and journals. A network of *madrasah*s promoting the Deoband *maslak* was later established all over South Asia.[13] Other religious institutions also developed on the same pattern, stressing on adherence to their respective *maslak*.

According to the report prepared by a National Committee for Religious Madaris in 1979, among the 1745 religious institutions, 354 belonged to the Deobandi *maslak* and 267 to the Barelwi, 126 to Ahl-i Ḥadīth, and forty-one' to the Shi'ite *maslak* (National Committee 1979, 61). Jamal Malik provides the following table showing the number of *madrasah*s according to these different *maslak*s in Pakistan and their growth during 1960-1984.

[9]Murad, "Dīnī madāris ka-niẓām-i taʻlīm", 24.
[10]Rizwi, "Tārikh dār al-ʻulūm Deoband", 57.
[11]Op. cit., 144.
[12]Op. cit., 144.
[13]Metcalf, *Islamic Revival in British India*.

Table 1

***Madrasahs* in Pakistan**

Year / *Maslaks*	1960	1971	1979	1983/ 1984	1984
Deobandi	233	292	354	945	1097
Barelwis	98	123	267	557	not available
Ahl-i Ḥadīth	55	47	126	56	76
Shi'ah	18	15	41	116	?
Jamā'at Islāmī	13	41	57	107	?
Not Categorized	55	390	900	?	?

Source: Malik, *Islamisierung in Pakistan*, 279.

Each of these schools teaches not only the religious catechesis of its own *maslak*, but also prepares for the debate and refutation of heretical sects, which often means *maslaks* other than their own. For instance the syllabus approved by the Deobandi Board (*Wafāq al-madāris al-'arabiyyah*) includes in its curriculum refutation of the following as a subject: Westernism, Socialism, Qadiyanism, Barelwism, Rafidism (Shi'ism), Ahl-i Ḥadīth, Christianity, Zionism and so forth. The Barelwi Board has recommended *al-Dawlah al-makkiyyah* and *al-Mu'taqad al-mustanad*, two polemical books written to refute the Deobandi and the Ahl-i Ḥadīth *maslaks* (National Committee 1979,124). There have been repeated attempts by various governments to unify the syllabi and curricula of religious education, but these could not succeed because, firstly, the *madrasahs* regard all such attempts as interference by the government in religious matters; secondly, most of them insist that by introducing modern sciences the religious character of these *madrasahs* would be eliminated. The government of Pakistan has not been able to unify the syllabus for religious education for the Sunnites and the Shi'ites in the regular schools directly controlled by the government either. Consequently, the students become sensitized to their religious denominations quite early in their education.

This exclusionist conception of religious education is clarified even more sharply in a report, *Na'ī Ta'līmī Pālīsī* prepared by Mufti Muḥammad Shāfi' and Mawlānā Yūsuf Bannūrī. This report also formulated recommendations for the Christian education in Pakistan. The report recommends special, separate schools for Christian pupils. Their syllabi, curricula, and system should accord to the general Pakistani governmental educational institutions. These schools would not be allowed to admit Muslim boys and girls. These institutions should be free to teach Christian beliefs, but they should not be allowed to condemn, refute, or ridicule Islam and its teachings in their books, class rooms, and educational activities.[14] These recommendations reflect an exclusionist concept of religious education, which does not allow the pupils of different faiths or sects to study together. In certain respects we find this exclusionist concept vehemently opposed in the Swann Report (1985) in Great Britain.

The Case of Great Britain: The Secular Approach to Religious Education

In Great Britain, Muslims called for separate schools for Muslim education, voluntarily aided (by private Muslim funds) and within the general British educational framework, but independent to frame their own curricula and syllabi for Muslim education. The freedom to give and receive religious education in Great Britain was guaranteed by the Education Act of 1944. The conception of religious education among Muslims in Great Britain has passed through several stages of transformation. Until approximately the 1970s, freedom of religious education was understood as the right of parents to demand school authorities for *ḥalāl* diet, separate classes for physical education for boys and girls, the parent's right to withdraw their children from sex education, music, dance and swimming classes, as well as the removal from assemblies for religious worship. They could also request for alternate religious education. It appears that religious education was defined in this period in quite simple terms that confused aspects of religious and cultural identity. It is significant to note that according to a survey of the 1970s, 47 per cent of Muslim parents in Great Britain agreed that Christianity influenced their children by attending assemblies at school with a Christian service, while 41 per cent disagreed with the statement. Among the pupils 50 per cent disagreed with the statement. One issue on which the overwhelming majority (83 per cent) of Asian parents agreed was single sex

---

[14]Shāfiʿ, *Naʾī Taʿlīmī Pālīsī.*

241

schools.[15] The categories of investigation also indicate that religious identity was conceived in the British society in terms of ethnic identity. Consequently religious education was perceived as a means to preserve this identity. This objective could be achieved by supplementing regular education by establishing "mosque *madrasahs*" on the pattern of Sunday schools.

Teachers belonging to the particular faith founded mosque *madrasahs*, as supplementary schools for religious education, to provide religious instructions. A survey conducted in 1982-83 found parents generally confused about this arrangement. A total of 50 per cent of parents found mosque *madrasah* education unsatisfactory, 30 per cent considered it sufficient. The researchers found that parents had different criteria for judging satisfactory religious education. The parents were mostly illiterate; the majority did not know English. Those who found the mosque *madrasah* system satisfactory were happy that their children could recite the Koran fluently. Those who were dissatisfied complained that the *madrasahs* and Islamic centres belonged to different sects or communities. A total of 80 per cent of parents complained that these schools created confusion in the minds of children.[16] The most important problems with the regular British schools, as pointed out by the majority of parents, again reflected a narrow perception of religious education. Among the 300 parents interviewed, the majority (165) counted food as the most important problem, while fifty mentioned prayers at assembly, forty-five swimming and sports, and eighteen misconceptions about Islam as crucial issues.

Dissatisfied with the concept of supplemental religious education in 1980s, Muslims in Great Britain called for separate Muslim schools. J. Mark Halstead has studied the issue in detail.[17] His comprehensive analysis of the literature on this issue in Great Britain, including the Swann Report of 1985, covers almost all aspects of the issue. The Swann Committee examined the issue in the framework of three concepts: cultural pluralism, cultural relativism, and multiculturalism. The Swann report supported cultural pluralism and considered separate Muslim schools dangerous; they would isolate the Muslim community from the British society. The Swann report did not see the problem of Muslim education as a religious problem. It

[15] Anwar, "Young Muslims in Britain", 113-5.
[16] Ali, "Teaching of Islam".
[17] Halstead, "To What Extent".

looked at it generally as a problem of ethnicity or cultural identity. It has insisted to view religion from a secular perspective.

The Case of the Netherlands: Between Christian Testimony and Religious Inclusivism

In the Netherlands, on the other hand, the issue of Muslim religious education grew largely within a Christian religious framework, probably because it was the Christian Church that first encountered the problem. For a short discussion of the situation in this country one may refer to a concise report on this issue by Jaap Kraan.[18] As far as Muslim parents' perception of problems in the religious education of their children is concerned, Kraan's findings correspond with most of Halstead's.

Christian schools in the Netherlands faced the question of whether they should admit Muslim children. A Christian school was not legally obliged to admit them, but the Church felt obliged not to refuse admission under the motive of "Christian hospitality". The Muslim parents on the other hand, were not obliged to send their children to Christian schools, but they found them better than secular schools because of their emphasis on religious values. While the Christian schools developed an "admission policy" to justify this new development and introduced certain conditions for the Muslim children, Muslim parents did not feel obliged to accept these conditions. The Christians schools kept deliberating on the issues. Finally, the Council of Churches came out with a paper "Roadmap for the meeting", which discussed three approaches to the problem. The "Testimony approach", which was common in most Christian schools, stressed on a Christian theological vision. Quite evidently, it could not admit Muslim pupils. The second approach, based on the concept of what was called a "Christian meeting school", admitted Muslim pupils suggesting the theological vision of dialogue as a basis for meeting. The third approach was called the "open Christian school". The paper favoured the second approach. It was, however, not possible under this policy to allow Islamic education for Muslim pupils. The third option, which was later called by a more popular name "intercultural educational policy" stressed on ethnic and cultural identity. It allowed Islamic education provided it was culturally oriented. In the end

---

[18]Kraan, "Muslims, Christians and Education".

Muslim organizations took the initiative to establish independent Islamic schools.

Kraan shows that not only Muslims, but also the Christians had to face some hard questions about admitting Muslim pupils in their schools. Kraan made a very significant observation saying: " It became clearer ... that (religious) identity, personal as well as collective, is per definition a dynamic notion, liable to change".[19] The point becomes particularly significant in the perspective of the following remark by Hendrik Procee quoted by Kraan:

"Education should not be focused on exclusive preparation for the existing society, nor on an equally exclusive initiation in the own (sub) culture, but on the future functioning in a partly still unknown and in many ways pluriform world".[20]

Kraan and Procee both seem to be proposing the adoption of an inclusive, rather than integrative or exclusive approach to the concept of identity. The term "inclusive" is distinguished here from "integrative", because the latter, according to the Protestant Education Policy Plan of 1970, meant "integration with the preservation of one's own cultural identity".[21] The integrative approach was therefore not much different from the exclusive one, the main difference being that the latter defined identity in theological terms, while integration defined it in cultural and ethnic terms. Kraan does not seem to favour this distinction between religious and cultural criteria, and therefore prefers to use the term "inclusive".

Conclusion: Comprehensive Religious Education in the Global Community

In a recent article on "Religious Education", Nimat Hafez Barzangi rightly speaks about ambiguity in the perception of religious education among Muslims. He argues that Islamic education should be distinguished from religious education. Islamic education is more sophisticated, comprehensive and universal.[22]

---

[19]Op. cit., 130.
[20]Op. cit., 133 (Kraan's translation of the Dutch original, slightly corrected).
[21]L.c.
[22]Barzangi, "Religious Education", 406.

It becomes clear from the above discussion that the issue of religious education has gained some ambiguity in the context of mass education. Religious education can be seen in three senses. First, there is religious education to train religious leaders like imams. It requires a professional training and a particular approach. This is not the objective for mass education. Second, religious education in the meaning of inculcating particular religious values in the mind of the pupils. That is again a particular project, for which schools cannot be held fully responsible. Religious communities may develop special programmes. Religious values may be the concern of mass education, but not those values which stress exclusivism. Third, religious education in the meaning of knowledge about beliefs and practices. Mass education cannot ignore this aspect. In fact, a pupil must know about his or her neighbours, their beliefs and practices so that the prejudices based on ignorance and negative information could be reduced.

In the global community towards which mankind is moving, it would be unfortunate if diversity was lost, but diversity does not mean isolation from the main stream, nor can it be achieved by focusing only on common or shared values. A better understanding in a pluralist society requires being sympathetically aware of the points of difference as well. Pluralism cannot be achieved by isolated educational systems, nor can a better mutual understanding be developed without learning about each other's beliefs and practices. A comprehensive religious education enlightens not only by removing misunderstandings and prejudices about each other, but in the process the person being educated may perhaps achieve even a better understanding of his or her own identity.

13 Seeking Knowledge unto China
Traditionalization, Modernity, and the State

Dru C. Gladney

We have made Italy, now we have to make Italians.
(Massimo d'Azeglio at the first meeting of the parliament of the newly united Italian Kingdom [in Hobsbawm, *Nations and Nationalism*, 144])

Introduction

How are Muslims "made" in China? This text suggests that while they are born at home (or in hospitals) they may very well be *made* in schools. There are at least two types of schools for Muslims in China: state-sponsored and mosque-sponsored (which sometimes receive state funding). As yet, there are few if any non-Muslim private schools in China to which Muslims have access. Although I and others have written extensively about Muslim minority identity and identification in China, few have specially addressed the role of education and the transmission of Islamic knowledge in the "making" of Muslims in China. This text examines the two sides of this transmission of knowledge about and among Muslims in China mentioned, namely the state education of Muslims as members of China's fifty-five minority nationalities as well as the Islamic education set up by Muslims for their own populations. In this way, we seek to some extent to answer John R. Bowen's question: "How do people negotiate among competing and conflicting sets of norms and ideals?"[1] With respect to the Muslims in China, they do it through public and private systems of education.

As has been noted, given that there are ten official Muslim nationalities in China (see Table 1), Muslim identities range widely, from Turkic to Indo-European, "Central Asian" to "East Asian," "northerner" to "southerner," rural to urban, religious to secular, and educated to illiterate. In addition to a shared Islamic heritage (much of which is forgotten by some, and denied

[1] Bowen, "The Forms Culture Takes", 1061.

247

to others), there are at least two main streams of educational training that to a remarkable extent bring these divergent Muslim nationalities together through a systematized fulcrum of socialization: state-sponsored education and traditionally maintained Islamic education. While both aspects of this educational socialization will vary for each of the ten Muslim nationalities, I would argue that the similarities at least bind them closer together than the Han Chinese majority and the other forty-five minority nationalities. While much of the data for this text is drawn from the Hui, shared Islamic concerns makes many of the traditions and debates among Muslims in China regarding education, modernization, and the state quite similar. At the same time, all Muslims in China, no matter what their language or nationality, have been subjected to the same government educational policy and centralized curricula. One factor of this relative similarity among all Muslims in China, is their representation as members of minority nationalities and specifically as Muslims. This Other- and Self-representation is perhaps the most public of the widespread transmission of knowledge about Islam in China and will be dealt with first. Corrections and confirmations of these representations will then be addressed in sections on China's education of minorities and then Muslims in China. We will then turn our attention to traditional and contemporary Islamic educational trends in China. The text will be concluded with a discussion of public and private discourse regarding Islam in China.

Education and China's Civilizing Mission

Recent writing on the minorities in China and the national identification programme have begun to focus on the "civilizing mission" of China's policy toward its "backward minorities".[2] In state-sponsored media and publications, and public representations, the Han majority are represented as the most "modern" and, by implication, the most "educated". The Han are frequently represented as somewhere near the "modern" end of a Marxist historical trajectory upon which the minorities of China must journey. Much of this derives from a continued commitment in Chinese social science to the

---

[2]See Anagnost, "The Politics of Displacement"; Borchigud, "The Impact of Urban Ethnic Education"; Gladney, "Transnational Islam"; *idem*, "Representing Nationality in China"; Harrell, *Cultural Encounters*.

study of minorities as "living fossils" indicating the origins of "primitive communism". Matrilineality, communal living and property holding, and even extra-marital sexuality among the minorities all become "proofs" of how far the Han have come. Chinese Marxist social science has been heavily influenced by stage evolutionary theory, particularly as represented in the writings of the American anthropologist Lewis Henry Morgan.[3]

The Han, as representative of "higher" forms of civilization, were thought to be more evolved, and were to lead the way for minorities to follow. While there are many nationalities in China, the Han are so-defined as to be in the cultural and technical vanguard, the manifest destiny of all the minorities. While many younger scholars, like Tong Enzheng, are beginning to challenge the dominance of the Marxist-Stalinist-Morganian paradigm, it still heavily influences the popular discourse regarding nationalism and Han superiority in China, as well as state policy.[4]

Minorities, generally less educated in the Chinese school system than the Han majority, are thought to lag somewhere behind the Han culturally. Education plays a privileged role in executing China's national integration project.[5] This is reflected in popular discussion about education and "culture" in China. One of the most difficult questions I had to ask in China was one regarding education. The way to pose the question in Chinese is, literally: "What is your cultural level?" (*nide wenhua chengdu duoshao*). "Culture" here, refers only to learning in state-sponsored schools and literacy in Chinese characters. In the volume of "nationality statistics" recently published by the Department of Population Statistics of the State Statistical Bureau and the Economic Department of the State Nationalities Affairs Commission, the educational sections are all listed under the category of "cultural levels" of the various minority nationalities as compared to the Han.[6] I still remember asking this question to an elderly Hui haji in Hezhou,

---

[3] In his famous 1878 treatise, *Ancient Society*, Morgan described in his first chapter, entitled the "Ethnical Period", the development of society from savagery, to barbarism, and then to civilization (see Yang *1992*).

[4] Tong Enzheng (Tong, "Morgan's Model", 182, 184), the Sichuanese anthropologist and museologist, was one of the earliest to criticize publicly the heavy reliance, almost reverence, of Chinese anthropology for this theory of societal evolution, in which Morgan's work was "canonized, and for the past 30 years has been regarded as something not to be tampered with.... therefore, to cast any doubt on it would be to cast doubt on Marxism itself."

[5] See Hawkins, *Education and Social Change*; Postiglione et al., "Basic Education".

[6] Dept. of Population Statistics, *Population*, 1994, 38-70.

who answered that he "had no culture". This Islamic scholar had spent twelve years living in the Middle East, was fluent in Persian and Arabic, as well as a master of the Islamic natural sciences. Efforts to integrate "nationality general history" (*minzu changshi*) into the state school curriculum do not even begin to address this issue of pervasive Han chauvinism. It may be a strong factor that keeps Hui children from wanting to go to mainly Han schools.

Recently, even the State Council of the People's Republic of China has admitted that despite what the government regards as fifty years of "favourable" policies toward minorities in China, most groups continue to lag far behind the Han majority in all areas of development, especially education. This is especially true in western China, where most Muslims live. The following statement comes from the first official document published in China admitting dramatic shortcomings in its minorities policies:

> China has been a united, multi-ethnic country since ancient times.... Although there were short-term separations and local division in Chinese history, unity has always been the mainstream in Chinese history.... In China, all normal religious activities ...are protected by law.... The state had offered 16.8 billion yuan [2.2 billion USD] of subsidies to minority areas by 1998.... The Chinese government is well aware of the fact that, due to the restrictions and influence of historical, physical geographical and other factors, central and western China where most minority people live, lags far behind the eastern coastal areas in development.[7]

Muslims, as minorities, are not only often less educated than the Han majority, but they are generally are portrayed as backward, exoticized, and even eroticized in the public media in a similar fashion as other minorities even though the Muslims are generally much more conservative socially and

---

[7]Information Office, *National Minorities Policy and Its Practice in China*, 2, 13-4, 41-2. This document, now known as the "Minority Policy White Paper," was released in September 1999, just prior to China's October 1 celebration of the fiftieth anniversary of the founding of the People's Republic. A national conference was called in Beijing, September 28-29, to discuss the "Nationalities Problem", which many believe had become increasingly important to Beijing following the demise of the former USSR in 1991 and the rise of the independent, mainly Muslim, Central Asian states on its border. Admission of the lack of development among Muslims in the western regions led to a new "Western Development Programme" that promises to resolve developmental and educational gaps between the largely rural west and the wealthy south-eastern coastal and urban areas.

morally.[8] This is quite remarkable given the long tradition of learning idealized by Muslims (the desire, as the Prophet said, to "Seek Knowledge, even unto China"), the proliferation of Muslim centres of learning in China, and the fact that at least two Muslim groups, the Tatar and Uzbek, are considerably better educated than the general populace including the Han Chinese (see below, Table 3 and 4). This is not unusual, however, given the fact that the Korean minority in China is also popularly perceived as a "backward minority" even though the Koreans in China possess the highest literacy and educational rates, far surpassing the Han and other groups.[9] The Koreans, like the Muslims, are members of the minorities of China, and they are consequently in need of education.

This may reflect also the view in China that education was the means to acculturation into Chinese civilization, and that depended on the learning of Chinese. Minorities and foreigners per force had less possibility of attaining such in depth knowledge of Chinese and would therefore always be on the periphery. Yet, this knowledge was not limited to elites. Myron Cohen argues that interaction between elites and common people in the Chinese educational system led to not just "a common culture in the sense of shared behaviour, institutions and beliefs," but also to "a unified culture in that it provided standards according to which people identified themselves as Chinese".[10] As long as one maintained these standards, one was Chinese. Yet, knowledge of those standards was communicated in Chinese, in state schools. In imperial China, exhortations and rituals articulating the standards set by those in power helped to extend the standards beyond a "tiny literate reef" in the midst of "illiterate oceans" of the general populace.[11] As David Johnson notes, "The values and beliefs of a dominant class take on the radiance of truth in the eyes of ordinary people."[12] Yet this top down view often excludes those it fails to inspire, particularly groups like Muslims, Tibetans, and Mongols who follow different moralities according to different religious texts. In other words, to learn Chinese meant one became Chinese. This notion has been shared by both Chinese and Western scholars who

---

[8]See Gladney, "Transnational Islam and Uighur National Identity"; *idem*, "Representing Nationality in China", 114-6.
[9]The proportional number of college students among the Korean population was three times higher than among any other nationality (see Yeo, op. cit., 25; Lee, op. cit.).
[10]Cohen, "Being Chinese", 114.
[11]See Woodside and Elman, "Introduction", 3.
[12]Johnson, "Communication, Class, and Consciousness", 47.

adhere to a Sinicization paradigm that links literacy and education with assimilation, the primary method of the "civilizing project" of China. As LaBelle and Verhine have theorized, access to education contributes to the nature of social stratification in many societies.[13] In China, Muslim minorities have increasing access, but as will be seen below, there seems to have been little progress in their educational development.

Representation of Muslims as Minority Nationalities

Muslims are grouped and displayed in all of China's many nationality publications, including the state-sponsored magazines *Minzu Huabao* (Nationality Pictorial) and *Minzu Tuanjie* (United Nationalities), as well as various collections, such as *Chinese Nationalities* (1989), *China's Minorities* (1994), *A Picture Album of Turpan Landscape and Custom* (1985), and *Nationality Style and Figures* (1985). A cursory examination of photos and paintings of Muslims in these state-sponsored publications reveals no real difference from the usual portrayal of minorities in China as "exotic" and "erotic".[14] Perceptive China scholars have noted the colourful portrayal of minorities in China as derogatory, colonial, and useful to the state.[15] Rarely have Muslims been distinguished from this corpus, since they are generally treated similarly as other minority subjects.

After the People's Republic of China was founded in 1949, the state embarked upon a monumental endeavour to identify and recognize as nationalities those who qualified among the hundreds of groups applying for national minority status. The question of one's nationality, which is registered in one's passport and on all official documents, is determined by Stalinist and historical criteria that determine if one is a member of a group that was ever linguistically, economically, geographically, or "culturally" distinct from the so-called Han majority population.[16] This recognition may make a considerable difference in obtaining certain privileges accorded to

[13]LaBelle and Verhine, "Education, Social Change, and Social Stratification".

[14]See Gladney, "Representing Nationality in China".

[15]Diamond, "The Miao and Poison"; Thierry, "Empire and Minority in China". However, this phenomenon extends to imperial times and is not particularly new (see Eberhard, *China's Minorities*).

[16]See Fei, "Ethnic Identification in China".

minorities, in some cases including permission to have more than one child, having access to local political office, special economic assistance, tax relief programmes, and, what is important for the educational focus of this text, priority and preference in higher education (with reduced entrance requirements, lower scores, and even "affirmative action" quotas). In minority autonomous areas, between 1952 and 1998, the government has increased the number of institutions of higher learning from eleven to ninety-four, secondary schools from 531 to 13,466, and primary schools from 59,597 to 90,704.[17] The number of students in institutions of higher learning has increased from 0.45 to 22.65 per ten thousand persons, in secondary schools from 20.94 to 529.64 per ten thousand persons, and in primary schools from 467.31 to 1,240.9 per ten thousand persons.[18] These schools, though in minority areas, also enrol Han students in the region, and tend to be in urban areas where the Han are most numerous. Primarily for minorities themselves (though some Han attend), the state has founded twelve "national minorities institutes" or "universities", fifty-nine teachers' training schools, 158 secondary schools, 3,536 middle schools, and 20,906 primary schools. These schools follow the centralized state curriculum, despite the high minority student population (i.e., there is no more teaching about Islam in a middle school in Urumqi city, Xinjiang Uyghur Autonomous Region, than there is in a Beijing middle school). Those who were recognized by the state are always portrayed in the state-sponsored media as happily accepting that objectivized identity.[19]

While one might be prepared to allow for the fact that South-Western minorities may have more "open" sexual practices than the Han in China today, they are not the only minorities portrayed as sensual and erotic. While the Thai women did traditionally bathe in the nude (though many may fear to now), and the Nuoso as a matrilineal society may very well have allowed extra-marital sexual practice at the matrilocal residence, the Uyghur and

---

[17]Information Office, op. cit., 20.
[18]L.c.
[19]A clear example is the caption for a photograph of several minorities in traditional costume pictured in a brochure introducing the "Nationalities Cultural Palace" (*Minzu Wenhua Gong*) in Beijing, reading: "The Happy People of Various Nationalities" (*Minzu Wenhua Gong*, 12). In one survey of Han Chinese college students, southern minorities often represented as happy and colourful, were ranked as "positive primitives" whose qualities included: "beauty, friendliness, singing and dancing, industry, primitivity, and ignorance" (Fong and Spickard, *1994*, 26).

other Muslim peoples can hardly be said to be more publicly erotic or sensual than the Han in their traditional culture.[20] Uyghur women are widely known throughout China to traditionally cover themselves with *pardah*s-like head scarves and wraps that envelope their entire faces and hair. Unlike the Middle East *pardah* where eyes and sometimes faces are exposed, Uyghur veils cover the entire face. As Muslims, they are generally much more conservative than Han Chinese in the public sexual sphere. Despite their protestations, these representations continue, underscoring the extraordinary contrast between the Han and minority spectacle in China. Muslims also protest about publications about Islam that they find denigrating, as evidenced by the "Chinese Salman Rushdie protest" of 1989, against an encyclopedic portrayal of Islam as sensual and eroticized in a book entitled *Sexual Customs*, a representation that has a long history in China.[21] Despite the government's crackdown on such publications, these kinds of representations of Islam and Muslims continue. For most Han Chinese, who have never darkened the door of a mosque and learn little about Islam in public schools, this representation in the "public sphere" is their only exposure to knowledge about Islam in Chinese or Muslim identities.

Like many tourist hotels, The Sheng Tang ("Ascendant Tang") Hotel in north-east Beijing has a tile mural of a Tang dynasty minority dancer, with accentuated nude breasts, in the centre of its main dining hall. On the opposite walls, erotic stylized murals from the Dunhuang Buddhist grottoes grace the dining room. Like many public places in China, the sensual "Flying *Absarases*" are an officially sanctioned art subject.[22] I once asked a group of Han scholars viewing this mural if they thought the dancers were minorities or Han, and they all said minorities, even though the theme is from the Buddhist caves of Dunhuang, supposedly the cradle of the *Chinese* Buddhist religious tradition. While Buddhism became transformed into a "Chinese" religion, its sensual representation in art and *absarases* have apparently remained an attribute of foreigners and minorities, not the Han.

---

[20]See Gladney, "The Ethnogenesis of the Uigur".
[21]See Gladney, "Salman Rushdie in China".
[22]J.L. Cohen, *The New Chinese Painting*, 17-20.

In the Chinese tourist pictorial, *A Picture Album of Turpan Landscape and Custom*, a Han artist, Gu Shengyue, portrays the sensual images of the Dunhuang caves, with floating female *absarases* and their accentuated breasts, hovering above him, almost as if to say: "Though these Uyghur claim to be Muslim, we know what they are really thinking about when they sing and dance."[23] They have become yet another landscape in the national repertoire of China. In another portrait from the same pictorial, erotic Buddhist figures are portrayed hovering above ecstatic Uyghur dancers.[24] Central Asian dance and artistic displayal come to represent a metaphor of sensuality and eroticism for Han China, even though the region is now dominated by Muslims.

Extremely realistic is the figure painting *Nude with Apples*, by Tang Muli.[25] The Realist painting of a complete frontal nude is clearly meant to portray a Central Asian minority, though the model may very well be Han. Perhaps Tang Muli knew that a Han woman could never be portrayed so vividly and realistically. Yet, Muslims are arguably the most conservative of all peoples in China, including the Han.

Muslim Self-Representation

As China does not yet have a free press, opportunities for Muslims to represent themselves in the public sphere entirely without state mediation is still impossible. Even recent popular novels such as Zhang Chengzhi's *A History of the Soul* (1991) and Huo Da's *Jade King* (1993) (or in Chinese, *Muslim Funeral*, 1992) which are written by Muslims about Muslim lives and conflicts have passed through state bodies of literary approval. Both of these works, though controversial in their own right, are remarkable in their serious and upright portrayal of Muslim society in general, modern attempts to reveal a Muslim morality related to the earlier interest of Chinese Muslims in Confucian ethics that will be discussed later.

---

[23]*Tulufan Fengqing Huaji*, 16.
[24]Op. cit., 18.
[25]In Cohen, op. cit., 101.

One recent pictorial published for charity by the China Islamic Association (1985), *A Collection of Painting and Calligraphy Solicited for Charity in Aid of the Disabled*, presents an entirely different view of Muslims than that found in Nationality Pictorial and the Yunnan Art School. Here, Muslims are represented as studious, hard-working, devout, and dedicated to the family and society. Other publications emphasize the interest of Chinese Muslims in education, scholarship, architecture, and art.[26]

These publications reveal that Muslims have a very different view of themselves than that found in most state-sponsored public media. They are not only a minority nationality, but members of a long religious and scholarly tradition that has contributed to Chinese culture and society. The transmission of this image of Islam and Islamic knowledge in China is a difficult task for a population that occupies only two per cent of the total, and one that has generally been stigmatized throughout much of Chinese history. Generally thought to be lower in "cultural level" than most Han Chinese and less "educated", their pride in their own tradition of Islamic learning is only now beginning to be communicated to non-Muslims. Moreover, as will be seen below, for most Muslim nationalities in China, including the Hui, Uyghur, Uzbek, and Tatar, their general Chinese education equals or exceeds that of the Han. However, this is not the general perception, and one that is only gradually changing in China.

Chinese Education of Muslims

International travel and exposure for China's Muslims in the twentieth century has meant a rush to attain both Chinese and Islamic education in hopes of "modernizing" the Muslim communities of China. In the early decades of the twentieth century, China was exposed to many new foreign ideas and in the face of Japanese and Western imperialist encroachment sought a Chinese approach to governance. Intellectual and organizational activity by Chinese Muslims during this period was also intense. Increased contact with the Middle East led Chinese Muslims to re-evaluate their

---

[26]Examples are the various publications by the China Islamic Association entitled *The Religious Life of Chinese Moslems* (1957, 1978, 1985), the Muslim sponsored pictorial, *Islamic in Beijing* (Hadi Su Junhui 1990), and the Xinjiang publication by the Uyghurs Jori Kadir and Halik Dawut, *Examples of Uyghur Architectural Art* (1983).

traditional notions of Islam. Pickens records that from 1923 to 1934 there were 834 known Hui Muslims who made the haj, or pilgrimage, to Mecca.[27] In 1937, according to one observer, over 170 Hui pilgrims boarded a steamer in Shanghai bound for Mecca.[28] By 1939, at least thirty-three Hui Muslims had studied at the prestigious al-Azhar University in Cairo. While these numbers are not significant when compared with pilgrims on the haj from other South-East Asian Muslim areas, the influence and prestige attached to these returning Hui haji was profound, particularly in isolated communities. "In this respect," Fletcher observed, "the more secluded and remote a Muslim community was from the main centres of Islamic cultural life in the Middle East, the more susceptible it was to those centres' most recent trends."[29]

As a result of political events and the influence of foreign Muslim ideas, numerous new Hui organizations emerged. In 1912, one year after Sun Yat-sen was inaugurated provisional president of the Chinese Republic in Nanjing, the Chinese Muslim Federation was also formed in that city. This was followed by the establishment of other Hui Muslim associations: the Chinese Muslim Mutual Progress Association (Beijing, 1912), the Chinese Muslim Educational Association (Shanghai, 1925), the Chinese Muslim Association (1925), the Chinese Muslim Young Students Association (Nanjing, 1931), the Society for the Promotion of Education Among Muslims (Nanjing, 1931), and the Chinese Muslim General Association (Jinan, 1934).

The Muslim periodical press flourished as never before. Although Rudolf Löwenthal reports that circulation was low, there were over one hundred known Muslim periodicals produced before the outbreak of the Sino-Japanese War in 1937.[30] Thirty journals were published between 1911 and 1937 in Beijing alone, prompting one author to suggest that while the traditional religious centre of Islam in China was still Linxia (Hezhou), its cultural centre had shifted to Beijing.[31] This took place when many Hui intellectuals travelled to Japan, the Middle East, and the West. Caught up in the nationalist fervour of the first half of the twentieth century, they published magazines and founded organizations, questioning their identity as

---

[27]Pickens, "The Four Men Huans", 231-5.

[28]Anonymous, "Peoples and Politics of China's Northwest", 127.

[29]Fletcher, "The Naqshbandiyya in Northwest China".

[30]Löwenthal, "The Mohammedan Press in China", 211-50.

[31]Anonymous, "Peoples and Politics of China's Northwest", 27.

never before in a process that one Hui historian, Ma Shouqian, has recently termed "The New Awakening of the Hui at the End of the 19th and Beginning of the 20th Centuries".[32] As many of these Hui hajis returned from their pilgrimages to the Middle East, they initiated several reforms, engaging themselves once again in the contested space between Islamic ideals and Chinese culture. This zeal for "modern" education led to the establishment of more modernist Islamic movements in China, including the *Ikhwān* (known in China as the *Yihewani*) and the Salafiyyah. The Yihewani differ from the traditionalist and Sufi Muslim groups in China primarily in ritual matters and their stress upon reform through Chinese education and modernism. Because of their emphasis on nationalist concerns, education, modernization, and decentralized leadership, the order has attracted more urban intellectual Muslims. The Yihewani are also especially numerous in areas like Qinghai and Gansu where they proliferated during the Republican period under the patronage of Hui warlords. Many of the large mosques and Islamic schools rebuilt with government funds throughout China in the late 1970s and early 1980s tend to be staffed by Yihewani imams.

It was this spread of Islamic reform movements in China during the late nineteenth century which saw the establishment of Beijing as the "cultural centre of Chinese Islam". These movements in many ways displaced Central and Western China (in places such as Hezhou, Yunnan, Kashgar, and Zhengzhou) as the main sites for Muslim learning, shifting many of the Muslims of China from traditionalist and Sufi Islamic associations to that of the modernist Yihewani. While Muslims in the North-West saw religious conservatism and revival as the answer to their social and cultural problems, the Muslims in many urban centres and especially in Beijing decided that education was the solution:

> [The decline of the Hui in Beijing] is associated with the following four things: 1) the degeneration of Islam among all religions; 2) the degeneration of China among the nations; 3) the degeneration of Beiping [the present Beijing] among the capitals; 4) the degeneration of Niujie where the Hui people are crowded together. In fact, it is not the degeneration of the people but the backwardness of their education.... The relationship between education and the living standard is one of cause and effect. Obviously, without education there would not be

---

[32]Ma Shouqian. "The Hui People's New Awakening".

people of talent, without talented personnel there would be no better means of livelihood.[33]

The question of what kind of education was debated throughout the Republican period, with various private Hui schools attempting different combinations of secular and religious education. By the early days of the People's Republic, these private schools became secularized and nationalized. Religious education was now the responsibility of the mosque and home, whereas secular education was the responsibility of the state. Shortly after the establishment of the People's Republic of China, the Beijing city government combined the Hui middle schools of Cheng Da Normal School, Northwest Middle School, and Yanshan Middle School into the Hui Institute (*Huimin Xueyuan*). In 1963 the Hui Institute was changed to the Hui Middle School. In 1979 it was reopened under that name after being divided up during the Cultural Revolution as the Capital Middle School and the Number 135 Middle School.

Post-1949 Chinese Education of Muslims

In 1949, there were nineteen Hui primary schools created out of former private "Muslim" (*Mu zi*) schools. By 1953 there were twenty-eight Hui elementary schools all of which were renamed during the Cultural Revolution. Children were required to attend the schools in the neighbourhoods where they lived. While this is still mainly the case for Hui primary schools, there are now thirteen Hui primary schools and six Hui nursery schools in Beijing, all in Hui concentrated neighbourhoods. Primary education, now universally required throughout Beijing, is the area of real gain. In 1949 there were only about 2700 Hui in primary school in Beijing. Now there are no Hui primary school-aged children out of school.

The curriculum in all of these state-run institutions is set by the Ministry of Education and is exactly the same as in other schools, with the main difference that no pork is served at the schools and no tuition charged to Hui students. In 1985 the State Commission for Nationality Affairs published the "nationality general knowledge" (*minzu changshi*) curriculum for the Hui Middle Schools. The goal of the state to strengthen education among

---

[33]Wang Shoujie, "Niu jie Huimin Shenghuo tan", 18-9.

minorities reflects the call in the 1930s: "This research explains that whenever nationality education work is seized upon (*zhua haole*), then nationality relations and nationality unity will be greatly strengthened".[34]

Despite a great deal of emphasis on minority education since the "golden period" of the 1950s, the Hui still lag behind the Han in Beijing, especially in post-primary education. Out of 364 Han who graduated from Beijing's Number One Middle School in 1982, there were forty-seven (twelve per cent) who went on to either college or higher technical schools. Out of the seven Hui who graduated, not one went on.[35] Table 2 gives differences in Hui and Han high school entrance from 1979 to 1981 in the Oxen Street District, a district representative for a Muslim neighbourhood in Beijing. We observe that there was a slight decline among both Han and Hui in High School during these years. Although the Hui occupy about one quarter of the Oxen Street population, they represent only five to fourteen per cent of those entering High School. Less than six per cent of the Oxen Street area Hui had attended middle school prior to 1955. Figures for 1982 and 1983 are similar.[36]

This brief examination of the educational situation of the Hui in Beijing is indicative of national trends for most Muslims in urban areas in China. Pertinently, it is clear that there are large gaps between the education of the rural and the urban Muslim population, which affects the national statistics. While it is generally true that Hui educational level is lower than that of the Han majority among whom they live, at the national level, Hui educational level has apparently fared fairly well. Table 3 reveals that in 1982 the Hui had kept pace with the national average, and are substantially better educated than the other Muslim minorities, with the exception of the Tatar and Uzbek. The main advantage the Hui have is language: other Muslim minorities have to contend with learning the Han language as a second language to enter middle school and university.[37] The Hui speak the Han dialects wherever they live.

Since 1982, Muslims have made some gains in public education in China compared to the rest of the population according to the 1990 census. Comparison with figures from the 1990 census (see Table 4) reveal that for

---

[34]Beijing City Sociology Committee et al. (ed.), "Beijing shi canzaju xiaoshu minzu jiaoyu wenti diaocha baogao", 19.

[35]Op. cit., 20.

[36]See op. cit., 21 for details.

[37]Note that the Dongxiang have the highest illiteracy rate in China, at 87 per cent.

the Hui, educational rates have remained basically the same. Significantly, college graduate rates for all Muslims except for the Tatar and Uzbek are similar to those for the rest of the Chinese population (about 0.5 per cent). The primary distinction for Tatar and Uzbek is that their numbers are small and that they are mainly concentrated in urban areas in Xinjiang. Though their college educational rates are extraordinary compared to the rest of the population (2.7 and 3.7 per cent respectively in 1990), there at least ten other minority groups with higher educational rates in China than the Han (including the Korean, Manchu, Russians, Daur, Xibe, Hezhe, Ewenke, and Oroqen). It is clear that the most rural Muslim groups (the Dongxiang, Baoan, and Salar in Gansu) and the still semi-nomadic or pastoralist (Kazakh and Kyrgyz) suffer from the least access to public schools, though there does seem to be some gains in primary school education among the Uyghur, Kazakh and Dongxiang. The gap between rural and urban, nomadic and sedentary, shows up most dramatically in illiteracy and semi-illiteracy rates. While Hui have made some gains between 1982 and 1990 (reduced from 41 to 33.1 per cent), the two groups with the highest illiteracy rates (in Chinese) in 1982, the Dongxiang (87 per cent) and the Baoan (78 per cent) have shown only marginal gains in literacy in 1990 (reduced to 82.6 per cent and 68.8 per cent). This compares to an overall illiteracy reduction in China between 1982 and 1990 from 32 per cent to 22 per cent. This dramatic drop has apparently not reached the Muslim communities in rural Gansu.

At the other extreme, when college educational levels among Muslims are compared with the rest of China, not only have they done comparatively well, but there have been some gains between 1982 and 1990, particularly for the most educated Muslims, the Tatar and Uzbek. Most remarkable gains have been among undergraduate education for the Uyghur, Kazakh, Kyrgyz, Salar, and Tajik. Whereas the Han undergraduate college population grew from 0.2 to 2.4 per cent, these groups experienced even greater gains (Uyghur, 0.1 to 2.1; Kazakh 0.2 to 3.3; Kyrgyz 0.1 to 2.9; Tajik 0.1 to 2.5).[38]

For the most part, however, we have not seen much change between 1982 to 1990 in state education for Muslims in China, despite significant state efforts to promote education in minority and Muslim areas. Not only

---

[38]Note that the 1982 census included a category for college education, whereas the 1990 census broke that category into "undergraduate" and "technical school" figures. For 1982 and 1990 comparisons, these figures have been combined.

are primary and secondary education provided in several primarily Muslim languages (especially Uyghur, Kazakh, Kyrgyz, and Tajik), but the state provides the normal minority nationality incentives for preferred college entrance. The state in China has made strong efforts to provide equal educational access for minorities and Han in rural and urban areas.[39] Nevertheless, it is noteworthy that second-language education is not widely available among the least educated Muslim populations concentrated in the Hexi corridor of Gansu, the Dongxiang, Baoan, and Salar. As these groups speak a mixture of Chinese, Turkish, and Mongolian, the state for the most part provides primarily Chinese language education. It has to be conceded that in all Muslim areas the state has sought to adapt to Muslim needs by providing "*qing zhen*" or *halāl* food that does not contain pork, and special "Hui" schools in urban areas. Yet even these efforts do not seem enough to raise Muslim minority education in China. This may have to do more with the content of education, which is set by the central education bureau, than with a lack of adaptation to local languages and Muslim customs.

For example, in my Beijing city research, many Hui parents in the Oxen Street district told me that, while they were glad of the Hui schools and the priority Hui are now receiving in education, they felt their children would be more motivated to study if there was more ethnic content. Many of them remember that Hui schools in the early 1950s often invited famous Hui scholars such as Bai Shouyi and Ma Songting to give lectures on Hui history and on historical Chinese Muslim personages. The Hui Middle school in Oxen Street also offered Arabic as a second language, so they did not have to go to the mosque to learn it. Beijing Hui parents are not tempted to withdraw their children from school and send them to the mosque for religious education like many North-Western Hui. Instead, they argue that there is more of a need to integrate secular and religious education in order to motivate their children. They also point out that the Islamic schools, even with the course for training imams at the Chinese Islamic Association in the Oxen Street district, cannot supply enough imams for as many mosques as need them. One of the reasons is that many young men upon graduation use their Arabic or Persian to become interpreters or translators overseas where they can travel and earn more money, instead of becoming imams. The distinction between ethnicity and Islam in the city is still too strong for most

---

[39]Kwong and Hong, "Educational Equality among China's Minorities".

Hui parents, and they think it might help the country if the two were brought closer together.

Like other minorities, the Hui in Niujie receive special consideration in their exams for entrance to middle school, high school, and college. In general, they receive two "levels" of ten points each for college entrance preference. For example, if the threshold for college entrance on the state exams is three hundred points, a Hui who scores 280 points will be accepted. This may make a difference. I knew a Hui who scored 281 on the exam and was admitted to Beijing Normal University (*Beijing Shifan Daxue*). His Han neighbour complained bitterly of this to me, as he scored 295 and was not admitted to the college of his choice, but had to go to a "television university" (*dianshi daxue*) where most courses are taught on video cassette. Athletes who are placed among the top six (*qian liu ming*) in provincial competitions are also given two stage preferences. Hence, it is conceivable that a Hui athlete could score 260 in the exam and still be admitted to college with a total score of 300 since he receives four stage preferences. Preference for high school and college minority education is just beginning to show long term effects, and 1990 records should reveal a significant improvement over the 1979 to 1981 figures cited above.

From the government's perspective, the most important stress has been placed upon raising the educational level of rural Hui villagers. In 1958, over 90 per cent of the Hui in Changying, one suburban village on the outskirts of Beijing, were found to be illiterate. By contrast, almost all of the children above the age of ten in the neighbouring Han villages could read. The commune had to send in outside accountants to handle the brigade paperwork for the Hui. By 1980, there were eight Hui college students from the village, 650 high school students, 3000 middle school students, and 3000 primary school students. The municipality and district government donated 300,000 yuan to build a Nationality Primary School (*Minzu xiaoxue*) in Changying, with the plan of making it into a cultural centre for all the Beijing suburban villages to emulate. The staff are paid a higher wage than at other primary schools and there is twice the budget for the children's meals and snacks. Out of 647 students, 85 per cent are Hui, a proportion higher than any other nationality school in Beijing. The faculty are 30 per cent Hui. A total of 95 per cent of the first class entered middle school, and 50 per cent of them tested into high school.

Indubitably progress, but there are still problems to overcome. The Hui principal said that Hui parents do not value education as much as do the

Han. They would rather have their children help out with the family side-line enterprise. The brigade government has developed special training programmes to help families realize the importance of a public education. One of the issues that the local officials have yet to address, however, is the nature of education for these Hui. The imam mentioned that while desire for "Han" learning was low, many of the younger Hui were quite motivated in studying Islamic history and Koranic languages. The party secretary countered that this was not regarded as education by the state and therefore could not be encouraged by state schools. In his eyes, it was part of religion.

For other Muslim minorities, efforts have been made to bring state education to the minority areas, including the pastoral areas, through the novel programme of setting up schools in the pastures, or more commonly, requiring Kazakh and Kyrgyz herders to leave their children in school until they can join them in the herding areas during vacation. Despite these efforts, Muslim illiteracy (with the exception of the Tatar and Uzbek) remains high, and there has been little overall change in Muslim minority education in the last eight years. According to Jacques Lamontagne's study comparing the 1982 and 1990 censuses, Muslim illiteracy continues to vary widely, with the Uzbek and Tatar among the ten most literate minority groups, and the Salar, Bonan, and Dongxiang among the least educated.[40] The Hui remain in the middle, predictably, as they are the most widespread and most urban of all the Muslim groups. Gerard Postiglione has also found that the 1990s did little to bridge the gaps of illiteracy in minority areas, especially between the wide divisions among Muslim groups.[41] Once again, the reason many Muslims lag behind may have more to do with "what" is taught, rather than "how" it is taught. The lack of nationality content and Muslim world history may be forcing Muslims interested in their people's history to go to the mosque rather than public schools and libraries for such "religious" knowledge. This is odd since other world religions are frequently mentioned in the public schools, including Buddhism and Christianity, though often in a critical fashion.

[40]Lamontagne, "Improving the Education".
[41]Postiglione, "China's National Minorities", 39.

The Gender Gap: Male/Female Education Discrepancies Among Muslim Nationalities

It is clear that the Chinese policy of co-education and mixing male and female students runs directly against traditional Muslim sensitivities. While it could be argued that Muslim women in China are more "liberated" than their Middle Eastern counterparts, in that they are not subject to the strict rules of *pardah* and seclusion, the 1990 data on education suggests a significant male/female discrepancy in access to state-sponsored education, at both ends of the spectrum. China, as a society dominated by male influence related to the East Asian tradition of patrilineal descent and patrilocal residence, is characterized by male preference in terms of birth, education, and social mobility.[42] For Muslims, this is even more significant in terms of public education. In terms of illiteracy and semi-illiteracy rates, Muslim females score nearly twice as high as Muslim males. While China's overall illiteracy rate is about 22.2 per cent, the Muslim average (excluding the Tajik and Uzbek) is about 45 per cent. The rates diverge even more across gender boundaries. Hui females score a 42.7 per cent illiteracy and semi-illiteracy compared to 23.7 per cent among Hui males and 12.3 per cent among Han males (Han females score 31.1 per cent). For the three least educated Muslim groups, the Dongxiang, Baoan, and Salar, the rates are even worse: Dongxiang males: 73.8 per cent, females: 92 per cent; Baoan males: 53.3 per cent, females: 85.3 per cent; Salar males: 49.2 per cent, females: 88.9 per cent. Earlier, Hawkins (1973) argued the importance of minority education for inter-group relations in China. This data reveals that high rates of illiteracy among females and males for at least three Muslim nationalities bodes ill for inter-group relations with Han Chinese and the Chinese state.

At the other extreme, college education among Muslim males and females reveals a similar gender gap. Whereas for Han males, 0.4 per cent have received university education, this is true for only 0.1 per cent of females. Among the least educated Muslim groups, this gap is negligible, since so few have attended college. But it is interesting to note that Kazakh · males attend college three times as much as females (0.35 to 0.1 per cent respectively), and Uyghur males twice as often (0.32 to 0.16 per cent

---

[42]Shih, "Cultural Tradition and Women's Participation".

respectively). Among the more educated Muslim minorities, the Uzbek male/female college ratio is equal (1.3 per cent for both males and females) and for the Tatar it is only slightly different (2 per cent for males and 1.5 per cent for females). This indicates that more educated Muslim tend to send both males and females to school together. This is not true, however, for the more rural and less educated Muslim populations.

Because Muslim males and females in China never pray together, it is no wonder they do not want their children to study together. Although China is distinguished in the Muslim world by having many women's mosques that are often attached to or even independent of men's mosques, it is clear that they rarely mix together for ritual or religious education. Only on one holiday, that of Faṭimah's birthday celebrated widely among Muslims in China, have I witnessed men and women praying together. In general, women pray at home, in the back or at the side of the mosque separated by a curtain, or in an adjacent or separate "women's mosque" (nu si).[43] While it is not clear how well educated China's Muslim women are in Islam, they are active in studying the Koran and in establishing mosques. This is not true of their participation in public education. It is clear that if China wants to improve the education of its Muslim population, it not only needs to consider a more inclusive curriculum of Muslim history, but it may need to end co-education in Muslim areas. An examination of traditional Islamic education in China, though generally equally exclusive toward women, shows it that is highly developed and permeates all of the Muslim communities, male and female in China. This cannot be said for public school education.

Traditional Islamic Education in China

In a recent paper, Ma Qicheng (a Hui Muslim scholar from Ningxia) and Gladney have argued that traditional Islamic education in China has been one of the primary catalysts in preserving and promulgating Hui Muslim

---

[43]For more on Muslim women in China, see the recent book by Jaschok, *The History of Women's Mosques in Chinese Islam*; also see Alles, "L'islam chinois"; Cherif, "Ningxia"; Pang, *The Dynamics of Gender, Ethnicity, and State*; Pillsbury, "Being Female in a Muslim Minority in China".

identity.[44] This can be considered a process of indigenization assisted by the rise of a system of "*jing tang jiaoyu*" (lit. "education in the Classics' Hall"), i.e., the *madrasah* Muslim educational system closely associated with the mosque.[45] It is interesting that mosque education in China was modelled on Confucian education, but instead of the lineage bearing responsibility, the entire community supported the mosque and its students. The system paralleled the Confucian literati training programme, but was not supported by imperial authorities and was not recognized by the imperial government. *Jing tang* is a *madrasah* (or a community school) established in and attached to the mosque. The leading *ahong* (Persian, "teacher" or imam) in the mosque is also the master of the *jing tang*. The aim of a *jing tang* is to train religious personnel, hence the Koran and other Islamic classics are the main textbooks. The emergence and development of *jing tang* education is closely related to the Hui effort in adapting Islam to the Chinese social milieu.

Early in the Tang and Song Dynasties, such religious positions as the *zhang jiao* (imam) or *aqadi* (from Arab *al-qāḍī*, judge) were fulfilled by the scholars among the Muslim "foreign guests" and their male children. This inheritance of religious authority extended into the Yuan Dynasty, but in the mid-Ming Dynasty, some drastic social changes made this traditional mode outdated. At this point in time, Hui Muslims enjoyed economic expansion, a population explosion, and increasingly widespread distribution. The expanding Hui communities required more mosques, which in turn required more religious specialists. The greatest problem was that, as most of the Hui had adopted Chinese as their language, fewer people could use Arabic and Persian. Even fewer could understand the Islamic classics in the original. The traditional "father to son" way of training could no longer satisfy their needs. Under these circumstances, the *jing tang* educational system was created especially to resolve the problem of more mosques without adequate and qualified personnel.

According to literature, the founding father of the mosque school system among the Hui was Hu Dengzhou (1522-1597), a Hui Muslim who lived in southern Shanxi Province during the reigns of the Ming emperors Jiajing and Wanli. Acutely alarmed by the fact that mosques everywhere were short of

---

[44]Gladney and Ma Qicheng, "Local and Muslim in China".
[45]For a list of educational terms and mosque personnel titles, see Gladney, *Qing Zhen*, 387-91, 394.

religious classics and specialists, he began to enrol Muslim students and lecture them in his own house. Soon, many mosques followed suit and a Hui Islamic educational system eventually evolved.

Mosque 1 education can be generally classified into three levels: that of the primary (school), the intermediate (middle school), and the advanced (college). The primary school (*jingwen xiaoxue*) teaches the alphabet and phonetics of Arabic; elementary Koranic knowledge, often referred to as the *khatim* (Arabic, "seal", referring to the complete reading of the Koran); and various readings on ritual practices, such as prayer, fasting, funerals, marriages, and so forth. Morning and evening, children are taught the rudimentary basics of prayer, ablution, and recitation. Rote memorization of the Koran is accomplished through assigning Chinese characters homophonically with Arabic syllables, leading to remarkably accurate pronunciation without any understanding whatsoever. In many Muslim communities it was traditionally compulsory for both boys and girls from age six to thirteen or fourteen.[46] Wang Jianping argues that graduation from primary school was more important than circumcision for recognition as members of the Islamic community for young Muslims in Yunnan. This clearly is not the case in most Muslim areas of China where mosque education is less developed.[47]

Middle-level mosque education is more seasonal. Incorporating students from twelve to eighteen years old, it equips Muslim young people with the core Islamic stipulations and morals. They learn both pedagogy (Arabic grammar, syntax, logic, rhetoric, and ethics) and theology (including the *sharī'ah* and Hadith). Students further their knowledge of elementary Arabic, the Koran, and classic religious works in Arabic or even Persian depending on the expectations and level of the community.

The "college" level is actually the real *jing tang*, in which the regular students (known as "*halifa*" [from Arabic *khalīfah*], or "*manla*") improve their knowledge of Arabic or Persian, rhetoric, commentaries on the Koran, and the Hadith. While many Muslim communities have primary and middle level training in the mosque, only large communities can support college level training. Ages range from eighteen to twenty-five, and even older,

---

[46]For an interesting comparison documenting the widespread standardization of this *madrasah* system even in Yunnan, see the recent thesis by Wang Jianping, *Concord and Conflict: The Hui Communities of Yunnan Society in Historical Perspective* (1996).
[47]Op. cit., 151

depending on the support from the community. Often the education depends on the mastering of five Arabic and Persian textbooks, including an examination and graduation ceremony, attended by the entire community.

The Islamic colleges in different regions have developed different centres and characteristics. The Shanxi school in the North-West represented by Feng Yangwu and Zhang Shaoshan has emphasized professional Arabic education, and concentrated on the way to recognize the True God (*ren zhu xue*); the scholars in Shandong and other internal areas represented by Chang Zhimei have taught in both Arabic and Persian, with an emphasis on Islamic law; the Yunnan school founded by Ha Fuchu has integrated the main traditions from both Shanxi and Shandong.

It is also important to point out that *jing tang* as an educational institution not only had religious functions. It was also a historical form of extra-Islamic education promulgated by the Hui people. It gives the Chinese-speaking Hui the possibility to continue their historical tradition of learning Arabic and Persian. The curricula of the mosque college, while heavily loaded with religious connotations, is extended beyond the religious sphere. It includes such fields in the humanities as the languages, linguistics, rhetoric, logic, history, and in the natural sciences as astronomy, mathematics, measurement, geography, and time-keeping. In addition, it has created a way to transcribe Arabic and Persian into Chinese and *vice versa*, thus constituting an ethnic feature of Chinese Muslim daily speech.

Finally, it also important to note that this *madrasah* system is characteristic of traditionalist and modernist or Yihewani Muslim communities. Sufi communities follow more personalized courses of instruction after the elementary stage, in which the Shaykh personally inducted the student (*manla*) into the generally esoteric practices and traditions of the order.[48] Three stages of initiation among Sufis are taught, and while debate often centres on which stage is most important, or in what order they should be followed, they are generally given as the first stage of *Jiaocheng* or *Changdao* (Arabic, the *shari'ah*); the middle stage of *Daocheng* or *Zhongdao* (Arabic, *tarīqah*); and the final stage of *Zhencheng* or *Zhidao* (Arabic, *haqīqah*). Individual Sufis would be initiated into each of these stages under the *Daozu* ("master of the Dao"), which often takes place in the *Dao Tang* (ritual centre of the Sufi shaykh).

---

[48]See Gladney, *Muslim Chinese*, 44-7; Ma Tong, *Zhongguo Yisilan*.

Confucianization and Islamic Knowledge

Gladney and Ma note that in addition to promulgating traditional Islamic knowledge in China, Muslim intellectuals engaged in the zealous learning of Confucian teachings.[49] The Confucian ideals of following the way set out by the ancient sages, advancing benevolence and personal duty, loyalty and tolerance, and the golden doctrine of the mean has attracted numerous Hui scholars since the time of the Yuan and Ming Dynasties. Many of them even became addicted to Confucianism and established themselves in this career. For example, the famous Hui scholar, Shan Si, in the late Yuan could "recite a thousand words from the classics daily" when he was only nine years old. He dedicated his life to the study of Confucianism and wrote dozens of books. He was especially good at expounding *The Book of Changes*.[50] His contemporary, Bo Yan, could recite *The Analects* and *The Book of Filial Piety* at six years old. Later, he became a renowned Confucian master and drew students from all over China. It was said, "He rendered answers to whatever questions and dispelled all the perplexities."[51]

Beside Confucian classics, Hui scholars studied and inherited Chinese literature and arts, achieving prominence in the fields of Tang poetry, Song music, Yuan opera, and traditional Chinese painting and calligraphy. Many Hui scholars competently established themselves among the celebrated Han scholars. In the Yuan, this included Gao Kegong, Sadula, Ma Jiugao, Ding Yefu; in the Ming, Ding Henian, Ma Shijun, Jin Dache, and Ding Peng.

The Hui adoption and assimilation of Han culture paved the way for the extensive synthesis of Islam and Chinese culture in the Ming and Qing Dynasties. As a result, a Chinese Islamic philosophy formed and a vast literature on its interpretation was produced. The typical Muslim scholars of this period, such as Wang Daiyu (1570-1660), Liu Zhi (about 1660-1720), Ma Zhu (1640-1711), and Ma Dexin (1794-1874), not only had Islamic expertise, but also were well versed in Confucianism, Buddhism, and Taoism.[52] They were celebrated as "learned in both Chinese and Arabic",

---

[49]Gladney and Ma, op. cit.

[50]"The Biography of Shan Si", in vol. 190 of *History of the Yuan Dynasty*.

[51]"The Biography of Bo Yan", In vol. 190 of *History of the Yuan Dynasty*.

[52]Reference is to works such as *Zhen jiao zhen quan* (The Genuine Elucidation of the Authentic Religion), *Qingzhen daxue* (The Advanced Learning of the Pure Religion), and *Xi zhen wen da* (Answers Concerning the Genuine Religion) by Wang Daiyu; *Tian fang xing li* (The Rationality of Allah), *Tian fang dian li* (The Ceremony of Allah), and *Tian*

"knowledgeable in the four religions" and "good at Confucianism". They believed that "the classics of Islam and Confucianism embody the same Way in distinct scripts, contain the same Meaning in different languages." For this reason, they "employed Chinese characters to translate the Arabic religious teachings, and make annotations at Confucian books to explore the meanings, so that a mutual understanding can be achieved." They adopted the introspective cognition in the traditional Chinese philosophy and the objective idealism developed by the Song scholars into the framework of recognizing the True God in Islam, and thus gave theology some philosophical connotations.[53] For instance, they combined the concept of "One God" with the Chinese concept of *tai ji* (the supreme ultimate), and established the Chinese cosmology of Islam. They adapted the Confucian notion of "investigating things to complete knowledge" to serve the Islamic notion of belief in the Only God (Allah). They elucidated the Islamic Five Virtues (*wu gong*) in the light of the Confucian Five Norms (*wu chang*), and merged it into traditional Chinese ethics, and thus harmonized the loyalty to the True God and to the Emperor. In this way, Islam as a religion became an integral part of Chinese culture.

The successful transplanting of Islam into China proper owes a great deal to these Hui Muslim scholars. It is their profound knowledge of traditional Chinese culture that rendered Islam in Chinese form. Without their efforts, the majority of illiterate Hui Muslims could not have had access to the extensive and profound philosophy of Islam and Islam itself would not be appealing to Chinese Muslims. This integration of the Islamic and Confucian cultures as a process was largely advanced during the transitional period between the Ming and the Qing dynasties (seventeenth century).

---

fang zhisheng shilu (The Record of the True God) by Liu Zhi; *Qingzhen zhinan* (The Compass of Islam) by Ma Zhu; *Si dian yao hui* (Essence of the Four Classics), *Da hua zong gui* (The Supreme Destiny of the Great Way) and *Xing shi zhen yan* (The Admonition to Awaken the World) by Ma Dexin.

[53]See Ma Qicheng: "Zhongguo yisilanjiao de da wenhua shuxing".

The Transmission of Islamic Knowledge and its influence on Traditional Chinese Culture

Muslim culture did not only adopt traditional Chinese culture. It also had an importance influence on Chinese culture. Since the Song and Yuan Dynasties, many Hui Muslim scholars helped to introduce Islamic astronomy, time-keeping, mathematics, medicines, and textiles to China, thereby greatly enriching Chinese culture.

The *Ying Tian Li* (*Heavenly Accordance Calendar*) prevalent in the early Song Dynasty, was influenced by a Muslim scholar named Ma Yize (921-1005), in which the system of seven days a week was first introduced, and thus laid a foundation for the conversion between the Chinese and the Islamic calendars. In the Yuan Dynasty, the *Wan Nian Li* (Eternal Calendar) compiled by the Muslim astronomer Zhama Luding was presented to the Khubilai Khan in 1267. Zhama Luding also made seven instruments, including the celestial and the terrestrial globes, for measuring the time when the sun crosses the equator, and to ascertain the beginning and end of the four seasons[54] The Hui scholars were also good at composing calendars. The cross-checking between the Great Sequential and the Islamic Calendars significantly enhanced the development of the calendar in the Ming Dynasty. Mathematics is the basis of calendar calculation. Thanks to the introduction of the Islamic calendar by Hui scholars, Yuan mathematicians developed quickly in calendar calculation, algebra, geometry, and spherical trigonometry. Arabic numerals were introduced to China by the early Hui Muslims. The Euclidean *Principles of Geometry* was first introduced into China by Hui Muslim scholars.

Hui medicine is also famous in China. In the early Yuan Dynasty, the Great Capital (Da Du, Beijing) and the Upper Capital (Shang Du, Duolun) each had an Institution of Hui Medicines. Later, the Beijing Institution was merged into the Department of Extensive Mercy (*Guang Hui Si*) and was carried out by Hui doctors with Islamic medications. Hui surgery and

---

[54]In his *Science and Civilization in China*, Joseph Needham introduced the terrestrial globe made by Zhama Luding. He says: "it seems this is something new. Except for the archaic terrestrial globe by Crates of Mollos, nothing is earlier than that recorded by Matein Bhaim in 1492. In comparison, Zhama Luding's design was 225 years earlier than that recorded by Matein Bhaim." (see Bai Shouyi, *Biographies of Renowned Hui Figures*, 37-39).

pharmaceuticals were especially famous for their effectiveness.[55] The Arabic Pharmaceutical Code was translated into Chinese in the Yuan Dynasty. The four incomplete volumes of *The Hui Remedies* preserved in the rare-books reading room of the National Library in Beijing were translated in the later Yuan and printed with wooden blocks in the early Ming. According to the text, it was adapted from the *Thirteen Tibb* [the Arabic Word for medicine] *Classics,* the only Hui book collected by the Yuan imperial library. This title refers to *al-Qānūn fī al-ṭibb* (The Code of Medicine) by Ibn Sīnā (980-1037), the renowned Persian philosopher-cum-scientist. Hui medicine was also popular in the folk society. In south China, many Hui doctors marketed their medicines and healing in the streets.

The Hui textile technology has also positively influenced China. Artisans constituted the major part of the Muslim immigrant population in China proper. Most of them were recruited into the official manufacturing guilds owned by the Yuan court or nobles. Their main occupations included construction, textiles, weaponry, leather, felt, and metal utensils. In the aspect of architecture, Yesu Dirding, the famous Hui architect, not only participated in the overall planning of the palaces of the Great Capital, especially the design of the Forbidden City, but also personally presided over the construction of the Qiong Hua Island project in the North Sea (today Beihai Park). These two projects have influenced the history of construction in China. Moreover, the Hui also left their impact on Chinese leather processing, incense-manufacturing, and cuisine in China.

From these interactions, we see that Hui and Han Chinese made substantial contributions to the transmission of Islamic and Chinese knowledge. The intermingling of the many cultures of the Hui, Han, and other ethnic groups in China over the last 1200 years has led to the rise of the Hui as an ethnic group and their indigenization in China. In state acknowledgment of this, the Hui were recognized very early by the founders of the People's Republic as a separate and distinct nationality, an official designation that has further strengthened their ethnic and indigenous identity.

---

[55]Tao Zongyi, vol. 22 of *Chuo Geng Lu* (Idle Recordings in the Slack Season).

The Rise of Islamic Education and its Influence on Chinese Education

It is clear from Tables 3 and Table 4 that Muslim education in China varies dramatically between groups. Not only were the Baoan and Dongxiang among the most illiterate groups in China in 1982 and 1990, but the Tatar and Uzbek continue to be among the most educated. As mentioned before, a significant discrepancy also existed between males and females. These trends were continuing in the 1990s, but with rising Islamic conservatism, there is some concern that gains in Chinese education may be lost. As I noted in my earlier study in Ningxia in the mid 1980s, rising Islamic conservatism led to a decline in interest in government-sponsored education. A decrease in public school enrolment, and an increase in the number of children studying the Koran in private *madrasah*s attached to local mosques is another phenomenon that had local Ningxia cadres concerned. This growing interest in pursuing religious education has not yet reached large proportions among the Hui in Na Homestead, as only ten school age children were not attending public school in 1985. Instead, they were studying the Koran at home privately. There are four officially permitted *manla*s in the village. Nevertheless, in more heavily populated Hui areas this is becoming a more noticeable trend.

This trend has become even more pronounced in conservative Muslim areas such as Linxia Hui Autonomous Prefecture, in Gansu Province, where Muslim minorities were 52.7 per cent of the population (1981).[56] School enrolment has regularly decreased since 1978. In addition to this gradual reduction throughout the years, a common practice in this region is that children attend school for the first few weeks of registration, but return full-time to the farm before completing the term.[57] In a *China Daily* front page article entitled "Keep rural girls in school," Liu Su,[58] the Vice-Governor of

---

[56]Out of a population of 1.3 million in 1981, the Hui were 35.2 per cent (489,571), the Dongxiang 15.9 per cent (223,240), the Baonan 0.53 per cent (7,683), and the Salar 0.27 per cent (4,364).

[57]For further information on the economic situation in Linxia, see Linxia Committee (ed.), *Linxia Huizu zizhizhou gaikuang.* Other helpful introductions to Hui Autonomous Counties that I have been able to collect include: Da Chang (1985); Min He (1986); Meng Cun (1983); Men Yuan (1984); Hua Long (1984); and Chang Ji Autonomous Prefecture (1985). For the Hui in Gansu, see Ma Tong, *Gansu Huizu shi gangyao.*

[58]All names used in this study are true unless indicated as pseudonyms.

Gansu Province, reported that out of 157,300 school-aged children not in school in Gansu, 85 per cent were girls.[59] Children leave school for a variety of reasons, including the need for income-producing labour on the farm under the newly-introduced responsibility system. Yet many Hui indicate traditional Islamic views that have made them reluctant to send their children, especially daughters, to public schools.

When asked about their reluctance to send their children to school, Na Homestead parents expressed doubts about "the value of learning Chinese and mathematics". "It would be much more useful," I was told by one mother, "for our children to learn the Koran, Arabic, and Persian." If a child excelled, he or she might become a *manla*, and eventually perhaps an *ahong*. Their status in the village would be much higher than the average middle school or even high school graduate, as would their income (estimated at 100 to 500 yuan a month for a well-known teaching *ahong*). Children who are in poor health are often kept at home to study the Koran. In large families with more than one son, generally one child is encouraged to study to become an *ahong*. Although the government officially allows each mosque to support from two to four full-time *manla*s — who should be at least eighteen years old and junior middle school graduates — many younger children study at home without official approval.

Ningxia, as the only autonomous region for Hui Muslims in China, tends to monitor *ahong* training and religious practice more closely than other areas where Hui are concentrated. In Weishan Yi and the Hui Autonomous County in Yunnan, several mosques had over twenty resident *manla*s studying under well-known *ahong*. In Linxia Hui Autonomous Prefecture in Gansu, at the South Great Mosque there were over 130 full-time students. In the Bafang district of Linxia City, where most of the Hui are concentrated, there were at least sixty full-time *manla*s in each mosque. Mirroring the spiritual importance of Mecca and the centrality of theological learning of the Iranian city of Qum for Hui Muslims in China, the famous mosques and scholars of Linxia attract students from all over China.[60]

---

[59]"Keep Rural Girls in School", *Cina Daily*, 17 April 1987, 1.

[60]Cf. Fischer, *Iran*. A rather new development is the sending of Hui *manla* to mosques in Xinjiang where Arabic language study is much more advanced because of the influence of the Arabic script in Uyghur and the proximity to Pakistan with its recently opened Karakoram highway. In September 1987 while visiting a mosque in Kashgar, I met a Hui *manla* from Hezhou who had been studying there for six years for precisely those reasons. He mentioned his desire to travel to Mecca through Pakistan and how much more

Renowned mosques in the Shadian and Weishan Counties in Yunnan tend to attract students from throughout the South-West, including Hainan Island. At an ordination (*chuanyi*) service I attended at the Xiao Weigeng Mosque in Weishan County in February 1985, the ten graduates included one Hainan Island student and six students from outside the county who had studied there for five years. The Hainan student had a brother studying the Koran in Beijing. The next class admitted thirty students, ten from the local village, ten from other villages, ten from outside the county, including one from outside Yunnan. The fact that these *manla*s travel long distances to study under celebrated *ahong*s demonstrates that national ties continue to link disparate Hui communities. It also reveals the growing importance of religious education in the countryside.

In the North-West, in addition to allowing from two to four students (*halifat*) to train privately in each mosque, the government has approved and funded two Islamic Schools (*yixueyuan*) in Yinchuan and Tongxin. In 1988 the state provided funding to establish a large Islamic seminary and mosque complex outside the West Gate of Yinchuan near Luo Village. Similarly, in Urumqi the Islamic college was established in 1985 and other regional and provincial governments have followed suit. This indicates a "regionalization" of state-sponsored Islamic education which until the 1980s had been officially concentrated at the China Islamic Affairs Commission in Beijing, established in 1956.

The increased promotion of exchange with foreign Muslim countries is exposing more urban Hui to international aspects of their religious heritage. Among urban Hui, Islamic knowledge tends to be higher than in rural areas, perhaps because of increased educational levels and more media exposure. The majority knew of Khomeini (Khumaynī) and the location of Mecca. Unlike the vast majority of Hui in rural areas, many urban Hui interviewed knew of and often read the magazine published by the Chinese Islamic Association, *Zhongguo Musilin* ("The Muslims of China"). Few were aware of and interested in the sectarian disputes in the Iran-Iraq conflict, but most knew of Shi'ism.

inexpensive and convenient the haj had become since the opening of the road. He served at the only Hui mosque among the 160 Uyghur mosques in the city.

Public and Private Discourse Regarding Islamic Knowledge in China

This text has examined the nature of the transmission of Islamic knowledge from two perspectives: first, that of the public state-sponsored representation and education of the Muslims in China, and secondly, that of the Muslims themselves, their self-representation and methods of Islamic education. It is clear that neither of these streams of Islamic knowledge transmission is separate from the other, both have intermingled, but they have never fully blended and as a result many Muslim communities continue to live in very different worlds from those of their Han and other nationality neighbours. The rise of private schools in China today may even see the return of private Muslim schools (*muzi xuexiao*) that arose in Beijing at the beginning of the twentieth century.

Until state education in China begins to incorporate more Muslim information about Islam, these streams will continue to run parallel, leading to continued misunderstandings and misrepresentations. In addition, until Chinese educational policy recognizes "cultural level" that is based on other knowledge traditions and languages, many more conservative Muslims might continue to resist sending their children — especially their daughters — to state schools. Given the money to be made in the free market economy, at which many Muslims are quite adept, there may be even less incentive to attract and keep those Muslim children in state schools. The mosque might become an even more practical source of an alternative education, a source of knowledge that has persisted throughout the Muslim regions of China since the Prophet Muhammad enjoined the new world Muslim community to seek knowledge even unto China.

Table 1

Muslim Nationality Populations in China, 1982-1990

Ethnonym	Location	Languages	1982 Census	1990 Census	Per Cent Growth
Hui (Dungan)	All China, esp. Ningxia, Gansu, Henan, Xinjiang, Qinghai, Yunnan, Hebei, Shandong	Sino-Tibetan	7,219,352	8,602,978	19
Uyghur	Xinjiang	Altaic (Turkic)	5,957,112	7,214,431	21
Kazakh	Xinjiang, Gansu, Qinghai	Altaic (Turkic)	907,582	1,111,718	24
Dongxiang	Gansu, Xinjiang	Altaic (Turkic)	279,397	373,872	34
Kyrgyz	Xinjiang, Heilongjiang	Altaic (Turkic)	113,999	141,549	24
Salar	Qinghai, Gansu	Altaic (Turkic)	69,102	87,697	27
Tajik	Xinjiang	Indo-European	26,503	33,538	27
Uzbek	Xinjiang	Altaic (Turkic)	12,453	14,502	16
Bonan	Gansu	Altaic (Mongolian)	9,027	12,212	35
Tatar	Xinjiang	Altaic (Turkic)	4,127	4,873	18
Total Muslim Minority Population			14,598,654	17,597,370	26
Total Minority Populations			67,295,217	91,200,314	35
Total Han Majority Populations			940,880,121	1,075,470,555	10

Note: Name(s) of group based on most commonly used and Chinese *pinyin* transliterations.
Sources: *Renmin Ribao*, "Guanyu 1990 nian renkou pucha zhuyao de gongbao", 14 Nov. 1991, 3; Gladney, *Muslim Chinese*, 20, 224.
Note that Muslim population estimates in China are based on the official census nationality categories, which do not include religion. Non-Muslim nationalities, such as the Han, may include believers in Islam, just as the so-called "Muslim Nationalities" may include those who do not believe in or practice Islam.

Table 2

Ethnic Composition of Entering High School Students from Beijing, Niujie (Oxen) Muslim district, 1979-81

	1979		1980		1981		Total	
	Han	Hui	Han	Hui	Han	Hui	Han	Hui
Students	54	3	37	2	35	2	123	10
Percentage of Ethnic Group	0.13	0.03	0.09	0.2	0.8	0.04	0.29	0.07
Percentage of Class	94.7	5.3	95.0	5.0	86.0	14.0	92.0	8.0

Source: adapted from Beijing City Sociology Committee et al. (ed.) "Beijing shi canzaju xiaoshu minzu jiaoyu wenti diaocha baogao", 21; See Gladney, *Muslim Chinese*, 214-9.

Table 3

Educational Level of Muslim Minorities in China in Per Cent, 1982

Educational Level	Hui	Uyghur	Kazakh	Dongxiang	Kyrgyz	Salar	Tajik	Uzbek	Baoan	Tatar	All Ethnic Groups	All China
University Graduate	.5	.2	.4	0	.3	.2	.2	2.1	.2	3.9	.2	.5
Undergraduate	2.5	.1	.1	0	.1	.2	.1	.9	.1	11	.1	.2
Senior Middle School	7	5	5	1	5	1	4	11	2	15	5	8
Junior Middle School	19	12	17	3	11	5	11	22	6	25	15	20
Primary School	30	37	49	8	40	18	38	40	12	40	37	40
Illiterate*	41	45	29	87	41	74	49	20	78	9	45	32

*Population age 6 and above who cannot read or can read very little (in Chinese).
Source: adapted from Population Census Office, *The Population Atlas of China*, XVI, 29; Gladney, *Muslim Chinese*, 20.

Table 4

Educational Level of Muslim Minorities in China in Per Cent, 1990

Educational Level	Hui	Uyghur	Kazakh	Dongxiang	Kyrgyz	Salar	Tajik	Uzbek	Baoan	Tatar	All China
University Graduate	.6	.5	.5	.05	.3	.3	.2	2.6	.2	3.6	.5
Undergraduate	.9	.4	.7	.08	.5	.3	.3	1.9	.1	2.5	2.4
Technical School*	1.6	1.6	2.6	.3	2.4	.9	2.1	4.7	1.0	5.8	17.6
Senior Middle School	6.2	3.5	5.5	.6	3.4	1.6	2.5	10.8	2.9	11.0	6.4
Junior Middle School	19.9	11.9	16.4	2.8	10.2	6.3	9.3	20.3	7.2	22.0	23.3
Primary School	29.1	43.3	43.9	12	43.4	18.8	40.4	33.7	16.2	32.7	37.2
Semi- or Illiterate	33.1	26.6	12.3	82.6	24.9	68.7	33.5	8.3	68.8	4.9	22.2

*Note that data for "Technical School" was not provided in 1982.
Source: adapted from Department of Population Statistics, *Population of China's Nationalities*, 70-3, 76-116.

14 The Institut Agama Islam Negeri at the Crossroads

Some Notes on the Indonesian State Institutes for Islamic Studies[1]

Johan Meuleman

Introduction

The Institut Agama Islam Negeri (IAIN) or State Institute for Islamic Studies[2] has played an important role in the religious and educational life of the Indonesian Republic and this role may even become more prominent in the future. The first IAIN was officially created in 1960 in Yogyakarta, with a branch in Jakarta.[3] Today, Indonesia has fourteen IAINs, comprising at least three faculties each. In addition, in 1997 thirty-three smaller Sekolah Tinggi Agama Islam Negeri (STAIN — State College for Islamic Sciences) were formed out of thirty-seven former outlying faculties of these IAINs and given autonomy.[4] Today, well above 100,000 students are enrolled in these IAINs and STAINs.

Outside Indonesia, little has been published so far on the IAIN. Margaret Gillett published an article entitled "The IAIN in Indonesian Higher Education", which formed the result of a short mission to Indonesia in preparation for the cooperation between the Institute of Islamic Studies of McGill University, Montreal, and the Indonesian Ministry of Religious Affairs in view of the development of the IAINs. This article offers a short presentation about the institution of the IAIN and points out some paradoxes

---

[1]Most of the written and oral information this text is based on was collected prior to the INIS conference of June 1996 at which it was originally presented. Information on some more recent developments was added later.

[2]The literal translation of the Indonesian name is "State Institute for Islamic Religion", but the common translation by "State Institute for Islamic Studies" explains the function of the institution better.

[3]Details on the historical background of this first IAIN will be given in the section "The IAIN Between State and Civil Society".

[4]Information obtained from the Indonesian Ministry of Religious Affairs; *Pelita* (daily, Jakarta), 1 July 1997; *Jum'at* (weekly supplement to the Jakarta daily *Republika*), 11 July 1997; *Ummat* (weekly, Jakarta), 21 July 1997.

and problems it is facing in its development.[5] Zamakhsyari Dhofier published an article entitled "The Intellectualization of Islamic Studies in Indonesia", which discusses the modernizing and intellectualizing trend of Islamic thought and studies in Indonesia during the 1980s, in which the IAINs played a prominent role. He places this development in a broader historical and social context.[6] Since 1989 the Indonesian-Netherlands Cooperation in Islamic Studies (INIS) has been publishing the *INIS Newsletter* (Leiden/Jakarta), of which each issue contains a section "Academic Life in 14 IAINs".[7] This probably forms the most detailed serial report available to an international public on current issues relating to curricular and institutional development and scholarly as well as social activities within a particular form of Islamic higher education.[8] In addition, Henri-Chambert Loir and I contributed a discussion of the IAIN to a recent French-language publication on Islamic education in various regions of the world.[9]

The present text will explain that, from various points of view, the IAIN is at the crossroads. Its being at the crossroads is understood here in the double sense of facing a crucial moment in its development and of being located at the interface of, firstly, different scholarly traditions, secondly, the state and civil society, and, thirdly, specifically religious learning and general education and science.

---

[5]Gillett, "The IAIN in Indonesian Higher Education". This article was originally presented as a paper at the VIIth World Congress of Comparative Education, Montreal, 26-30 June 1989.

[6]Zamakhsyari, "The Intellectualization of Islamic Studies", republished, together with some other articles of which most also touch on the IAIN, in Muhaimin (ed.), *Zamakhsyari Dhofier on: Tradition and Change in Indonesian Islamic Education*, 61-86. References in this text are to the latter edition.

[7]The *INIS Newsletter* was scheduled to be published twice yearly, but since 1994 some delay has occurred. The last issue published so far is no. 15, published in 1998 and covering the period from October 1995 to April 1996. Since April 2001 a new version of the *INIS Newsletter* has been presenting a daily selection from Indonesian newspaper articles on Islam in Indonesia through the Internet.

[8]The *INIS Newsletter* is scheduled to be published twice yearly, but since 1994 some delay has occurred, which should be caught up with later this year.

[9]Chambert-Loir and Meuleman, "Les instituts islamiques publics indonésiens".

The IAIN between Different Scholarly Traditions

In his article referred to above, Zamakhsyari Dhofier explains that the relations between Islam in the Indonesian Archipelago and in the Middle East were always strong, especially from about the beginning of the fifteenth century until the middle of the seventeenth century of the Christian era and again from the end of the nineteenth century. Between both periods mentioned, Dutch colonization, by its very economic and political domination as well as by concrete restrictive measures, brought about the relative isolation of the Archipelago. The main factor of the reintensification of the contacts from roundabout 1870 was the improvement in transport, in particular because of the opening of the Suez Canal (1869) and the development of steamships. Scholarly and educational interaction occupied a prominent place in these contacts. By the end of the nineteenth century, more than 5,000 Indonesians were studying in the Middle East, mostly in Mecca or Medina. Therefore, the influence of the Middle Eastern tradition of Islamic learning, especially from the Hijaz, on Islamic education in the Archipelago was very strong. The main institution of Islamic education in the Archipelago was the *pesantren* or Islamic boarding school. It existed at several levels, up to the advanced level of what nowadays would be called higher education. The same author also explains that this Middle Eastern scholarly tradition was the rather closed and static tradition that developed after the decline of the intellectual dynamism found once in centres such as Cordoba and Baghdad: philosophy and logic were discarded and the curriculum was concentrated on *tafsīr* (Koran exegesis), theology, linguistic study of the Koran, and — probably most of all, one should add — *fiqh* (Islamic jurisprudence). Reproduction superseded production.[10] To complete the description of this tradition, it should be mentioned that natural sciences were no longer part of the ordinary curriculum of most Muslim scholars, but that *tasawwuf* (Islamic mysticism), both in its ritual as well in its theoretical and doctrinal aspect, was.[11]

[10]Zamakhsyari, op. cit., 65 ff.
[11]The negative attitude towards natural sciences is also mentioned in op. cit., 69. The strong integration of mystical learning and studies in other religious subject matters, as well as the strong links in both fields between the Hijaz and South-East Asia appears clearly from Azyumardi, *The Transmission of Islamic Reformism.*

Whereas the Hijaz tradition differed from the earlier Cordoba-Baghdad tradition, by the end of the nineteenth century yet another, reformist approach to Islamic education and learning developed. Its centre was al-Azhar of Cairo. From that time, a growing number of Indonesians went to study at al-Azhar and their interest in studying in the Hijaz diminished. The main causes of this shift in orientation were the following: firstly, Wahhabi thought, which was opposed by most Muslim scholars in the Indonesian Archipelago brought up in the previous tradition, began to be dominant in the Hijaz; secondly, the new, reformist approach to Islamic Studies corresponded better with the needs and mentality of the contemporary Muslim population of the Netherlands Indies, especially the growing group living in an urban environment; in addition, this approach formed a more convincing alternative to Dutch-style education, which was made available to a limited group of indigenous inhabitants of the Dutch colony, than the previous tradition.[12]

It is this reformed al-Azhar which became one of the main references for the IAIN when this latter institution was created. Three of the IAIN faculties are identical to faculties existing in al-Azhar since the 1930s: the faculties of *Usūl al-Dīn* (Islamic Theology), *Sharī'ah* (Islamic Law) and *Ādāb* (Arts). The institution of yearly examinations was also adopted from al-Azhar.[13] One of the factors which contributed to the influence of the al-Azhar model was that many prominent positions within the Indonesian Ministry of Religious Affairs, which worked out the creation of the IAIN, were occupied by al-Azhar graduates.[14]

This does not mean to say that the al-Azhar model was adopted blindly. In order to satisfy the national needs of agents and teachers of religious development, two more faculties were created: a Faculty of *Tarbiyah*, i.e. education or teachers' training, and a Faculty of *Da'wah* (Propagation of the Faith). The latter began as a department within the Faculty of *Usūl al-Dīn* and was later upgraded into an independent faculty. At a more fundamental level, a particular Indonesian element of the IAIN is that the education of

---

[12]Zamakhsyari, op. cit., 67 f. Recently, much research on Indonesian students at al-Azhar has been done by Mona Abaza; see in particular her *Islamic Education*.

[13]On the successive reforms of al-Azhar, see Reid, "Al-Azhar". For a brief history of the IAIN, see *Informasi Institut Agama Islam Negeri (IAIN)*, 1 ff., which was at the same time made available in an English edition: *Information on State Institute for Islamic Studies (IAIN)*.

[14]Zamakhsyari, op. cit., 71.

specialists in religious sciences who, among other roles, should contribute to the development of harmonious relations between the different communities of the variegated Indonesian society, is mentioned as one of the objectives of the IAIN.[15] At the doctrinal level, one reason why many Indonesian Islamic scholars stress the need for an autonomous development of higher education in Islamic Studies, is their conviction that Islam has developed in various ways, in conformity with different historical and cultural contexts, and that it should continue to do so in future. Therefore, Islamic learning in Indonesia should not follow the Middle Eastern model or any other reference blindly. Finally, at the social level, the fact that a large part of the IAIN students originates from *pesantren*s, adds to the weight of the particular Indonesian tradition of Islamic education within the IAINs. This observation remains valid even after the early 1990s, when a diploma from a general secondary school (*sekolah menengah atas — SMA*) or a *madrasah* (an institute with a mixed curriculum of religious and "secular" subjects) became a condition for admission to an IAIN. Many *pesantren* pupils nowadays follow a *SMA* or *madrasah* education besides their more traditional *pesantren* studies.

In addition to the Middle Eastern, in particular al-Azhar, tradition and to the indigenous one, the IAIN underwent the influence of the Western tradition of higher education. This was evident, first of all, in the structure of the studies. Based on the Dutch academic tradition, the first study programmes lasted five years, divided into a three-year course for a *sarjana muda* ("young scholar", i.e. bachelor) degree and a further two years for a *doctorandus* degree, offering its holder the right to prepare a doctorate. Although this system was later abandoned, the Dutch practice was again the main source of inspiration for the replacement of the al-Azhar system of annual examinations with a system based on the accumulation of a certain number of credit points.

Of more fundamental importance, however, were several reforms in the contents of the study programme and the methods of instruction. Looking first at the contents of the programme, the principal change was the introduction of a general introductory course to Islamic religious studies and

---

[15]For example in the report of the Team in Charge of Carrying Out a Feasibility Study on the [Project] to Develop the IAIN into an Islamic State University (Tim Penyusun Studi Kelayakan Pengembangan IAIN Menjadi Universitas Negeri), Tim Penyusun Studi Kelayakan, *Laporan*, 2.

an increase in the attention paid to Western and Muslim philosophy. In the case of the teaching methods, rational, critical, and independent thinking as well as discussion were stimulated in order to replace the blind imitation of the teacher and more or less classical texts. Most of these reforms were introduced during the rectorship (presidency) of Harun Nasution at IAIN Syarif Hidayatullah (1973-1984) and spread at a slower rate to the other IAINs.[16] They were inspired both by the policy of national development, within which a rational and dynamic religious life was considered a necessary spiritual component, and the Western academic tradition. The fact that Harun Nasution, for example, had studied at al-Azhar, but on a later occasion, disappointed by this institution, followed courses at *al-Dirasāt al-islāmiyyah* in the same city, then obtained his PhD from the Institute of Islamic Studies of McGill University, was undoubtedly one of the factors behind these reforms.[17] At the same time these reforms stressed that the IAINs should become institutes for the development of religious sciences, rather than centres of Islamic doctrine. During the earlier period of its development, the nature of the IAIN had not yet clearly taken shape.[18]

An indubitable indication of the plural orientation of the IAIN as an institution is its international cooperation. As explained above, traditionally Indonesia's international scholarly contacts in the field of religious studies were most intensive with the Middle East. This goes for the IAINs too. Up to the present day, a number of IAIN graduates pursue graduate studies in the Middle East and several IAIN lecturers have received all or part of their education, at undergraduate or postgraduate level, in the Middle East. Despite this tendency to follow tradition, an increasing number of IAIN lecturers and/or graduates are sent to the West for advanced studies. This phenomenon had already begun during the 1960s, but has become increasingly important since the late 1980s. Most of these students and researchers are sent to McGill and Leiden Universities, smaller numbers are sent to several universities in the USA, Australia or other Western countries. One of the main reasons for this new policy, as stated on several occasions by officials of the IAINs and the Indonesian Ministry of Religious Affairs,

---

[16]Ahmad Syadali, "Harun Nasution dan Perkembangan IAIN", 276; Mastuhu, "Harun Nasution dan Identitas IAIN Jakarta", 280 ff.

[17]Cf. Harun Nasution's autobiography, edited on the basis of a series of interviews by Zaim Uchrowi and Ahmadie Thaha and published with the title "Menyeru Pemikiran Rasional Mu'tazilah".

[18]Mastuhu, op. cit., 280 f.

has been the desire to bridge the cultural and intellectual gap between those Indonesians, most of them Muslims, who were specialized in non-religious subjects and had been educated largely in the Western scholarly tradition and partly in the West, and those educated at institutes of Islamic higher education, especially at IAINs. A further reason, which has much in common with the previous one, was the wish to widen the intellectual horizon of the Indonesian students of Islamic religious science and introduce them to the Western tradition of critical scholarship in their field.[19] The general trend at the Indonesian Ministry of Religious Affairs became to send Indonesians for undergraduate studies to the Middle East, mainly Saudi Arabia and Egypt, where more stress is put on doctrine and the forming of a Muslim personality, and for postgraduate studies to the West.[20]

Now the pattern is changing and in recent times the development of new cooperation projects for postgraduate studies by the Indonesian Ministry of Religious Affairs, although concentrated on Western partners, has not been limited to them. In the mid 1990s, it signed several agreements with Middle Eastern partners. A group of recent IAIN graduates was scheduled to be sent to Riyadh in the second half of 1996 to study for a master's degree. This new project received particular attention from the ministry and it selected the best male participants — no female candidates were invited — from the Arabic language group of its most recent pre-departure training programme for prospective lecturers. Apparently, this cooperation is part of a more general policy to develop the good relations between both countries. The relations between Indonesia and Saudi Arabia are intensive, in particular because for some years now Indonesia has been sending the largest contingent of haj pilgrims. Relations between the two countries are complicated because of the difference in cultural and religious traditions and open to strain because of the bad treatment of part of the numerous Indonesian female immigrant workers in the kingdom. It is noteworthy that most or all of the candidates for advanced studies in Saudi Arabia received the news of their selection with disappointment.[21] Later, it appeared that none of the selected candidates could leave for the kingdom because of a failed follow-up to the ministerial agreement in principle by the Saudi

[19]See Zamakhsyari, op. cit., 61 ff. and Zamakhsyari, "The Role of Traditional Islamic Educational Institutions", 56.
[20]This policy was explained on several occasions by Munawir Syadzali, the Indonesian minister of religious affairs from 1983 to 1993.
[21]Discussion with one of the candidates.

authorities.[22] Some of them still had what they considered the good luck to leave for postgraduate studies in a Western country.

An interesting development concerning undergraduate studies is that from the mid 1990s plans have been elaborated to open al-Azhar sections within Indonesian IAINs. They will offer programmes largely modelled on the al-Azhar curriculum, with Arabic as working language. Although this project seemed to be in contradiction with the principle of Indonesian national sovereignty in matters of education as understood in that period, the idea was adopted by the Indonesian authorities as a means to control the large group of Indonesians who are interested in an al-Azhar education and, up to now, have been leaving for Egypt instead of enrolling at IAINs or other Indonesian institutes of higher education.[23] After protracted discussions on details, in September 1999 al-Azhar University and IAIN Syarif Hidayatullah, Jakarta signed a memorandum of understanding for this type of cooperation.

As a conclusion of this section, it is possible to state that during the history of the IAIN, various educational and scholarly traditions and perspectives — national, Western, and several Middle Eastern — have been combined in changing proportions. Although changes in emphasis will probably continue in the future, none of the elements mentioned is likely to be abandoned totally. In principle the process of combining different traditions is fruitful, but it has not been completed yet, nor has it always been run in a consistent way.

The IAIN between State and Civil Society

Although, by its very definition, from its origin the IAIN has been a state institution, it was not created out of nothing by public authorities. In many ways it is the heir to the highest level of *pesantren* education in colonial and pre-colonial times. More directly, the IAIN can be considered as the successor to private initiatives, such as the project of Satiman Wirjosandjojo before the Second World War to create a "*pesantren luhur*" (high level *pesantren*), which was never realized, and the Sekolah Tinggi Islam (Islamic

---

[22]Oral information, Indonesian Ministry of Religious Affairs.
[23]Discussions with Prof. Dr. M. Quraish Shihab, Rector IAIN Syarif Hidayatullah, Jakarta, and Prof. Dr. Mastuhu, Deputy Rector IV of the same IAIN.

College), later Universitas Islam Indonesia (Indonesian Islamic University), established in 1945 by a private foundation with Mohammad Hatta as chairman and Mohammad Natsir as secretary. In 1950 the Faculty of Religious Studies of the latter institute was taken over by the state and transformed into the Perguruan Tinggi Agama Islam Negeri (PTAIN — State College for Islamic Studies). This decision was considered a gesture of appreciation from the government towards the "Muslim" group of the population, after the "secular" element of the population had been offered the creation of the Gadjah Mada University of Yogyakarta.[24] In 1957 the government created the Akademi Dinas Ilmu Agama (ADIA — Academy for [Islamic] Religious Science Service) to educate teachers of Islamic religion for senior high schools. The IAIN was created in 1960 as a merger and further development of the PTAIN and the ADIA.[25] Therefore, the IAIN, although a state institution, was created in close contact with traditions and aspirations of the Muslim "civil society".[26]

It should not be forgotten that the main objective of the public authorities in creating the IAIN was to form specialists which would become agents of the state in guiding and developing the religious life of the Muslim community, in conformity with values and aims established by these authorities. Among these values and aims are the creation of harmonious relations between the different religious communities of the country as well as within the Muslim community. This harmony should be realized by avoiding the development of religious ideas that were considered — by the public authorities or the majority of the population — fanatical or unorthodox and by creating a spiritual attitude which was simultaneously conducive to national development and would check its degeneration.

In order to realize this aspiration, the Indonesian government not only steadily developed the IAINs both in quantity and in quality, but also extended its influence on the other institutes of Islamic education. The IAIN curriculum was made compulsory for private institutes of higher Islamic

---

[24]*Rencana Induk Pembangunan IAIN*, 5 f. In fact, most members of the "secular" group were Muslims too, but they laid less stress than the "Muslim" group on the specifically Islamic character state and society should adopt after the recently gained independence.
[25]*Informasi Institut Agama Islam Negeri*, l.c.
[26]In this text, without further reference to any particular theoretical discussion of the concept, the term "civil society" is used in the sense of the population of a country, with their organizations and initiatives, as partners — or in certain cases adversaries — of the state, with its authorities and further agents, apparatus, and policies.

religious education that aspired to official recognition and these institutes were brought under the supervision of the regional IAIN within the framework of what is known as the Koordinasi Perguruan Tinggi Agama Islam (Kopertais — Co-ordination of Islamic Higher Education). The influence of the IAIN was made effective at the lower levels of Islamic education by the rule, referred to earlier, that all IAIN students should have an *SMA* or *madrasah* diploma. This was one of the reasons why an increasing number of *pesantren* pupils followed parallel education at an *SMA* or *madrasah* and many *pesantren* leaders opened schools of this type within their institute. However, it was neither the only nor the first reason. These trends had started within the *pesantren* milieu long before.[27] Although the new regulation on admission to IAIN education aroused some protest, the proportion of IAIN students with a — partly — *pesantren* background remained large.[28] On the other hand, a not negligible number of *pesantren* leaders and other *pesantren* teachers are IAIN graduates.[29] Therefore, the relation between IAINs and *pesantren*s may be characterized as one of interaction and mutual influence.

In the final analysis, whether in future the IAIN will function as a means of pressure, or even of oppression, by the state on the Muslim community or as a catalyst of social dynamics and development in the positive and broad sense of the word will depend on the development, or absence thereof, of a larger political and social openness in Indonesia in general. One important problem that remains to be solved is the gap between IAIN graduates and Islamic religious leaders educated in traditional centres of religious education in the Middle East or without any advanced religious education at all.

---

[27]As stressed in particular by Zamakhsyari in his "The Role of Traditional Islamic Educational Institutions", 50, and Zamakhsyari, "Pesantren and the Development of Islam".

[28]Because of the new regulation, IAIN students are no longer registered as former *pesantren* pupils and therefore no statistical data are available on their number. My contention that their number is still important is based on experience as an IAIN lecturer and discussions with IAIN students and colleagues. For a protest action of April 1992 against the new regulation at IAIN Syarif Hidayatullah of Jakarta, where its application was delayed longer than at other IAINs, see *INIS Newsletter*, 7 (1992), 15 f.; this report was republished in Darul Aqsha et al., *Islam in Indonesia.*, 410 f.

[29]In 1986 about 10 per cent of the Indonesian *pesantren*s were led by IAIN graduates (Zamakhsyari, "Pesantren and the Development of Islam", 99, referring to a survey conducted by the Perhimpunan Pengembangan Pesantren dan Masyarakat [P3M — Association for *Pesantren* and Community Development]).

The IAIN between Religious Studies and General Education

In Indonesian public administration, the IAINs and institutes with an important part of religious subject matters at a lower level, in particular the *madrasahs*, fall primarily within the competence of the Ministry of Religious Affairs, whereas institutes of general, i.e. non-religious, education, from primary schools to universities, fall basically within the cognizance of the Ministry of Education and Culture. According to some authors, among others Karel A. Steenbrink and C.E. Beeby, this complicated situation has created a relationship fraught with competition and envy between both ministries, related to a difference in cultural background and attitude.[30] Zamakhsyari Dhofier, again referring to this question, rather emphasizes the harmony that existed.[31] In the present text, this question will not be discussed in a general way, but some of its aspects are worth further consideration.

In March 1989 the Indonesian president signed the Law on the National Educational System, which had been under discussion since 1978. This law fixes a general framework for all educational institutes in the country, general as well as religious. In other words, it has integrated institutes of religious education, including the IAIN, into the one unified system of education. By doing so, up to certain limits, it put an end to the dualism between religious and general education that basically went back to the Dutch colonial policy of introducing Dutch-style educational institutes.[32] There is some compromise in that the Ministry of Religious Affairs remains in charge of the management and development of the IAINs.[33]

Another aspect of the relationship between religious and non-religious education that needs consideration is the theory that general universities are a "present" for the "secular" group in the Indonesian society and the IAIN a "present" for the "Muslim" group. Firstly, the division of the Indonesian population — of which the large majority is Muslim — into both these groups

---

[30]Steenbrink, *Pesantren Madrasah Sekolah.*, 89 ff.; Beeby, *Assessment of Indonesian Education*, 231, as mentioned in Gillett, op. cit., 25. It should be noted that both authors speak of a relatively early stage of the development of the Indonesian post-colonial administration.

[31]Zamakhsyari, "The Role of Traditional Islamic Educational Institutions", 49 ff.

[32]On the history of this dualism, see Steenbrink, op. cit., chapter 1.

[33]Only for certain matters, such as the promotion of IAIN lecturers to the rank of professor, is the consent of the Ministry of Education and Culture needed.

291

is imprecise and superficial.[34] Secondly, the idea that these two, partially imaginary, groups should be satisfied each with its own "present", seems to correspond to an unhealthy and unfruitful way of political thinking. The question is of actual relevance because the idea is one of the elements that plays a role in the discussion about the transformation of the IAIN into an Islamic State University, which will be discussed below.

Another question related to the place of the IAIN on the scala between the poles of pure religious studies and general education is that of the subject matter covered. Above it was mentioned that from its creation in 1960, in addition to the three faculties adopted from the al-Azhar model, the IAIN has housed a Faculty of *Tarbiyah* or teachers' training. Up to the present, the majority of IAIN students register in this faculty because its programme is easier: it offers more practical and less theoretical subjects and demands a less profound mastering of Arabic than the other faculties. Within this faculty, the Department of *Tadris Umum* (general teaching), which educates teachers in non-religious subjects, such as the natural sciences, mathematics, Indonesian, English, and the social sciences, especially at *madrasah*s, and was opened in the early 1980s, was the most popular. This is no longer the case, because as from the academic year 1989/1990 most IAINs do not accept new students for this department and have expressed the wish to close it down gradually. One reason given for this decision was that the *madrasah*s no longer suffered from a lack of teachers in these subjects and many *tadris umum* graduates could find no jobs.[35] A tendency of the IAINs to concentrate on religious subjects, to improve their quality in this field, and to leave other subjects to the institutes under the authority of the Ministry of Education and Culture, was another reason put forward.[36]

From the viewpoint of the subject matter offered, the IAIN seems to be proceeding in a zigzag course because recently plans were developed to

---

[34]For a criticism of this schematism from a historical point of view, see Shiraishi, *An Age in Motion*.

[35]Some IAINs do continue to accept students in this department. Although, after finishing their studies, they are not accepted as civil servants in public schools, they still find employment as teachers at private schools. It is precisely in regions where private religious schools still need many new teachers that IAINs continue to accept new *tadris umum* students (discussion with Drs. Choliluddin A.S., Deputy Dean I, Faculty of *Tarbiyah*, IAIN Syarif Hidayatullah, Jakarta).

[36]For details see *INIS Newsletter*, 2 (1989), 9; 6 (1991), 12 f.; republished in Darul Aqsha et al., op. cit., 386 f., 399.

enlarge the scope of the IAIN and transform at least two of them into Islamic State Universities with several faculties in the field of the social and the natural sciences. A similar project was already considered in the 1970s by Harun Nasution and the then minister of religious affairs, Mukti Ali, but it got no further than the drawing board.[37] At the end of 1992, Sutan Takdir Alisjahbana, then rector of the Universitas Nasional (National University) of Jakarta, declared that he deplored the closing of the Department of *Tadris Umum* in IAINs. Instead, he argued, in order that its graduates should have a broad horizon and that a revival of science and technology should take place in Indonesian Muslim circles, the IAINs should open faculties in fields other than religious sciences.[38] After preparatory discussions within the Ministry of Religious Affairs, in which Zamakhsyari Dhofier, then Director for the Development of Islamic Religious Education, was one of the main participants, in January 1994 the Minister of Religious Affairs, Tarmizi Taher, announced that the IAINs would be transformed into general universities. A commission to survey the feasibility of this project was created by ministerial decision of 25 August of that year.[39]

Except for the fact that the development of the IAINs seems to follow a zigzag line, the recent plans to transform them into Islamic state universities raises a number of questions for another reason too: varying reasons are cited for the project and no clear and uniform idea seems to have developed yet on its objectives and the procedure for its implementation.

On different occasions, two very different reasons are mentioned for the project to transform IAINs into Islamic universities. The first one is to satisfy the Muslim community or concede it a more important place in national education.[40] This argument is related to the theory of the existence of a "secular" and a "Muslim" component of the Indonesian society, which should each be satisfied with particular "presents". Above it has been explained that this theory needs to be reconsidered. The argument may also be related to certain political analyses which claim that during the recent period the Muslim community has obtained a more prominent and respected position in the Indonesian political and social structure. It also seems related to the aspiration of a group of highly educated Muslims to take a more

---

[37]*Republika* (daily, Jakarta), 5 Jan. 1996.
[38]*INIS Newsletter*, 9 (1993), 18; republished in Aqsha et al., op. cit., 424 f.
[39]*INIS Newsletter*, 9 (1995), 14; Tim Penyusun Studi Kelayakan, op. cit., 80 ff.
[40]Tim Penyusun Studi Kelayakan, op. cit., 8.

prominent part in national development and the creation, within this framework, of the Ikatan Cendekiawan Muslim Se-Indonesia (ICMI — All-Indonesian Association of Muslim Intellectuals). All these questions are related, but all are still subject to controversy and open to further analysis.[41] A clearer and less speculative argument for the development of Islamic state universities is that the success of national development depends largely on the quality of the Muslim community, which is the largest religious community of the country.[42]

The second reason cited is the aspiration to reunify science and technology with religion after they had been separated by modern Western thought.[43] This ambition has been inspired by discussions outside Indonesia on the "Islamization of science" and related themes. However, neither have these discussions abroad led to any agreement on several fundamental questions, nor have the participants in the discussion on the transformation of the IAIN gone beyond general statements about the reunification aspired to. A related argument is the aspiration to bridge the gap between Indonesian Muslims educated at general universities and at IAINs, which, as we have seen above, is not new.[44] Finally, one particular reason why it becomes increasingly important to bridge the gap between science and technology and, on the other hand, religion is the growing risk of the negative effects of a development process that might run out of control.[45]

No clarity has yet been reached either about the procedure to implement the transformation of IAINs into Islamic state universities. Since 1994 pilot projects at the IAINs of Jakarta and Yogyakarta have been announced,[46] but so far they have not commenced. Furthermore, it is not clear whether the transformation into universities will remain limited to these two IAINs for ever. The IAIN Development Master Plan for the period 1994/1995-2018/2019 presupposes this.[47] The rub is that a limitation to only part of

---

[41]On the political and social meaning of the creation of the ICMI, see Saiful Muzani, "Kultur Klas Menengah". This article clearly shows that the last word has not been said yet on the development of the ICMI.

[42]Tim Penyusun Studi Kelayakan, op. cit., 7.

[43]Op. cit., 4, 6, 27, 29 ff., 34; "Lesehan 38 Tahun IAIN Kita".

[44]This argument is mentioned in Tim Penyusun Studi Kelayakan, op. cit., 27.

[45]Op. cit. 1, 6.

[46]INIS Newsletter, 11 (1995), 14.

[47]Rencana Induk Pembangunan IAIN, 31.

the IAINs for practical reasons is in contradiction to the fundamental aspiration to put an end to the separation between science and religion.

No single opinion seems to exist either about the faculties which should be created within the IAINs in order to realize the transformation. In his statement of 1992, Sutan Takdir Alisjahbana suggested the creation of faculties of medicine, economics, law, and political sciences.[48] In January 1994, the Minister of Religious Affairs mentioned economics and banking as possible new fields of study. Other officials of this ministry, as well as the Minister himself on a later occasion, proposed to begin with the opening of faculties of psychology and sociology.[49] In its report of January 1995, the Team in Charge of Carrying Out a Feasibility Study, in order to comply with the existing regulation on universities, proposed three faculties in the field of the natural sciences (mathematics and the natural sciences, engineering, medicine) and three other ones in the social field (psychology, economics, the social and political sciences).[50] The discussion on the procedure of the transformation of IAINs into general universities cannot be closed before more clarity is obtained about the objectives of this project.

From the discussion on this subject, for example at a seminar on "*Iptek Islami*" (Islamic Science and Technology) held on 22 October 1994 in the IAIN of Jakarta, it appears that no elaborated conception of the nature of the education and science that should be offered by the future Islamic state universities has yet been reached. The ideas voiced still remain very general and sometimes vague. Some participants point out religious values that should guide the development of science within these institutes or provide it with an ethical and moral basis.[51] It is also mentioned that religion should offer the metaphysical and ontological background for science.[52] On the other hand, on several occasions it was emphasized that the objectivity of the scholarly activities within these universities should be guaranteed.[53] Nobody has yet come up with the answer to the question in which way medicine or civil engineering, for example, as developed, taught, or applied by a Muslim

---

[48]*INIS Newsletter*, 9, l.c.

[49]*INIS Newsletter*, 9, l.c.; *Pelita* (daily, Jakarta), 21 April 1994; *Republika*, 23 April 1994.

[50]Tim Penyusun Studi Kelayakan, op. cit., 12. The *Rencana Induk Pembangunan IAIN*, Annexe II, proposes a faculty of communications, containing a department of *da'wah* and a department of communications, and a faculty of economics.

[51]Tim Penyusun Studi Kelayakan, op. cit., 8, 35.

[52]Op. cit., 35, 46 ff., 63.

[53]Op. cit., 34 f.; cf. op. cit., 9; *Rencana Induk Pembangunan IAIN*, 10.

scholar at one of the existing Indonesian universities and by a scholar at one of the projected Islamic state universities, will be different.

Which existing foreign institutes of Islamic higher learning will be taken as a model, and to what degree, is another question that is still pending. Three members of the Team in Charge of Carrying Out a Feasibility Study visited various institutes of higher learning in India, Iran, and Malaysia for a comparative study.[54] No detailed conclusions or proposals were submitted as a result of this mission. Nevertheless, an examination of the structure of the future Islamic state university as proposed in the final report of the Team in Charge of Carrying Out a Feasibility Study presents the clue that it is closest to the model of the Iranian University of Teheran and Ferdowsi Masyad University, where faculties of religious studies exist beside other faculties, but with certain compulsory religious subject matters, including Muslim philosophy and Muslim history and civilization.[55] This is rather interesting because in general the Indonesian government and most Indonesian Muslims do not take Iran as their model. The present al-Azhar, which contains a large number of faculties in non-religious subjects and, therefore, has changed much from the al-Azhar model which became an important source of inspiration at the creation of the IAIN, is another foreign institute of which the Indonesians take notice. However, its social status in contemporary Egyptian practice is not considered inspiring. This is because, in the eyes of many people, al-Azhar functions as a last choice for people who have failed to be admitted elsewhere and that, within this giant university, the traditional religious faculties have been reduced to an inferior status among the numerous more recently created ones.[56] Another criticism is that the al-Azhar model has only brought together religious and non-religious faculties within one institution, without really overcoming the dichotomy between both scholarly traditions.[57]

---

[54]The institutes visited were Jamia Millia Islamia and Aligarch Muslim University in India; Imām Ṣādiq University, the University of Teheran and Ferdowsi Masyad University in Iran; and Universitas Kebangsaan Malaysia (National University of Malaysia) and the International Islamic University Malaysia in Malaysia (Tim Penyusun Studi Kelayakan, 65 ff.).

[55]Cf. Tim Penyusun Studi Kelayakan, op. cit., 10, 69 f.

[56]Discussion with Dr. Azyumardi Azra, Deputy Director of the Centre for the Study of Islam and Society of IAIN Syarif Hidayatullah, Jakarta. Cf. Zamakhsyari, "The Intellectualization of Islamic Studies", 73.

[57]This was stated in an article in *Institut*, the student monthly of IAIN Syarif Hidayatullah, Jakarta (January 1996, 15). Cf. also Muarif, "Dikotomi Ilmu, antara Fardlu Ain dan

Conclusion

This short discussion has made clear that the Indonesian State Institute for Islamic Studies functions at the crossroads of the indigenous and several foreign scholarly traditions, state and civil society, as well as general and religious studies. Therefore, the IAIN is a very interesting and probably unique institution, but it is also exposed to several tendencies and pressures. Many questions concerning the IAIN need further reflection. This is particularly true of the recent project to transform the IAIN into an Islamic state university. This project crucially places the IAIN at a crossroads in its forty-year development.

Fardlu Kifayah" [Dichotomy of Sciences, between *Fard al-'Ayn* and *Fard al-Kifāyah*; signed "rif": Muarif], *Republika*, 5 January 1996 and other articles in the same *Republika* issue; Ali Anwar, "Universitas Islam Negeri: Lembaga Pendidikan Kelas Dua?" [Islamic State University: a Second Class Educational Institute?], 19.

15 The Interaction of Religion and State in Indonesia

The Case of the Islamic Courts

Muhamad Hisyam

Introduction

In spite of the fact that the overwhelming majority of its population is Muslim, the development of the Islamic judiciary in Indonesia has been fraught with controversy. The ambiguous relationship between Islam and state has been at the core of a series of conflicts. On the one hand the effectiveness of Islamic law requires state intervention and Islamic jurisprudence demands that the Islamic judges should be appointed by the government. On the other hand state intervention is typically inspired by the interests of various groups as well as the interest of the state itself. Conflicts relating to the Islamic judiciary owe much of their intensity to the way the colonial administration affected the development of this body. This text will briefly narrate the development of the Islamic courts in Indonesia. Special reference will be made to the interaction between Islam and the state and to conflicts which were basically a result of colonial government policy. The development of the Islamic judiciary since independence, as is the case for other legal institutions, has been deeply influenced by the legacy of the colonial situation. The aims of legal development are not only to emancipate the administration of justice from the colonial past, but also to accommodate it to the demands of a modern society.

The Origin and Development of Islamic Courts as a Result of the Interaction of Islam and State

The history of Islamic courts in Indonesia started a long time ago, once the Islamic kingdoms were firmly established, if not already at the very beginning of the formation of Muslim communities.[1] This was a consequence of the character of Islam, which is not limited to the domain of religious belief and rituals, but also concerns social and political matters. The development of Muslim societies was intrinsically followed by the advance of *sharī'ah* law, a set of regulations formulated on the basis of Islamic principles. No Muslim community in the world disregards the *sharī'ah*. In this respect, Indonesia is no exception. Therefore, Indonesian Muslim society is coloured more by *sharī'ah* law than by theological or mystical thought. Indonesian Muslim intellectuals are typically experts on *fiqh*, the systematic elaboration of *sharī'ah* in jurisprudence.

Fiqh had been their primary field of interest since the formation of Muslim society in the archipelago. As in other Muslim countries, the implementation of *fiqh* has led to the perpetual creation of new institutions. One of the most important ones was that of the *qāḍī* (judge). The obligation to judge (*qāḍā*) every dispute among the Muslims led to the creation of courts of justice. At an early stage, conflicts between people in the Muslim society were brought before the *imām* or leader of the Muslim community. When the necessity to pursue a more orderly form of social life resulted in a kind of government administration, the office of *qāḍī* was created. *Fiqh* established this office as a mandatory institution. It then determined that the *qāḍī* should be appointed by the government, by means of *tawliyah* (delegation of sovereign authority).

In the old Islamic states of the Indonesian Archipelago, the *qāḍī* institution appeared under a variety of names. In Java, where this institution emerged most visibly, this *qāḍī* or *ḥākim* was called a *pangulu*, and his office *pangulon*. In Aceh it was called *kali malikun ade'*, in South Kalimantan *kerapatan kadi*, in South Sulawesi *imang*, and in Ternate *penghulu*. In these old Islamic states the *qāḍī* held an absolute competence to judge all kinds of conflicts among the population under his jurisdiction.

When the Vereenigde Oost-Indische Compagnie (V.O.C. — Dutch East India Company) gradually subjugated West-Java, in the early seventeenth century, the Dutch rulers began to erect courts of justice in each newly conquered principality in order to exercise their power in the field of legal affairs. They introduced a dual system, consisting of *qāḍī* courts on the one

---

[1] The best example of the *qāḍī* during the early process of Islamization is probably the myth of *Penghulu Jipang* in the *Hikayat Banjar*. See Ras, *Hikajat Bandjar*, 417-425. Cf. Jones, "Ten Conversion Myths", 144-146.

hand and Dutch district civil courts (*landraden*, sg. *landraad*) on the other. The first was competent in religious cases among the Muslim population and the latter in "secular", civil and criminal, cases. In criminal cases involving the death penalty for Muslims, the *landraad* was obliged to ask the *qāḍī* for advice, however. Meanwhile, the Javanese *kraton* (sultan's palace), which remained free from Dutch control, continued to employ the single *pangulu* court, at least until the second decade of the eighteenth century. Then Dutch influence led to its division into a religious court (*pangadilan surambi*) and a secular court (*pangadilan kepatihan/pradhoto*).[2]

The Dutch policy towards the *qāḍī* institution was to allow it to function following the indigenous custom. Until the late nineteenth century the predominant vision among Dutch scholars and administrators was that Islamic law was the legal system adhered to by the Muslim indigenous population. Although a large diversity was observed in the extent to which Islam was observed in religious practice, all Muslims in the colony seemed to share the faith in Islam as the supreme religion. This supremacy was symbolized by the authority of the *penghulu*, who handled civil and criminal cases. It was also manifested in the close relationship between religion and the state, both in the Malay world of Sumatra and in Java. Diponegoro's close relationship with the Muslim religious leaders prior to and during the Java War was the best illustration of this unity.[3]

The Java War (1825-1830) was a turning point in Dutch awareness of the political potency of Islam in Java. The war shocked the Dutch rulers out of their complacency and prompted them to investigate the relationship between religion and the state in the Javanese realm. It was time to make an effort to understand Islam. Undeniably the war made the Dutch realize the danger inherent in militant Islam, but, warned by the feelings it had aroused, it caused them to act gradually and with more circumspection and sensitivity towards the religious community. The policy henceforth became to break in a careful way not only the sense of unity between religion and the *kraton*, but also the relationship between the "devout" Muslims and the more "syncretic" Muslim groups.

The efforts to understand Islam were further intensified during the Padri war in West Sumatra (1830-1835) and the Aceh War (1873-1904). These wars were caused mainly by the conflict between the emerging group of

---

[2] Jonker, *Javaansch strafrecht*, 7-9.
[3] See Carey, "Santri and Satria.", 271-318.

"purified" young Muslims and the old "syncretic" establishment, as well as between *'ulamā'* (Islamic religious scholars) and *uleubalang* (*adat*, i.e. customary, leaders). Learning from these conflicts and the scholarly writings of government advisors such as L.W.C. van den Berg and C. Snouck Hurgronje, the Dutch formed the opinion that, from a religious point of view, the indigenous Muslim population could basically be divided into two groups, which potentially confronted each other, the "devout" or "universalist" and the "syncretic" or "vernacularist" Muslims, especially in the Javanese context often referred to as *santri* and *abangan*. In conflicts between the two groups, the Dutch inevitably took the side of the latter category. This tendency became a characteristic of Dutch colonial policy throughout the archipelago during the second half of the nineteenth century and was intensified in the twentieth century.

The institution of the Islamic court was also affected by the new attitude adopted by the colonial rulers towards Islam. As a symbol of unity between the two groups as well as between religion and state, the *penghulu* (*pangulu* in Javanese) institution in Java became the object of particular attention for the Dutch. Their policy towards the Islamic judiciary in Java should be considered as an attempt to prevent the "danger" of other wars, which would drain still more wealth and energy. The first measure in this framework dated from 1830. It made the Islamic courts in Java subordinate to the *landraden*, set up by the Dutch. The *landraad* was the only court which could order the execution of contested decisions (*executoir verklaring*), including those of Islamic courts.[4]

Despite such innovations, the bond between the head of the Islamic court and the local aristocratic rulers, and therefore the state, remained strong. In Java the head of the Islamic court also presided over the mosque administration. He was appointed by the sultan or the regional aristocratic leader, the *bupati*. The *penghulu* appointed was often chosen from the family circle of the *bupati*. In conformity with the colonial policy designed to emancipate the native authorities from Islam, in 1882 the colonial government reorganized the Islamic courts in order to make them independent of the native ruler. Although the *bupati*s were consulted about the appointment of *penghulu*s, henceforth it was the Dutch *resident*s who decided on their appointment. The transfer of the authority over the *penghulu*s from the *bupati*s to the Dutch *resident*s loosened the bonds

---

[4]Lev, *Islamic Courts*, 11.

between the Islamic officials and their *priyayi* (Javanese aristocrat) overlords and brought the Islamic courts firmly under Dutch control.[5] The reorganized Islamic court was named *priesterraad* (priests' council), a label which was later strongly criticized by Snouck Hurgronje who pointed out the misunderstanding of the Dutch about Islam this designation betrayed: Islam, this scholar explained, has no priestly office.[6] Among the indigenous masses, the new court was called "*raad agama*" (religious council).

At the beginning of the twentieth century, an increasing number of independent *'ulamā'* with modern ideas became active as teachers in religious schools (*pesantrens*) and involved themselves in popular movements. From this circle fierce criticism was levelled against the religious officials because they not only served a non-Islamic (Dutch) administration, but also acted as Islamic judges without a solid education in Islamic law. Facing such criticism, the *penghulus* found themselves in a confusing situation. Although the colonial administration had established the *priesterraad* and made its members formally independent of the native authorities, it did not provide any means for the education of religious judges or for their salaries. The Islamic popular movement the Sarekat Islam (SI), for instance, urged the government to improve the Islamic courts and threatened that, if this did not happen, it would set up independent Islamic courts.[7]

In reaction to this wave of criticism, in 1922 the colonial government appointed a commission to study ways to improve the status of the *priesterraad* and its members.[8] The commission recommende that an independent "*Raad Ulama*", as suggested by the SI, not be created and that the collegial *priesterraad* be changed into a court with a single judge. This new Islamic court would be called *penghoeloegerecht* (*penghulu* court) and would consist of a single *penghulu* as a judge, assisted by no more than two assessors and a clerk. Furthermore, they recommended that the colonial government should provide the salary of the court personnel and a budget for its proper functioning. A regulation based on these recommendations was

---

[5]Op. cit., 14.

[6]See Snouck Hurgronje, "Rapport over de godsdienstige rechtspraak op Java en Madoera", 201-24.

[7]*Sarekat Islam Congres (1e Nationaal Congres)*, 39-40. See also *Neratja*, 1, 90 (10 November 1917).

[8]*Verslag van de Commissie van advies nopens de voorgenomen herziening van de Priesterraad-Rechtspraak.*

issued in 1931,[9] but the *penghoeloegerecht* never became operational because plans for its implementation were disrupted by the economic crisis. Daniel Lev argues that, besides financial difficulties, concerns about reactions from Muslim circles were also behind the postponement of its functioning.[10]

On the other hand, the development of law studies which were based on the dichotomy of "*adat*" and "Islam", gave rise to the new theoretical concept of *receptio* (reception [of Islamic law within *adat* law]).[11] This *receptio* theory, which was originally developed by Snouck Hurgronje at the end of nineteenth century, implied that the effective law among the indigenous Muslim population was not Islamic law, but law based on *adat* (custom, a Malay term derived from the Arabic *'ādah*).[12] Indeed, *adat* had been penetrated by the law of Islam, but isolated fragments of Islamic law only possessed a legal force after they had been accepted as part of *adat* law. This theory was followed and elaborated by C. van Vollenhoven (Leiden University), B. ter Haar (Batavia Law College) and their students, among whom Raden Soepomo. The Leiden-cum-Batavia school of *adat* law had a deep influence among the decision makers in the Netherlands East Indies. In 1927, the concept of *adat* law was accepted by the East Indies government and from that time Dutch colonial policy was marked by what Soepomo called a "systematic step backwards to create a dynamic dualism".[13] The efforts to preserve *adat* law were supported by systematic initiatives to investigate and codify the many regional varieties of *adat* law. This "*adatrechtspolitiek*" (*adat* law policy) received a great deal of support among the Javanese *priyayi* and among aristocratic groups elsewhere in the Netherlands East Indies.[14]

Among the *santri* groups, however, the aim of this policy was viewed not only as to preserve *adat* as such, but also to protect it from the attacks

---

[9]*Staatsblad van Nederlandsch-Indië*, 1931, no. 53.

[10]Lev, op. cit., 21.

[11]Many Western writers present Islam and *adat* as two opposites within indigenous Muslim society, which they generally relate to two equally opposite social groups, the *santri* and the *abangan*. A number of contemporary Indonesian writers, like Taufik Abdullah, consider the terms *adat* and Islam not as referring to mutually exclusive legal or ideological systems, but to complementary principles of the whole structure and way of life. See Abdullah, "Adat and Islam".

[12]Vollenhoven, *Het Adatrecht van Nederlandsch-Indië*, vol. 1, 8.

[13]Soepomo, *Bab-Bab Tentang Hukum Adat*, 5.

[14]Lev, op. cit., 26.

launched against it by modern Islam. Indubitably, the development of the reformist Muslim movement put indigenous cultural elements under pressure, and this was especially true of *adat* which did not correspond to the ideals of Islamic purity it sought to attain. It was understandable that the Dutch were afraid of the expansion of Islamic reformism, since they realized it would have a wider impact in stimulating the intellectual life and the emancipation of the indigenous population and, more than this, it had the potential to unify the various ethnic groups in the colony. Another germ of unrest was that the concept of egalitarianism in reformist Islam to some extent could weaken the hold of feudalism, which tended to be bolstered by various constituent parts of *adat* law.

One of the most significant steps taken by the reformist Muslim group in reaction to the *adat* law policy was a motion issued by the twentieth congress of the Partai Sarekat Islam, in 1934. The motion called for the abolition of ancient *adat* pertaining to the field of family relations, marriage, and inheritance if this did not conform to the *sharī'ah* and the requirements of modern society.[15] Cogently, the motion was not only addressed to the government of the Netherlands East Indies, but to the Indonesian community in general. This was because the tension between *adat* and Islam was generated not only by a conflict between the colonial government and the Muslim community, it also emerged from frictions between traditionalist and progressive or more puritan adherents of Islam within this community. The latter group considered the *sharī'ah* more in conformity with modern times than various local customs which it considered obsolescent.

The most crucial problem arose after the decision of 1937 to transfer inheritance cases from the competence of the *penghoeloegerecht* to the *landraad*. In this year the government of the Netherlands East Indies promulgated a regulation which created an Islamic Appeals Court (*Hof voor Islamitische Zaken*), but they detracted from this by referring inheritance cases to the *landraden*, which based their decision on the *adat* law.[16] The reason stated was that Islam had not in fact deeply influenced the rules of inheritance within Muslim families. As a consequence of the new regulation,

[15]The Partai Sarekat Islam was a political party issued in 1923 from the Sarekat Islam (Islamic Association, created in 1912, continuing the Sarekat Dagang Islam [Islamic Commercial Association] established in 1911) mentioned earlier. This congress (*madjlis tachkim*) was held from 20 to 26 May 1934 in Bandjarnegara. See *Djedjak Langkah Hadji A. Salim*, 176-89.

[16]*Staatsblad van Nederlandsch-Indië*, 1937, no. 116.

the *penghulu*s would not only be deprived of the most significant part of their job, but they would also lose the legal basis by which they could sustain the application of Islamic law in this respect. The regulation was issued on February 19, 1937, and soon after its promulgation, on May 16, 1937, the *penghulu*s from all over Java and Madura organized a congress in Solo to protest about the law. In fact, the objection to the law was pronounced not only by the association of *penghulu*s (Perhimpunan Pangulu dan Pegawainya — Association of *Penghulu*s and Their Staff), which was established during the congress, but also by other organizations of Indonesian Muslims. The first Islamic congress (*Kongres Al-Islam I*, Surabaya 1938) which was organized by the High Council of Indonesian Islam (*Majlis Islam A'la Indonesia*) and attended by all important Indonesian Muslim associations issued a motion which expressed disagreement with the transfer of competence in inheritance disputes to the *landraad* and asked the government to return this competence to the "*Raad Agama*".[17]

To no avail and the fate of the Islamic courts remained unaltered until the Japanese military occupied Indonesia in 1942. During the Japanese occupation, the military rulers showed a marked concern about Islamic affairs, but in the case of the Islamic court they did no more than change the name: *Raad Agama* was called *Sooryo Hooin* and the *Hof voor Islamitische Zaken Kaikyo Kotoo Hooin*.[18] Because of the high expectations aroused by the promises made by the Japanese rulers to those members of the Indonesian population prepared to cooperate with them, the Muslim associations gave less priority to their demand that inheritance disputes should be returned to the jurisdiction of the Islamic courts. Furthermore, Lev argues that in 1944, when Soepomo was assigned by the Japanese administration to provide recommendations on this subject, he still continued to reiterate pro-*adat* views. He referred particularly to the opinion of Ter Haar given in the advisory commission of 1922 that the *landraden* should not try inheritance cases according to Islamic law because this legal system was in no way part of the Indonesian sense of justice. The *landraden* should only apply an Islamic rule if it had become integrated into *adat* law in the

---

[17]*Damai*, 1, 3 (March 1938), 69-71.
[18]For more details on the functioning of the Islamic courts during the Japanese occupation, see Kartodirdjo, "De Rechtspraak op Java en Madoera".

course of the years. This was the formula which had been accepted by the government at the time.[19]

Entering the era of independence, the institution of Islamic courts remained weak in Indonesia. Not only were inheritance cases still excluded from its competence, its functioning also continued to diverge throughout the country. Groups with secular tendencies, which had grown stronger after the successful end of the struggle for independence, opposed any efforts to solve the crucial problem of bringing back inheritance disputes under the jurisdiction of the Islamic courts. The lack of human resources prevented these courts from gaining a high authority and expanding uniformly throughout the new republic. The absence of a provision for salaries for the judges and their assistants also continued to be a problem.

During the preparation of Indonesia's independence in the last years of the Japanese occupation, many Muslims considered a ministry of religious affairs to be a natural part of the future government. During the debates of the Preparatory Committee for Indonesian Independence, however, the non-Muslim group and the religiously neutral nationalists seemed to reject such an institution and the majority of the committee members voted against the idea. Therefore, in the first cabinet formation in 1945, no office of minister of religious affairs was included. The Ministry of Religious Affairs was only established on January 3, 1946, in accordance with a proposal to the Central Indonesian National Committee. Officially, the founding of the Ministry of Religious Affairs was based on Art. 29 of the Constitution 1945. This article states that the State is based on the belief in the Oneness of God and guarantees the freedom of every inhabitant to embrace his or her own religion and to worship according to this religion. Legally, the establishment of the ministry was necessary to implement the constitution, although it was hampered by some of the drafters. Although the Ministry of Religious Affairs administers all five religious denominations generally recognized in Indonesia i.e. Islam, Protestantism, Roman Catholicism, Hinduism, and Buddhism, Islam benefits most from it. This is because most sections of the ministry deal with Islamic affairs, whereas the other religions only have their representatives in order to guarantee that their interests are protected. Therefore, the ministry clearly shows that although the Indonesian state is basically not Islamic, it holds Islam in a high position.

---

[19]See Lev, op. cit., 20-1, footnote no. 17.

When the Ministry of Religious Affairs was established, Islamic courts existed all over Java and Madura and in parts of the islands of Sumatra and Kalimantan. As mentioned before, an association of Islamic judges had even existed since 1937. During the Japanese occupation, as under the preceding Dutch administration, the Islamic courts were organized under the colonial justice departments. The head of the Islamic Appeals Court, and the founder of the Perhimpunan Pangulu dan Pegawainya, K.H. Mohamad Adnan, was asked by the Minister of Religious Affairs, Muhammad Rasjidi, to transfer the Islamic courts into his ministry. Mohamad Adnan agreed on the condition that this transfer would imply the restoration of independent Islamic courts and would also guarantee an improvement in their jurisdiction. [20]High expectations were aroused by the transfer to the new ministry, but in reality changes remained limited to improvements in the sphere of salaries. After the Dutch government finally recognized the passing of sovereignty to the Indonesian authorities, in 1949, the Ministry of Religious Affairs expanded the number of Islamic courts outside Java and Madura, a process which had to overcome a number of stumbling blocks.

The Religious Judicature Bill and the Reactions of the Non-Muslim Factions

On January 28, 1989 the Indonesian government submitted a draft legislation on Islamic courts to the People's Representative Council (Dewan Perwakilan Rakyat — DPR). The bill is a natural consequence of the Law on the Basic Rules of the Judiciary of 1970, which establishes that (Islamic) religious courts and the three other types of courts (civil courts, military courts, and administrative courts) have an equal status and are all placed under the authority of the Supreme Court (Mahkamah Agung). After more than 150 years of the subordination of the religious courts to the civil courts, more than fifty years of the exemption of inheritance disputes from their competence, and forty-three years of independence without substantial progress in this matter, this bill aroused new expectations among the Indonesian Muslims that the government wished to restore the authority of

---

[20]The transfer of the Islamic Appeals Court and all Islamic courts from the control of the Ministry of Justice to the Ministry of Religious Affairs took place on March 25, 1946 under Governmental Decree No. 5/SD. See Lev, op. cit., 86.

the Islamic courts. Moreover, in the climate of diminishing tension between *santri* and *abangan* and increasing tolerance between Muslims and non-Muslims which had developed during the New Order administration of President Soeharto, many Muslims assumed that the DPR debate on the bill would run smoothly. In fact, however, while the DPR was discussing the bill, the debate aroused fierce reactions outside the DPR.

Both within the DPR and in the public debate at large, a sharp contention arose between those who were in favour of the bill and those who were not. Almost all Islamic groups supported it, whereas the non-Muslim groups opposed it. The Christian lobbyists, including the Christian members of the Partai Demokrasi Indonesia (PDI — Indonesian Democratic Party) and the semi-governmental Golkar (Golongan Karya — Functional Groups), denounced the draft law as being contrary to the basic principles of the *Pancasila* and the Constitution of 1945.[21] Through newspapers with a Christian background, Christian scholars argued that the bill would endanger the unity of the nation. It was undeniable that the bill yielded part of the state authority to a particular religion and it was glaringly contradictory to the national consensus. The latter argument referred in particular to the decision of 18 August 1945 not to include the "seven words" stating that Muslim citizens would be obliged to practise Islamic *sharī'ah* in the preamble to the constitution.[22]

It was not astonishing that the Muslim *abangan* voiced a reaction to the bill which closely resembled the objections raised by the Christians. R.

---

[21]*Pancasila* (the "Five Pillars") is the name of the official ideology of the Indonesian Republic. Golkar, short for Golongan Karya (Functional Groups), was a semi-governmental association of various functional, i.e. professional, social, and even religious, groups which functioned as the dominant political party in New Order Indonesia.

[22]The "seven words" — *dengan kewadjiban mendjalankan sjari'at Islam bagi pemeluk-pemeluknja* (with the obligation for adherents of Islam to implement its *sharī'ah*) [various sources offer slightly differing formulations] — were included in the so-called Jakarta Charter. This charter was framed in June 1945 by a group of prominent Indonesians in preparation for independence and used as a draft for the preamble to the constitution of the new republic. In July this clause had been agreed upon by all members of the Preparatory Committee for Indonesian Independence, but on 18 August 1945, i.e. one day after the proclamation of independence, it was dropped from the draft constitution because a Christian minority considered it unacceptable.

Some of the Christian voices opposing the 1989 bill were Magnis-Suseno, Franz, in *Kompas*, 16 June 1989; Widjojo, S. in *Majalah Hidup*, 1989, no. 7 (17 February) and no. 10 (5 March); Suwarno, P.J., in *Suara Pembaruan*, 6 April 1989.

Suprapto, a former Governor of Metropolitan Jakarta, and one of the vice-presidents of the People's Consultative Assembly (MPR), wrote an official statement to the president of the DPR and the presidents of all its factions urging them to reject the bill.[23] He argued that the bill ran contrary to the *Pancasila* and the Constitution of 1945. He stated in particular that the state did not have the right to regulate their fulfilment of religious duties by Muslims.[24] Amir Mahmud, a former president of the MPR, supported Suprapto's point of view. He argued that the bill would destroy national unity.[25]

A number of experts in law who had indicated that they belonged to the *abangan* group voiced a similar outlook. However, those who were well versed in law and *adat* seemed to approach the bill in a subtle way. They had to find their way out of a quandary which had been generated because, although the existence of the Islamic courts was deeply rooted in tradition, they were in favour of the principle of legal unification as characteristic of a modern state. In their serach for a solution they differentiated between court and judicature. The first refers to an institution, and the second to the implementation of law. They tended to reject the Islamic court, but to accept Islamic judicature. Therefore, they proposed that civil courts should provide an Islamic section, but not all civil disputes of Muslims should be judged by this section. They rejected an obligation for Muslims to opt for the Islamic section of the civil court.[26]

The objections to the bill expressed by the *abangan* and non-Muslim groups arose from the fear that, when passed into law, it would have the same impact as the Jakarta Charter, which specifically stipulated the obligation for Muslim citizens to have recourse to Islamic law. Therefore, President Soeharto needed to assure the nation that this was not the objective of the government. He explained that the bill was an implementation of the

---

[23]The Majelis Permusyawaratan Rakyat (MPR — People's Consultative Assembly) is the highest body of people's representation. It elects the state president and vice-president and in what are usually annually recurring sessions establishes the fundamental principles of state policy. The smaller Dewan Perwakilan Rakyat (DPR — People's Representative Council) exercises its legislative function through sessions throughout the year.

[24]See Center for Strategic and International Studies, *Dokumentasi Kliping Tentang Rancangan Undang-Undang Peradilan Agama*, 43-49.

[25]*Suara Karya*, 16 June 1989.

[26]For example, Prof. Padmo Wahjono in *Suara Pembaruan*, 26 May 1989, Prof. Sri Sumantri in *Suara Pembaruan*, 14 June 1989, Prof. Sudikno Martokusumo in *Suara Pembaruan*, 6 July 1989.

1945 Constitution and the *Pancasila*. The State would continue to guarantee its citizens the freedom to perform their religious beliefs. He expatiated on the fact that a special law on Islamic judicature was necessary because Islam is not only a matter of worship, but it also comprises rules on family and inheritance.[27] The government took the extra step of guaranteeing that the bill, if passed, would not interfere with the life of non-Muslims since it affected only Indonesian Muslims. Munawir Sjadzali, the Minister of Religious Affairs, added that the bill only dealt with the procedures and structure of the religious courts, of which the jurisdiction would be limited to marriage, inheritance, religious endowment (*waqf*) and alms giving (zakat and *sadaqah*) among Muslims.[28]

In the DPR itself the bill was discussed with great care, since it contained sensitive issues. The fierce criticism from outside the DPR, particularly expressed in newspapers with a Christian background such as *Kompas* and *Suara Pembaruan*, had no significant impact on the DPR debate. After the government presented the bill, the discussion seemed to reach agreement within the various DPR factions. In their general overviews on the bill, the Golkar, Partai Pembangunan Persatuan (PPP — United Development Party), PDI, and Armed Forces faction all commented the initiative taken by the government which reflected its commitment to update obsolete laws. After the revision of a number of ambiguous clauses, all factions approved the bill. The draft law on religious judicature was ratified by President Soeharto on December 29, 1989 as Law no. 7, 1989. It fulfilled more than the demands of the Indonesian Muslims since colonial times. The law established the legal basis of an Islamic court institution and it laid down its procedures. It implemented the principle of equality of the Islamic courts with the other types of courts of justice. It returned to them the jurisdiction over hereditary disputes. Finally, it provided for the appointment of bailiffs within the religious courts, who could enforce the execution of their decisions. Following the promulgation of the Law on Islamic Courts, President Soeharto issued a presidential instruction (Inpres no. 1/1991) concerning the material law of these courts. This instruction established a standard *Kompilasi Hukum Islam* (Compilation of Islamic Law) as a reference for all judges involved in Islamic courts. Previously, these judges

[27] *Antara*, 29 May 1989.
[28] *Jakarta Post*, 20 June 1989.

had referred to a variety of *fiqh* works, which sometimes led to inconsistency among judges and Islamic courts.

By promulgating the Law on Religious Judicature (1989) and the Marriage Law (1974), Indonesia now has two laws concerning Muslim interests. Both laws strengthen each other. The latter needs the former, since the former is the place where the latter should be administered. Important though this reciprocity is, the debates when the two laws were proposed to parliament took a different tack. In the case of the Marriage Law discussions, both inside and outside the DPR, the strongest reactions came from Muslims. This was a consequence of the fact that the bill was proposed by the Ministry of Justice and had been framed by secular experts who failed to take Islamic law into consideration, whereas the bill would administer the marriages of all Indonesian citizens, the majority of whom were Muslim. Under the influence of the Muslim PPP faction in the DPR and several Muslim leaders outside, the originally secular character of the bill was islamized before it was approved by the DPR. In contrast, the bill on religious judicature, when presented to the DPR, had already taken Islamic principles in full consideration. This was partly a consequence of the fact that the law was designed to administer the Muslim concern only. Learning from its experience of 1974, in 1989 the DPR seemed to have overcome the conflict between Islamic and non-Islamic parties. In the 1989 debates, all Muslim parliament members, members of the PPP, Golkar, PDI, and Armed Forces factions alike, had a similar view on the bill. Therefore it came as no surprise that the bill was approved unanimously.

The Islamic Courts and Their Role in the Future

When the president of the DPR pounded his gavel to mark the end of the session, the controversy about the political and legal basis of the Islamic courts had apparently ended. During the last ten years the Indonesian Muslim population has experienced the benefits and the efficacy of the law. This has confirmed the assurance of the Indonesian government that the law was a technical matter and not a re-implementation of the Jakarta Charter, nor would interfere in the religious life of other religious communities. It covered cases relating to marriage and divorce, religious endowments and alms of all Muslim citizens, both "*santri*" and "*abangan*", and it made litigation in Islamic courts about inheritance cases optional for Muslim citizens. This symbolized a victory for conservatism in terms of its adherents' efforts to islamize the state. This victory was achieved at a time by which Islamic political parties had already been abolished. This circumstance strengthened the conviction of a number of modernized Muslim intellectuals that the aspirations of the Muslim population were better served in the absence of Islamic political parties.[29]

What has been achieved by the Muslim community in Indonesia contrasts with the development in other Muslim countries. In Turkey and North African countries, as well as in Pakistan, Islamic law and Islamic judiciary institutions have undergone various changes during the past few decades. In most of these countries, Islamic judicial institutions, if not completely abolished, have been facing increasing restrictions on their competence, and civil courts have taken over their place in the application of Islamic family law and the Islamic courts were brought under the legislative authority of civil institutions.[30] In contrast, in Indonesia the Islamic courts seem not only to have improved their status and obtained equality with other courts, but they also have taken over part of the jurisdiction of civil courts.

Although the Law on Religious Judicature was complemented by the Compilation of Islamic Law, its function stretches far beyond this compilation of traditional *fiqh*. The contemporary situation is characterized by intensive interaction with the global environment. By means of the mass media, new means of transportation, and economic relations, the world has been unified. This development not only has constructive effects, but also disruptive ones. Among the disturbing effects is the menace of foreign mass media to the integrity of family life.[31] In this respect the Islamic courts play an important role in Indonesia. Family law is the last and most critical stronghold of the *sharī'ah* and indubitably the family is still the core of social structure. To save the family from disintegration is the most important task of the Islamic courts. The importance of this role will still increase during the twenty-first century. Nor should it be forgotten that the global media also provide the opportunity to spread the values of the Islamic law.

---

[29]Sjadzali, Munawir, *Muslim Interests are Better Served in The Absence of Muslim Parties: Indonesian Experience*, Ministry of Religious Affairs, Jakarta, 1992.
[30]Lev, op. cit. 229.
[31]Ahmed, *Postmodernism and Islam, passim.*

At the level of the legal and political system, the Indonesian Law on Religious Judicature does show a tendency towards conservatism. While the present situation is characterized by globalization, a local appropriation has emerged. It is probably in conformity with the general trend at the end of the twentieth and the opening of the twenty-first century that the dialectic of globalization and local appropriations has become part of the internal dynamic of Islam in Indonesia.

16 The *'Ulamā'*, the Government, and Society in Modern Indonesia
The Indonesian Council of 'Ulamā' *Revisited*

Mohamad Atho Mudzhar

Introduction

This text attempts to understand the nature of the interactions between the Indonesian Council of *'Ulamā'* (Majelis Ulama Indonesia, abbreviated as MUI), the government, and society in Indonesia during the period of 1989 to 1996. A postcriptum has been added to cover the period of 1996 to 2000. The point of departure for the analysis is a study by the same author covering the period from 1975, when the MUI was established, to 1988.[1] With this purpose in view, first the findings of the previous study will be summarized, next a comparison will be made with more recent developments.

The Findings of the Previous Study (1975-1988)

For the period covered by the original study, 1975-1988, it was found that four basic objectives determined the activities of the MUI:
1. the desire to gain acceptance within society and good relations with Muslim organizations;
2. the desire to maintain good relations with the government;

---

[1]Mudzhar, *Fatwa-fatwa Majlis Ulama Indonesia*. This study was originally a PhD dissertation entitled *Fatwas of the Council of Indonesian Ulama': A Study of Islamic Legal Thought in Indonesia 1975-1988*, submitted to the University of California, Los Angeles, USA, 1990. Although the study focuses on the fatwas (legal pronouncements) of the MUI, one of the main functions of the MUI, to some degree it also depicted the role of the MUI in general. All materials presented in this text on the 1975-1988 period are derived from this study, unless otherwise indicated.

3. the desire to encourage a higher participation of Muslims in national development;

4. the desire to maintain harmonious relations with non-Muslim religious groups.

A short survey of the MUI policy in view of these four objectives and its results will be presented below.

In pursuance of the first objective, to gain acceptance within society and develop good relations with other Muslim organizations, MUI functionaries visited the central committees of other Muslim organizations or invited them to meetings at the MUI office in order to discuss various issues. Although some Muslim leaders were initially reluctant to support the creation of the MUI for fear of its being used as a political instrument by the government, the MUI was gradually accepted by both the Muslim masses and Muslim organizations. The credibility of its first general chairman, Hamka (Haji Abdul Malik Karim Amrullah; 1975-1981), contributed greatly to this acceptance. The credibility of the second general chairman, Syukri Ghozali (1981-1984), was not less important at least for the fact that he was well versed in Islamic law and came from the largest traditional segment of the Muslim community, the Nahdlatul Ulama (NU). The credibility of the third general chairman, Hasan Basri (1985-1990), relied heavily on his eloquent speeches and gentle dealings with both the people and the government. The role the MUI played in the discussion of the two bills of Education and of Religious Courts, in 1988 and 1989 respectively, also enhanced the prestige of the MUI as the guardian of the Muslims' interests. The MUI furthermore engaged in cooperation with other Muslim organizations in the field of *da'wah* (religious propagation) and *ukhuwwah islāmiyyah* (Islamic fraternity). The international dimension of some of its activities helped to establish the authority of the MUI. These activities consisted in the issuing of statements or fatwas on problems facing various parts of the Muslim world as well as the sending of delegates to international Islamic conferences and the receiving of foreign Muslim guests in Indonesia.

The relationship of the MUI with the government was rather complicated. It commenced on the wrong foot when the suggestion mooted by the government in 1970 that the MUI be created went largely unnoticed and was even considered with suspicion by many Muslim leaders until 1974. The provincial councils of *'ulamā'* were only created in 1974 and the national one in 1975. There were a number of reasons behind this suspicious attitude: (1) most Muslim leaders were associated with Islamic political parties and their defeat in the 1971 general election increased suspicions about the government's intention to create the MUI; (2) the amalgamation of the numerous Islamic political parties in 1973 into one, the Partai Persatuan Pembangunan (PPP — United Development Party or PPP), which no longer had any specific reference to Islam in its name or symbol, made many Muslims suspect that the creation of the MUI was just another step in the process of reducing the role of the Muslim community; and (3) the introduction of the originally secular marriage bill in 1973 had outraged the Muslims.[2] After the creation of the MUI, it was often felt that the government put the MUI under pressure to justify some of its controversial policies, such as in the case of the Christmas celebrations in 1981 and the Porkas lottery in 1986.[3] Whatever the truth of this, the government constantly demonstrated its high regard for the MUI and extended its financial support, while the MUI tried to maintain good contacts with the president, ministers, military leaders, and other government officials. With respect to this attitude, it was not surprising to see that a number of fatwas of the MUI were very supportive of government policies. Out of twenty-two fatwas examined for the period of 1975-1988, eight were supportive and only three were opposed to government policies, while the remaining eleven may be considered neutral.[4] In general, the relationship between the MUI and the government improved considerably during this period.

The desire of the MUI to encourage the participation of the Muslim community in national development manifested itself partly in the fatwas it

---

[2]After some protests and demonstrations by Muslim students, as well as deliberations between Muslim leaders and President Soeharto, the bill of marriage was finally revised and passed by the Parliament in 1974 to the satisfaction of the Muslims.

[3]In the framework of its general policy of improving the harmonious co-existence of citizens from different religious communities, the government took a positive attitude to the habit of an increasing number of Muslims to attend Christmas celebrations, whereas many Muslim leaders and organizations considered this practice as contrary to Islamic doctrine or as part of a Christianization campaign among Muslims citizens. The Porkas Sepakbola (Soccer Pools or "Forecast") was a national lottery considered widely as being in contradiction to the Islamic ban on games of chance.

[4]Fatwas falling in the supportive category of government policies are: (1) the fatwa on Jeddah and King 'Abd al-'Aziz Airport as the places of $m\bar{\imath}q\bar{a}t$ in the pilgrimage; (2) the fatwa on three pronouncements of $talaq$ (divorce) at once; (3) the fatwa on the mechanical slaughtering of animals; (4) the fatwa on the lawfulness of rabbit meat; (5) the fatwa on frog-breeding and consumption; (6) the fatwa on family planning in general; (7) the fatwa on the lawfulness of the use of IUDs; and (8) the fatwa on the Shi'ah movement in Indonesia.

issued and in its advice to the Muslim masses in support of the enhancement of their social welfare. Furthermore, in view of this objective, the MUI went as far as to issue a number of joint decrees with various ministers, such as the one with the Ministers of Religious Affairs, and of Cooperatives in 1985 on the introduction of cooperatives in Islamic organizations and educational institutions.

Finally, the desire of the MUI to maintain harmonious relations with non-Muslim religious groups was important in view of the complicated relations or even rivalry between the Muslim and the Christian communities in particular. The tension between both groups began at the latest early in the twentieth century, when the Dutch colonial administration offered discriminatory treatments and subsidies to religious groups in the Indonesian archipelago. This was then followed by the rumour of Christianization of Muslims in the early 1960s and culminated in a much publicized failing inter-religious meeting on November 30, 1967. In the mid seventies, Hamka, was apparently still concerned about the issue of Christianization. In 1978, in order to reduce tensions between different communities, the Minister of Religious Affairs, Alamsjah Ratuprawiranegara, issued two decrees, on missionary activities and on international support to religious bodies in Indonesia respectively. In 1980 an agreement was reached between Muslims and non-Muslims to create an inter-religious consultative body in which each of the five generally recognized religious groups (Muslims, Protestants, Roman Catholics, Hindus, and Buddhists) was represented to discuss issues of common concern and to develop religious harmony. Initially the Muslims seemed to feel uncomfortable about sitting on an equal footing with other, much smaller, religious groups in the consultative body, considering the fact that they constituted the majority (88 per cent) of the population, but later they adapted to the situation. In 1981 the consultative body succeeded in producing draft directives on how to hold religious celebrations. In 1983 some Christian voices were still heard asking the government to revoke the two ministerial decrees of 1978. In the early eighties, a programme was set up by the Ministry of Religious Affairs to sponsor regional tours for the members of the consultative body and other religious leaders at the national level; this programme was a success.[5]

---

[5]Since 1998 violent conflicts between different religious communities have developed in the province of Maluku (Moluccas). Although most observers agree that these conflicts were triggered off by local political and economic factors, religious identity has come to

The MUI Revisited (1989-1995)

For the period under revisitation (1989 onwards), the basic attitude of the MUI has remained the same, with some changes in intensity and manifestation. The desire of the MUI to win the acceptance of the Muslim society at large and to have good relations with other Muslim organizations seems to have been fulfilled to a level where the MUI is very comfortable. The 1990-1995 leadership of the MUI was designed in such a way as to represent intellectuals, regional Muslim leaders, and major Muslim organizations such as the Muhammadiyah and the Nahdlatul Ulama. The participation of these two largest Muslim organizations in the leadership of the MUI was crucial. Although the basic attitude of these organizations towards the MUI has been a little ambivalent, for fear of losing their own identities and its becoming a supra-structural body above other Muslim organizations, the MUI was finally well accepted by these Muslim organizations. In the 1995-2000 leadership of the MUI such representation of the two largest Muslim organizations has slightly decreased and the MUI seems to have become more independent.

The nature of the programmes of the MUI also seems to have developed. In 1975, the MUI was not intended to be an organization launching programmes by itself, but limited itself instead to providing advice and to acting as a point of contact and coordination. Since 1990 however, this has changed. The MUI has gradually embarked itself on launching its own practical programmes. Its involvement in the sending of *dā'īs* to transmigration areas, the creation of the Bank Muamalat Indonesia (BMI – Indonesian bank for *Mu'āmalah*, or social interaction, in this context meaning business on an Islamic basis; 1991), the establishment of the Indonesian Board of Arbitration for *Mu'āmalah* (Badan Arbitrase Muamalat Indonesia – BAMUI; 1993), and the establishment of the Assessment Institute for Food, Drugs, and Cosmetics (Lembaga Pengkajian Pangan, Obat-obatan dan Kosmetika Majelis Ulama Indonesia – LPPOM-MUI; 1989) are cases in point.[6] The involvement of the MUI in the BMI went so far as to having its leadership sit as members of the *Sharī'ah* (Islamic Law) Board of the bank. The involvement of the MUI in the certification of *ḥalāl* food is even more elaborate; it welcomes applications for *ḥalāl* food certificates,

play an important role.
[6]MUI, *20 tahun Majelis Ulama Indonesia*, 242-57.

visits and checks the facilities and the production process of the food, carries out laboratory analyses, and finally issues the *ḥalāl* certificates. By the year 2000 the institute has issued about 500 *ḥalāl* certificates, which has added to the authority of the MUI at the international level, as the applicants for the certificates are not limited to domestic food producers, but include foreign importers. The LPPOM-MUI has already been invited by and visited food producers in New Zealand, the United States of America, Japan, and Thailand. for the purpose of certification of their products to be marketed in Indonesia.[7] At times, local branches of multinational food companies and restaurant chains have insisted on having *ḥalāl* certificates issued by the MUI.[8] This does not mean that the MUI enjoys the exclusive right to produce *ḥalāl* certificates. In fact, the Ministry of Health considers that *ḥalāl* certification should not be issued by private organizations but by the Ministry.[9] Evidence of a compromise on this question was a news report of 1995 quoting the Minister of Food, Ibrahim Hasan, as having said that President Soeharto had indicated his approval to having *ḥalāl* labelling included in the bill on food being drafted.[10] The rule that food destined for the Indonesian Muslim community should be provided with a *ḥalāl* label was in fact included in the 1996 Food Law.

After the 1995 national conference, the MUI has changed the nature of its programmes more consciously. The 1995 conference outlined that there were two kinds of programme for the MUI to pursue in the 1995-2000 period: functional and institutional programmes. The functional programmes

---

[7]*Halal*, 2, 7 (Sept.-Nov. 1995), 25.

[8]The Kentucky Fried Chicken (KFC) restaurant in Bukittinggi, West Sumatra, was reported to have had only a few customers for some time after its grand opening, because the management forgot to display the *ḥalāl* label. After the *ḥalāl* label was shown, the number of customers grew rapidly. This was admitted by Mr Soeharlie, Manager of Quality Control, PT Fastfood Indonesia. KFC now has 116 branches all over Indonesia. A similar situation was admitted by PT Indofood Sukses Makmur Indonesia which produces over twentu-six types of product, ranging from food and drinks, to spices. See *Gatra Magazine*, May 4, 1996. The McDonald's restaurant, according to the Manager, Bambang Rahmadi, was also given the *ḥalāl* certificate as of October 11, 1994 (see *Halal*, 1, 2 [15 Nov. – 15 Jan. 1995]).

[9]This was expressed by Drs. Ading Suryana, Director of Food Control, Ministry of Health, at the National Seminar on Islamic Medicine held on 25-26 November 1995 in Bandung, but many participants of the seminar were opposed. See *Halal*, 2, 8 (Dec. 1995 - Jan. 1996).

[10]*Halal*, 2, 9 (Feb. – March 1996), 33; see also Zuhdi, "Angin Segar Makanan Halal", 26-9.

refer to the original functions of the MUI as a provider of advice to both the Muslim *ummah* (community) and the government, while institutional programmes refer to the practical activities carried out by the MUI itself. The functional programmes cover the areas of *ukhuwwah islāmiyyah* (Islamic fraternity), *da'wah islāmiyyah* (propagation of the Islamic faith), *tarbiyyah islāmiyyah*, (Islamic education), *iqtisādiyyah islāmiyyah* (Islamic economy), and *shakhsiyyah islāmiyyah* (Islamic character). The institutional programmes include plans to develop pilot projects on *da'wah bi al-ḥal* (*da'wah* through deeds, i.e. community development), to create a *bayt al-māl* (lit. money house, i.e. a lending institution) and a *bayt al-tamwīl* (financing house), and to extend the *'Ulamā'* Training Centre.[11]

The desire of the MUI to maintain good relations with the government has manifested itself in a positive cooperation. A number of factors have contributed to this. First, the policy to limit the issuance of fatwas, introduced in 1986, is still effective, which reduces the room for possible contradictions with government policy. Secondly, the controversial permits for the Porkas or Sumbangan Dana Sosial Berhadiah (SDSB – Social Philanthropic Contribution with Prizes) have been revoked by the government, causing all pressures on the MUI to protest against these institutions to cease. Thirdly, the Broad State Guidelines of 1993 produced by the People's Consultative Assembly explicitly stipulated that faith in God was the basis of Indonesian national development. Fourthly, the representation of the Muslim community in the cabinet increased, which was considered by many Indonesian Muslims to be more in conformity with composition of the total Indonesian population.

The desire of the MUI to encourage a higher participation of Muslims in national development coincided with the its cooperative attitude towards the government. In addition to its direct involvement in various projects such as the creation of the Bank Muamalat Indonesia mentioned earlier, the MUI also gave advice on a wide range of issues to the government and the *ummah*. It advised, for instance, on how to preserve national vigilance and resilience, how to collect and distribute zakat, how to develop mutual respect among members of society, how to control the distribution of *ḥalāl* food in the market, and how to preserve the family as the basis of society.[12]

---

[11]Sekretariat MUI, "Keputusan Musyawarah Nasional V Majelis Ulama Indonesia".
[12]MUI, *15 Tahun Majelis Ulama Indonesia*, 214-29; *idem, 20 Tahun*, 137-61.

The desire of the MUI to maintain harmonious relations with non-Muslim religious groups manifested itself in inter-religious cooperation and mutual respect. The joint regional tours sponsored by the government have continued and are participated in by religious leaders of different levels and from a wider spectrum. Each religious group was able to guard itself from the possible penetration of political and economic problems into religious issues. Religious harmony was being nurtured and developed in such a way as to preserve national integration and unity. Pertinently, this did not mean that the Muslims were no longer concerned about inter-religious issues. In the 1989 national conference of the MUI, some concerns were still expressed about the need for each religious group to follow all the regulations laid down by the government with regard to inter-religious relations. Special reference was made to the joint ministerial decree of the Minister of Interior and the Minister of Religious Affairs of 1969 on procedures for the construction of houses of worship, and both decrees of the Minister of Religious Affairs of 1978 mentioned earlier. The issue of Christmas celebrations remained a concern of the MUI, which emphasized that the term "joint Christmas celebrations" widely used in public or in the media should not mean the joint participation of Muslims and Christians in the celebrations but rather be limited to the joint participation of Protestants and Roman Catholic Christians. The MUI urged religious leaders to follow the Joint Agreement on Religious Celebrations produced by the Inter-Religious Consultative Body in 1981.[13]

Postcriptum: A Second Revisitation (1996–2000)

After 1995 there where moments where the fatwas of the MUI touched on political issues of high sensitivity and, therefore, triggered off controversies. The first one was associated with the fatwa on non-Muslim candidates for the legislative body. The fatwa was not designated a proper fatwa but called itself a *tausiah* (Arabic *tawṣiyah*) or a recommendation.[14] The fatwa was issued on June 1, 1999, just six days before the June 7, 1999 General Election. Four points were stated in the fatwa:

---

[13]MUI, *20 Tahun*, 145 f.

[14]The fatwa was signed by Prof. K.H. Ali Yafie and Drs. H. A. Nazri Adlani, respectively as the General Chairman and the Secretary-General of the MUI.

322

1. Muslims are advised to exercise their right to vote in the June 7, 1999 General Election freely and responsibly, in favour of political parties that promise to articulate the interests of Muslims;

2. Muslims are advised to vote for political parties that mostly promote Muslim candidates;

3. Muslims are advised to be constantly alert to the latent danger of communism, authoritarianism, and secularism disguised in certain political parties;

4. Muslims are advised to pray to God for the free and democratic implementation of the June 7, 1999 General Election.

Some questioned whether the fatwa dealt with issues of Islamic law at all. However, the MUI was correct in addressing this question because the issue of leadership is part of the chapter of *qadā'* (leadership) in *fiqh* (Islamic jurisprudence) discussions. Some segments of the community were alarmed by the fatwa. Abdurrahman Wahid, then the General Chairman of the Executive Board of the Nahdlatul Ulama and the declarator of the creation of the National Awakening Party (Partai Kebangkitan Bangsa — PKB) accused the MUI of intervention in practical political matters.[15] The spokesman of the Indonesian Democratic Party for the Struggle (Partai Demokrasi Indonesia Perjuangan – PDIP), Didi Supriyanto, accused the MUI of inciting social disharmony, which was punishable under Article 151 of the Criminal Code.[16] The Golkar (Golongan Karya — Functional Groups) party did not feel itself targeted by the fatwa, and therefore, did not react to it, because its non-Muslim legislative candidates were not dominating as they were in the PDIP. The argument of the fatwa was that many Koranic verses had stipulated the prohibition of acquiescing in non-Muslim leadership, including the People of the Book, by Muslims.[17] In spite of the controversy the fatwa triggered off, it did show the MUI's firm commitment to serve the interest of the Indonesian Muslim community at the political level.

The second moment worth observing was associated with the issue of the eligibility of women to become the president of Indonesia. In this case the controversy was not related to the MUI's issuance of a fatwa, but rather

---

[15] *Jateng Pos*, 4 June 1999.

[16] *Republika*, 7 June 1999.

[17] Some of these Koranic verses are surah 4:141, 5:51, 5:57, and 60:1. The Koranic expression "People of the Book" (*ahl al-kitāb*) refers to adherents of other revealed religions, primarily Jews and Christians.

to its non-issuance. A request for a fatwa was submitted in 1998 by the Congress of Indonesian Muslim Community (Kongres Umat Islam Indonesia – KUII). Surprisingly, until its national meeting in July 1998, about a year before the June 7, General Election, the MUI did not issue any fatwa on this question. This was reminiscent of its silence about the Porkas lottery question for a relatively long period of time, from 1986 to 1991. The silence was not because of its being ignorant or impartial about the issue, but it revealed a reluctance to contradict government policy. This time, on the issue of female leadership, the best that the MUI could come up with was press statements by two of its leaders. K.H. Ibrahim Hosen, the chairman of the fatwa committee of the MUI, stated that Islam forbade a woman to become president of a country if its constitution was Islamic. This rather reluctant position was expressed more clearly in the statement made K.H. Ali Yafie, the general chairman of the MUI, who declared that no agreement had been reached among the MUI leaders on whether a woman could become the president or vice-president of Indonesia.

It may well be asked why the MUI was reluctant to take a stand on the issue. The MUI seemed aware that the Indonesian Muslim community was divided over the issue. The majority of the Nahdlatul Ulama leaders, in a conference in Baturaden, Central Java, in July 1999, attended by some 200 'ulamā', agreed to that it would be acceptable for Indonesia to have a woman as president.[18] In fact, they had in mind Megawati Soekarnoputri, the leader of the PDIP, with which the PKB of Abdurrahman Wahid and other prominent NU figures would ally itself. Nurcholish Madjid, a non-partisan Muslim leader, did not question the sex of the presidential candidate. All that mattered, he declared, was the ability of the person to manage the country. During the KUII there was a strong tendency to reject female presidency, although it finally passed over the question to the MUI. Again, the MUI was undecided about such an important issue, probably for fear of being accused of interventionism in political issues.

Another moment in this period worth observing was related to the issue of the independence of the MUI. The issue was discussed and agreed upon in a national conference of the MUI held from July 25 to 29, 2000. The MUI was determined to free itself from the influence of the government. In order to realize this objective, a number of steps have been taken: first, to remove the Minister of Religious Affairs and other ministers from being ex

---

[18]*Republika*, 19 July 1999.

officio members of the advisory body of the MUI; secondly, to strengthen the lines of organizational coordination between the central MUI and its regional counterparts by transforming them from consultative to instructional ones; and thirdly, to issue independent fatwas. While the effectiveness of the first two steps is still to be seen, the bewildering nature of the third step has already been drawn attention to. K.H. Ibrahim Hosen, the fatwa committee chairman, wrote a book defending in fact that the fatwas the MUI had issued since its creation in 1975 had always been independent and in no case influenced by government policies. This was a courageous statement indeed, after the findings of some studies pointing to the opposite.[19]

Concluding Remarks

The foregoing discussion has led to the conclusion that the nature of the interactions between the MUI, the government, and the society in Indonesia since 1989 is basically the same as that during the 1975-1988 period. The four basic objectives of the MUI found in the previous study have continued to prevail in the period under discussion. The difference lies only in the intensity and manifestation. The MUI is now much more accepted in Muslim society as well as Indonesian society at large and by Muslim organizations than ever before. Moreover, the MUI is now more rigorous in launching its own programmes like any other independent Muslim organizations, without abandoning its original functions of giving fatwas and advice. However, in the period of 1996 to 2000, the MUI has been tempted to take sides on political issues, which has been at the cost of its credibility among the nationalist Muslim masses.

The relationship of the MUI with the government has improved substantially because of the lifting of various potential sources of discord that existed in the previous period. The increase in the participation of the Muslims population in national development is only a logical consequence of this improved relationship. Rumour had it that K.H. Ali Yafie, who had led the MUI since the end of 1998, did not enjoy a good relationship with President Abdurrahman Wahid. Therefore, he refused to be re-elected in the

---

[19]Whatever is the truth about the preceding periods, the above discussion shows that the MUI has changed in the 1996-2000 period. Although some of the changes are still subject to further factorial developments, a firm position has been adopted that it considers itself as an independent body.

July 2000 national conference, giving way to K.H. Sahal Mahfudz, a prominent NU leader, to be the MUI's general chairman for the period 2000-2005.[20]

The harmonious relations between the MUI and non-Muslim religious groups have largely been achieved through the Inter-Religious Consultative Body, though concerns about Christianization continue to be expressed. Although serious conflicts with a strong religious element do occur in a number of regions, such as Maluku and Poso (Central Sulawesi), at the central level the contacts between the MUI leaders and their non-Muslim counterparts remain good. Indeed, hopes are high that the MUI and the Inter-Religious Consultative Body will play a greater role in the future to re-establish the inter-religious harmony in Indonesia. Religious leaders should now be more concerned with the issue of national unity than ever before.

---

[20]K.H. is the abbreviation of *Kiai Haji*, a honorific title used especially in front of the names of Javanese *'ulamā'*, but also, quite exceptionally, predicating the name of the Sulawesi-born Ali Yafie.

17 Contemporary South-East Asian Muslim Intellectuals

An Examination of the Sources for Their Concepts and Intellectual Constructs

Howard M. Federspiel

Introduction

South-East Asia is usually characterized as a peripheral region of the Muslim world and "mainstream" studies of Islamic history, doctrine and character generally do not make much reference to the region. This is not different, of course, from other "peripheral" regions, like Africa South of the Sahara or the Balkans; as regions outside of the Middle and Near East they too are seen as outlying areas relegated in the scholarly realm to "specialists". This is not to deny the work of several prominent scholars, such as Frederick M. Denny[1] and John O. Voll,[2] who have attempted to see the Muslim world in very wide terms. On the other hand, much of the exclusiveness of research on South-East Asian Islam probably rests with the scholars who deal with that region themselves, who frequently make the point that conditions are "different" and subject to other rules of interpretation than prevail in the "central Muslim world". The work in customary law by Dutch scholars at the turn of the twentieth century, such as Cornelis van Vollenhoven,[3] and examination of social sectors in the 1950s done by Clifford Geertz,[4] have been important markers in this trend. Still, there have always been scholars working on that region who have seen clear relationships among Muslims in South-East Asia and those elsewhere, such

---

[1] Denny, *Introduction to Islam.*
[2] Voll, *Islam.*
[3] Holleman, *Van Vollenhoven on Indonesian Adat Law.*
[4] Geertz, *Religion of Java.*

as the famed Christiaan Snouck Hurgronje[5] earlier, and Fred von der Mehden[6] recently.

Assumptions and Approaches

This study starts from the assumption that South-East Asian Muslims do have their own environment, a social history that is unique, and a distinct economic and political configuration affecting their community. At the same time there have been very clear lines of contact among Muslims in South-East Asia and those elsewhere that have allowed the universal character of Islam to be expressed in South-East Asia as much as anywhere else. The pilgrimage, long-term immigration to South-East Asia by Arabs, and South-East Asian student travel in the Middle East are three of the most observable factors showing this inter-regional connection. The purpose of this text is to test just one specific point of contact, expressed through the passage of ideas from elsewhere in the Muslim world to the intellectuals of the South-East Asian region.

As a second assumption this text defines a "Muslim Zone" in South-East Asia, generally consisting of the modern countries of Brunei, Indonesia, and Malaysia, parts of Thailand and the Philippines as well as, to a certain extent, Singapore that have Muslim populations. With the caveat that large groups of non-Muslims live in the region described above, the "Zone" can be considered to be one where the Muslims of South-East Asia are concentrated. Most scholars working on the South-East Asian region implicitly or explicitly accept the existence of such a Muslim Zone. For this study the small Muslim enclaves in Cambodia, Vietnam, and Burma are not included.

This text examines the relationship of South-East Asian Islam with other regions of the world. It builds on an earlier study[7] which put forward the thesis that four groups of Muslim intellectuals operate in South-East Asia and their writings serve as a source for the viewpoints and aspirations of the wider community of Muslims living in the Zone. That earlier study used the definition of Edward Shils who stated that "intellectuals are ... persons ...

---

[5]Snouck Hurgronje, *Verspreide Geschriften.*
[6]Von der Mehden, *Two Worlds of Islam.*
[7]Federspiel, "Muslim Intellectuals in Southeast Asia".

who employ in their communication and expression ... symbols of general scope and abstract reference concerning man, society, nature and the cosmos."[8] The four groups that were identified as existing among South-East Asian Muslims consisted of 1) those dealing with matters of religious doctrine, practice and usage, often defined as *'ulamā'*, but actually broader in classification than that term usually implies; 2) those dealing with the production of "revivalist" literature, both in the traditional sense of repackaging old texts for new inspiration and of seeking new converts to enlarge the Muslim community; 3) those producing special studies of examination and analysis, generally described as academic studies, but again, the group includes many who are not necessarily connected with institutions of learning; and 4) those writers aiming at the goals of society or political activity, who attempt to reconcile religious principles with the functioning of society. The earlier study stressed that intellectuals were those among these four groups of producers who gave guidance and coherence to the writers in their category and consisted of only a small group of all the writers involved in any specific category. These four groups will be used in this study as an instrument of the investigation.

The point of investigation of the present text is the relationship of the South-East Asian Muslim Zone with other world regions as seen through the writings of the four intellectual groups. The hypothesis consists of three principal points:

First, the strongest source of influence on South-East Asian Islam is the Middle East, an assertion based on the long-term contacts and passage of the literary tradition of the Middle East to the Zone.

Second, the emerging influence on South-East Asia is from the West, which has been highly influential in shaping educational and economic institutions. Much of the vocabulary of development, from the use of technology to social sciences concepts, is derived from the West as well.

Third, there is a strong, but lessening influence of local concerns and values that still play an important role in the definition of values and goals by Muslim intellectuals of the region.

These points will be revisited at the conclusion of the text. The analysis will be based on textual materials, that is, drawn from the writings of specific

---

[8]Shils, "Intellectuals".

intellectuals. In each category two writers have been chosen, one from Indonesia, the largest single group of Muslims in the region, and one from elsewhere in the Zone. The writings themselves have been selected to deal with general themes concerning Islam so that special problems of the Zone do not unduly skew the results. As an example, much of the writing of Chandra Muzaffar is concerned with the political and social events of Malaysian society and government, but the work examined here deals with his theoretical views on the concept of justice in Islam. The examination itself seeks to ascertain the point of origins of many of the base arguments and assumptions made by the selected authors. This exercise is intended to move beyond the simple reading of footnotes over to recognizing the specific arguments and ultimate sources of the authors, whether they are found in other writings in South-East Asia or elsewhere. Obvious cases are selected and an attempt to trace subtle argumentation is avoided.

The Investigation

Intellectuals Dealing with the Presentation of the Standard Islamic Message

Intellectuals seeking to give guidance to *'ulamā'* and other teaching/pastoral groups using religious literature are difficult to identify, simply because the group is easily confused with those who wish to undertake revivalist activities. The two groups have always been close historically, so there is every reason for them to be close today, but there is some distinction. Intellectuals in this first group are interested in the explanations of religious texts and the correctness of the doctrines and practices that they are seeking to impart. While they may wish for some renewal of spirit among those receiving the teachings of Islam, they are more concerned with the content of the message than they are about the renovation, as would be the case among revivalists. Some of their work is aimed at other *'ulamā'*, some is intended for general teachers of religion in schools and nearly all of it is intended for use by the general public itself. The two sources chosen for this exercise are Ahmad Sonhadji Mohammad of Singapore and the staff of the *Al-Muslimun* magazine from East Java in Indonesia.

330

Ahmad Sonhadji Mohammad[9] is a prominent religious scholar located in Singapore, who was born in Indonesia, trained in traditional boarding schools in Indonesia, and has taught in Singapore, Malaysia, and Brunei. He reflects modernist[10] Muslim approaches in his use of scripture, but is firmly grounded in the sources used among the traditionalist Muslim groups of the Zone. His works are a good place to begin, since they reflect a general orthodoxy found in the region among the people working in this category of activity. Ahmad's specific contributions have been in the field of Koranic explanation, especially in making the material clear to users in schools and to the general public. The first text examined here, *Kursus Tafsir Al-Qur'an*,[11] was intended for use among school-age teenagers and the second, *Tafsir al-Quran*,[12] was originally a series of radio lessons aimed at the general public. Both are intended to be used with those audiences by general teachers of religion.

Both studies are very basic, intended as they are for lay groups, and they rely heavily on basic definitions and on paraphrasing the sections of the Koran under study. The religious message and the intent of the scripture are the central points of investigation and the author makes few references to the sources of his lessons and perceptions. His brief, often tangential references, indicate that he is in the mainstream of Sunnite tradition, both because of the particular material he presents and the standard way he presents it. His text occasionally alludes to general categories of older scholars in the traditional scholarship, such as the "writers of commentaries" (*ahli tafsir*) and the "historians" (*ahli tarich*), and at other times to specific individuals such as al-Ghazālī, al-Shāfi'ī and Ibn Khaldūn. On occasion he uses more specific references, such as the *Tafsīr al-Khāzin* and the *Tafsīr Ibn 'Abbās*. On only one occasion does he cite a modern Muslim scholar, i.e., Muhammad Farīd Wajdī, an Egyptian of the early twentieth century, that being a reference to an entry in his dictionary. Only once is a Western scholar mentioned, again

---

[9]Sonhadji is also spelt Sonhaji; Mohammad (his father's name) is also spelt Mohamad and Mohamed.

[10]Terms such as "modernist," "traditionalist," and other indicators of theoretical and philosophical labelling, are used is this essay with the general understanding given such terms in the *Oxford Encyclopedia of the Modern Islamic World* and Haddad, *Contemporary Islam*.

[11]Sonhaji, *Kursus Tafsir Al-Quran*.

[12]Sonhadji, *Tafsir Al Quran di Radio*.

an unspecific reference to a textbook on psychology by a person, obviously a Western writer, simply identified as "McDougall".[13]

The material presented by Ahmad Sonhadji Mohammed is reflective of the Middle Eastern sources that he cites. His explanations of Koranic verses use a special category of hadiths that deal with Koran explanation and are replete with examination techniques laid down by the scholars of Hadith in early Islam. Consequently, there is some discussion of the importance of the first three generations of Islam and of presentation of teachings using references to some of the prominent individuals in those formative generations. Second, standard teachings of this class of Muslim scholars in earlier Islam are again presented here without dispute, such as the treatment of the Koran as a major miracle and the listing of the names and importance of the twenty-five prophets mentioned in the Koran. Without much question, the primary sources for this writer are from the Middle East and are strongly reflective of scholarship done there by classical and medieval scholars. Explanations from recent writers or those filtered through a Westernized prism are not included. In this particular set of studies no attempt is made to draw on local scholarship nor are there allusions to local conditions.

The second case in this first category is different. *Al-Muslimun*[14] is a journal dedicated to the exploration of *fiqh*, the Islamic science of jurisprudence, but as seen through the twin sources of Koran and firm hadiths of the Prophet. This reflects a modernist Muslim outlook, which eschews the wider jurisprudence based on the formulations of the writers from the Islamic classical and middle periods, which are found in the Shafi'ite, Malikite, Hanafite, and Hanbalite schools. Located in East Java, it has a subscription list of nearly 60,000 throughout Indonesia and parts of Malaysia. The editors and chief writers are products of the boarding school with which the magazine is associated, with some additional education in Islamic institutions in the Middle East, often al-Azhar in Egypt, or in South Asia. None have been to the West for any study opportunities or for general contacts.

The core of *Al-Muslimun* is advice to readers and three primary methods are used to attain that goal. First, there are several sections dedicated to the examination of specific issues in standard Islamic teachings: proper worship,

---

[13]Probably referring to William McDougall (1871-1938), born in Great Britain and professor at Harvard.

[14]*Al-Muslimun* [The Muslims] (Bangil, 1963-).

the role of rite and celebration, and meeting standards of good Muslim behaviour. Discussions on the poor tax, the structure of ritual for the major Islamic day of celebration ('*Īd al-Fiṭr*), and control of sexual desire are representative of these discussions. Second, there are answers to letters from readers, usually about proper ritual, but sometimes about matters of behaviour. Third, there are articles from authors outside the organization, frequently Indonesian or overseas Muslim writers, on subjects of general interest to the Muslim community. Significant among this last group is a series of articles by the mid-twentieth-century Egyptian scholar Muṣṭafā al-Sibā'ī on the role of women in Muslim society and the particular limits that women should have in career fields to preserve the importance of the family institution and women's heavy responsibility in that endeavour. An article by the Indonesian scholar Afan Gaffar talked about the responsibility of intellectuals to interpret Islamic values properly in Indonesian society.

There are frequent citations in the text to the sources for the material presented, but these references do not always support the arguments made or the particular decisions asserted. This is not an oversight on the part of the editors, because the standpoint of *Al-Muslimun* is well known to its readers. It regards only Koran and firm hadiths as proper sources of Islamic thinking and these two sources are adequately identified by the usual markers, that is, chapter (*sūrah*), verse (*āyah*) in the case of the Koran; first recorder and major collector in the case of hadiths. The editors maintain that other sources could be used to add perspective on an issue under consideration, but certainly could not be considered as authoritative. Consequently, in discussions where advice is being given about the application of maxims in specific teachings, references are only to the two scriptures and any comparisons would include only further references to Koran and hadiths. Occasionally reference is made to previous discussions made in *Al-Muslimun* or books by authors associated with *Al-Muslimun*; obviously such studies may cite the fuller record of sources found in scripture. However, in some articles designed to impart general teachings about Islam a wider group of references is employed. An example is a presentation on flawed and weak hadiths, where three standard commentators are cited repeatedly: Muḥammad al-Ḥākim al-Naysābūrī, Shams al-Dīn al-Dhahabī, and Muḥammad Nāṣir al-Dīn al-Albānī. In a similar discussion in another issue the author cites Muhyī al-Dīn al-Nawāwī, Ibn Ḥajar al-Haytamī, and Ibn Qayyim al-Jawziyyah. Modern Muslim writers and Western writers are not used by the editors as sources.

The information provided by *Al-Muslimun* is stark, stripped of sophisticated reasoning, and specific. It makes the language of the Koran and Hadith quite explicit and seldom differentiates between admonition and injunction. It is a reflection of the fundamentalist approach it espouses. At the same time, despite its commitment to standard Islam, there is a strong degree of identification with the South-East Asian environment and an understanding of conditions there, as witnessed in some of its guest articles. The precise thinking of that side of *Al-Muslimun* character is open to several interpretations and will not be dealt with here because of its peripheral value to the study at hand.

Intellectuals Dealing with Revivalist Messages and Goals

The two authors dealing with revivalist activity are quite different in their approaches to the subject. Like the two cases in the previous category, the lessons of Islam are important as the central principle in defining Muslims as distinct from other peoples and as making the pious Muslim one who is different from the Muslim who regards his religious obligations casually. Unlike the cases in the previous category the tone of the message is important and the impact of the message on the reader is of first importance. The effort is to renovate the Muslim's attitude and raise it to greater commitment to Islam. Amran Kasimin from Malaysia and Syahminan Zaini from Indonesia are the two authors used in this investigation.

Amran Kasimin attended an Islamic college in Malaysia and did graduate work in Scotland. He has been a teaching staff member at the National University of Malaysia and also occupied administrative posts in religious affairs in Johore. He has written extensively on Koran and *sunnah*, on the study of Arabic and on the state of polygyny in Malaysia. For analysis in this essay one volume of his book titled *Tanya Jawab Agama*[15] is examined here. The book is a collection of newspaper articles written over a span of time which attempt to explain basic teachings about practical Islam. The book is an attempt to relate proper beliefs and practices to Muslims who seek to deepen religious consciousness in their own lives. He does this by answering the questions regarding proper behaviour raised by his readers.

---

[15]Kasimin, *Tanya Jawab Agama Mingguan Malaysia.*

One volume in the series deals with twenty-seven separate queries, each answered in five to seven pages of text. The queries themselves deal with a wide variety of matters. One group of questions addresses interpretations of scripture, such as meanings of the *al-kursī* text, and the essence of *sūrah* Yā' sīn as "the heart of the Koran". A second group discusses specific rites and obligations, such as the recitation of teaching to the dead (*talqīn*), the giving of the poor tax (*zakāh*), and "unacceptable" forms of worship. A third group reviews several matters of belief, including "determinism" and the concept of "martyr for the faith".

The responses prepared by Amran Kasimin are technical and reflective of teaching found in a traditionalist style of thinking. He refers everywhere to the classical and medieval writers of Islam. Accordingly, the terms *ulama salaf* and *mazhab Ash-Shafie* are mentioned regularly as sources for his responses. By *ulama salaf* he is referring to the esteemed scholars in the classical period of the eighth to twelfth centuries who shaped orthodox Sunnite Islam; among them Amran Kasimin specifically mentions Ḥasan al-Baṣrī, al-Ṭabarī, al-Ghazālī, Aḥmad b. Hanbal, and Mālik b. Anas. By *madzhab Ash-Shafie*, he is referring to the primary writers of the school of jurisprudence founded by al-Shāfi'ī, that extends from the tenth century of the Christian era, when al-Shāfi'ī wrote, all the way to the twentieth century. At times Amran Kasimin is specific about particular scholars of the Shafi'ite school, such as Ibn Ḥajar al-Haytamī where he draws heavily on his major works. Mostly, references are generalized to an accepted body of knowledge, best described as *fiqh* of the al-Shafi'ite school and the writings of the orthodox teachings of Sunnite Islam.

Within this framework of authoritative reference, another set of scholarly markers are used as well, that is references to the words and actions of the Prophet Muhammad as recorded in the Hadith literature, where many of the lessons laid down by the *ulama salaf* and the Shafi'ite writers had their ultimate source. In the citation of specific hadiths, the early collector is cited, such as Ibn Mas'ūd, Abū Sa'īd al-Khudrī, or 'Abd Allāh b. 'Umar. At other times the later, major collector was given, such as al-Tirmidhī and al-Bukhārī. But regardless of the collection, in all cases hadiths are introduced with the name of the first relator. Citations of the Koran in Amran Kasimin are sparse and only used when accompanied by the explanation of a known authority, that is, by a hadith, by a member of the *ahli salaf* or a member of the Shafi'ite *madhhab*. This passage of authority through a series of reliable writers is regarded as essential and Amran Kasimin implies that his own interpretation is part of that living tradition. He concludes with a short list of books in Malay, published in Malaysia within the previous five years, accompanied by a statement that the reader might find those books useful as additional reading. All are listed by title, with no authors given. Again the reference is to the total pool of knowledge, not necessarily to an individual author or a particular document.

The second author in this section, Syahminan Zaini was educated at a State Institute for Islamic Studies (IAIN) in Indonesia and has been a member of its staff since then. He has been particularly active in revivalist activities connected with the Muhammadiyah movement and has done extensive writing on basic Islamic matters to support that revivalist effort, generally referred to as *dakwah* (Arabic *da'wah*, Islamic religious propagation). His writing on the meaning of the Koran to contemporary Indonesian lay Muslims grew out of that effort. In *Isi Pokok Ajaran Al-Qur'an*,[16] Syahminan Zaini attempts to project the Koran as a guide for everyday life for believers in Indonesia. Accordingly, it is broken into three chapters which deal with "Allah," "Humankind," and "The World" respectively. Syahminan Zaini maintains that God is the originator and sustainer of all that exists and that humans have been created especially to operate the world, while acknowledging that it belongs to God. The message is the usual one among those concentrating on *da'wah*, namely, that, without God, the universe has no meaning and that only by accepting the truth of the revelation that came via Muhammad can humans find fulfilment and purpose in life.

The style used in *Isi Pokok* is meant to be informative and persuasive, as one would expect from a *dā'ī* (*da'wah* agent). Hence a whole series of themes are developed in each main section of the book. For example, under the "Humankind" chapter, some of the themes are "the meaning of humankind," the "requirements placed on humans," "the path not to be taken," "how humans were created," the characteristics of humanness," "the ends of humanity," and "fulfilling human goals". Each theme is described with ample citations from the Koran and then with short pithy expressions from famous writers, historical and modern, who amplify the statements of the author.

---

[16]Zaini, *Isi Pokok Ajaran Al-Qur'an*.

There are several hundred references to various writers in the book and Syahminan Zaini draws heavily on them for his arguments. Among them, Syahminan Zaini refers to a group of Egyptian scholars popular during the middle and second half of the twentieth century as a common source for his chief theme that humans reflect divine creation and have consequent duties to observe God's commands. Among others, he cites al-Sayyid Sābiq to the effect that it is God who has given spiritual freedom to humans. It is this unique gift to humans which gives them the ability to differentiate good from bad in their lives and, when they aspire to lead godly lives, to achieve several levels of spiritual attainment and piety. Syahminan Zaini also quotes 'Abbās Maḥmūd 'Aqqād to the effect that humans have been designated as creatures with specific responsibilities to God Himself. He also cites Maḥmūd Shaltūt that Islam constitutes a regulation establishing the relationship between God and humans, among humans, and between humans and the world around them. This is reflected in all aspects of life, including events of the political environment.

A second group of writers chosen by Syahminan Zaini consists of Indonesian scientists and Western authors who comment on the philosophical quandaries of the West with science and the moral choices by humans that relate to the use of science. He cites Achmad Baiquni, an Indonesian scientist, concerning the ordering of the universe according to the competing theories of natural randomness and divine order. Achmad Baiquni asserts that divine order is the more obvious way to believe, because of the evidence of natural physical laws and the power of human reason, which suggest a single creator operating behind the system. Syahminan Zaini also paraphrases the French physician, Alexis Carrel, as stating that modern science has not been developed in a way that recognizes human spirituality and that only through reference to a religious message is science brought into such a context. In the same way Syahminan Zaini draws on the French writer, Roger Garaudy, who states that Western reason, based as it was on Greek philosophy and the rules of examination, is bound to the limits found in human experience. As a result of such transitory experience, the Western world has flirted with absolute destruction because it has no spiritual centre upon which to base its moral decisions. Garaudy is cited as stating that science needs to have the moral teachings of the East, such as that of Islam, to provide a more suitable guideline for the techniques of investigation provided by Western thought.

The third group of writers used by Syahminan Zaini are inspirational writers from the West, such as Dale Carnegie and Norman Vincent Peale.

Their common theme is that humans need guidance for their own personal lives and that those themes should be developed from the relevant religions and moral sources at hand. Syahminan Zaini suggests that the Koran provides the best of all possible alternatives for such development. Finally, Syahminan Zaini draws heavily on the Koran to justify his basic framework of values that he puts forward in this book. In this sense he uses the same technique as Fazlur Rahman (Faḍl al-Raḥmān) in his *Major Themes of the Qur'an*, making assertions about the meaning that scripture has for contemporary humankind. He occasionally cites a hadith as backup to a specific record but shows no particular interest in evaluation of Hadith sources. He does not refer to the historical and jurisprudential works of belief as support for his own viewpoint.

Intellectuals Employing "Academic" Writing

Muslim intellectuals employing "academic" writing are interested in providing insight and perspective concerning Islamic subjects or matters relating to Islam for other scholars or, in some cases, for the public at large. Their studies often have conclusions that may be useful to policy makers but they are really intended to describe what does or did exist, without reference to the functioning of contemporary society. Intellectuals in this category are often concerned with the history of Islam and have contributed significant insights to national histories through their analysis of the contributions of Muslims in the region. Equally, they study the institutions of Islam and often relate them to the nation-states of the region. The two scholars chosen for this examination are Kuntowijoyo from Indonesia and Carmen A. Abubakar from the Philippines.

Kuntowijoyo attended a national university in Indonesia and then undertook graduate work in the United States. His career has centred on academic writing concerning Islam, on literary criticism, on creative writing (novels and plays), and on some general writings dealing with Islamic teachings. *Dinamika Sejarah Umat Islam Indonesia*[17] belongs to the first genre and uses social science methodology. That social science prism is held by a committed Indonesian Muslim scholar and he makes the display consistent

---

[17]Kuntowijoyo, *Dinamika Sejarah Umat Islam Indonesia*.

with standard Muslim values, even if the methodology and the sources are heavily Western in orientation.

The examination by Kuntowijoyo pursues two themes: history and contemporary institutions. His history owes much of its orientation to Daniel Lerner and his assertions about the passage from "traditional," through "transitional" to "modern" society in the Indonesian nation-state. Accordingly, his studies of Muslim passage along this continuum focus on the type of social identifications that were apparent as change occurred in Indonesia in the last two hundred years. In this context Lerner regards the authority of the religious teacher-scholar (*kiai*) important in an agricultural period, but giving way to a more narrow spiritual guidance role later as urbanization and industrialization occur. The believer finds himself moved from an all-embracing community in the agricultural village over to a fractionalized existence in urban life. In the urban areas, religious identity is broken into components, so that the Muslim association has importance, but it controls the believer only part of the time. In his examination of modern institutions, such as the mosque and the organization of scholars, Kuntowijoyo uses this approach to expand and develop the basic observations of Lerner.

The sources cited by Kuntowijoyo are those common to the Western social science field and probably are drawn from his earlier graduate readings in the United States. Significantly, he uses these sources appropriately, but, nevertheless, qualifies them in light of his own Muslim viewpoint. For example, he cites Arnold Toynbee and his theory of the radiation of cultures. In this context he notes that in the passage of Westernism to the East in the nineteenth century the concepts of technology passed easily, but that other aspects of Western culture were slow to transfer or were hardly accepted at all in the East. Christian values, for example, hardly passed over at all. Nationalism, which was very strong in the West, was adopted, but underwent a permutation to make it fit with prominent political and social features of Eastern societies. Kuntowijoyo uses this theory of cultural radiation to explain how the development of modernization in the Netherlands East Indies of the nineteenth century concentrated on the adaptation of technology, while rejecting the Western values that were part of modernization as it developed in its Western context.

In another essay Kuntowijoyo confronts the issue of political identification in Indonesia to the thinking of a series of Western social scientists. Using references to Ralf Dahrendorf, Hans-Dieter Evers, Karl

Jackson, and Barrington Moore, he shows how different groups in Indonesian society at the mid-twentieth century moved in different directions, causing a particular schism about the year 1945. Reflecting this approach Kuntowijoyo states, for example, that the relationship of the military to Big Business, in particular, put the military at odds with the older middle-class entrepreneurs who were the Muslim traders. In the same way, the bureaucratic necessities of the new [Indonesian] state ultimately created a new organization, i.e. Golkar (Golongan Karya — Functional Groups), which could act as an agent for the new administrative class. This, too, precluded identification of Muslim bureaucrats with Muslim political entities and associations. The arguments of Kuntowijoyo are replete with social science terminology, such as "social consciousness," "ideology," "primordial," "big labour," "strategic group," "bureaucratic society," "ruling class," "crisis syndrome", and "wartime mentality".

At some points in his analysis, when he builds interpretations of Indonesian institutions and events, Kuntowijoyo turns to several Indonesian scholars, but always those who have strong ties with Western methodology, such as Dawam Rahardjo, Nurcholish Madjid, and Deliar Noer. Strikingly Kuntowijoyo does not draw on Middle Eastern authors who have responded to Western intellectual writings. He includes one essay in which he examines the themes and position of the prominent Iranian scholar, 'Alī Sharī'atī. Significantly, Kuntowijoyo does not cite Sharī'atī himself very much, even in that article, and in a subsequent essay on Muslim intellectuals, where 'Alī Sharī'atī's views are relevant, he is not cited at all.

Finally, Kuntowijoyo cites the Koran occasionally. Most often this usage consists of a prominent verse to set a theme or serve as a lead-in for a particular essay. At other times he uses Koranic citations as backup for an Islamic standard or point of reference he wishes to make. Kuntowijoyo avoids references to hadiths and does not refer to the writers of *fiqh* at all. Any mention of classical scholars is made without regarding them as a revered group, but only as individual scholars with particular outlooks and messages.

The second academic writer, Carmen A. Abubakar, is a teaching staff member of the Institute of Islamic Studies at the University of the Philippines. She has been the editor of the journal *Ayat az-Zaman*, a scholarly publication of her faculty, and she was once the acting dean of the faculty. She exhibits the style and breadth of an academic writer in "The

Birth of Muslim States".[18] In it she lays out a hypothesis which juxtaposes two themes in Muslim political organization. The first is the theoretical construct with the name "*khilāfah* state," favoured by some contemporary Muslim political thinkers. This construct features a single international community (*ummah*) with an all embracing political organization, headed by a leader *(khalīfah)*, reflecting that institution in classical Muslim history. The second theme is the popularity of the existing nation-state common to most of the twentieth century, including areas where Muslim populations reside. In the course of her investigation Carmen Abubakar uncovers strong support for the *khilāfah* state among important Muslim thinkers of the twentieth century, such as al-Fārūqī, Khumaynī, and Mawdūdī. At the same time she marshals the views of a number of other scholars and political leaders, such as Datuk Musa Hitam of Malaysia and 'Allāl al-Fāsī of Morocco, who argue for continued recognition of the nation-state as a practical reality and as compatible with overall aspirations of Muslim unity. She concludes that there is no consensus on which form should ultimately prevail among Muslims.

Abubakar relies heavily on four writers of the contemporary era — Murtaḍā Garyā, Ismā'īl al-Fārūqī, Ziauddin Sardar, and James Piscatori. Murtaḍā Garyā, an Iranian, regards the Muslim political mission as a necessary part of Muslim endeavours and, to that end, he asserts, the Muslim states should aim at translating the divine will into practice. Al-Fārūqī is quoted as the foremost voice of the *khilāfah* model, a view which flows from his emphasis on *tawḥīd* as the overarching standard of Islam. He asserts that *tawḥīd*, the unity of all things in God, expresses the singularity of purpose in Islam to God and to a single *ummah*. The *ummah*, as the repository of all things regarding community, would include political obligations as well as those of religious obligations. Sardar, a South Asian scientist, is used to express the general commitment of a Muslim scientist to the concept of unity. Sardar's argument begins with five key points, contrasting the *khilāfah* state with the nation-state, and concludes with support for an *ummah* state, which would be a hybrid nation-state which builds towards the more idealistic *khilāfah* state. Piscatori, an American political scientist, is used only as the collector of views from throughout the Muslim world. The different Muslim voices are grouped by category, with those still supporting the nation-state in one section and those favouring the *khilāfah* state in another.

---

[18]Abubakar, "The Birth of Muslim States".

Abubakar is sparse in her use of scripture, quoting the Koran twice near the beginning of her article to set the stage for presentation of the *khilāfah* model. There are no references to standard Islamic texts and only writers of the contemporary period are used in her presentation.

Societal Intellectuals

Societal intellectuals are concerned about the goals of their own society and civilization, that is, how the values that they espouse fit with the social, educational, economic, and political systems that operate in their nations and in the world in general. Here, Muslim intellectuals of this category can be expected to provide insight into how Islam fits, or could fit, with the national goals of Indonesia, Malaysia and other nations of the region and, also, to comment on the aims of Muslim civilization in general. The two people chosen to represent this group are Chandra Muzaffar from Malaysia and Nurcholish Madjid from Indonesia.

Chandra Muzaffar was once a political science lecturer at the Universiti Sains Malaysia at Penang and now associates with several "think-tanks" analysing political events and trends in Malaysia. He is a keen analyst of Muslim progress in Malaysia and has provided several studies which examine and measure the state of Islam in national affairs of that country. The work reviewed here, titled "The Implementation of Justice in Politics",[19] is more theoretical than what he generally writes, but is used because it shows the principles behind his analysis and provides certain insights about the place and condition of Islam in the current world order.

The article asserts that the Koran, as a holy book, is deeply concerned about the well-being of humans and commands the followers of Islam to erect a system of justice for giving substance to human conduct. A first step in this endeavour is to make sure that Muslims themselves are familiar with the teachings of the Koran and that they are capable of using its principles to regulate their public behaviour. Governments as well — which need to be based on democratic principles — are bound to follow the principles set forth in the Koran. *Tawhīd*, the great unifier of all things Islamic, fortifies that belief system and sets all Muslim thinking into context. Chandra asserts that

[19]Muzaffar, "Administration of Justice in Politics".

in the past Muslim rulers were not always dedicated to the principles of the Koran and came up short in supplying these standards for Muslim nations. At particular historical times, Muslim rule was so wanting as to be considered "decadent". Today, he asserts, Muslims are faced with a world where Islam has a bad reputation among Westerners, where Western values of secularism prevail, and where uneven distribution of world wealth patently works against Muslim societies. Chandra regards Islam as offering a way through the moral miasma of the age, especially in redefining gender relations, ethnic differences, economic justice, environmental issues, and international cooperation.

The sources of his arguments are fairly broad. He cites a number of important Western scholars who express sympathy with Islam — Roger Garaudy, John Esposito, and Arnold Toynbee. He draws on some strong fundamentalist writers, such as ʿAlī Sharīʿatī, Abū al-Aʿlā Mawdūdī, Murtaḍā Muṭahharī, and Maḥmūd Ṭāliqānī. He also cites Muslims reared in Muslim societies who live and write in the West, such as Fazlur Rahman and Seyyed Hossein Nasr (Sayyid Ḥusayn Naṣr). He also indicates his preference in a section of text where he lists a group of Muslim scholars he finds important enough to be translated into all prominent languages used by Muslims; among them he names Shāh Walī Allāh, Muḥammad Iqbāl, and Abū al-Kalām Āzād from pre-Partition India; ʿAlī Sharīʿatī, Maḥmūd Ṭāliqānī, and Muḥammad Bāqir Ṣadr from the Revolutionary Iranian Era; and Fazlur Rahman from Pakistan-United States.

Among these he draws specifically on the writings of ʿAlī Sharīʿatī, Mawdūdī, Fazlur Rahman, and Murtaḍā Muṭahharī and also the much earlier Ibn Khaldūn to provide a basis for his own argumentation. Ibn Khaldūn is used for his commentary concerning the cycle of rule in a dynasty. Ibn Khaldūn notes that founders of a dynasty are often simple, hard-working, and admirable, while later leaders become dissolute and lose the moral fibre of their predecessors. Chandra uses the citation to speak about the poor showing of Muslim rulers in working for the public welfare of their subjects. He quotes Muṭahharī as the source for basic discussion on *tawḥīd*, who holds that *tawḥīd* is not an abstract belief, but a part of social reality for Muslim society, spelling out obligations in law, politics and justice. Chandra uses this context to expand on Muslim obligations of the contemporary era. Tied closely to this contention is Mawdūdī's concept of the Islamic state which asserts that consultation (*shūrā*) by Muslim rulers with their subjects is a requirement. Furthermore, Chandra quotes ʿAlī Sharīʿatī to the effect that transcendent Islamic law, i.e. the *sharī'ah*, has served historically as a protective shield for Muslim rights against arbitrary rule. Finally he quotes Fazlur Rahman for his view that the Koran promotes a standard for an ethical, egalitarian social order opposed to both economic disparities and to social inequalities. Chandra infers scriptural reference, but seldom actually does much citation. In this particular essay he uses a small number of verses from the Koran, using Yusūf 'Alī's English rendition.

The second societal intellectual, Nurcholish Madjid undisputedly ranks as the leading Muslim intellectual of Indonesia. He was educated in a "modern" *pesantren* (Islamic boarding school), attended a national university, and did his graduate work in the United States. His work, clearly within the neo-modernist Muslim pattern, reflects that found elsewhere in the Muslim world, but relates clearly to the Indonesian context. Since his first foray at the "secularization" of Islamic knowledge in the early 1970s, he has attempted to refine his thinking in articles, conference presentations, and books. Here we examine *Islam: Doktrin dan Perababan*,[20] a 600-page work seeking to place Islam into the setting of the twentieth century and to show that it is compatible with the mainsprings of Indonesian national development.

The books consists of two parts that, while related, each stands on its own as an independent intellectual statement. The introduction of 120 pages is a major essay explaining the particular challenges and role of Islam in the contemporary era, particularly in Indonesia. The second part, which is the main body of the book, tracks through the historical context of Islam, reflects on the primary doctrinal demands of the religion and asserts that modernization, modernity, and local variation are possible for Muslims to achieve, while staying rooted in religious tradition.

The introductory essay seems designed for readers who are familiar with the Western scholarly tradition. It lays great stress on Western sources as a justification for Nurcholish's argumentation that Islam is a modern religion capable of providing guidance, which will allow Indonesia to assume a major role in the international community that its political leaders project for early in the next century. His thesis rests on four main points. The first, taken from Joseph Campbell, reflects that the modern world emerged from an earlier world of myth and unproven belief through a process of

---

[20]Madjid, *Islam: Doktrin dan Perabadan.*

demystification that was an important turning point in history. The second, from Robert Bellah, recognizes the early Muslim community as having been a unique moment in history, attuned to modernization through recognition of "true" science. However, the community was too early in history to succeed, but the principles produced at that time remained for later use by others. In the third argument Nurcholish moves to the Indonesian context and draws on the Indonesian Christian theologian Sidjabet, who spelled out the importance of the nationalist ideology — *Pancasila* — to the religions that are found in Indonesia. Sidjabet regards the "Belief in God" principle of the slogan as being especially important and as opening the way for religion itself to play an important role in the development of Indonesian society and government policy. Finally, Nurcholish invokes *ukhuwwah islāmiyyah,* the concept of Islamic brotherhood, which brings all Muslims into a common effort to assert their collective identity, based on Islam, and thereby assume important status in the world.

The larger work, that is, the main text of the book, rests on a somewhat different basis than the introduction. It is reflective of the neo-modernist Muslim, although there are references to Western, South Asian, and Middle Eastern intellectual authors. The first feature of the work is the heavy use of Koranic citation, reflecting Fazlur Rahman's admonition to follow the example of earlier Muslim scholars, who used the Koran to examine their own civilization and as a tool in improving and developing that civilization. Nurcholish Madjid does this. Second, he contends that commentary about the Koran is important and to this end Nurcholish cites two South Asian writers, ʿAbd Allāh Yūsuf ʿAlī (A. Yusuf Ali) and Abū al-Kalām Āzād to place the Koran into the context that he finds important. Furthermore, he uses Ibn Taymiyyah as the "explainer" of early Islam, drawing on that scholar's analysis for the doctrinal positions and historical relationships of early groups in Islamic history. These three factors — Koran, Koranic commentary and historical commentary — are the workhorses of the text that Nurcholish evolves. Alongside this, four viewpoints are prominently mentioned and serve as anchor points for the book. First is the contention made by Yūsuf ʿAlī, and generally accepted by all elements of contemporary Muslim thought, that the Koran conveyed a clear message of purpose to the early Muslim community and, accordingly its members were able to use it to their advantage. The second, by Āzād is that the Koran should be interpreted according to its meaning to early believers, who regarded their religion as the most important point of their own communal identification. Third, by Ibn

345

Taymiyyah, that truth cannot be determined through logic or inductive reasoning alone; it must be demonstrated in empirical evidence as well.

Revisiting the Hypotheses

1. The first hypothesis stated that the strongest influence on South-East Asian Islam stems from the Middle East, an assertion based on the long-term contacts and passage of the literary tradition of the Middle East to the Zone. In this study this contention was not fully proven and qualifications are needed. So far as intellectual sources in the study of eight intellectuals are concerned, the Middle East was a very important source for some writers, but by no means dominant among all of them. As the foregoing discussion shows, not all writers in our group found Middle Eastern sources important, and even among those who did, they were not all referring to the same sources.

In fact, three different major categories of Middle Eastern sources were used. The first group of references were the classical and medieval thought pattern used by Ahmad Sonhadji Mohammad and Amran Kasimin and to some extent by the *Al-Muslimun* staff. This is the traditionalist approach in its new form; neo-traditionalism might be a good name for it. It tries to stylize the old scholars, draw selectively on them, without necessarily accepting all of their teachings.

A second Middle Eastern group are Iranian writers, roughly described as belonging to the Revolutionary Era: ʿĀlī Sharīʿatī, Maḥmūd Tāliqānī, and Murtaḍā Muṭahharī. These are used extensively by Chandra Muzaffar, less so by Carmen Abubakar and lightly by Kuntowijoyo. The arguments and constructs of these Iranians are used in the appropriate sense of how they were intended. Chandra is most effective in this regard.

A third Middle Eastern group, that of modern Egyptian writers, is surprisingly limited to only one real user among our group. Syahminan Zaini draws appropriately on the authors and uses their constructs in a way those Egyptian authors would find applicable.

In sum, the Middle East authors exist on a wide spectrum, with three quite different source groups identified. There is a historical dimension to one group — the traditional one — and an ideological difference between the two contemporary groups. All groups were used seriously, however, so that the Middle East constituted an important source of information for many members of the group.

2. The second hypothesis states that the emerging influence on South-East Asia is from the West, particularly the United States, which has been influential in providing concepts in comparative religion and the social sciences that have been widely adopted. This contention needs qualification as well. There was an awareness of the West shown by nearly all the writers and some writers were heavily influenced by Western intellectual trends. Nevertheless, the use of Western writing differs significantly among the South-East Asian Muslim intellectuals reviewed in this study. Two authors, Kuntowijoyo and Nurcholish Madjid, used it intellectually, calling on a series of modern social scientists and comparative religion specialists to give shape and coherence to their own intellectual constructs. Both drew from the essence of these Western intellectuals in ways that Western intellectuals themselves would deem appropriate. The arguments by Kuntowijoyo and Nurcholish Madjid also stand clearly within the framework of these Western intellectuals so far as methodology and terminology is concerned, although their findings and conclusions reflect an Islamic value system.

Two writers — Syahminan Zaini and Chandra Muzaffar — drew on selected Western writers, those who gave words of praise to Islam or who gave support to particular outlooks put forward by these two intellectuals. Quoting Maurice Bucaille or Garaudy for their sympathy towards Islam appears to be very selective use of Western sources. The use of situational ethics from Western authors, such as Norman Vincent Peale, is sometimes taken out of context, since Peale and the other authors did not have Islam in mind at all as the source of moral power they promote in their writings.

Furthermore, there is the use of studies made by Westerners of the Muslim world itself. Carmen Abubakar does this with Piscatori, who is used simply as a source book for information about political thinking in the Muslim world. Of course in such cases some of the Westerners' intellectual filters may inadvertently be taken over by Muslim users, but probably not to a very high degree. This appears to be an appropriate use of Western sources.

Finally, there is respect for and use of Muslim intellectuals, such as Fazlur Rahman, Seyyed Hossein Nasr, and Ismā'īl al-Fārūqī, who were born elsewhere but thought, wrote, and taught within the Western academic tradition. Syahminan Zaini, Carmen Abubakar, Nurcholish Madjid, and Chandra Muzaffar belong to this category. Like the earlier case of the social science and comparative religion intellectuals, the citations and argument from these authors are expressed correctly and are meant to reflect their core arguments.

In sum, concerning Western sources, it can be said that they were sometimes selectively used without regard for the real arguments, but in a significant number of cases two clear groups are seen as highly influential on South-East Asian Muslim intellectuals.

3. The third hypothesis stated that there is a strong, but lessening influence of local concerns and values that still play an important role in the definition of values and goals by Muslim intellectuals. This was neither proved nor disproved in the course of this study. In fact, South-East Asian sources are not plentiful among the writers examined in this study and only a handful of local intellectuals are cited. As in the case of other world regions, South-East Asian references can be divided into two groups. The first are merely used for confirming statements concerning the writer's own views, as Achmad Baiquni, the Indonesian scientist, is for his views on God being the creator of the universe. The second involves a serious adoption by Nurcholish Madjid and the staff of *Al-Muslimun* of political and philosophical constructs made by particular South-East Asian authors. Even in these cases that usage is limited, however.

4. An important exception to the original hypotheses became apparent during investigation and analysis, that is, the importance of South Asian scholars as a source of intellectual thinking. They were noted by many of the eight Muslims intellectuals studied in this report and two of them — Chandra and Nurcholish Madjid — cited them extensively. Both took key intellectual constructs from Abū al-Kalām Āzād, Yūsuf 'Alī, and Muḥammad Iqbāl. Significantly, all these authors were prominent prior to Indian Partition in 1947. Mawdūdī, who first appeared in that era, but transcended it, was recognized by several writers as providing valuable insights. Still, his influence was less than his reputation might have been expected to engender.

5. As a sidelight the investigation revealed that there were three general approaches to the use of Islamic scripture. The first and most common type of reference involved the approach often identified with the neo-modernists, where direct reference is made to the Koran and the Hadith literature is not used. In this approach, the references are placed in direct support of the author's arguments or intellectual constructs. This is common to the

academic and societal intellectuals[21] and to Syahminan Zaini in the revivalist category. The second and least common usage was to Koran and Hadith, as advocated earlier by the Muslim modernists, where careful argumentation is built on the basis of both sources. This was the approach of *Al-Muslimun*. The third approach, common to Amran Kasimin and Ahmad Sonhadji Mohammed, makes references to Koran and Hadith, but only in the context of the interpretations made by accepted classical and medieval Muslim theologians and legalists. This is essentially the approach used by the traditionalists.

Summary

South-East Asian Muslim intellectuals draw widely for their inspiration and support of their concepts. The South Asian Muslim scholars were used most openly and in an unqualified manner. The writers in the West were regarded with some reserve, even by those South-East Asian intellectuals using Western sources as the primary basis for their studies. The West was seen as a place of danger and its views on Islam and intellectual activity as able to be taken only with caution and special care as to usage. There was similar reserve concerning Iranian writers from the Revolutionary Period, but this suspicion was not as extensive as the trepidation about the West. On the other hand, classical and medieval writers of the Middle East were readily accepted by nearly all the writers, but a different respect was assigned them according to the writers themselves. The "neo-traditionalists" in this study regarded them as pure sources of the true understanding of Islam. The neo-modernists saw individual scholars from the classical and medieval periods as having applied the lessons of Islam to their times and therefore having performed a role similar to that which they themselves were attempting to accomplish.

South-East Asian Muslim intellectuals are not uniform in the sources they use in developing their concepts or in supporting their arguments. Given the different kinds of training and the trend of influences on South-East Asia

---

[21]One should be on one's guard against making too many inferences on this study that would assign particular characteristics to particular intellectual groups (i.e., academics, *da'wah*, etc.). Other research suggests that, while there are some tendencies, none of the groups are monolithic.

from other regions — not studied here, but generally known — this could be expected in general. The study confirms this, but adds perspective to the attitudes of intellectuals in South-East Asia regarding other regions and the usefulness of learning in those regions to their own studies. The diversity is itself interesting and suggests that South-East Asian Muslims in general are under the influence of a very complicated web of influences that reflects the universal state of Islam today; no one centre of Islamic thought prevails, and contending centres of scholarship and activity compete with one another for the loyalty of individuals and groups of Muslims. The study here gives us some views of the patterns that exist in this multipolar world of Islamic thinking.

Finally, it can be stated that South-East Asian intellectuals are not bound by tradition, by geography, or ideology. They exist in an intellectual environment which is dynamic and they draw on a wide scope of intellectual thinking from the Muslim world and the West to make their arguments. They are hardly united in outlook; indeed their views are disparate, but still they are currently not at ideological odds with one another either. What does unite them is the search for solutions which aim at addressing contemporary issues while staying within the bounds of orthodox Islam.

18 Between *Ummah* and Home Country

The Indian Transnational Muslim Diaspora in the Caribbean Countries

Mohan K. Gautam

Introduction

It is a well-known fact that since the inception of Islam the concept *ummah* (Muslim brotherhood or community) has played a unique role in uniting the Muslims all over the world under a single Islamic umbrella. In South Asia, Islam became known when Muḥammad b. al-Qāsim took the kingdom of Multan (Punjab, India) in AD 711. However, the expansion of Islam took place only after 1192 when Muʿizz al-Dīn Muḥammad b. Sām, also known as Muḥammad Ghūrī, defeated the emperor of India, Prithviraj Chauhan. Soon afterwards followed a wave of Islamic conversion of Hindus. Though the new converts followed Islam seriously, they could not isolate themselves from the innate Hindu culture and traditional practices of their forefathers. In name they were Muslims, but in their traditional practices they were not different from their cognate Hindus. More in particular, although Islam does not believe in a caste system, the Indian Muslim community became a caste society. Indian Muslims used caste names no different from the Hindu caste names. In this way, the affirmation of their new Muslim identity was built on the prevailing traditions. After all, the Indian Muslims remained in the same villages, continued their same professions, and maintained the same social interactions with the neighbouring Hindus. Adherents of both religious communities were part of the same kinship group and these kinship groups were a source of pride in village life. The new converts became agents of change in creating a Hindu-Muslim synthesis in arts, architecture, language, administration, diet system, and other fields.[1] Indian Islam also absorbed various groups of Muslims who came to India as immigrants and were known as Turkish, Iraqi, Persian, and Afghan Muslims, but the civilization of India moulded them into a single group under the label of Indian

[1] Rizvi, *The Wonder that Was India*, 277-307.

351

Muslims. In other words, intercultural discourse, social commitment, and the feeling of belongingness to the region (*mulk*) of India became characteristics of the Indian Muslims. They were first Indian and then Muslim in their identities. The same situation prevailed in many other countries which were far away from the Arab world and all these countries gradually developed the same type of identities where their communicational language, in which they could laugh and weep, also became the language of their Muslim identity.

This gradual development of a Muslim identity, closely connected to their specific lands, raises two vital questions. First, to what extent does the concept of *ummah* still play a role among the South Asian Muslims? Second, how do the Indian Muslims define their identity when they live outside India? This text will address these questions and attempt to demonstrate a connection between the social basis of the Muslim identity and the cultural heritage of the country of origin of the Muslim emigrants of Surinam, Trinidad, and Guyana.

The Background of Muslims in India

Islam proclaims the universal principle of Muslim brotherhood, the *ummah*, and admits no differentiation of human beings except on the basis of their piety (*taqwah*). Given the historical circumstances outlined above, in India the principle of Islamic brotherhood, which would imply a casteless society, has remained operative only in theory, while in practice Islam has developed a different shade, based on local regional customs and traditions of the Hindu civilization. This does not mean that the five fundamental duties of Islam — the profession of faith (*shahādah*), ritual prayer (*salāh*), zakat, fasting, and haj — are not observed by the Indian Muslims, but in practice their religion has been submitted to processes of regionalization and localization. In India the Muslim society is not homogeneous and the observance of Islamic duties and rites varies in degree. Borrowing Robert Redfield's concepts, one might argue that Indian Islam during the last 700 years of history is the product of a constant interaction between the Islamic "Great Tradition" and Indo-Islamic "Little Tradition". Under the Islamic Great Tradition the ideals of Islam are followed and under the Indo-Islamic Little Tradition, the regional, folk, unwritten customs and traditions which have been handed down through the family (*khāndān*), caste (*zāt*), and community (*birādarī*) still continue.[2] In other words, the historical and cultural accommodation of Islam with its local environment in India has brought profound changes in its substance and fundamentally altered the practice and mode of thinking of its local adherents. In a way, it has also created a wide gap between Islamic law and actual practice.

By adhering to the Hindu notion of *jāt-birādarī* (caste brotherhood), an endogamous social unit which links them together with distant Hindu relatives, the Indian Muslims continue to practise the local customs and traditions in the hope of enhancing their social status and recognition within Indian society at large. The term for this notion varies and is generally known in India as *jāti* in Sanskrit and in North Indian languages, *qaum* in the north-western region, *jamāt* in West Gujarat, and expressed by the terms *zāt* and *birādarī* in the whole of India.

One of the most important elements of the Muslim social structure in India is the recruitment pattern for marriage (*nikāḥ* or *shādī*). Muslims always marry their daughter in their own regions in order that her family-in-law should speak the same language and observe the same customs. Moreover, the geographical nearness makes contacts easy. Migration within India or even abroad has not brought any change: when the time of marriage arrives, the partners are mostly selected in the region of the forefathers.

In this way Indian Muslims to some extent maintain the principle of endogamy. The Hindu avoidance of "purity-pollution" has penetrated into the social structure of the Muslim community.[3] For example, the Meo of Rajasthan, the Bengali Muslims of Calcutta, and the Siddique sheikhs of Allahabad constantly emphasize their descent and *jāti* membership and prohibit the inter-marriage with other Muslims. This attitude stresses the "regional identity", as is the case of the Tamil Muslims in Tamil Nadu, who identify themselves as part of the region together with the Hindu Tamil society. In such cases the concept of *mulk* (region or country) becomes a paramount factor in defining the self-identity. Therefore, when a Muslim in India declares he believes in the concept of *ummah*, he refers to the Muslim community within his region only.

It is often said in India that Islam has seventy-two denominations. The origin of this idea needs further research. It may be related to similar theses

---

[2] Ahmad, *Caste and Social Stratification*, I-XXII; Eaton, *Rise of Islam*, 305 ff.; Farzana, *Community and Consensus*, 1-9.
[3] Dumont, *Homo Hierarchicus*, 260 ff.

in classical Islamic heresiography. It may also refer to the occupational castes. Without arguing about exact numbers, Indian Islam is definitely characterized by the multitude of its denominations. Their primary distinctive feature is regional origin. Adherence to a particular school of jurisprudence or theology, such as the Hanafite, Shafi'ite, Ismaili, Deobandi, or Barelwi traditions, only comes next and often strengthens regional differences and geographical differences.

The Hindu system in India has divided the population into four *varṇas* (social orders or broad categories of castes). Similarly, Muslims in India are also divided into four categories, defining their descent and social status. These are the *sheikhs* (*shaykhs*), *sayeds* (*sayyids*), *mughals*, and *pathāns*. Those who pretend to have an Arabic genealogy call themselves *sheikhs* and *sayeds* and relate their ancestry with the family of the Prophet Muhammad. The title of *sheikh* is primarily used for religious scholars. *Mughals* are those who are known as Mirza or Beg and relate their ancestry with the Mughals of India, who came from Central Asia. *Khān* is a very common name found among *pathāns* in Central Asia, Persia, Afghanistan, and the North-West Frontier Province of Pakistan. All these Muslims consider themselves of high and middle class level in society. They are known as "*ashraf*" (from Arabic *ashrāf*, sg. *sharīf* — noble, distinguished) Muslims. Finally, the majority of the Muslims are descendants of converts from low caste Hindu artisans. In distinction from the four categories of *ashraf*s, they are called and considered "*ajlaf*s" (from Arabic *ajlāf*, sg. *jilf* — boorish, uncivil). The division of the Indian Muslim community is further enhanced by the frequent discriminatory attitude of *ashraf*s towards the *ajlaf*s. A remarkable fact is that, in order to enhance their social status, many descendants of high caste Hindus converted to Islam trace their genealogy to Arab origins. During the time of the Mughal Sultan Akbar in particular, many high caste Hindus were converted and afterwards were given the high status of *sheikh*s and *sayed*s.[4] In a way similar to the Hindu form of climbing upwards (called "sanskritization" by Mysore Srinivas[5]), the Indian Muslims have taken the names of Quereshi, Ansari, and Momin. The majority of Indian Muslims marry within their own category and region.

---

[4]Ahmad, l.c., ; *idem*, "Economic Change among the Muslims", 59 ff.; Malik, "Muslim Identities", 2 f.; Ansari, *Muslim Caste in Uttar Pradesh*.
[5]Srinivas, *Remembered Village*, 183.

Among the other Hindu traditions incorporated into the Muslim social system are the customs of dowry (*jahez*), *neg* (offering of money to sisters), and *barāt* (bridegroom's party to the house of the bride). All these traditions enhance the identity as members of a particular group. During the time of the Mughal emperors Akbar and Jahangir, Hindu ladies who married Muslims were allowed to carry on their own Hindu customs and rites, such as worship of the gods by maintaining an altar, fire sacrifices, and the celebration of festivals in their *zanānā* (ladies apartments).

Caribbean Muslims of Indian Origin

Between AD 1836 and 1916, many Indian Muslim families, both Muslim and Hindu, emigrated as indentured labourers to British colonies such as Mauritius (starting from 1834), Guyana (1838), Trinidad (1845), and Fiji (1879), the Dutch colony of Surinam (1873), and French colonies like Réunion (1830) and Guadeloupe (1845). There, they worked on sugar, cacao, coffee, cotton, banana, and other plantations for periods of five years. During their contract period, the Muslim indentured labourers maintained the form of Islam they had known in India. Since in Surinam, Guyana, and Trinidad most of these labourers originated from North Indian regions, i.e. from the present states of Uttar Pradesh (formerly known as Agra and Oudh), Bihar, and the surrounding states, they spoke a sort of Hindustani, a variant of Hindi/Urdu, and observed the same customs and traditions. Having lived together at a distance of about 15,000 km from their original villages, they minimized their regional differences and dialectical barriers and developed a proud Indian identity. Since most of them were uneducated, they kept alive their Indo-Muslim Little Tradition. At that time there were no imams, few religious books, and not even sufficient women. The British government restricted the immigration of women to a maximum of forty per cent. In practice however, they were far less than thirty per cent and their number mostly depended upon the recruiters in India and the transport ships. Those who stayed in Surinam, Guyana, and Trinidad after the end of their contract period started consciously to develop a Muslim society. By 1900 some sort of informal *madarsā*s (schools, from Arabic *madrasah*) were founded and attached to the mosques. When in 1921 the last contractors left for India, the newly settled Indian Muslims started creating *jamāt*s (brotherhood associations) and in their gatherings on the occasion of festivals or life cycle

355

ceremonies discussed the future of their children and Indian Islam. Almost until the 1930s Hindus and Muslims used to live together and share each other's joys and sorrows. After 1930 a rift between Hindus and Muslims began to emerge owing to the introduction of the Hindu revivalist movement known as Arya Samaj. The conflict continued until the 1940s.[6]

The Indian Muslims have developed a syncretic type of Islam blended with folk Hinduism. Their Indian identity has become even stronger because of fictive kinship bonds the Indian Muslims developed during the time of emigration as *dipuā bhāī* (brotherhood of the sub-depot and depot in Calcutta and Paramaribo) and *jahājiyā bhāī* (ship brotherhood) relationships.[7] When struck by grief and in life cycle ceremonies, frequent use is made of local Indian forms of religious practices such as the use of *tābīz* (amulets) and Koranic verses for healing, reverence to Hindu deities and shrines, and the consulting of fortune tellers and Sufi saints. When crises are not averted, often Hindu priests with their horoscopes are consulted. In most countries, Muslims of Indian origin practise monogamy and divorce is not popular. Feasts like *Shab-i barāt* (a feast in which the spring is welcomed with vigils and Koran recitation) have adopted the decor of the Hindu feast of *Divali* (festival of lights). Similarly, the feast of *Nav Roz* (New Year) has been combined with the Hindu feast of *Basant Pancamī* (Spring Festival). In Trinidad the feast of *mouloud* (*mawlūd*, also *mawlid* — the Prophet Muhammad's birthday, celebrated with religious songs) is celebrated by sitting on the floor on a white clean sheet listening to recitations in Urdu and in Arabic. Sufism in India developed as a syncretic phenomenon including elements from the Vedanta and *bhakti* (devotion to god Viśṇu). The Sufi idea of *tawhīd* (in the meaning of union with God), the use of the *tasbīḥ* (rosary), and the practice of *dhikr* (repetition of formulas in praise of God, similar to the practice of ecstasy by Hindu Yogis) have been influenced by the Hindu tradition.

A point in case is the work of Munshi Rahman Khan (1874-1972), a Muslim of Indian origin living in Surinam, who was well-known for his knowledge of the *Rāmāyaṇa*, a classical Hindu epic. He taught Hindus and Muslims Hindi and always emphasized the moral education for the betterment of the new generation. He wrote a biography of the Prophet Muhammad on the model of the *Rāmāyaṇa*, which was recited in gatherings

---

[6]Gautam, *Munshi Rahman Khan.*
[7]Gautam, "The Construction of Indian Image in Surinam".

and was written by Goswami Tulsidasa (1532-1623) in Avadhi, the mother tongues of many Indians.[8] Munshi Rahman Khan's suggestion was that Muslims should recite the story of the model life of their Prophet in a way similar to the Hindu epic. Moreover, in 1942 he published a work propagating three concepts which he had discovered in a book published in 1933 in Bombay by Ashfak Hussain.[9] He wrote in Hindi with the help of his son, Chote Khan, with an idea of helping his Indian Muslim brothers (*birādarī*). These three concepts were expressed in the Arabic terms of *takdīr*, *tadbīr*, and *tarkīb*, but their understanding as respectively the fortune to be born as Indian, the solution of problems, and realization of this solution was strongly influenced by the Hindu tradition. In other words, the idea of *apan zāt apan mulk aur apan tehzīb* (our people, our country, and our culture) remained the inseparable constituent of Indian Muslim identity in Surinam.[10] The situation was similar in Trinidad and Guyana.

The threat of loss of identity in an environment dominated by Christians was an important factor in the development of the notion of *mulk* among the Caribbean Muslims of Indian origin. The reference to their particular language and culture provided them with psychological security. In the case of Surinam, for example, most Creoles and Dutch workers in the administration of the plantations and the government were Christians. This is why until 1890 Indian Muslims refused to send their children to the Christian schools. During the initial years of immigration (1873 -74), eight ships brought 4954 Indian indentured labourers from Calcutta. They were distributed to the plantations, but, because of poor medical care, a lack of interpreters, and other shortcomings, twenty per cent died. In view of the high mortality rate of the Indian emigrants, in June 1874 the British government stopped the sea traffic to Surinam for a period of two years. Starting from this period, the socio-religious norms of the Indian community were consciously reconsolidated by a few Indian Muslim and Hindu leaders on their own plantations. The bonds of *jahājiyā bhāī* and *dipuā bhāī* were evoked and the notion of *mulk* became very prominent. Since the Muslims of Indian origin retained a strong awareness of India as the land of their forefathers (*ājā-ājīs*), the notion of Muslim brotherhood (*ummah*) became

---

[8]Gautam, "Ramayan in Surinam"; *idem, Munshi Rahman Khan.*
[9]Khan, Rahman; Munshi; and Chote Khan, *Khun ke Ansu.*
[10]Gautam, "Ramayan in Surinam"; *idem, Munshi Rahman Khan; idem,* "The Construction of Indian Image".

associated with the concept of *mulk*. This particular understanding has also provided the Muslims the feeling that India is not an ordinary geographical entity, but *dār al-aḥad*, *dār al-amān*, and *dār al-'ulūm* (land of unity; land of security or peace; and land of sciences or knowledge). Many Muslim families in Surinam send their children to India for religious education. Similar phenomena existed during the initial years of immigration in Trinidad and Guyana.[11]

A word should be added about the division of Indian Muslims into Sunnites, Shi'ites, and Ahmadis. During the last few decades, the Ahmadis have generally not been considered Muslims and their activities have been banned in Pakistan. In Caribbean countries, however, Ahmadis claim to be true Muslims and have their own schools and mosques. Moreover, in spite of their doctrinal differences, in Caribbean practice the various Islamic denominations work together when they face a common crisis. This is manifested in their attitude towards their black co-religionists.

A community of black Muslims has developed in Trinidad. This community is supported by the Muslims of the United States of America, but social intercourse and marriages between the Indian and the black Muslims are almost out of question. Each group had its own mosques and *madarsās*, where they can speak their mother tongue and listen to the preachings of their respective imams.

In July 1990, when Afro-Trinidadian Muslims who belonged to Jamat-e-Musliman attempted a coup and seized the parliament for six days, they obtained no support from the Indian Muslims. The black leader, Abu Baker, justified the overthrow of the government with Koranic injunctions, saying that Allah has laid down the laws and that, when people are oppressed, they should act to redress the situation. However, Dr M.A. Aziz of the Trinidad Muslim League, considered close to the Lahore branch of the Ahmadiyyah, together with the United Islamic Organization, which united thirteen small orthodox Muslim groups, vociferously condemned it and stated that "this brand of armed uprising and terrorism with hostage taking has nothing to do with Islam as a religion or ideology and must be condemned by right-thinking persons."[12]

---

[11]Gautam, *The Role of Bhojpuri and Avadhi*; cf. Gautam, "Maintenance Mechanism of Indian (Hindustanis) Ethnic Identity".
[12]Khan, *Islam as a Social Force*, 9; Ryan, *The Muslim Grab for Power*, 52 ff.

From the 1950s, these differences have created conflicts among the various Muslim communities in the Caribbean countries. Although the Caribbean Muslims of Indian origin endorse the notion of *ummah*, in practice the use of this term denotes the Muslims of East Indian origin only and excludes the black Afro-Muslims in Trinidad as well as in Guyana. In Surinam the other Muslim community is composed of the Muslims of Javanese origin. During feasts, Javanese and Indian Muslims in Surinam all meet together, but the regular religious observances take place in their respective mosques and so do the marriage ceremonies. It has to be said that, although using a different language and observing different socio-cultural practices, related to their respective country of origin, the Javanese (also referred to as "Malay") and the Indian Muslim community feel close to each other owing to their oriental set-up. When in the 1950s political parties started to be created, Indians and Javanese adhered to the same political party, known as the Verenigde Hervormings Partij (VHP — United Reform Party).

Conclusion

Indian Muslims construct their identity with reference to their country and region of origin as well as caste-like social status groups and they enhance their particular identity through the use of their language and rituals. Brotherhood bonds play an important role as source of honour, respect, and status. The way Muslims of Indian origin in the Caribbean countries conceive the concept of *ummah* has been profoundly coloured by the notion of *mulk-birādarī* and has provided them with psychological security.

Glossary

Note: technical terms used in a particular contribution and explained there are not listed in this glossary.

Abbreviations used:
A: Arabic
E: English
I: Indonesian
M: Malay
U: Urdu

abangan (I): Muslims whose beliefs and customs are strongly influenced by the pre-monotheist Javanese tradition (Java)

adat (M/I; A *'ādah*): custom(s)

birādarī (U): endogamous social unit and status group (Pakistan)

da'wah (A): propagation or intensification of the Islamic faith

dhikr (A): (mystical drills for the) commemoration of God

dīnī madāris (U): Islamic religious schools (Pakistan)

fatwa (A *fatwā*): qualified advice or opinion on a question of Islamic law

fiqh (A): Islamic jurisprudence

hadith (A *hadīth*): report on sayings or acts of the Prophet Mohammed

Hadith (A *hadīth*): the collection of reports on sayings or acts of the Prophet Mohammed

halāl (A): permissible (Islamic law)

ijtihād (A): independent development of Islamic law

Institut Agama Islam Negeri (IAIN) (I): State Institute for Islamic Studies (Indonesia)

jinn (A): spiritual being

kiai (I): honorific title for Islamic religious scholar and *pesantren* leader (Indonesia, esp. Java)

madrasah (A): Islamic religious school

mashāyikh (A/U, plural): elders, chiefs, leaders of mystical orders

mufti (A *muftī*): person empowered to give fatwas

mullā (A/U): Islamic religious scholar (Pakistan et al.)

New Order: regime headed by Soeharto (Indonesia, 1965/6-1998)

pardah (U, E also "purdah"): curtain to screen women; veil

pesantren (I): traditional Islamic boarding school (Indonesia)

pīr (U): saint, venerated person (Pakistan et al.)

qāḍī (A): Islamic judge

Reformasi (I): the recent reform movement against the Soeharto regime (Indonesia)

santri (I): *pesantren* pupil; "orthodox" Muslim (Indonesia)

sayyid (A/U/I): descendant of the Prophet Mohammed, esp. through Ḥusayn b. Abī Ṭālib

sharī'ah (A): Islamic law

sunnah (A): the tradition of the Prophet Mohammed and the first generations of his followers

ulama (I): Indonesian form of *'ulamā'*, used both in a singular and a plural sense

'ulamā' (A; sing. *'ālim*): Islamic religious scholar

waqf (A): religious endowment (Islamic law)

zakat (A *zakāh*): alms tax (Islamic law)

Bibliography

Anonymous, Manuscript without title: On Islamic teachings, Brunei, AH 1325 (AD 1907) (appendix to Malay translation of Ibn 'Aṭā' Allāh al-Iskandarī, *Kitāb al-ḥikam*; Library of the Brunei History Centre, Bandar Seri Begawan).

Anonymous, *Peoples and Politics of China's Northwest*, unpublished report, Office of Strategic Services, Research and Analysis Branch: Washington, DC: 1945.

Abaza, Mona, *Cultural Exchange and Muslim Education: Indonesian Students in Cairo*, diss., University of Bielefeld, 1990.

----, *Changing Images of Three Generations of Azharites in Indonesia*, Singapore: ISEAS, 1993.

----, *Islamic Education. Perceptions and Exchanges. Indonesian Students in Cairo*, Paris: Association Archipel, 1994 (adapted version of the author's 1990 dissertation).

----, "Islam in South-east Asia. Varying Impact and Images of the Middle East", in Hussin Mutalib and Taj ul-Islam Hashmi (eds), *Islam, Muslims and the Modern State; Case-Studies of Muslims in Thirteen Countries*, London: MacMillan and New York: St. Martin Press, 1994.

Abdul Aziz et al. (eds), *Gerakan Islam Kontemporer di Indonesia* [Contemporary Islamic Movements in Indonesia], Jakarta: Pustaka Firdaus, 1991.

Abdul Aziz Juned, Pehin Tuan Imam, *Islam di Brunei* [Islam in Brunei], Bandar Seri Begawan: Brunei History Centre, 1992.

Abu Hamid, *Syekh Yusuf Makassar. Seorang Ulama, Sufi dan Pejuang* [Sheykh Yusuf Makassar. A Religious Scholar, Sufi, and Warrior], Jakarta: Obor, 1994.

Abu Bakar (ed.), *Undang-Undang Ugama 1955* [Religious Law of 1955], Bandar Brunei: Star Press, 1955.

Adams, Cindy, *Sukarno; An autobiography as told to ----* , Jakarta: Gunung Agung, 1966.

Ade Armando, "Sialnya, Ada Muchtar Pakpahan" [Shit, There is This Muchtar Pakpahan], *Republika* (daily, Jakarta), 5 July 1998, 2.

Adviezen van den adviseur voor inlandsche zaken betreffende de Vereeniging "Sarekat Islam" [Advices of the Advisor for Native Affairs Concerning the Association "Sarekat Islam"], Batavia: Landsdrukkerij, 1913.

Ahmad Syadali, "Harun Nasution dan Perkembangan IAIN Syarif Hidayatullah Jakarta" [Harun Nasution and the Development of IAIN Syarif Hidayatullah of Jakarta], in Aqib Suminto et al., *Refleksi Pembaharuan Pemikiran Islam. 70 Tahun Harun Nasution* [Reflection on the Renewal of Islamic Thought. Harun Nasution 70 Years], Jakarta: LSAF, 1989, 271-9.

hmad Sonhaji Mohamad, *Kursus Tafsir Al-Quran* [A Course of Koran Exegesis], Kuala Lumpur, Percetakan Simal, 1983.

----, *Tafsir Al Quran di Radio* [Koran Exegesis on the Radio], Kuala Lumpur, Pustaka Al-Mizan, 1988.

Ahmad, Imtiaz, *Caste and Social Stratification among the Muslims*, Delhi: Manohar, 1973.

----, "Economic Change Among the Muslims" in Dietmar Rothermund (ed.), *Islam in Southern Asia. A Survey of Current Research*, Wiesbaden: Franz Steiner, 1975, 59-61.

Ahmed, Akbar S., *Postmodernism and Islam, Predicament and Promise*, London: Routledge, 1992.

---- and Hastings Donnan, "Islam in the Age of Postmodernity", in Akbar S. Ahmed and Hastings Donnan (eds), *Islam, Globalization and Postmodernity*, London and New York: Routledge, 1994, 1-20.

Ahsan, Aitzaz, *The Indus Saga and the Making of Pakistan*, Karachi etc.: Oxford University Press, 1996.

Aishah Md. Yusof, *Pusat Da'wah Islamiah dan Islamisasi di Brunei Darussalam* [Centres of Propagation of the Islamic Faith and Islamization in Brunei], MA thesis, IAIN Syarif Hidayatullah, Jakarta, 1993.

Al-Khayyat, Sana, *Honour and Shame. Women in Modern Iraq*, London: Saqi Books, 1990.

Al-Muslimun (monthly, Bangil), 1963-.

Algemeen Rijksarchief (ARA – General State Archives, the Netherlands).

Ali, M. Mumtaz, "Teaching of Islam to Muslim Children and Youth in Great Britain", *Muslim Education Quarterly* (Cambridge, UK), 4 (1987), 2, 28-39.

Ali, Yusuf Talal, "Draft Chapter on Islamic Education for Inclusion in the Report of the President's Task Force on Education", mimeo, Islamabad, 1982.

Ali Anwar, "Universitas Islam Negeri: Lembaga Pendidikan Kelas Dua?" [Islamic State University: a Second Class Educational Institute?], *Hikmah* (Bandung), 1 March 1996, 19.

Alkaff, Thohir Abdullah, "Perkembangan Syiah di Indonesia" [The Development of Shi'ism in Indonesia], in Abduh and Away (eds), *Mengapa Kita Menolak Syi'ah*, Jakarta: Lembaga Penelitian dan Pengkajian Islam, 1998, 54-74.

Alles, Elisabeth, "L'islam chinois: femmes ahong", *Etudes Orientales* (Paris), 13/14 (1994), 163-68.

Alvi, Anjum, *Bearers of Grief: Death, Kinship, Gift Exchange, and Women in Muslim Punjab*, diss., Freie Universität Berlin, 1999.

Amran Kasimin. *Tanya Jawab Agama Mingguan Malaysia* [Religious Questions and Answers from the weekly *Mingguan Malaysia*], Kuala Lumpur: Dinie Publishers, 1993.

Anagnost, Ann S., "The Politics of Displacement", in Charles Keyes, Laurel Kendal, and Helen Hardacre (eds), *State and Religion in East and Southeast Asia*, Honolulu: University of Hawai'i Press, 1994.

Anderson, Benedict, *Imagined Communities*, London: Verso Press, 1983.

364

Ansari, Ghaus, *Muslim Caste in Uttar Pradesh (A Study of Culture Contact)*, Lucknow: Ethnographic and Folk Culture Society, 1960.

Antara (Indonesian public news agency).

[*Laporan Penelitian*] *Antisipasi Agama Terhadap Trend Globalisasi Pembangunan Regional dan Lokal* [(Research Report) on the Religious Anticipation of the Globalization Trend in Regional and Local Development], Jakarta: Badan Penelitian dan Pengembangan Agama, Departemen Agama (Religious Research and Development Agency, Ministry of Religious Affairs), 1992-94 (a series of research reports by a team of this government agency).

Anwar, Muhammad, "Young Muslims in Britain", in Mohammad Wasiullah Khan (ed.), *Education and Society in the Muslim World*, Jeddah: King Abdul Aziz University, 1981, 100-121.

ARA: see *Algemeen Rijksarchief*.

Asad, Talal, *Genealogies of Religion: Discipline and Reasons of Power in Christianity and Islam*, Baltimore and London: John Hopkins University Press, 1993.

Azyumardi Azra, "'Ulama' Indonesia di Haramayn. Pasang Surut Sebuah Wacana Intelektual" [The Indonesian *'Ulamā'* in the *Ḥaramān* (the two holy cities: Mecca and Medina). The Development and Decline of an Intellectual Discourse], *Ulumul Qur'an* (Jakarta), 3, 3 (July-Sept. 1992), 76-85.

----, "Darul Arqam: A Historical Reflection", *Jakarta Post* (daily, Jakarta), 31 August 1994.

----, *Gerakan-gerakan Kontemporer Islam di Indonesia. Upaya Memahami Neo-Revivalisme dan Fundamentalisme* [Contemporary Islamic Movements in Indonesia. An Effort to Understand Neo-Revivalism and Fundamentalism], paper presented at the Center for Policy and Development Studies (CPDS), Jakarta, 1994.

----, "Guarding the Faith of the Ummah: Religio-Intellectual Journey of Mohammad Rasjidi", *Studia Islamika. Indonesian Journal for Islamic Studies* (Jakarta), 1, 2 (April-June 1994), 87-119.

----, *The Transmission of Islamic Reformism to Indonesia: Networks of Middle Eastern and Malay-Indonesian 'Ulamâ' in the Seventeenth and Eighteenth Centuries*, diss., Columbia University, New York, 1992 (to be published by KITLV, Leiden; Indonesian translation: *Jaringan Ulama. Timur Tengah dan Kepulauan Nusantara Abad XVII dan XVIII. Melacak Akar-Akar Pembaruan Pemikiran Islam di Indonesia*, Bandung: Mizan, 1994).

----, "Dari Haramayn ke Kairo" [From the *Ḥaramān* (the two holy cities: Mecca and Medina) to Cairo], in Mahasin, Aswab et al. (eds), *Ruh Islam dalam Budaya Bangsa* [The Islamic Spirit within the National Culture], Jakarta: Yayasan Festival Istiqlal, 1995, vol. 3 (*Wacana Antar Agama dan Bangsa* [Interreligious and International Discourse]), 88-106.

----, "Melacak Pengaruh dan Pergeseran Orientasi Tamatan Kairo" [Tracing the Influence and Shift of Orientation of Cairo Graduates] (review article of Abaza, *Islamic Education*),

Studia Islamika. Indonesian Journal for Islamic Studies (Jakarta), 2, 3 (July-Sept. 1995), 199-219.

----, *Perbukuan Islam di Indonesia: Merambah Intelektualisme Baru* [The Production of Books in Indonesia: Steps Towards a New Intellectualism], paper presented at the Istiqlal Festival II, Jakarta, 1995.

----, "Syi'ah di Indonesia: Antara Mitos dan Realitas" [Shi'ism in Indonesia: Between Myth and Reality], *Ulumul Qur'an* (Jakarta), 6, 4 (Oct.-Dec. 1995), 4-19.

----, "Two Worlds of Islam: Interaction between Southeast Asia and the Middle East" (book review), *Journal of Islamic Studies* (Oxford), 6 (1995), 2, 301-4.

----, "Darul Arqam: Tradisionalisme vs Reformisme", in *idem, Menuju Masyarakat Madani*, Bandung: Rosda Karya, 1999, 163-5.

----, "The Islamic Factor in Post-Soeharto Indonesia", in Chris Manning & Peter van Diermen (eds), *Indonesia in Transition: Social Aspect of Reformasi and Crisis*, Canberra: Research School of Pacific and Asian Studies, Australian National University and Singapore: Institute of Southeast Asian Studies, 2000, 309-318.

----, "Sustaining the Transition from Authoritarian Rule to Democracy: A Special Reference to Indonesia", paper presented at the International Conference of the International Council on Human Rights Policy, Jakarta, 16 March 2001.

----, "Islamic Perspective on the Nation-State: Political Islam in Post-Soeharto Indonesia", in Virginia Hooker and Amin Saikal (eds), *Islamic Perspective on the New Millennium*, Canberra: Australian National University and Singapore: Institute of Southeast Asian Studies, forthcoming.

Badaruddin P. Hj. Othman, Hj., *Ugama dengan Pegawai Kerajaan* [Religion with State Officials], Bandar Seri Begawan: Information Department, 1982.

----, *Ugama Rasmi: Latar Belakang dan Sumbangan Pegawai Kerajaan* [Official Religion: Its Background and the Contribution of State Officials], Bandar Seri Begawan: Information Department, 1983.

Bahādur: see Muḥammad Ṣiddīq Ḥasan Khān Bahādur.

Bai Shouyi and Yang Huaizhong (eds), *Huizu renwu zhi, Yuan dai* [Annals of Hui Personages. Yuan Dynasty], Yinchuan: Ningxia People's Publishing Companya, 1985.

Bamualim, Chaider S. et al., *Laporan Penelitian Radikalisme Agama dan Perubahan Sosial di DKI Jakarta* [Research Report on Religious Radicalism ans Social Change in the Special Capital City Region of Jakarta], Jakarta: Pusat Bahasa dan Budaya [Centre for Language and Culture], IAIN Jakarta and Badan Perencanaan Pembangunan Daerah DKI Jakarta [Regional Planning and Development Agency of the Special Capital City Region of Jakarta], 2001.

BAR: see *State of Brunei Annual Report*.

Barton, Greg, "Neo-Modernism: A Vital Synthesis of Traditionalist and Modernist Islamic Thought in Indonesia", *Studia Islamika. Indonesian Journal for Islamic Studies* (Jakarta), 2, 3 (July-Sept. 1995), 1-75.

Barzangi, Nimat Hafiz, "Religious Education", in John L. Esposito (ed.-in-chief), *The Oxford Encyclopedia of the Modern Islamic World*, New York and Oxford: Oxford University Press, 1995, vol. 1, 406-11.

Basu, Amrita (ed.), *The Challenge of Local Feminisms. Women's Movements in Global Perspective*, Boulder: Westview, 1995.

Baumann, Zygmunt, *Modernity and the Holocaust*, Cambridge: Polity Press/Ithaca: Cornell University Press, 1989.

Beeby, C.E., *Assessment of Indonesian Education: A Guide in Planning*, Wellington: New Zealand Council for Educational Research in association with Oxford University Press, 1979.

Beijing City Sociology Committee et al. (ed.), "Beijing shi canzaju xiaoshu minzu jiaoyu wenti diaocha baogao" (Research Report on the Problem of Education among Dispersed Minorities in Beijing City), *Central Institute for Nationalities Journal* (Beijing), 1 (1984), 18-26.

Bell, Diane; Patricia Caplan; and Wazir Jahan Karim (eds), *Gendered Fields. Women, Men and Ethnography*, London and New York: Routledge, 1993.

Bellah, Robert N., *The Broken Covenant. American Civil Religion in Time of Trial*, New York: Seabury, 1975.

Bescheiden betreffende de Vereeniging "de Indische Partij" [Documents Concerning the Association "de Indische Partij"], Batavia: Landsdrukkerij, 1913.

Bintang Soerabaia (daily, Surabaya), probably 1861-1919 or beyond.

Bluhm, Jutta E., A preliminary statement on the dialogue established between the reform magazine al-Manar and the Malayo-Indonesian world. *Indonesia Circle* (London), 32 (Nov. 1983), 35-42.

Boland, Bernard Johan, "Historical Outline", in: *idem* and I. Farjon, *Islam in Indonesia: A Bibliographical Survey*, Dordrecht: Foris, 1-56, 1983.

Borchigud, Wurlig, "The Impact of Urban Ethnic Education on Modern Mongolian Ethnicity, 1949-1966", in Stevan Harrell (ed.) *Cultural Encounters on China's Ethnic Frontiers*, Seattle: University of Washington Press, 1995, 278-300.

Borneo Bulletin: see *The Borneo Bulletin*.

Bouamama, Said and Hadjila Sad Saoud, *Familles maghrébines de France*, Paris: Desclée de Brouwer, 1996.

Bowen, John, "The Forms Culture Takes: A State-of-the-field Essay on the Anthropology of Southeast Asia", *The Journal of Asian Studies* (Ann Arbor) 54 (1995), 4, 1004-68.

Braighlinn, G., *Ideological Innovation under Monarchy*, Amsterdam: V.U. University Press, 1992.

Braudel, Fernand, 'The expansion of Europe and the "longue dureé"', in H.L. Wesseling (ed.), *Expansion and Reaction. Essays on European Expansion and Reactions in Asia and Africa*, Leiden: Leiden University Press, 1978, 17-27.

367

----, *Civilisation matérielle, économie et capitalisme. XVe-XVIIIe siècle*, Paris: A. Colin, 1979, 3 vols.

----, *La Méditerrannée et le monde méditerranéen à l'époque de Philippe II*, Paris: A. Colin, ⁵1985, 2 vols (¹1949).

Bruinessen, Martin van, *Tarekat Naqsyabandiyah di Indonesia* [De Naqshbandiyyah Order in Indonesia], Bandung: Mizan, 1992.

Bruinessen, Martin van, *Globalization and Particularism in Indonesian Muslim Discourse*, paper presented at the Conference on Changing Life-Styles in Asia: Consumption/Media/Religion in Contemporary India and Indonesia, International Institute of Asian Studies, Leiden, 1994.

al-Bukhārī: see *Ṣaḥīḥ al-Bukhārī.*

Bushkov, Valentin I., "The Population of Northern Tajikistan between 1870 and 1990", in Vitaly Naumkin (ed.), *State, Religion and Society in Central Asia. A Post-Soviet Critique*, Reading: Ithaca Press, 1993, 219-44.

Cahill, James, "Figure, Bird, and Flower Painting in China Today", in Lucy Lim (ed.), *Contemporary Chinese Painting*, San Francisco: Chinese Culture Foundation, 1983.

Carey, Peter, "Santri and Satria. Some Notes on the Relationship between Dipanegara's Kraton and Religious Supporters During the Java War (1825-30)", in T. Ibrahim Alfian (ed.), *Dari Babad dan Hikayat Sampai Sejarah Kritis* [From *Babad* and *Hikayat* to Critical History], Yogyakarta: Gadjah Mada University Press. 1987. 271-318.

Carley, Patricia M., "The Price of the Plan. Perceptions of Cotton and Health in Uzbekistan and Turkmenistan", *Central Asian Survey* (Oxford), 8 (1989), 4, 1-38.

Carmen A. Abubakar, "The Birth of Muslim States", *Ayat az-Zaman*, 2 (1990), 40-51.

Chambert-Loir, Henri and Johan Hendrik Meuleman, "Les instituts islamiques publics indonésiens", in Nicole Grandin and Marc Gaborieau (eds), *Madrasa. La transmission du savoir dans le monde musulman*, Paris: Arguments, 1997, 199-216.

Chandra Muzaffar, "Administration of Justice in Politics", in Aidit Ghazali, *Islam and Justice*, Kuala Lumpur: Institute of Islamic Understanding, 1992/1993, 159-82.

Chang, Arnold, *Painting in the People's Republic of China. The Politics of Style*, Boulder: Westview, 1980.

Cherif, Leila, "Ningxia, l'école au féminin", *Etudes Orientales*, 13/14 (1994), 156-62.

China Islamic Association, *A Collection of Painting and Calligraphy Solicited for Charity in Aid of the Disabled*, Beijing: China Islamic Association, 1985.

China Daily (daily, Beijing), 1981-

Chinese *Nationalities*, Beijing: China Nationality Photography and Art Press, 1989.

Chow, Rey, "Violence in the Other Country. China as Crisis, Spectacle, and Woman", in C.T. Mohanty et al. (eds), *Third World Women and The Politics of Feminism*, Bloomington: Indiana University Press, 1991, 81-100.

Cohen, Joan Lebold, *The New Chinese Painting 1949-1986*, New York: Harry N. Abrams, 1987.

----, *The Yunnan School, Jiang, He Neng*, Minneapolis: Fingerhut, 1989.

Cohen, Myron L., "Being Chinese: The Peripheralization of Traditional Identity", *Daedalus* (Boston), 120 (1991), 2, 113-34.

Craumer, Peter R., "Agricultural Change, Labor Supply, and Rural Out-Migration in Soviet Central Asia", in Robert A. Lewis (ed.), *Geographic Perspective on Soviet Central Asia*, London and New York: Routledge, 1992.

Crossley, Pamela Kyle, "Thinking about Ethnicity in Early Modern China", *Late Imperial China* (Pasadena), 11 (1990), 1, 1-35.

Daniel, Norman, *Islam and the West. The Making of an Image*, Edinburgh: Edinburgh University Press, 1966.

Damai (monthly, Perhimpunan Penghulu dan Pegawainya, Surakarta), 1938-39.

Darul Aqsha, Dick (Theodorus Cornelis) van der Meij, and Johan Hendrik Meuleman, *Islam in Indonesia: A Survey of Events and Developments from 1988 to March 1993*, Jakarta: INIS, 1995.

De Expres: alphabetically arranged as *Expres*.

Dekmejian, R. Hrair, *Islam in Revolution: Fundamentalism in the Arab World*, Syracuse: Syracuse University Press, [2]1995.

De Locomotief: alphabetically arranged as *Locomotief*.

Demographic Situation & Population Projections: Bandar Seri Begawan: Economic Planning Unit, 1994.

Denny, Frederick Mathewson, *An Introduction to Islam*, New York: Macmillan and London: Collier Macmillan, 1985.

Deutsch, Karl Wolfgang, "Social Mobilization and Political Development", *American Political Science Review* (Baltimore), 55, 3 (September 1961), 493-514.

Diamond, Norma, "The Miao and Poison: Interactions on China's Southwest Frontier", *Ethnology* (Pittsburg), 27 (1988), 1, 1-25.

Dijk, C. [Cornelis = Kees] van, *Rebellion under the Banner of Islam. The Darul Islam in Indonesia*, 's-Gravenhage: Nijhoff, 1981.

Djanko. T. A., "Sem'ya i byt narodov Sredney Azii i Kazakhstana" [Family and Life Styles of the Peoples of Central Asia and Kazakhstan], in K.D. Basaeva, N. Bikbulatov, V.N. Birin et al. (eds), *Semeyny byt narodov SSSR* [Family Life Styles of the Peoples of the USSR], Moscow: Nauka, 1990, 440-512.

Djedjak Langkah Hadji A. Salim. Pilihan Karangan, Utjapan dan Pendapat Beliau dari Dulu Sampai Sekarang [Footprints of Haji A(gus) Salim. A Choice from His Works, Statements, and Opinions from the Past till Today], Jakarta: Tintamas, 1954.

Dokumentasi Kliping Tentang Rancangan Undang-Undang Peradilan Agama [Clipping Documentation on the Bill on Religious Judicature], Jakarta: Center for Strategic and International Studies, no. 181/H/VII/1989.

Dreyfus, Hubert and Paul Rabinow, *Michel Foucault: Beyond Structuralism and Hermeneutics*, Chicago: University of Chicago Press, 1982.

Dumont, Louis, *Homo hierarchus. Essai sur le système des castes*, Paris: Gallimard, 1967.

----, *Essays on Individualism: Modern Ideology in Anthropological Perspective*, Chicago and London: University of Chicago Press, 1986.

Eaton, Richard, *The Rise of Islam and the Bengal Frontier, 1204-1760*, Berkeley etc.: University of California Press, 1993.

Eberhard, Wolfram, *China's Minorities. Yesterday and Today*, Belmont, CA: Wadsworth, 1982.

Education for All: The Report of the Committee of Inquiry into the Education of Children from Ethnic Minority Groups (chairman: Lord Swann), presented to Parliament by the Secretary of State for Education and Science by command of Her Majesty, London: Her Majesty's Stationery Service, 1985

Eglar, Zekiye, *A Punjabi Village in Pakistan*, New York: Columbia University Press, 1960.

Eickelman, Dale F., "Mass Higher Education and the Religious Imagination in Contemporary Arab Societies", *American Ethnologist*, 19, 4 (Nov. 1992), 643-55.

----, and James Piscatori, *Muslim Politics*, Guildford: Princeton University Press, 1996.

Eisenstadt, Samuel N., "European Expansion and the Civilization of Modernity", in H.L. Wesseling (ed.), *Expansion and Reaction. Essays on European Expansion and Reactions in Asia and Africa*, Leiden: Leiden University Press, 1978, 167-86.

Eliade, Mircea, *Le mythe de l'éternel retour: archétypes et répétition*, Paris: Gallimard, 1947.

Esposito, John L., *The Islamic Threat: Myth or Reality?*, New York etc.: Oxford University Press, 1973.

---- (ed.), *The Iranian Revolution: Its Global Impact*, Miami: Florida International University Press, 1990.

---- (ed.), *Oxford Encyclopedia of the Modern Islamic World*, New York: Oxford University Press, 1995.

Evans-Pritchard, Edward Evan, *Theories of Primitive Religion*, Oxford: Clarendon Press, 1965.

De Expres (daily, Bandung), 1912-14.

Farzana, Shaikh, *Community and Concensus in Islam, Muslim Representation in Colonial India, 1860-1947*, Cambridge/New York: University of Cambridge Press, 1989.

Federspiel, Howard, "Muslim Intellectuals in Southeast Asia", *Studia Islamika. Indonesian Journal for Islamic Studies* (Jakarta), 6, 1 (Jan.-March 1999), 41-76.

Fei Xiaotong, "Ethnic Identification in China", in Fei Xiaotong (ed.), *Toward a People's Anthropology*, Beijing: New World Press, 1981.

Fischer, Michael M.J., *Iran: From Religious Dispute to Revolution*, Cambridge, MA: Harvard University Press, 1980.

Fletcher, Joseph, "The Naqshbandiyya in Northwest China", unpublished manuscript, Harvard University, s.a.

Gansu, Lanzhou: Gansu People's Publishing Society, 1982.

Gautam, Mohan K., "Maintenance Mechanism of Indian (Hindustanis) Ethnic Identity in Surinam and the Netherlands: Strategies of Segregation and Integration in Defining the Solidarity of the Community" in Uttama Bissoondoyal and S.B.C. Servansing, *Indian Labour Immigration. Papers Presented at the International Conference on Indian Labour Immigration (23-27 October, 1984)*, Moka, Mauritius: Mahatma Gandhi Institute, 1986, 265-288.

----, "Ramayan in Surinam" in V. Sagar (ed.), *Focus on Surinam: Mother Children India Abroad*, New Delhi: ICFIC, 1991, 48-56.

----, *Munshi Rahman Khan (1874-1972): An Institution of the Indian Diaspora in Surinam*, paper presented at the Conference on Challenge and Change: the Indian Diaspora in its Historical and Contemporary Contexts, University of the West Indies, St. Augustine, Trinidad, 1995.

----, "The Construction of Indian Image in Surinam: Deconstructing Colonial Derogatory Notions and Reconstructing Indian Identity" in Mahin Gosine and D. Narine (eds), *Sojourners to Settlers: Indian Migrants in the Caribbean and Americas*, New York: Windsor, 1999, 125-79.

----, *The Role of Bhojpuri and Avadhi in the Reconstruction of Surinami Indian Culture*, paper presented at the Second World Bhojpuri Convention, Moka, Mauritius, 24-29 Feb. 2000.

Geertz, Clifford, *The Religion of Java*, Glencoe: The Free Press, 1960.

----, *Islam Observed: Religious Development in Morocco and Indonesia*, New Haven etc.: Yale University Press, 1968.

Gellner, Ernest, "Flux and Reflux in the Faith of Men", in *idem*, *Muslim Society*, Cambridge: Cambridge University Press, 1981, 1-85.

----, *Postmodernism, Reason and Religion*, London and New York: Routledge, 1992.

----, *Conditions of Liberty. Civil Society and Its Rivals*, Harmondsworth: Penguin, 1994.

----, "Foreword" to Akbar S. Ahmed and Hastings Donnan (eds), *Islam, Globalization and Postmodernity*, London and New York: Routledge, 1994, XI-XIV.

Giddens, Anthony, *The Consequences of Modernity*, Cambridge: Polity Press/Stanford: Stanford University Press, 1990.

----, *Beyond Left and Right: The Future of Radical Politics*, Cambridge and Oxford: Polity Press/Stanford: Stanford University Press, 1994.

Gillett, Margaret, "The IAIN in Indonesian Higher Education", *Muslim Education Quarterly* (Cambridge, UK), 8 (1990), 1, 21-32.

Gilmartin, David, *Empire and Islam: Punjab and the Making of Pakistan*, Berkeley et al.: University of California Press, 1988.

Gladney, Dru C., "Muslim Tombs and Ethnic Folklore: Charters for Hui Identity", *The Journal of Asian Studies* (Ann Arbor), 46 (1987), 3, 495-532.

----, *Qing Zhen: A Study of Ethnoreligious Identity Among Hui Muslim Communities in China*, diss., University of Washington, Seattle, 1987.

----, "The Ethnogenesis of the Uigur", *Central Asian Survey* (Oxford), 9 (1990), 1, 1-28.

----, *Muslim Chinese: Ethnic Nationalism in the People's Republic*. Cambridge, MA: Harvard University Press, Council on East Asia, 1991.

----, "Transnational Islam and Uighur National Identity. Salman Rushdie, Sino-Muslim Missile Deals, and the Trans-Eurasian Railway", *Central Asian Survey* (Oxford), 11 (1992), 3, 1-18.

----, "Representing Nationality in China: Refiguring Majority/Minority Identities", *The Journal of Asian Studies* (Ann Arbor), 53 (1994), 1, 92-123.

----, "Salman Rushdie in China: Religion, Ethnicity, and State Definition in the People's Republic", in Charles F. Keyes, Laurel Kendall, and Helen Hardacre (eds), *Religion and the Modern States of East and Southeast Asia*, Honolulu: University of Hawai'i Press, 1994, 255-78.

---- and Ma Qicheng, *Local and Muslim in China: The Making of Indigenous Identities among the Uygur and Hui*, paper presented to the Annual Association of Asian Studies Meetings, Honolulu, Hawai'i, 10-14 April 1996.

Government of Pakistan, Ministry of Religious Affairs, *Riport-i qaumī kamūī barā-ye dīnī madāris-i Pākistān* [Report of the National Committee on Religious Schools in Pakistan], Islamabad: Ministry of Religious Affairs, 1979.

"Guany nian renkou pucha zhuyao de gongbao" [Report Regarding the 1990 Population Census Primary Statistics], *Renmin Ribao* (daily, Beijing), 14 November 1991.

Guillaume, Alfred, *The Traditions of Islam*, reprint Beirut: Khayats, 1966 (originally Oxford: Clarendon, 1924).

Habel, Shelley, *The 'Folklore of a Regime' and Other Minority Tales*, unpublished seminar paper, University of Hawai'i at Manoa, 1996.

Habermas, Jürgen, *Der philosophische Diskurs der Moderne*, Frankfurt a.M.: Suhrkamp, 1985.

Hadi Su Junhui, *Islamic in Beijing*, Beijing: Beijing Nationality Pictoral Academic Society, 1990.

Halal (bimonthly journal of the Lembaga Pengkajian Pangan, Obat-obatan dan Kosmetika Majelis Ulama Indonesia [LPPOM-MUI) — Assessment Institute for Food, Drugs, and Cosmetics], Jakarta), 1994-.

Halstead, J. Mark, "To What Extent is the Call for Separate Muslim Voluntary Aided Schools in the U.K. Justifiable?", *Muslim Education Quarterly* (Cambridge, UK), 3 (1986), 2, 5-26; 3, 3-40.

Hamand, Jeremy, "Working for Change in the Arab World", *Challenges. Journal of the International Planned Parenthood Federation* (London), 1 (1996), 5-7.

Hamdan Hassan, *Tarekat Ahmadiyah di Malaysia: Suatu Analisis Fakta Secara Ilmiah* [The Ahmadiyyah Order in Malaysia: An Analysis of Facts in a Scientific Way], Kuala Lumpur: Dewan Bahasa dan Pustaka, 1990.

Handelingen, Verslag van de ---- der Staten Generaal [Report of the Proceedings of the States-General], 's-Gravenhage (The Hague): Algemeene Landsdrukkerij, 1814-.

Haque, Ziaul, "Muslim Religious Education in Indo-Pakistan". *Islamic Studies* (Karachi). 14 (1975), 1, 271-92.

Harris, Colette, "Women of the Sedentary Population of Russian Turkestan through the Eyes of Western Travellers", *Central Asian Survey* (Oxford), 15 (1996), 1, 75-96.

----, *Control and Subversion: Gender, Islam, and Socialism in Tajikistan*, diss., University of Amsterdam, 2000.

Hassan, Riffat, "Made from Adam's Rib. The Woman's Creation Question", *al-Mushir (The Counselor). Theological Journal of the Christian Study Centre* (Rawalpindi), 27, 3 (Autumn 1985), 124-55.

Hawkins, John N., "The Politics of Intergroup Relations: Minority Education in the People's Republic of China", in Murray Thomas (ed.), *Politics and Education*, New York: Pergamon Press, 1973.

----, *Education and Social Change in the People's Republic of China*, New York: Praeger, 1983.

Heer, David M. and Judith S. Bryden, "Family Allowances and Fertility in the Soviet Union", *Soviet Studies* (Glasgow), 18, 2 (Oct. 1966), 153-63.

Hefner, Robert W., "Islam and Nation in the Post-Suharto Era", in Adam Schwarz and Jonathan Paris (eds), *The Politics of Post-Suharto Indonesia*, New York: Council on Foreign Relations Press, 1999, 40-72.

Hobsbawm, Eric J., *Nations and Nationalism since 1780: Programme, Myth, and Reality*, Cambridge: Cambridge University Press, 1991.

Hodges, H.A., *The Philosophy of Wilhelm Dilthey*, Westport: Greenwood, 1952.

Holleman, J.F., *Van Vollenhoven on Indonesian Adat Law*, 's-Gravenhage (The Hague), Martinus Nijhoff, 1981.

Hoodfar, Homa, "Reforming from Within: Islamic Women Activists in Iran", in Shirkat Gah (ed.), *Reconstructing Fundamentalism and Feminism: The Dynamics of Change in Iran*, Lahore: Shirkat Gah (special bulletin Women Living under Muslim Laws), October 1995, 12-36.

Hooks, bell [Gloria Watkins], *Yearning: Race, Gender and Cultural Politics*, Boston: South End, 1990.

Hopper, Jeffery, *Understanding Modern Theology. Reinterpreting Christian Faith for Changing Worlds*, Philadelphia: Fortress, 1987.

Horkheimer, Max and Theodor W. Adorno, *Dialektik der Aufklärung. Philosophische Fragmente*, Frankfurt a.M.: Fischer Taschenbuch Verlag, 1988 (original publication Amsterdam: Querido, 1947).

Hübinger, Paul Egon (ed.), *Bedeutung und Rolle des Islam beim Übergang vom Altertum zum Mittelalter*, Darmstadt, Wissenschaftliche Buchgesellschaft, 1968.

Hull, Gloria and Barbara Smith, "The Politics of Black Women's Studies", in G.T. Hull, P. Bell Scott, and B. Smith (eds), *All The Women Are White, All the Blacks Are Men, but Some of Us Are Brave: Black Women's Studies*, New York: Feminist Press, 1982.

Humm, Maggie (ed.), *Modern Feminisms: Political, Literary, Cultural*, New York: Colombia University Press, 1992.

Hunter, James, *Culture Wars. The Struggle to Define America*, New York: Basic Books, 1991.

Huo Da, *The Jade King: History of a Chinese Muslim Family*, Beijing: Panda Press, 1992.

----, *Musilin de Zangli* [Muslim Funeral], Beijing: Beijing Changpian xiaoshuo zhuang zuo congshu, ed. 1993 (¹1988).

Hurgronje, Christiaan Snouck, "Rapport over de godsdienstige rechtspraak op Java en Madoera" [Report on the Religious Judicature in Java and Madura], in Christiaan Snouck Hurgronje, *Adatrechtbundel*, vol. 1, 's-Gravenhage: Nijhoff, 1910.

Ibrahim Abu Bakar, "Islamic Studies in Malaysian Universities and Colleges: An Overview", in Isma-ae Alee, Imtiyaz Yusuf et al. (eds), *Islamic Studies in ASEAN. Presentations of an International Seminar*, Pattani: College of Islamic Studies, Prince of Songkla University, 2000, 7-25.

Iik Arifin Mansurnoor, "Brunei Sebagai Sebuah Pusat Jaringan (*Network*) Intelektual Islam di Asia Tenggara" [Brunei as a Centre of an Islamic Intellectuel Network in South-East Asia], in Abu Bakar Apong (ed.), *Sumbangsih UBD* [The Contribution of the University of Brunei Darussalam]: *Essays on Brunei Darussalam*, Bandar Seri Begawan: Academy of Brunei Studies, 1992, 148-163.

----, "Historiography and Religious Reform in Brunei During the Period 1912-1959", *Studia Islamika. Indonesian Journal for Islamic Studies* (Jakarta), 2, 3 (July-Aug. 1995), 77-113.

----, "Socio-religious Change in Brunei after the Pacific War", *Islamic Studies* (Islamabad) 35 (1996), 1, 45-70.

----, European Views of the *Jawah:* Brunei and the Malays in the Nineteenth and Early Twentieth Centuries", *Oxford Journal of Islamic Studies* (Oxford), 9 (1998), 2, 178-209.

----, "Recent Trends in the Study of Islamic Revivalism in Contemporary Malaysia", *Asian Research Trends* (Tokyo), 7 (1998), 39-73.

Informasi Institut Agama Islam Negeri (IAIN), Jakarta: Departemen Agama RI, Direktorat Jenderal Pembinaan Kelembagaan Agama Islam, Direktorat Pembinaan Perguruan Tinggi

Agama Islam (Ministry of Religious Affairs of the Indonesian Republic, Directorate-General for the Development of Islamic Institutions, Directorate for the Development of Islamic Higher Education), 1988/1989 (English version: *Information on State Institute for Islamic Studies (IAIN)* — see below).

Information Office of the State Council of the People's Republic of China, *National Minorities Policy and Its Practice in China*, Beijing: Information Office of the State Council of the People's Republic of China, 1999.

Information on State Institute for Islamic Studies (IAIN), Jakarta: Departemen Agama RI, Direktorat Jenderal Pembinaan Kelembagaan Agama Islam, Direktorat Pembinaan Perguruan Tinggi Agama Islam (Ministry of Religious Affairs of the Indonesian Republic, Directorate-General for the Development of Islamic Institutions, Directorate for the Development of Islamic Higher Education), 1988/1989 (Indonesian version: *Informasi Institut Agama Islam Negeri (IAIN)* — see above).

INIS Newsletter (1989-1990 three-monthly, 1990-1998 about six-monthly, Jakarta and Leiden; since April 2001 a new, daily version has been presented through the Internet at http://www.iias.nl/host/inis/INL/).

Institut (students monthly, later more irregular, IAIN Syarif Hidayatullah, Jakarta), 1984-.

Iqbal, Muhammad, *The Reconstruction of Religious Thought in Islam* (Lahore: Shaikh Muhammad Ashraf), 1962.

Israeli, Raphael, *Fundamentalist Islam and Israel*, Lanham: University Press of America, 1993.

Izutsu, Toshihiko, *The Structure of Ethical Terms in the Koran*, Mita et al.: Keio Institute of Philosophical Studies, 1959.

Jakarta Post (daily, Jakarta), 1983-.

Jaschok, Maria, *The History of Women's Mosques in Chinese Islam*, London: Curzon Press, 2000.

Jateng Pos (daily, Surakarta), 1999.

Jayawardena, Kumari, *Feminism and Nationalism in the Third World. In the Early 19th and 20th Centuries*, London: Zed Books, 1988.

Jihād Muḥammad Abū Najā (Jehad Muhammad Abu Naja), "Manāhij al-taʻlīm al-islāmī fī Tāyland" [Methods of Islamic Education in Thailand], in Isma-ae Alee, Imtiyaz Yusuf et al. (eds), *Islamic Studies in ASEAN. Presentations of an International Seminar*, Pattani: College of Islamic Studies, Prince of Songkla University, 2000, 243-65.

Johns, Anthony H., "Islam in Southeast Asia. Reflections and New Directions", *Indonesia* (Ithaca), 19 (April 1975), 33-55.

----, "The Role of Sufism in the Spread of Islam to Malaya and Indonesia", *Journal of the Pakistan Historical Society* (Karachi), 9 (1981), 3, 143-60.

Johnson, David, "Communication, Class, and Consciousness in Late Imperial China", in David Johnson, Andrew J. Nathan, and Evelyn Rawski (eds), *Popular Culture in Late Imperial China*, Berkeley: University of California Press, 1985, 34-72.

Jones, Ellen and Grupp Fred W., *Modernization, Value Change and Fertility in the Soviet Union*, Cambridge: Cambridge University Press, 1987.

Jones, Russell, "Ten Conversion Myths from Indonesia", in Nehemia Levtzion (ed.), *Conversion to Islam*, New York and London: Holmes and Meier, 1979, 129-58.

Jonker, Johann Christoph Gerhard, *Over Javaansch strafrecht*, Amsterdam: De Roever-Krober-Bakels, 1882.

Jum'at (weekly supplement to the Jakarta daily *Republika*).

Kandiyoti, Deniz (ed.), *Gendering the Middle East. Emerging Perspectives*,Syracuse, NY: Syracuse University Press/London: Tauris, 1996.

Kaptein, Nico, "Meccan *fatwâs* from the End of the Nineteenth Century on Indonesian Affairs", *Studia Islamika. Indonesian Journal for Islamic Studies* (Jakarta), 2, 4 (April-June 1995), 141-60.

----, "Sayyid 'Uthmân on the Legal Validity of Written Evidence", *Bijdragen tot de Taal-, Land- en Volkenkunde* (Leiden), 153 (1997), 1, 85-102.

Karam, Azza Mostafa, "Islamismen/feminismen" (Islamisms/Feminisms), *Lover* (Amsterdam), 22, 3 (Sept. 1995), 10-6.

----, *Women, Islamisms and the State: Contemporary Feminism in Egypt*, New York: St. Martin's Press/Basingstoke etc.: MacMillan, 1998.

Kartodirdjo, Oerip, "De Rechtspraak op Java en Madoera tijdens de Japansche Bezetting, 1942-1945" [The Administration of Justice in Java and Madura during the Japanese Occupation, 1942-1945], *Tijdschrift van het Recht* (Batavia), 1 (1947), 8-21.

Kaufman, Gordon Dester, *Theology for a Nuclear Age*, Philadelphia: Westminster Press, 1985.

"Keep Rural Girls in School", *China Daily* (Beijing), 17 April 1987.

Kepel, Gilles, *La revanche de Dieu. Chrétiens, juifs et musulmans à la reconquête du monde*, Paris, Seuil, 1991.

Kessler, Clive S., *Islam and Politics in a Malay State. Kelantan 1838-1969*, Ithaca and London: Cornell University Press, 1978.

Khan, Wasiullah M., *Education and Society in the Muslim World*, Jeddah: King Abdul Aziz University, 1981.

Khan, F., *Islam as a Social Force in the Caribbean*, paper presented at the Conference of the History Teachers Association, Trinidad, 1987.

Khan, Rahman; Munshi; and Chote Khan, *Khun ke Ansu*, manuscript in Hindi, Paramaribo, 1942 (originally written by Ashfak Hussain; Bombay, 1933).

Khayyat, Sana al-: see Al-Khayyat, Sana.

Kompas (daily, Jakarta), 1965-.

Kon, Igor S., *The Sexual Revolution in Russia. From the Age of the Czars to Today*, New York and London: Free Press, 1995 (translated from the Russian by James Riordan).

Kraan, Jaap, "Muslims, Christians and Education: The Example of the Netherlands", in Gé Speelman et al. (ed.), *Muslims and Christians in Europe, Breaking New Ground*, Kampen: Kok, 1993, 125-37.

Kristeva, Julia, "Le temps des femmes", *34/44: Cahiers de recherche de sciences des textes et documents* (Paris: Université de Paris VII), 5 (Winter 1979), 5-19.

----, *Pouvoirs de l'horreur. Essai sur l'abjection*, Paris: Seuil, 1980.

Kuntowijoyo, *Dinamika Sejarah Umat Islam Indonesia* [Historical Dynamic of the Indonesian Muslim Community], Yogyakarta: Shalahuddin Press, 1985.

Kurin, Richard, "Morality, Personhood and the Exemplary Life. Popular Conceptions of Muslims in Paradise", in Barbara Daly Metcalf (ed.), *Moral Conduct and Authority: The Place of Adab in South Asian Islam*, Berkeley et al.: University of California Press, 1984.

Kwong, Julia and Hong Xiao, "Educational Equality among China's Minorities", *Comparative Education* (Oxford), 25 (1989), 2, 229-43.

LaBelle, Thomas and Robert E. Verhine, "Education, Social Change, and Social Stratification", *Harvard Education Review* (Cambridge, MA), 45 (1975), 3-71.

Laing, Ellen Johnston, *The Winking Owl: Art in the People's Republic of China*, Berkeley: University of California Press, 1988.

Lajoinie, Simone B., *Conditions de femmes en Afghanistan*, Paris: Editions Sociales, 1980.

Lamontagne, Jacques, "Improving the Education of China's National Minorities", in Douglas Ray and Deo Poonwassie (eds), *Education and Cultural Differences. New Perspectives*, New York: Garland Publishing, 1992, 183-209.

Landau, Jacob M., *The Politics of Pan-Islam: Ideology and Organization*, Oxford: Clarendon Press, 1990.

Lawrence, Bruce, *Defenders of God. The Fundamentalist Revolt Against the Modern Age*, San Francisco: Harper and Row, 1989.

Leach, Edmund, "Ourselves and the Others", *Times Literary Supplement* (London), 6 July 1973, 771 f.

Lee, Chae-Jin, *China's Korean Minority: The Politics of Ethnic Education*, Boulder: Westview, 1986.

"Lesehan 38 Tahun IAIN Kita. Pendirian UIN Perkecil Dikotomi Ilmu Agama dan Umum" [An Informal Meeting on the Occasion of the 38th Anniversary of Our IAIN. The Creation of an Islamic State University to Reduce the Dichotomy between Religious and General Sciences], *Akrab* (monthly of the Jakarta Office of the Ministry of Religious Affairs, Jakarta), 12, 152 (February 1996), 6.

Leur, Jacobus Cornelis van, "On Early Asian Trade", in *idem, Indonesian Trade and Society. Essays in Asian Social and Economic History*, 's-Gravenhage: Van Hoeve, 1955 (reprint Dordrecht/Providence, Foris, 1983 [K.I.T.L.V.-reprint]), 1-144; translated from the Duth original: *Eenige beschouwingen betreffende den ouden Aziatischen handel*, Middelburg: Den Boer, 1934).

Lev, Daniel S., *Islamic Courts in Indonesia. A Study in the Political Bases of Legal Institutions*, Berkeley et al.: University of California Press, 1972.

Liddle, R. William, "Media Dakwah Scripturalism: One Form of Islamic Political Thought and Action in New Order Indonesia", in Liddle, *Leadership and Culture in Indonesian Politics, Sydney: Allen and Unwin in cooperation with Asian Studies Association of Australia (ASAA)*, 1996.

Linxia Hui Autonomous Prefectural Basic Situation Committee (ed.), *Linxia Huizu zizhizhougaikuang* (Linxia Hui Autonomous Prefectural Basic Situation), Lanzhou: Gansu Nationalities Publishing Society, 1986.

De Locomotief (twice a week from 1863, with increasing frequency, daily from 1870; Semarang), 1863-1956 or beyond.

Lombard, Denys, "L'horizon insulindien et son importance pour une compréhension globale de l'Islam", *Archipel* (Paris), 29 (1985), 35-52.

----, *Le carrefour javanais. Essai d'histoire globale*, Paris: Ecole des Hautes Etudes en Sciences Sociales, 1990.

Lorde, Audre, *Sister Outsider. Essays and Speeches*, New York: Crossing Press, 1984.

Löwenthal, Rudolf, "The Mohammedan Press in China", in *idem* (ed.), *The Religious Periodical Press in China*, Peking [Beijing]: Synodal Committee on China, 1940, 211-50 (originally in *Digest of the Synodal Commission*, Peking: Synodal Commission, 11, 9-10 (Sept.-Oct. 1938), 867-94).

Lufkin, Felicity, *Images of Minorities in the Art of the Peoples Republic of China*, MA thesis, University of California, Berkeley, 1990.

Luke, Carmen and Jennifer Gore (ed.), *Feminisms and Critical Pedagogy*, London and New York: Routledge, 1992.

Ma Shouqian, *The Hui People's New Awakening at the End of the Century and Beginning of the 20th Century*, paper presented at The Legacy of Islam in China: An International Symposium in Memory of Joseph F. Fletcher, 14-16 April 1989.

Ma Qicheng, "The Extensive Cultural Characteristics of Islam in China" (*zhongguo yisilanjiao de da wenhua shuxing*) in *Journal of the Central Institute of Nationalities* (Beijing), 2 (1993), 21-32.

Ma Tong, *Zhongguo Yisilan jiaopai yu menhuan zhidu shilue* [A History of Muslim factions and the *menhuan* system in China], Yinchuan: Ningxia People's Publishing Society, ed. 1983 ([1]1927).

----, *Gansu Huizu shi gangyao* [An Outline of Gansu Hui History], Lanzhou: Gansu Provincial Commission for Nationality Affairs, Gansu Provincial Nationalities Research department, s.a.

Majalah Hidup (weekly, Jakarta), 1946-.

Majalah Jabatan Hal Ehwal Ugama [Journal of the Department of Religious Affairs] (Bandar Seri Begawan: Jabatan Hal Ehwal Ugama), 1962-1977 (no. 1-40; from June 1977 [no. 41] continued as *Al-Huda*).

Majelis Ulama Indonesia (MUI), *15 Tahun Majelis Ulama Indonesia: Wadah Musyawarah Para Ulama. Zuama. dan Cendekiawan Muslim* [Fifteen Years the Indonesian Council of *'Ulamā'*: A Consultative Body of Muslim *'Ulamā'*, (Political) Leaders, and Intellectuals], Jakarta: MUI, 1990.

----, *20 tahun Majelis Ulama Indonesia* [Twenty Years the Indonesian Council of *'Ulamā'*], Jakarta: MUI, 1995.

----: see also Sekretariat Majelis Ulama Indonesia.

Makdisi, George, *The Rise of Colleges. Institutions of Learning in Islam and the West*, Edinburgh: Edinburgh University Press, 1981.

Makdisi, George, "The Juridical Theology of Shāfiʿī: Origins and Significance of Uṣūl al-Fiqh", *Studia Islamica* (Paris), 59 (1984), 5-47 (reprinted as chapter 2 in George Makdisi, *Religion, Law and Learning in Classical Islam*, Hampshire: Variorum, 1991).

Makhlouf Obermeyer, Carla, "Islam, Women, and Politics: The Demography of Arab Countries", *Population and Development Review* (New York), 18 (1992), 1, 33-57.

Malik, S. Jamal, *Islamisierung in Pakistan 1977-84, Untersuchungen zur Auflösung autochthoner Strukturen*, Stuttgart: Steiner Verlag, 1989.

----, "Dynamics among Traditional Religious Scholars and their Institutions in Contemporary Pakistan", in: Nicole Grandin and Marc Gaborieau (eds), *Madrasa. La transmission du savoir dans le monde musulman*, Paris: Arguments, 1997, 168-82.

----, *Colonialization of Islam*, New Delhi: ²1998.

Malik, T., "Muslim Identities Suspended between Tradition and Modernity", *Comparative Studies of South Asia, Africa and the Middle East* (Durham), 16, (1996), 2, 1-10.

Wan Kadir Che Man, *Muslim Separatism. The Moros of Southern Philippines and the Malays of Southern Thailand*, Singapore, Oxford, and New York: Oxford University Press, 1990.

Mascia-Lees, Frances E., Patricia Sharp, and Colleen Ballerino-Cohen, "The Postmodernist Turn in Anthropology: Cautions From a Feminist Perspective", *Signs. Journal of Women in Culture and Society*, 15, 1 (autumn 1989): 7-33.

Mastuhu, "Harun Nasution dan Identitas IAIN Jakarta" [Harun Nasution and the Identity of the IAIN of Jakarta], Aqib Suminto et al., *Refleksi Pembaharuan Pemikiran Islam. 70 Tahun Harun Nasution* [Reflection on the Renewal of Islamic Thought. Harun Nasution 70 Years], Jakarta: LSAF, 1989, 280-90.

Maududi, A.A. ['Abd al-Aʿlā Mawdūdī], *The Meaning of the Qur'an*, Lahore: Islamic Publications, 1976.

McDonnell, Mary Byrne, *The Conduct of Hajj from Malaysia and Its Socio-economic Impact on Malay Society: A Descriptive and Analytical Study, 1860-1981*, diss., Columbia University, 1986.

Md. Zain Hj. Serudin, Pehin Dato Hj., *Brunei Darussalam: Persepsi Sejarah dan Masyarakatnya* [Brunei Darussalam: Its Vision of History and Society], Bandar Seri Begawan: Azza, 1992.

379

Media Indonesia (daily, Jakarta), 1986-.

Mehden, Fred R. von der, "Malaysian and Indonesian Islamic Movements, and the Iranian Connection", in John L. Esposito (ed.), *The Iranian Revolution. Its Global Impact*, Miami: Florida International University Press, 1990, 233-54.

----, *Two Worlds of Islam. Interaction between Southeast Asia and the Middle East*, Gainsville: University Press of Florida, 1993.

Mehden, Fred R. von der, *Two Worlds of Islam: Interaction between Southeast Asia and the Middle East*, Gainesville: University Press of Florida, 1993.

Mernissi, Fatima, *Beyond the Veil*, Cambridge: Schenkman, 1975 (revised edition: *Beyond the Veil: Male-Female Dynamics in Modern Muslim Society*, Bloomington: Indiana University Press, 1987).

----, *La peur modernité. Conflit islam-démocratie*, Paris: A. Michel, 1992.

Metcalf, Barbara D., *Islamic Revival in British India: Deoband, 1860-1900*, Guildford: Princeton University Press, 1982.

Meuleman, Johan Hendrik, "Analisis Buku-Buku tentang Wanita Islam yang Beredar di Indonesia" [An Analysis of Books on the Muslim Woman which Circulate in Indonesia] in Lies M. Marcoes-Natsir and Johan Hendrik Meuleman (eds), *Wanita Islam Indonesia dalam Kajian Tekstual dan Kontekstual* [The Indonesian Muslim Woman Studied from a Textual and a Contextual Point of View], Jakarta: INIS, 1993, 175-205.

----, "Reactions and Attitudes towards the Darul Arqam Movement in Southeast Asia", *Studia Islamika. Indonesian Journal for Islamic Studies* (Jakarta), 3, 1 (Jan.-March 1996), 43-78.

----, "IAIN di Persimpangan Jalan", *PERTA. Jurnal Komunikasi Perguruan Tinggi Islam* (Jakarta), 1, 1 (Sept. 1997), 24-37.

----, "Indonesian Islam between Particularity and Universality", *Studia Islamika. Indonesian Journal for Islamic Studies* (Jakarta), 4, 3 (July-Sept. 1997), 99-122.

Mimbar Fatwa [Fatwa Tribune] (irregular, Bandar Seri Begawan: Jabatan Hal Ehwal Ugama [Department of Religious Affairs]), 1975-.

Mines, Mattison, *Public Faces, Private Voices. Communality and Individuality in South India*, Berkeley et al.: University of California Press, 1994.

Ministry of Health of the USSR, *The System of Public-Health Services in the USSR*, Moscow: Ministry of Health, 1967.

Minzu Wenhua Gong [The Cultural Palace of Nationalities], Beijing: Beijing Xinguang Caiyinchang, 1990 (full colour brochure).

Moghadam, Valentine M., *Modernizing Women. Gender and Social Change in the Middle East*, Boulder and London: Lynne Rienner, 1993.

Mohamad Atho Mudzhar, *Fatwa-fatwa Majlis Ulama Indonesia: Sebuah Studi tentang Pemikiran Hukum Islam di Indonesia, 1975-1988* [The Fatwas of the Indonesian Council of 'Ulamā': A Study on Islamic Legal Thought in Indonesia], Jakarta: INIS, 1993 (bilingual, Indonesian and English, edition).

Mohanty, Chandra Talpade, "Introduction. Cartographies of Struggle. Third World Women and the Politics of Feminism", in Mohanty, Russo, and Lourdes (eds), *Third World Women and the Politics of Feminism*, 1-47.

----, "Under Western Eyes: Feminist Scholarship and Colonial Discourses", in Mohanty, Russo, and Lourdes (eds), *Third World Women and the Politics of Feminism*, 51-80.

----, Ann Russo, and Torres Lourdes (eds), *Third World Women and the Politics of Feminism*, Bloomington and Indianapolis: Indiana University Press, 1991.

Mohd. Jamil al-Sufri, Pehin Dato Hj., *Liku-Liku Perjuangan Pencapaian Kemerdekaan Negara Brunei Darussalam* [The Roundabouts of the Struggle to Obtain the Independence of the State of Brunei Darussalam], Bandar Seri Begawan: Brunei History Centre, 1992.

Morgan, Lewis Henry, *Ancient Society or Researches in the Line of Human Progress from Savagery through Barbarism to Civilization*, New York: Holt, 1878.

Muhammad Siddīq Hasan Khān Bahādur, *Husn al-uswah bi-mā thabata min Allāh wa-rasūlih fī al-niswah* [The Good Example of What Has Been Established from God and His Prophet on Women], Constantinople: Matba'ah al-Jawā'ib, AH 1301 (AD 1884).

Muarif, "Dikotomi Ilmu, antara Fardlu Ain dan Fardlu Kifayah" [Dichotomy of Sciences, between *Fard al-'Ayn* and *Fard al-Kifāyah*, *Republika* (daily, Jakarta), 5 January 1996.

MUI: see Majelis Ulama Indonesia

Murād, Khurram. "Dīnī madāris ka-nizām-i ta'līm", *Tarjumān al-Qur'ān* (Lahore), 121 (1995), 7, 21-48.

Murād, Khurram, "Na'ī Salībī Jang, Dīnī Madāris ke Darwazon par" [A New Crusade, at the Door of the *Dīnī Madāris*], *Tarjumān al-Qur'ān*, 121 (1995), 5, 1-14.

Musallam B. F., *Sex and Society in Islam: Birth Control Before the Nineteenth Century*, Cambridge: Cambridge University Press, 1983.

Muslim: see *Sahīh Muslim*.

Nagata, Judith. *The Reflowering of Malaysian Islam*, Vancouver: University of British Columbia Press, 1984.

Nasr, Seyyed Hossein, *Islamic Sciences, An Illustrated Study*, London: World of Islam Festival, 1976.

Nasr, Seyyed Vali Reza, *Mawdudi and the Making of Islamic Revivalism*, New York and Oxford: Oxford University Press, 1996.

National Committee for Religious Education, *Dini Madaris Committee Report*, Islamabad: Ministry of Religious Affairs, 1979.

Nelson, Benjamin, *On the Roads to Modernity. Conscience, Science, and Civilizations* (selected writings by B. Nelson, ed. by Toby E. Huff), Totowa, NJ: Rowman and Littlefield, 1981.

Neratja (daily, Weltevreden).

Nicholson, Linda J. (ed.), *Feminism/Postmodernism*, London and New York: Routledge, 1990.

Nicholson, Linda J., and Nancy Fraser, "Social Criticism Without Philosophy: An Encounter Between Feminism and Postmodernism", in Nicholson (ed.), *Feminism/Postmodernism*, 19-38.

Noer, Deliar, *The Modernist Muslim Movement in Indonesia 1900-1942*, Singapore et al.: Oxford University Press, 1973.

Noorhaidi Hasan, "Islamic Radicalism and the Crisis of the Nation-State", *ISIM Newsletter* (Leiden), 7 (March 2001), 12.

Nurcholish Madjid, *Islam: Doktrin dan Perabadan* [Islam: Doctrine and Civilization], Jakarta: Yayasan Wakaf Paramadina, 1992.

----, "Beberapa Renungan tentang Kehidupan Keagamaan untuk Generasi Mendatang" [Some Reflections on Religious Life for the Future Generations]. *Ulumul Qur'an* (Jakarta), 4, 1 (Jan.-March 1993), 4-25.

----, "Islamic Roots of Modern Pluralism", *Studia Islamika. Indonesian Journal for Islamic Studies* (Jakarta), 1, 1 (April-June 1994), 55-78.

Nurjuliyanti, Dewi and Arief Subhan, "Lembaga-lembaga Syi'ah di Indonesia" [Shi'ite Institutions in Indonesia], *Ulumul Qur'an* (Jakarta), 6, 4 (Sept.-Dec. 1995), 20-6.

Omran, Abdel Rahim, *Family Planning in the Legacy of Islam*, London and New York: Routledge/UNFPA, 1992.

Ong, Aihwa, "Colonialism and Modernity. Feminist Representations of Women in Non-Western Societies", *Inscriptions*, (Santa Cruz), 4 (1988), 3.

Pakatan: Antologi Sajak [Pakatan: An Anthology of Verse], Bandar Seri Begawan: Dewan Bahasa and Pustaka, 1976.

Palmier, Leslie H., *Social Status and Power in Java*, London and New York: The Athlone Press, 1969.

Pang Keng-Fong, *The Dynamics of Gender, Ethnicity, and State Among the Austronesian-speaking Muslims (Hui-Utsat) of Hainan Island*, unpublished diss., University of California, Los Angeles, 1992.

Pelita (daily, Jakarta), 1974-.

Pelita Brunei (biweekly created 1956, weekly since 1965; Bandar Seri Begawan).

Pickens, Claude L., "The Four Men Huans", *Friends of Moslems* 16 (1942), 1, 12-22.

Pillsbury, Barbara, "Being Female in a Muslim Minority in China", in Lois Beck and Nikki Keddie (eds), *Women in the Muslim World*, Cambridge, MA: Harvard University Press, 1978.

Poerwokoesoemo, Soedarisman, *Daerah Istimewa Yogyakarta* [Special Region of Yogyakarta], Yogyakarta: Gadjah Mada University Press, 1984.

Polanyi, Michael and Harry Prosch, *Meaning*, Chicago: University of Chicago Press, 1975.

Population Census Office' of the State Council of the People's Republic of China and the Institute of Geography of the Chinese Academy of Sciences, *The Population Atlas of China*, Oxford: Oxford University Press, 1987.

Postiglione, Gerard A., "China's National Minorities and Educational Change", *Journal of Contemporary Asia* (Nottingham et al.), 22 (1992), 1, 20-41.

----, Teng Xing, and Ai Yiping, "Basic Education and School Discontinuation in National Minority Border Regions of China", in Gerard A. Postiglione and Lee Wing On (eds), *Social Change and Educational Development. Mainland China, Taiwan and Hong Kong*, Hong Kong: Centre of Asian Studies, University of Hong Kong, 1995, 186-206.

Puisi Hidayat, Bandar Seri Begawan: Jabatan Hal Ehwal Ugama, vol. 1 1971; vol. 2 1975.

Qvortrup, Jens, "Modernisation and Standards of Living in Soviet Central Asia", in Ewa A. Chylinski (ed.) *Soviet Central Asia, Continuity and Change*, Esbjerg (Denmark): South Jutland University Press, 1984, 89-117.

Rahman, Fazlur, *Major Themes of the Qur'an*, Minneapolis: Bibliotheca Islamica, 1980.

Ras, Johannes Jacobus, *Hikajat Bandjar, a Study in Malay Historiography*, 's-Gravenhage: Smits and Nijhoff, 1968.

Razali Judin, *Tarekat Ahmadiyah-Idrissiyah dan Tanggapan Masyarakat Kampung Beribi Terhadap Kewujudannya* [The Ahmadiyyah-Idrisiyyah Order and the Reaction of the Society of the Beribi District against Its Existence], unpublished essay, Universiti Brunei Darussalam. 1993.

Reid, Anthony, *Southeast Asia in the Age of Commerce. 1450-1680*, New Haven and London: Yale University Press, vol. 1 1988; vol. 2 1993.

Reid, Donald Malcolm, "Al-Azhar", in John L. Esposito (ed.-in-chief), *The Oxford Encyclopedia of the Modern Islamic World*, New York and Oxford: Oxford University Press, 1995: vol. 1, 168-171.

Rencana Induk Pembangunan IAIN [Master Plan for IAIN Development], unpublished document Departemen Agama RI, Direktorat Jenderal Pembinaan Kelembagaan Agama Islam, Direktorat Pembinaan Perguruan Tinggi Agama Islam (Ministry of Religious Affairs of the Indonesian Republic, Directorate-General for the Development of Islamic Institutions, Directorate for the Development of Islamic Higher Education), Jakarta, s.a. [1993 or 1994].

Republic of Tajikistan, *Human Development Report*, Dushanbe: UNDP/Government of Tajikistan, 1995.

Republika (daily, Jakarta), 1993-.

Rich, Adrienne, "Toward a Woman-Centred University", in *idem, On Lies, Secrets, Silence: Selected Prose 1966-1978*, London: Virago, 1980, 125-155 (originally in Florence Howe (ed.), *Women and the Power to Change*, New York: McGraw-Hill, 1975).

Rizvi, Saiyid Athar Abbas, *A History of Sufism in India*, vol. 2: *From Sixteenth Century to Modern Century*, New Delhi: Munshiram Manoharlal, 1983.

----, *The Wonder that Was India*, vol. 2: *1200-1700*, New Delhi: Rupa, 1994.

383

Rizwī, S. Maḥbūb, *Tārikh dār al-'ulūm Deoband* [The History of Dār al-'ulūm Deoband], published as a special issue (vol. 8 [1980], 4/5) of *al-Rashīd* (Sahiwal).

Robson, Stuart Owen, "Java at the Crossroads. Aspects of Javanese Cultural History in the 14th and 15th Centuries", *Bijdragen tot de Taal-, Land- en Volkenkunde* ('s-Gravenhage), 137 (1981), 259-292.

Rodinson, Maxime, *Islam et capitalisme*, Paris: Seuil, 1966.

Roff, William R., "Islam Obscured? Some Reflections on Studies of Islam and Society in Southeast Asia", *Archipel* (Paris), 29 (1985), 7-34.

----, "Islam di Asia Tenggara dalam Abad 19" [Islam in South-East Asia in the Nineteenth Century], in Azyumardi Azra (ed.), *Perspektif Islam di Asia Tenggara* [The Islamic Perspective in South-East Asia], Jakarta: Yayasan Obor Indonesia, 1989.

Rostow, Walt Whitman, *The process of economic growth*, New York: Norton, 1952.

Rothermund, Dietmar (ed.), *Aneignung und Selbstbehauptung. Antworten auf die europäische Expansion*, München: Oldenburg, 1999.

Ryan, Selwyn, *The Muslim Grab For Power. Race, Religion and Revolution in Trinidad and Tobago,* Port of Spain: Inprint Caribbean, 1991.

Ṣaḥīḥ al-Bukhārī (*al-Jāmi' al-ṣaḥīḥ* or compilation of sound hadiths of Muḥammad b. Ismā'īl al-Bukhārī, AH 194-256/AD 810-870), various editions.

Ṣaḥīḥ al-Bukhārī, in the English translation by Muhammad Muhsin Khan, Lahore: Kazi Publications, 1971.

Ṣaḥīḥ Muslim (*al-Jāmi' al-ṣaḥīḥ* or compilation of sound hadiths of Abū al-Ḥusayn Muslim al-Ḥajjāj, probably AH 206-261/AD 821-875), various editions.

Ṣaḥīḥ Muslim, in the English translation by Abdul Hamid Siddiqi, Lahore: Shaikh Muhammad Ashraf, 1972.

Said, Edward, *Orientalism: Western Conceptions of the Orient*, London: Penguin Books, 1978.

----, *The World, The Text and The Critic*, London: Vintage, 1983.

Saiful Muzani, "Di Balik Polemik "Anti Pembaruan" Islam. Memahami Gejala "Fundamentalisme" Islam di Indonesia" [Behind the Muslim "Anti-Renewal" Polemic. Understanding the Phenomenon of "Fundamentalism" in Indonesia], *Islamika* (Jakarta), 1, (July-Sept. 1993), 126-42.

----, "Kultur Klas Menengah Muslim dan Kelahiran ICMI: Tanggapan Terhadap Robert W. Hefner dan Mitsuo Nakamura" [The Culture of the Muslim Middle Class and the Birth of the ICMI: A Reaction against Robert W. Hefner and Mitsuo Nakamura], *Studia Islamika. Indonesian Journal for Islamic Studies* (Jakarta), 1, 1 (April-June 1994), 207-35.

----, "Mu'tazilah Theology and the Modernization of the Indonesian Muslim Community", *Studia Islamika. Indonesian Journal for Islamic Studies* (Jakarta), 1, 1 (Jan.-April 1994), 91-131.

Salam (1955-February 1973 weekly, 1973- biweekly; Kuala Belait, Brunei).

Saleh Aljufri, *Panji-Panji Muhammad SAW* [The Banner of Muhammad, May God Bless Him and Grant Him Salvation], Surabaya: Lembaga Penerangan dan Laboratorium Islam Sunan Ampel, 1989.

Sarnapi, "SMU Plus Mutahhari. Setetes Embun di Musim Kemarau Mutu SMU" [General Senior High School "Plus" Mutahhari. A Dewdrop in the Dry Season of General Senior High School Quality], *Hikmah*, week 3 of May 1996, 25.

Sangren, Steven P., "Rhetoric and the Authority of Ethnography. 'Postmodernism' and the Social Reproduction of Texts", *Current Anthropology* (Chicago), 29 (1988), 3 (June): 405-24.

Sarekat Islam Lokal, Jakarta: Arsip Nasional Republik Indonesia (Penerbitan sumber-sumber sejarah no. 7), 1975.

Sarekat Islam Congres (1e Nationaal Congres), 20-27 October 1917 te Batavia. Geheim voor de dienst, behoort bij de missive der Regeeringscommissaris voor Inlandsche en Arabische Zaken van 23 Augustus 1918, No. 416 [Sarekat Islam Congress (1st National Congress), 20-27 October in Batavia. Secret Service Document, Belonging to the Missive of the Government Commissioner for Native and Arab Affairs of 23 August 1918, No. 416], Batavia: Landsdrukkerij, 1918.

Schleiermacher, Friedrich [Daniel Ernst]. *Über die Religion. Reden an die Gebildeten unter ihren Verächtern*, new edition by Rudolf Otto, Göttingen, Vandenhoeck und Ruprecht, 1899 (several reprints).

Schneider, David M., "What is Kinship All About?", in Priscilla Reining (ed.), *Kinship Studies in the Morgan Centennial Year*, Washington, DC: The Anthropological Society of Washington, 1972, 32-63.

Scully, Diana and Pauline Bart, "A Funny Thing Happened on the Way to the Orifice. Women in Gynecology Textbooks", *American Journal of Sociology* (Chicago), 78 (1973), 4, 1045-50.

Segala Soal Jawab atas Masalah Tiada Harus Mehukumkan Talak dengan Semata-mata Tulisan Saksi-saksi yang telah Mati, s.l., s.a.

Sekretariat Majelis Ulama Indonesia [Secretariat of the Indonesian Council of *'Ulamā'*(MUI)], *Keputusan Musyawarah Nasional V Majelis Ulama Indonesia, 21-25 Juli 1995* [Decision of the Fifth National Consultation of the Indonesian Council of *'Ulamā'*, 21-25 July 1995], unpublished document.

Shāfi', Muftī Muḥammad and Mawlānā Muḥammad Yūsuf Banūrī, *Na'ī Ta'līmī Pālīsī* [New Educational Policy], s.l., s.a.

Shafruddin Hashim, "Ide Kenegaraan dan Negara Kecil: Satu Pengalaman Brunei Darussalam" [The Idea of Statehood and a Small State: An Experience of Brunei Darussalam], in Abdul Latif Haji Ibrahim et al., *Purih: A Collection of Essays on Brunei Darussalam*, Bandar Seri Begawan: Academy of Brunei Studies, 1996, 337-42.

Shi Jinghuan, "China's Cultural Tradition and Women's Participation in Education", in Gerard A. Postiglione and Lee Wing On (eds), *Social Change and Educational Development. Mainland China, Taiwan and Hong Kong*, Hong Kong: Centre of Asian Studies, University of Hong Kong, 1995, 139-49.

Shils, Edward, "Intellectuals", in David Sills (ed.), *International Encyclopedia of the Social Sciences*, New York: Macmillan and Free Press, vol. 7, ed. 1968, 399-424.

Shiraishi, Takishi, *An Age in Motion: Popular Radicalism in Java, 1912-1926*, Ithaca: Cornell University Press, 1990.

Shishov, A., *Sarty* [Sarts], Tashkent: 1904.

Shishov, A., *Tadjiki* [Tajiks], Tashkent: 1910.

Sjadzali, Munawir, *Muslim Interests Are Better Served in the Absence of Muslim Parties. Indonesian Experience*, Jakarta: Ministry of Religious Affairs, 1992.

Snouck Hurgronje, Christiaan, *Nederland en de Islam* [The Netherlands and Islam], Leiden: Brill, second, elaborated edition, 1915.

----, "Een rector der Mekkaansche universiteit" [A Rector of the University of Mekka], in: *idem, Verspreide Geschriften* [Miscellaneous Writings], vol. 3, Bonn und Leipzig: K. Schroeder 1923, 65-122 (previously published in *Bijdragen tot de Taal-, Land- en Volkenkunde* ('s-Gravenhage), 5 (1887), 2, 344-404).

----, *Verspreide Geschriften* [Miscellaneous Writings], Bonn and Leipzig: K. Schroeder, 1923-1927, 6 vols.

----, *Mekka in the Latter Part of the 19th Century; Daily Life, Customs and Learning. The Muslims of the East-Indian Archipelago*, transl. by J.H. Monahan, Leiden: Brill, 1970 (reprint of the 1931 English translation of the second volume of the 1888-1889 German original).

Soeharto, *Soeharto. Pikiran, Ucapan dan Tindakan Saya*, Jakarta: Citra Lamtoro Gung Persada, 1989.

Soepomo, *Bab-Bab Tentang Hukum Adat*, Jakarta: Pradnya Paramitha, [12]1989.

Soeriokoesoemo, Soetatmo, "Taal en kleding" [Language and Dress], *De Indiër. Weekblad gewijd aan het geestelijk en maatschappelijk leven van Indië en Oost Azië* ('s-Gravenhage), 2, 3/4, (12 Nov. 1914), 9-11.

Soetatmo Soeriokoesoemo: see Soeriokoesoemo, Soetatmo.

Sonius, Harko Willem Johannes, "Introduction", in: Johan Frederik Holleman (ed.), *Van Vollenhoven on Indonesian Adat Law. Selections from* Het adatrecht van Nederlandsch-Indië [Adat Law of the Dutch Indies], 2 vols, The Hague: Nijhoff, 1981, XXIX-LXVII.

Srinivas, Mysore Narasimhachar, *The Remembered Village*, Berkeley etc.: University of California Press, 1987.

SSJ: see *Segala Soal Jawab atas Masalah Tiada Harus Mehukumkan Talak dengan Semata-mata Tulisan Saksi-saksi yang telah Mati.*

Staatsblad van Nederlandsch-Indië [Law Gazette of the Dutch East Indies] (Batavia).

Stafford, Charles, "Chinese Nationalism and the Family", *Man* (London), New Series, 27 (1992), 2, 362-74.

State of Brunei Annual Report (*BAR*) (Bandar Seri Begawan), 1906- (since 1974 with Malay title).

Steenbrink, Karel A., *Pesantren Madrasah Sekolah. Pendidikan Islam dalam Kurun Moderen* [*Pesantren, Madrasah,* School. Islamic Education in the Modern Period], Jakarta: LP3ES, 1986 (partial translation of a dissertation at the Catholic University, Nijmegen, Netherlands, 1974).

Stevan Harrell (ed.), *Cultural Encounters on China's Ethnic Frontiers,* Seattle: University of Washington Press, 1995.

Strassberg, Richard E., *Inscribed Landscapes: Travel Writing from Imperial China,* Berkeley: University of California Press, 1994.

Suara Pembaruan (daily, Jakarta), 1987-.

Suara Karya (daily, Jakarta), 1971-.

Suhaili H. Mohidin, *Penyelewengan dari Dasar Aqidah Ahli Sunnah pada Masa Sekarang* [Deviations from the Sunnite Doctrinal Fundament Today], Bandar Seri Begawan: Islamic Da'wah Centre, 1986 (reprint 1994).

Sukarno: see Adams, Cindy.

Swann Report: see *Education for All: The Report of the Committee of Inquiry into the Education of Children from Ethnic Minority Groups.*

Sweeney, P.L. Amin (ed.), "Silsilah raja-raja Berunai" [Genealogy of the Kings of Brunei], *Journal of the Malaysian Branch of the Royal Asiatic Society* (Kuala Lumpur) 41, 2 (= no. 214; Dec. 1968), 1-83.

Swidler, Leonard, *Biblical Affirmations of Woman,* Philadelphia: Westminster Press, 1979.

Syahminan Zaini, *Isi Pokok Ajaran Al-Qur'an* [Basic Contents of the Teaching of the Koran], Jakarta: Kalam Mulia, 1986.

Tao Zongyi (born AD 1316), *Chuo Geng Lu* [Idle Recordings in the Slack Season].

Tapper, Nancy, *Bartered Brides: Politics, Gender and Marriage in an Afghan Tribal Society,* Cambridge: Cambridge University Press, 1991.

Taufik Abdullah, "Adat and Islam: An Examination of Conflict in Minangkabau", *Indonesia* (Ithaca), 1, 2 (October 1966), 1-24.

Tempo (weekly, Jakarta), 1971-94.

The Constitution of the State of Brunei: Bandar Seri Begawan: Brunei Museum, 1959.

The Borneo Bulletin (weekly created 1953, daily since 1990; Kuala Belait, Brunei).

Thierry, François, "Empire and Minority in China", in Gérard Chaliand (ed.), *Minority Peoples in the Age of Nation-States,* London: Pluto Press, 1989, 76-99.

Tibi, Bassam, *Die Krise des modernen Islams. Eine vorindustrielle Kultur im wissenschaftlich-technischen Zeitalter,* München: Beck, 1981.

Tim Penyusun Studi Kelayakan Pengembangan IAIN Menjadi Universitas Negeri [Team in Charge of Carrying Out a Feasibility Study on the (Project) to Develop the IAIN into an Islamic State University], *Laporan Hasil Studi Kelayakan Pengembangan IAIN Menjadi Universitas Islam Negeri* [Report Resulting from the Feasibility Study on the

Development of the IAIN into an Islamic State University], Jakarta, Departemen Agama, Proyek Perguruan Tinggi Agama IAIN Syarif Hidayatullah Jakarta [Ministry of Religious Affairs, Project Institute for Islamic Higher Education IAIN Syarif Hidayatullah, Jakarta], 31 Jan. 1995.

Time Magazine (weekly, Chicago, later New York), 1923-.

Tong Enzheng, "Morgan's Model and the Study of Ancient Chinese Society", *Social Science in China* (Beijing), 3, (Summer 1989), 182-205.

Tulufan Fengqing Huaji [Picture Album of Turpan Landscape and Custom], Urumqi: Sinkiang People's Press, 1985.

Turkestanskie Vedomosti [Gazette of Turkestan] (Tashkent).

Umar Abduh and Kittos Away (eds), *Mengapa Kita Menolak Syi'ah* [Why We Refuse Shi'ism], Jakarta: LPPI, 1998.

Ummat (weekly, Jakarta), 1995-1999.

United Nations, *The World's Women 1970-1990: Trends and Statistics*, New York: UN, 1991.

Van Bruinessen: see Bruinessen, Martin van.

Van Dijk: see Dijk, C. [Cornelis = Kees] van.

Van Leur: see Leur, Jacobus Cornelis van.

Van Vollenhoven: see Vollenhoven, Cornelis van.

Verslag van de Commissie van advies nopens de voorgenomen herziening van de Priesterraad-Rechtspraak [Report of the Advisory Commission on the Intended Revision of the *Priesterraad* Judicature; under the presidency of Hoesein Djajadaningrat], Weltevreden, 28 April 1926.

Voll, John O., *Islam: Continuity and Change in the Modern World*, Boulder: Westview, 1982.

Vollenhoven, Cornelis van, *Het Adatrecht van Nederlandsch-Indië* [Adat Law of the Dutch East Indies], vol. I, Leiden: Brill, 1918.

Wallerstein, Immanuel M., *The Modern World System. Capitalist Agriculture and the Origins of the European World Economy in the Sixteenth Century*, New York et al.: Academic Press, 1974.

Wang Shoujie "Beiping shi Huimin Gaikuang" (A Survey of the Hui People of Beiping), *Li Gong* (Shanghai), 1 May 1937.

Wang Shoujie, "Niu jie Huimin Shenghuo tan" [Discussion of the Lifestyle of the Oxen Street Hui], *Yue Hua* (Shanghai), 25 May, 5 July 1930.

Wang Jianping, *Concord and Conflict: The Hui Communities of Yunnan Society in Historical Perspective*, Lund: Almquist and Wiskell, 1996.

Waseem, Mohammad, *Politics and the State in Pakistan*, National Institute of Historical and Cultural Research, Islamabad, 1994.

Watkins, Gloria: see Hooks, Bell.

Weber, Max, *The Protestant Ethic and the Spirit of Capitalism*, New York: Scribners, 1958 (translated into English by Talcott Parsons; original version: "Die Protestantische Ethik und der Geist des Kapitalismus", *Archiv für Sozialwissenschaft und Sozialpolitik* (Tübingen), 21 (= new series 3; 1905), 1, 1-54 and 2, 1-110.

Welch, Claude, *Protestant Thought in the Nineteenth Century*, New Haven and London: Yale University Press, 1972.

Westkott, Marcia, "Women's Studies as a Strategy for Change: Between Criticism and Vision", in Gloria Bowles and Renate Duelli-Klein (eds), *Theories of Women's Studies*, London: Routledge, 1983.

Wild, Colin and Peter Carey, *Born in Fire. The Indonesian Struggle for Independence*, Athens: Ohio University Press, 1988.

William Miller, *The First Liberty: Religion and the American Republic*, New York: Paragon, 1985.

Wink, André, *Al-Hind. The Making of the Indo-Islamic World*, Leiden: Brill, 1990 vv. (2 of the planned 5 volumes appeared so far).

Woodside, Alexander and Benjamin A. Elman, "Introduction", in Alexander Woodside and Benjamin A. Elman (eds), *Education and Society in Late Imperial China, 1600-1900*, Berkeley: University of California Press, 1994, 1-15.

Woodward, Mark, "Conversations with Abdurrahman Wahid", in Mark Woodward (ed.), *Towards a New Paradigm. Recent Developments in Indonesian Islamic Thought*, Tempe: Arizona State University, (Program for Southeast Asian Studies Monograph Series), 1996, 133-53.

Woodward, Mark, *Islam in Java. Normative Piety and Mysticism in the Sultanate of Yogyakarta*, Tucson: University of Arizona Press, 1989.

Yahya M.S., *Perjalanan Malam Kalimantan Menuju Siang* [A Nightly Journey in Kalimantan until Daybreak], Bandar Seri Begawan: Dewan Bahasa and Pustaka, 1988.

Yeo Kwang-Kyoon, *The Koreans in China: The Most Educated Minority and Its Ethnic Education*, unpublished seminar paper, University of Hawai'i at Manoa, 1996.

Youssef, Nadia H., "The Status and Fertility Patterns of Muslim Women", in Lois Beck and Nikki Keddie (eds), *Women in the Muslim World*, Cambridge, MA: Harvard University Press, 1978, 69-99.

Yvonne Haddad, *Contemporary Islam and the Challenge of History*, Albany: SUNY Press, 1982.

Zaim Uchrowi and Ahmadie Thaha (eds), "Menyeru Pemikiran Rasional Mu'tazilah" [A Call for the Rational Thinking of the *Mu'tazilah*] [an autobiography of Harun Nasution edited on the basis of a series of interviews], in Aqib Suminto et al., *Refleksi Pembaharuan Pemikiran Islam. 70 Tahun Harun Nasution* [Reflection on the Renewal of Islamic Thought. Harun Nasution 70 Years], Jakarta: LSAF, 1989, 30-80.

Zamakhsyari Dhofier, *Tradisi Pesantren*, Jakarta: LP3ES, 1980.

----, "The Intellectualization of Islamic Studies in Indonesia", *Indonesia Circle* (London), 58 (June 1992), 19-31, republished in A.G. Muhaimin (ed.), *Zamakhsyari Dhofier on: Tradition and Change in Indonesian Islamic Education*, Jakarta, Office of Religious Research and Development, Ministry of Religious Affairs, 1995, 61-86.

----, "Pesantren and the Development of Islam in the New Order", in A.G. Muhaimin (ed.), *Zamakhsyari Dhofier on: Tradition and Change in Indonesian Islamic Education*, Jakarta, Office of Religious Research and Development, Ministry of Religious Affairs, 1995, 87-104.

----, "The Role of Traditional Islamic Educational Institutions in the Universalization of Basic Education in Indonesia", in A.G. Muhaimin (ed.), *Zamakhsyari Dhofier on: Tradition and Change in Indonesian Islamic Education*, Jakarta, Office of Religious Research and Development, Ministry of Religious Affairs, 1995, 36-60.

Zhang Chengzhi, *Xinling Shi* [A History of the Soul], Beijing: Huacheng Publishing Society, 1991.

Zhongguo Minzu Renkou Ziliao (1990 nian Renkou Pucha Shuju) [Population of China's Nationality (Data of 1990 Population Census)] (Department of Population Statistics of State Statistical Bureau and Economic Department of State Nationalities Affairs Commission, People's Republic of China), Beijing: China Statistical Publishing House, 1994.

Zuhdi, "Angin Segar Makanan Halal" [A Wind of Change in the Matter of *Halāl* Food], *Mimbar Ulama* (Jakarta), 211 (March 1996), 26-9.

Index